LONGMAN
KEYSTONE

B

Anna Uhl Chamot

John De Mado

Sharroky Hollie

PEARSON
Longman

LONGMAN KEYSTONE B

Pearson Education, 10 Bank Street, White Plains, NY 10606

Staff credits: The people who made up the Longman Keystone team, representing editorial, production, design, manufacturing, and marketing, are John Ade, Rhea Banker, Liz Barker, Danielle Belfiore, Don Bensey, Virginia Bernard, Kenna Bourke, Anne Boynton-Trigg, Johnnie Farmer, Maryann Finocchi, Patrice Fraccio, Geraldine Geniusas, Charles Green, Henry Hild, David L. Jones, Lucille M. Kennedy, Ed Lamprich, Emily Lippincott, Tara Maceyak, Maria Pia Marrella, Linda Moser, Laurie Neaman, Sherri Pemberton, Liza Pleva, Joan Poole, Edie Pullman, Monica Rodriguez, Tania Saiz-Sousa, Donna Schaffer, Chris Siley, Lynn Sobotta, Heather St. Clair, Jennifer Stem, Siobhan Sullivan, Jane Townsend, Heather Vomero, Marian Wassner, Lauren Weidenman, Matthew Williams, and Adina Zoltan.

Smithsonian American Art Museum contributors: Project director and writer: Elizabeth K. Eder, Ph.D.; Writer: Mary Collins; Image research assistants: Laurel Fehrenbach, Katherine G. Stilwill, and Sally Otis; Rights and reproductions: Richard H. Sorensen and Leslie G. Green; Building photograph by Tim Hursley.

Text design and composition: Kirchoff/Wohlberg, Inc.

Text font: 11.5/14 Minion
Acknowledgments: See page 468.
Illustration and Photo Credits: See page 470.

Library of Congress Cataloging-in-Publication Data
Chamot, Anna Uhl.
  Longman keystone / Anna Uhl Chamot, John De Mado, Sharroky Hollie.
    p. cm. -- (Longman keystone ; B)
  Includes index.
  ISBN 0-13-239444-8 (v. B)
  1. Language arts (Middle school)--United States. 2. Language arts (Middle school)--Activity programs. 3. Language arts (Secondary)--United States. 4. English language--Study and teaching. I. Demado, John II. Hollie, Sharroky III. Title.
  LB1631.C4466 2008
  428.0071'2--dc22
               2007049279

ISBN-13: 978-0-13-239444-4
ISBN-10: 0-13-239444-8

PEARSON LONGMAN ON THE WEB

Pearsonlongman.com offers online resources for teachers and students. Access our Companion Websites, our online catalog, and our local offices around the world.

Visit us at **www.pearsonlongman.com**.

Printed in the United States of America
6 7 8 9 10 11 12—V063—12 11 10

About the Authors

Anna Uhl Chamot is a professor of secondary education and a faculty advisor for ESL in George Washington University's Department of Teacher Preparation. She has been a researcher and teacher trainer in content-based second-language learning and language-learning strategies. She co-designed and has written extensively about the Cognitive Academic Language Learning Approach (CALLA) and spent seven years implementing the CALLA model in the Arlington Public Schools in Virginia.

John De Mado has been an energetic force in the field of Language Acquisition for several years. He is founder and president of John De Mado Language Seminars, Inc., an educational consulting firm devoted exclusively to language acquisition and literacy issues. John, who speaks a variety of languages, has authored several textbook programs and produced a series of music CD/DVDs designed to help students acquire other languages. John is recognized nationally, as well as internationally, for his insightful workshops, motivating keynote addresses, and humor-filled delivery style.

Sharroky Hollie is an assistant professor in teacher education at California State University, Dominguez Hills. His expertise is in the field of professional development, African-American education, and second-language methodology. He is an urban literacy visiting professor at Webster University, St. Louis. Sharroky is the Executive Director of the Center for Culturally Responsive Teaching and Learning (CCRTL) and the co-founding director of the nationally acclaimed Culture and Language Academy of Success (CLAS).

Reviewers

Sharena Adebiyi
Fulton County Schools
Stone City, GA

Jennifer Benavides
Garland ISD
Garland, TX

Tracy Bunker
Shearer Charter School
Napa, CA

Dan Fichtner
UCLA Ed. Ext. TESOL Program
Redondo Beach, CA

Trudy Freer-Alvarez
Houston ISD
Houston, TX

Helena K. Gandell
Duval County
Jacksonville, FL

Glenda Harrell
Johnston County School Dist.
Smithfield, NC

Michelle Land
Randolph Middle School
Randolph, NJ

Joseph E. Leaf
Norristown Area High School
Norristown, PA

Ilona Olancin
Collier County Schools
Naples, FL

Jeanne Perrin
Boston Unified School Dist.
Boston, MA

Cheryl Quadrelli-Jones
Anaheim Union High School Dist.
Fullerton, CA

Mary Schmidt
Riverwood High School
Atlanta, GA

Daniel Thatcher
Garland ISD
Garland, TX

Denise Tiffany
West High School
Iowa City, IA

Lisa Troute
Palm Beach County School Dist.
West Palm, FL

Dear Student,

Welcome to LONGMAN KEYSTONE

Longman Keystone has been specially designed to help you succeed in all areas of your school studies. This program will help you develop the English language skills you need for language arts, social studies, math, and science. You will discover new ways to use and build upon your language skills through your interactions with classmates, friends, teachers, and family members.

Keystone includes a mix of many subjects. Each unit has four different reading selections that include literary excerpts, poems, and nonfiction articles about science, math, and social studies. These selections will help you understand the vocabulary and organization of different types of texts. They will also give you the tools you need to approach the content of the different subjects you take in school.

As you use this program, you will discover new words, use your background knowledge of the subjects presented, relate your knowledge to the new information, and take part in creative activities. You will learn strategies to help you understand readings better. You will work on activities that help you improve your English skills in grammar, word study, and spelling. Finally, you will be asked to demonstrate the listening, speaking, and writing skills you have learned through fun projects that are incorporated throughout the program.

Learning a language takes time, but just like learning to skateboard or learning to swim, it is fun! Whether you are learning English for the first time, or increasing your knowledge of English by adding academic or literary language to your vocabulary, you are giving yourself new choices for the future, and a better chance of succeeding in both your studies and in everyday life.

We hope you enjoy *Longman Keystone* as much as we enjoyed writing it for you!

Good luck!

Anna Uhl Chamot
John De Mado
Sharroky Hollie

Learn about *Art* *with the* Smithsonian American Art Museum

Dear Student,

At the end of each unit in this book, you will learn about some artists and artworks that relate to the theme you have just read about. These artworks are all in the Smithsonian American Art Museum in Washington, D.C. That means they belong to you, because the Smithsonian is America's collection. The artworks were created over a period of 300 years by artists who responded to their experiences in personal ways. Their world lives on through their artworks and, as viewers, we can understand them and ourselves in new ways. We discover that many of the things that concerned these artists still engage us today.

Looking at an artwork is different from reading a written history. Artists present few facts or dates. Instead, they offer emotional insights that come from their own lives and experiences. They make their own decisions about what matters, without worrying if others agree or disagree. This is a rare and useful kind of knowledge that we can all learn from. Artists inspire us to respond to our own lives with deeper insight.

There are two ways to approach art. One way is through the mind—studying the artist, learning about the subject, exploring the context in which the artwork was made, and forming a personal view. This way is deeply rewarding and expands your understanding of the world. The second way is through the senses—letting your imagination roam as you look at an artwork, losing yourself in colors and shapes, absorbing the meaning through your eyes. This way is called "aesthetic." The great thing about art is that an artwork may have many different meanings. You can decide what it means to you.

This brief introduction to American art will, I hope, lead to a lifetime of enjoyment and appreciation of art.

Elizabeth Broun
The Margaret and Terry Stent Director
Smithsonian American Art Museum

Glossary of Terms

You will find the following words useful when reading, writing, and talking about art.

abstract a style of art that does not represent things, animals, or people realistically

acrylic a type of paint that is made from ground pigments and certain chemicals

background part of the artwork that looks furthest away from the viewer

brushstroke the paint or ink left on the surface of an artwork by the paintbrush

canvas a type of heavy woven fabric used as a support for painting; another word for a painting

composition the way in which the different parts of an artwork are arranged

detail a small part of an artwork

evoke to produce a strong feeling or memory

figure the representation of a person or animal in an artwork

foreground part of the artwork that looks closest to the viewer

geometric a type of pattern that has straight lines or shapes such as squares, circles, etc.

mixed media different kinds of materials such as paint, fabric, objects, etc. that are used in a single artwork

oil a type of paint that is made from ground pigments and linseed oil

paintbrush a special brush used for painting

perception the way you understand something you see

pigment a finely powdered material (natural or man-made) that gives color to paint, ink, or dye

portrait an artwork that shows a specific person, group of people, or animal

print an artwork that has been made from a sheet of metal or a block of wood covered with a wet color and then pressed onto a flat surface like paper. Types of prints include lithographs, etchings, aquatints, etc.

symbol an image, shape, or object in an artwork that represents an idea

texture the way that a surface or material feels and how smooth or rough it looks

tone the shade of a particular color; the effect of light and shade with color

watercolor a type of paint that is made from ground pigments, gum, and glycerin and/or honey; another word for a painting done with this medium

Contents

How does the natural world affect us? 2

Reading 1: Novel Excerpt

Prepare to Read **4**
    Vocabulary Focus: *Literary Terms, Academic Words*
    Reading Focus: *Predict*

from ***Project Mulberry*** **by** Linda Sue Park.........................**8**

Review and Practice **12**
    Speaking and Listening Focus: *Reader's Theater*
    ✔**Progress Monitoring:** *Response to Literature*

Grammar and Writing **14**
    Grammar Focus: *Order of Adjectives*
    Writing Focus: *Describe an Object*

Reading 2: Informational Text/Science

Prepare to Read **16**
    Vocabulary Focus: *Key Words, Academic Words*
    Reading Focus: *Preview*

Ecosystems: *The Systems of Nature* INFO TEXT **20**

Review and Practice **26**
    Speaking and Listening Focus: *In Your Own Words*
    ✔**Progress Monitoring:** *Read for Fluency*

Grammar and Writing **28**
    Grammar Focus: *Comparison Structures*
    Writing Focus: *Describe a Place*

Reading 3: Short Story and Poetry

Prepare to Read **30**
    Vocabulary Focus: *Literary Terms, Academic Words*
    Reading Focus: *Visualize*

Ali, Child of the Desert by Jonathan London **34**
Desert Women by Pat Mora **41**

Review and Practice **42**
    Speaking and Listening Focus: *Reader's Theater*
    ✔ **Progress Monitoring:** *Response to Literature*

Grammar and Writing **44**
    Grammar Focus: *Simple and Compound Sentences*
    Writing Focus: *Describe a Person*

Reading 4: Informational Text/Science

Prepare to Read **46**
    Vocabulary Focus: *Key Words, Academic Words*
    Reading Focus: *Identify Main Idea and Details*

Water and Living Things INFO TEXT **50**

Review and Practice **54**
    Speaking and Listening Focus: *In Your Own Words*
    ✔ **Progress Monitoring:** *Read for Fluency*

Grammar and Writing **56**
    Grammar Focus: *Subject-Verb Agreement: Simple Present*
    Writing Focus: *Describe an Event or Experience*

Link the Readings **58**
    ✔ **Assessment Practice:** Critical Thinking, Discussion
    🔍 **The Big Question:** Wrap-Up Discussion
    ✔ **Fluency Check**

Projects and Further Reading **59**

Put It All Together

Listening & Speaking Workshop: Presentation **60**

Writing Workshop: Descriptive Essay **62**

Smithsonian American Art Museum: The Language of Art

    Painting the American Landscape **66**

Contents

UNIT 2

Where can a journey take you? **68**

Reading 1: Myth

Prepare to Read **70**
Vocabulary Focus: *Literary Terms, Academic Words*
Reading Focus: *Identify Problems and Solutions*

from *Tales from the Odyssey* retold by Mary Pope Osborne **74**

Review and Practice **78**
Speaking and Listening Focus: *Reader's Theater*
✔**Progress Monitoring:** *Response to Literature*

Grammar and Writing **80**
Grammar Focus: *Simple Past: Regular and Irregular Verbs*
Writing Focus: *Write a Story from a Different Point of View*

Reading 2: Informational Text/Social Studies

Prepare to Read **82**
Vocabulary Focus: *Key Words, Academic Words*
Reading Focus: *Use Visuals*

Early Explorers INFO TEXT **86**

Review and Practice **90**
Speaking and Listening Focus: *In Your Own Words*
✔**Progress Monitoring:** *Read for Fluency*

Grammar and Writing **92**
Grammar Focus: *Passive Voice: Omitting the by-Phrase*
Writing Focus: *Write a Personal Narrative*

Reading 3: Informational Texts/Science

Prepare to Read **94**
Vocabulary Focus: *Key Words, Academic Words*
Reading Focus: *Recognize Cause and Effect*

Migrating Caribou  INFO TEXT **98**

Magnets in Animals by Darlene R. Stille INFO TEXT **101**

Review and Practice **102**
Speaking and Listening Focus: *In Your Own Words*
✔**Progress Monitoring:** *Read for Fluency*

Grammar and Writing **104**
Grammar Focus: *Prenominal and Postnominal Adjectives*
Writing Focus: *Write a Story with a Starter*

Reading 4: Novel Excerpt

Prepare to Read **106**
Vocabulary Focus: *Literary Terms, Academic Words*
Reading Focus: *Make Inferences*

from ***The Journal of Wong Ming-Chung*** by Laurence Yep **110**

Review and Practice **116**
Speaking and Listening Focus: *Dramatic Reading*
✔**Progress Monitoring:** *Response to Literature*

Grammar and Writing **118**
Grammar Focus: *Adverb Clauses of Time*
Writing Focus: *Write a Personal Letter*

Link the Readings **120**
✔**Assessment Practice:** Critical Thinking, Discussion
The Big Question: Wrap-Up Discussion
✔**Fluency Check**

Projects and Further Reading **121**

Put It All Together

Listening & Speaking Workshop: Personal Narrative **122**

Writing Workshop: Fictional Narrative **124**

Smithsonian American Art Museum: The Language of Art

Traveling the Electronic Superhighway **128**

Contents

What defines success?

.................130

Reading 1: Informational Text/Social Studies
Prepare to Read 132
Vocabulary Focus: *Key Words, Academic Words*
Reading Focus: *Connect Ideas*
Success Stories INFO TEXT 136

Review and Practice 140
Speaking and Listening Focus: *In Your Own Words*
✔**Progress Monitoring:** *Read for Fluency*

Grammar and Writing 142
Grammar Focus: *Independent and Dependent Clauses*
Writing Focus: *Write to Compare and Contrast*

Reading 2: Interview and Poetry
Prepare to Read 144
Vocabulary Focus: *Literary Terms, Academic Words*
Reading Focus: *Distinguish Fact from Opinion*
An Interview with Naomi Shihab Nye by Rachel Barenblat 148
Making a Mosaic by Naomi Shihab Nye 151

Review and Practice 152
Speaking and Listening Focus: *Dramatic Reading*
✔**Progress Monitoring:** *Response to Literature*

Grammar and Writing 154
Grammar Focus: *Gerunds as Subject or Object*
Writing Focus: *Write a Problem-and-Solution Paragraph*

Reading 3: Short Story

Prepare to Read **156**
    Vocabulary Focus: *Literary Terms, Academic Words*
    Reading Focus: *Predict 2*

The Marble Champ by Gary Soto **160**

Review and Practice **168**
    Speaking and Listening Focus: *Reader's Theater*
    ✔ **Progress Monitoring:** *Response to Literature*

Grammar and Writing **170**
    Grammar Focus: *Infinitives and Infinitives of Purpose*
    Writing Focus: *Write a Critique*

Reading 4: Informational Text/Science

Prepare to Read **172**
    Vocabulary Focus: *Key Words, Academic Words*
    Reading Focus: *Ask Questions*

Students Win Robotics Competition by Karina Bland INFO TEXT **176**

Review and Practice **180**
    Speaking and Listening Focus: *In Your Own Words*
    ✔ **Progress Monitoring:** *Read for Fluency*

Grammar and Writing **182**
    Grammar Focus: *Expressions of Quantity*
    Writing Focus: *Write a News Article*

Link the Readings **184**
    ✔ **Assessment Practice:** Critical Thinking, Discussion
    🔍 **The Big Question:** Wrap-Up Discussion
    ✔ **Fluency Check**

Projects and Further Reading **185**

Put It All Together

Listening & Speaking Workshop: Interview **186**

Writing Workshop: Expository Essay **188**

Smithsonian American Art Museum: The Language of Art

Self-Portraits **192**

Contents

THE BIG QUESTION

Can we see change as it happens? 194

Reading 1: Informational Text/Science
Prepare to Read 196
  Vocabulary Focus: *Key Words, Academic Words*
  Reading Focus: *Scan*
Changing Earth **INFO TEXT** 200

Review and Practice 206
  Speaking and Listening Focus: *In Your Own Words*
  ✔**Progress Monitoring:** *Read for Fluency*

Grammar and Writing 208
  Grammar Focus: *Present Perfect*
  Writing Focus: *Write an Advertisement*

Reading 2: Letters
Prepare to Read 210
  Vocabulary Focus: *Literary Terms, Academic Words*
  Reading Focus: *Identify Author's Purpose*

The Intersection by Dina Anastasio 210

Review and Practice 218
  Speaking and Listening Focus: *Dramatic Reading*
  ✔**Progress Monitoring:** *Response to Literature*

Grammar and Writing 220
  Grammar Focus: *Future with* will *or* won't *for Prediction*
  Writing Focus: *Write a Letter to the Editor*

Reading 3: Informational Text/Social Studies

Prepare to Read **222**
Vocabulary Focus: *Key Words, Academic Words*
Reading Focus: *Draw Conclusions*

from ***Through My Eyes*** by Ruby Bridges ......................... **226**

Review and Practice **232**
Speaking and Listening Focus: *In Your Own Words*
✔**Progress Monitoring:** *Read for Fluency*

Grammar and Writing **234**
Grammar Focus: *Conjunctions:* and, but, or
Writing Focus: *Write a Persuasive Paragraph*

Reading 4: Essay, Art, and Poetry

Prepare to Read **236**
Vocabulary Focus: *Literary Terms, Academic Words*
Reading Focus: *Recognize Sequence*

Harlem: Then and Now by James Baldwin............... **240**

Tar Beach by Faith Ringgold **244**

Harlem and ***Dreams*** by Langston Hughes............... **245**

Review and Practice **246**
Speaking and Listening Focus: *Dramatic Reading*
✔**Progress Monitoring:** *Response to Literature*

Grammar and Writing **248**
Grammar Focus: *Nouns, Pronouns, and Possessive Adjectives*
Writing Focus: *Write a Review*

Link the Readings...**250**
✔**Assessment Practice:** Critical Thinking, Discussion
🗨**The Big Question:** Wrap-Up Discussion
✔**Fluency Check**

Projects and Further Reading............................**251**

Put It All Together

Listening & Speaking Workshop: Speech.................**252**

Writing Workshop: Persuasive Essay **254**

Smithsonian American Art Museum: The Language of Art
Moving Through Time...**258**

Contents

UNIT 5

Why do we explore new frontiers?.. 260

Reading 1: Novel Excerpt, Song, and Poetry
Prepare to Read 262
   Vocabulary Focus: *Literary Terms, Academic Words*
   Reading Focus: *Make Generalizations*
from ***River to Tomorrow*** by Ellen Levine 266
River Song by Bill Staines... 272
Morning Prayer Song by Ronald Snake Edmo 273
Review and Practice 274
   Speaking and Listening Focus: *Dramatic Reading*
   ✔**Progress Monitoring:** *Response to Literature*
Grammar and Writing 276
   Grammar Focus: *The Past Perfect and the Simple Past*
   Writing Focus: *Write a Cause-and-Effect Paragraph*

Reading 2: Informational Text/Social Studies
Prepare to Read 278
   Vocabulary Focus: *Key Words, Academic Words*
   Reading Focus: *Take Notes*
Maps and Compasses INFO TEXT 282
Review and Practice 286
   Speaking and Listening Focus: *In Your Own Words*
   ✔**Progress Monitoring:** *Read for Fluency*
Grammar and Writing 288
   Grammar Focus: *Imperatives*
   Writing Focus: *Write Instructions*

Reading 3: Informational Text/Social Studies

Prepare to Read **290**
Vocabulary Focus: *Key Words, Academic Words*
Reading Focus: *Summarize*

The Cowboy Era INFO TEXT **294**

Review and Practice **298**
Speaking and Listening Focus: *In Your Own Words*
✔Progress Monitoring: *Read for Fluency*

Grammar and Writing **300**
Grammar Focus: *Modals:* could *for Past Ability;* could *and*
might *for Possibility*
Writing Focus: *Write a Summary*

Reading 4: Tall Tale Excerpt

Prepare to Read **302**
Vocabulary Focus: *Literary Terms, Academic Words*
Reading Focus: *Skim*

from *Pecos Bill: The Greatest Cowboy of All Time*

by James Cloyd Bowman **306**

Review and Practice **312**
Speaking and Listening Focus: *Reader's Theater*
✔Progress Monitoring: *Response to Literature*

Grammar and Writing **314**
Grammar Focus: *Comparison Structures:*
-er/-est, more/the most + *adjective*
Writing Focus: *Write a Classifying Paragraph*

Link the Readings **316**
✔Assessment Practice: Critical Thinking, Discussion
The Big Question: Wrap-Up Discussion
✔Fluency Check

Projects and Further Reading **317**

Put It All Together
Listening & Speaking Workshop: Group Presentation **318**

Writing Workshop: Instructional Essay **320**

Smithsonian American Art Museum: The Language of Art
The Roots of Frontier Culture **324**

UNIT 6

Contents

How do we know what is true?

How do we know what is true? 326

Reading 1: Myth
Prepare to Read 328
   Vocabulary Focus: *Literary Terms, Academic Words*
   Reading Focus: *Compare and Contrast*
How Glooskap Found the Summer 332
Persephone and the Pomegranate Seeds 334

Review and Practice 336
   Speaking and Listening Focus: *Reader's Theater*
   ✔**Progress Monitoring:** *Response to Literature*

Grammar and Writing 338
   Grammar Focus: *Modals to Express Ability, Necessity, and Permission*
   Writing Focus: *Write an Introductory Paragraph*

Reading 2: Informational Text/Social Studies
Prepare to Read 340
   Vocabulary Focus: *Key Words, Academic Words*
   Reading Focus: *Evaluate New Information*
Early Astronomers `INFO TEXT` 344

Review and Practice 348
   Speaking and Listening Focus: *In Your Own Words*
   ✔**Progress Monitoring:** *Read for Fluency*

Grammar and Writing 350
   Grammar Focus: *Participial Adjectives*
   Writing Focus: *Support the Main Idea with Facts and Details*

Reading 3: Play Excerpt
Prepare to Read 352
   Vocabulary Focus: *Literary Terms, Academic Words*
   Reading Focus: *Analyze Text Structure*
from *The War of the Worlds* by H. G. Wells, adapted by Howard Koch ... 356

Review and Practice **364**
  Speaking and Listening Focus: *Dramatic Reading*
  ✔**Progress Monitoring:** *Response to Literature*

Grammar and Writing **366**
  Grammar Focus: *Punctuation of Quoted Speech*
  Writing Focus: *Include Quotations and Citations*

Reading 4: Informational Text/Science
Prepare to Read **368**
  Vocabulary Focus: *Key Words, Academic Words*
  Reading Focus: *Classify*

Earth's Orbit INFO TEXT **372**

Review and Practice **378**
  Speaking and Listening Focus: *In Your Own Words*
  ✔**Progress Monitoring:** *Read for Fluency*

Grammar and Writing **380**
  Grammar Focus: *Cause and Effect Structures*
  Writing Focus: *Support the Main Idea with Examples and Explanations*

Link the Readings **382**
  ✔**Assessment Practice:** Critical Thinking, Discussion
  🔍**The Big Question:** Wrap-Up Discussion
  ✔**Fluency Check**

Projects and Further Reading **383**

Put It All Together
Listening & Speaking Workshop: Play **384**

Writing Workshop: Research Report **386**

Smithsonian American Art Museum: The Language of Art
Otherworldly Art **392**

Handbooks and Resources **395**
Glossary **456**
Index of Skills **462**
Index of Authors, Titles, Art, and Artists **467**
Acknowledgments **468**
Credits **470**
Smithsonian American Art Museum List of Artworks **473**

THE BIG QUESTION

How does the natural world affect us?

This unit is about nature. You will read literature and science texts about living things such as animals and plants. You will also read about nonliving things such as water and sand. Learning about these topics will help you become a better student. It will also help you practice the language you will need to use in school.

READING 1: Novel Excerpt
- From *Project Mulberry* by Linda Sue Park

READING 2: Science Article
- "Ecosystems: The Systems of Nature"

READING 3: Short Story and Poetry
- "Ali, Child of the Desert" by Jonathan London
- "Desert Women" by Pat Mora

READING 4: Science Article
- "Water and Living Things"

Listening and Speaking

At the end of this unit, you will make a **presentation** about the steps in a process.

Writing

In this unit you will practice **descriptive writing**. This type of writing describes things, or tells what things look, sound, feel, smell, or taste like. After each reading you will learn a skill to help you write a descriptive paragraph. At the end of the unit, you will use these skills to write a descriptive essay.

QuickWrite

Make a list of some living and nonliving things you see in your neighborhood every day.

Prepare to Read

What You Will Learn

Reading

■ Vocabulary building:
*Literary terms,
word study*

■ Reading strategy:
Predict

■ Text type: *Literature
(novel excerpt)*

**Grammar, Usage,
and Mechanics**
Order of adjectives

Writing
Describe an object

THE BIG QUESTION

How does the natural world affect us? How do humans and animals relate to each other? Do humans learn from animals? Do animals learn from humans? Work with a partner. Make a list of the ways humans and animals relate to each other in everyday life.

BUILD BACKGROUND

This reading is an excerpt from the novel ***Project Mulberry.*** An excerpt is a small part of a long text. It is about two students who are raising silkworms for a contest at a state fair. Raising silkworms is easy to do at home. You will need a lot of mulberry leaves—that is the only thing silkworms eat. You will also need time to feed and take care of them. Silkworms produce a silk cocoon for their protection. Learning about silkworms will teach you a lot about nature and life cycles.

▲ A silkworm spinning a cocoon

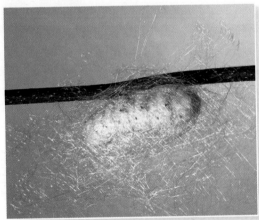

▲ A silkworm inside a cocoon

Learn Literary Words

Imagery is descriptive language that creates word pictures for readers. A writer creates imagery by using sensory details. These are details of sight, sound, smell, taste, or touch. Sensory details can help you visualize, or imagine, a scene in a story or poem. This can make you feel like you are really experiencing what the writer is describing.

The poem below includes sensory details that appeal to your senses of sight and touch. "A host of golden daffodils" appeals to your sense of sight. "Fluttering and dancing in the breeze" appeals to your sense of touch and sight.

Literary Words

imagery
sensory details

▲ Daffodils

> When all at once I saw a crowd,
> A host, of golden daffodils;
> Beside the lake, beneath the trees,
> Fluttering and dancing in the breeze.
> —*William Wordsworth*

The chart below gives an example of a sensory detail for each of the five senses.

Sight	Sound	Smell	Taste	Touch
a **blue** ribbon	a **squeaky** sound	a **sweet** smell	a **salty** taste	a **silky** scarf

Practice

 **Workbook Page 1**

Work with a partner. Take turns reading the sensory details below. Which of the five senses does each description appeal to? Some could appeal to a few senses.

baking bread	fluffy fur	sour lemons
beating drums	shiny buttons	sparkling water
buttery popcorn	silky hair	whistling wind

Learn Academic Words

Study the red words and their meanings. You will find these words useful when talking and writing about literature. Write each word and its meaning in your notebook. After you read the excerpt from *Project Mulberry,* try to use these words to respond to the text.

cycle = a set of events that happen again and again	➡	The life **cycle** of a moth is *egg, worm, cocoon,* and finally *moth.*
dramatic = sudden and noticeable	➡	In a few days the change to the caterpillars was **dramatic**. They were covered in layers of silk.
percent = an amount out of every hundred	➡	I answered 100 **percent** of the questions correctly on my science test!
project = a plan to do something	➡	The class is working on a **project** to learn about the life cycle of a frog.

Practice  Workbook Page 2

Work with a partner to answer these questions. Try to include the red word in your answer. Write the sentences in your notebook.

1. Name one stage in the life cycle of a moth.

2. Why was the change to the caterpillars dramatic?

3. Suppose you answered all the questions on a test correctly. What percent of the answers did you get right?

4. What was the last project that you worked on in class?

◀ The life cycle of a frog

Word Study: Prefixes *in-*, *re-*, *over-*, *un-*

A prefix is a group of letters that is added to the front of a base word and changes the meaning of that word. Some common prefixes are *in-*, *re-*, *over-*, and *un-*. Knowing the meaning of these prefixes helps you to understand the meaning of many words.

Prefix	Meaning	Base Word	New Word	Definition
in-	not	visible	invisible	not able to be seen
re-	again	write	rewrite	to change a text
over-	too much	priced	overpriced	too expensive
un-	not	certain	uncertain	not yet known

Practice  Workbook Page 3

Work with a partner. Take turns reading the words in the box. Look up the definition of each word and use the word in a sentence.

inaccurate	reappear	overactive	unable
inactive	recharge	overdue	uncomfortable
incomplete	reheat	overload	unpleasant

READING STRATEGY PREDICT

Predicting helps you better understand and focus on the text. Before you read, predict (or guess) what the story will be about. To predict, follow these steps:

- Stop reading from time to time and ask yourself, "What will happen next?"
- Look for clues in the story and illustrations.
- Think about what you already know. Make a prediction.
- As you read, check to see if your prediction is correct.

  Read the first two paragraphs of *Project Mulberry*. What do you predict the students are so excited about?

 Workbook Page 4

Set a purpose for reading What does Julia learn about the natural world? How does it make her feel?

from

Project Mulberry

Linda Sue Park

Julia Song and her friend Patrick want to win first prize at the state fair. Julia's mother suggests raising silkworms, something she did when she was a young girl in Korea. Julia is not happy about the idea at first—it seems too Korean, and she wants to do an American project.

I opened the cardboard window one last time, took out the same caterpillar, and put it into a little glass jar. We'd poked air holes in the metal lid. We kept the jar in the aquarium alongside the egg cartons, and I put a cup upside down over it so it would be dark most of the time. But whenever Patrick wanted to film, we took the jar out for a few minutes.

---

caterpillar, young form of insect, which looks like a worm with many legs
aquarium, large glass box in which fish live

8

It was *so* cool. My parents came out to see, and Patrick's parents brought Hugh-Ben-Nicky over that evening to have a look. The porch was very crowded; I worried that all those people would upset the caterpillar. But it didn't seem to care, not even when both the twins started jumping up and down and screeching with excitement.

The caterpillar moved its head constantly. Sometimes fast, sometimes a little slower, but never stopping—it looked like really hard work. The silk came out of its mouth just as Patrick had said.

At first the silk was almost invisible. You could see the strands only if you looked really hard.

By the next morning, though, the caterpillar had already wrapped itself in a layer of silk. It looked like it was living inside a cloud. We could see its black mouth moving, moving, moving, busy, busy, busy. Patrick wanted to stay up all night to film it, but both our moms vetoed that idea. The following morning he was at our house in his pajamas again. The silk was almost solid; now we could barely see the black mouth moving inside.

I was glad Patrick was taping it; I'd be able to watch it again as many times as I wanted. But I knew it would never be as special on tape as it was now, happening right in front of me, those wispy threads at first barely more than air, and then like a cloud, the caterpillar spinning layer after layer after layer, each layer made of one hundred percent real silk thread.

I stood with a piece of paper held behind my back. "I am a genius," I said to Patrick.

It was the afternoon of the third day of the spinning, a Sunday. Patrick was sitting on the couch in our living room. I'd told him to sit there while I went and got the paper from my room. He raised his eyebrows at me but didn't say anything.

"I've decided what I'm going to embroider. I'm going to do"—I paused dramatically, then whipped out the paper—"the Life Cycle of the Silkworm."

I held up the sketch I'd drawn.

"Egg. Worm. Cocoon. Moth." I pointed to the drawings one by one. "And wait till you hear the best part. I'm going to use regular embroidery floss to do the egg and the worm. And the moth, too. But for the cocoon, I'm going to use the thread we make. The cocoon is made of silk in real life, and it will be made of silk in the picture too, get it?"

Patrick grinned, a really huge grin.

He got it, all right. I almost felt like hugging him. He put his hands up in the air and bent forward a few times like he was bowing to me.

---

vetoed, refused to allow
wispy, soft and thin
embroider, sew pictures onto cloth using thread

✔ **LITERARY CHECK**
*How does the author use **imagery** to describe the caterpillar?*

BEFORE YOU GO ON

1. Where did the silk come out of the caterpillar?
2. What kind of thread does Julia plan to use to embroider the cocoon?

On Your Own
How are silkworms and mulberry leaves connected to the natural world?

9

"Julia Song, you *are* a genius. We are absolutely, positively, going to win a prize at the fair."

I made a silly curtsy back at him. "Thank you, thank you." I'd thought of doing the life cycle a while back. But it was the caterpillar that had given me the idea for the cocoon part. I'd watched it spin for a while right before I went to bed, and I'd woken up that morning with my genius plan.

I had known right away that it was perfect. There was just something so completely *right* about it. It wasn't American, like the flag—but it wasn't Korean, either.

Or maybe it was both?

Patrick took the sketch from me and studied it for a second. Then he looked up. "It's almost like an exact picture of the whole project, right?"

I nodded. "That's what I was thinking."

"Okay, so if it's supposed to be just like the project, you should leave out the moth at the end."

"Why would I leave out the moth? That's the final stage, right?"

"The final stage of the silkworm life cycle, yeah. But not the final stage of our project."

"What are you talking about?"

"We're not going to have any moths."

"Of course we're going to have moths," I said. "Look how great they're doing—they're almost done spinning their cocoons."

"But we want thread. So you can sew with it."

"Yeah, so?" What was Patrick's problem?

Patrick rolled his eyes at me. "Oh, I get it. You never read the book, did you."

"I did so. I mean, I didn't read every word, but I looked through it. I studied the pictures a lot—I traced one for the caterpillar sketch."

"Jules. If you'd read the book you'd know."

"Patrick, *what* are you talking about?"

He shook his head. "If you want to get silk from the cocoons, you have to kill the—the creatures inside. *Before* they come out as moths."

What?

I stared at him. I could feel the blood going out of my face. "You have to *kill* them?"

Patrick nodded. "You have to boil the cocoons. For about five minutes, to dissolve all the sticky stuff that keeps them together. Then you can unwind the silk. But the boiling kills them—the pupae."

---

curtsy, act of respect done by putting one foot forward and bending the knees
final stage, last period in a process
dissolve, break up or melt
pupae, insect in the middle stages of its development

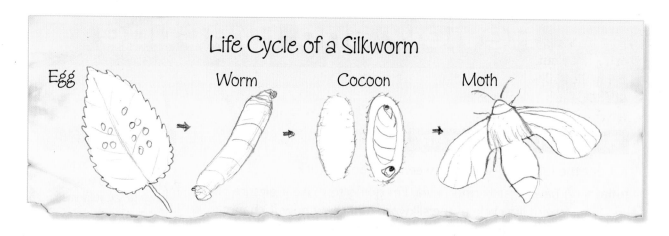

Life Cycle of a Silkworm

Egg → Worm → Cocoon → Moth

For once, there was no jostling in my head because there was only one thought, with nothing else for it to bump into.

Kill them.

We'd have to kill them.

My hands were freezing cold. I closed them into fists—open, shut, open, shut—while I tried to get my brain to work.

"Patrick, wait. Why can't we unwind the cocoons *after* the moths come out?"

"Jules. It's all in the book."

"Okay, okay. I didn't read the stupid book! Tell me!" I almost screamed.

Patrick spoke slowly, like he was trying to calm me down. "The moth gets out by making a hole in the cocoon, right? To make a hole it has to chew through the silk—well, it doesn't actually *chew*, it spits out this chemical that dissolves the silk and makes a hole. And the hole goes through *all* the layers of silk, see? So instead of one nice long thread, you'd end up with a million tiny short pieces that you couldn't sew with. Silk farmers never let the moths come out—it would ruin everything. Get it?"

I got it, all right. I closed my eyes because I felt dizzy.

I hadn't known that I didn't know.

ABOUT THE **AUTHOR**

Linda Sue Park was born in Illinois to Korean immigrant parents. At a very young age she developed a love for writing poetry and stories. She earned her degree in English from Stanford University while also competing on the school's gymnastics team. Her first children's book, *Seesaw*, was published in 1999. *A Single Shard* was a 2002 Newbery Medal winner. She lives with her family in western New York.

✔ **LITERARY CHECK**

*How does the author use **sensory details** to describe Julia's feelings?*

BEFORE YOU GO ON

1 How are the caterpillars killed?

2 Why is Julia confused? Explain the problem.

💡 **On Your Own**
Did you ever find out something surprising when you were doing a project?

Review and Practice

READER'S THEATER

Listening TIP

Listen carefully to the other actor so you know when to say your lines.

Act out the following scene between Julia and Patrick.

Julia: I have a really good idea. I'm going to make a picture of the entire life cycle of the silkworm. I'll show how it changes from an egg to a worm, and finally to a moth.

Patrick: That's a great idea! There's only one problem. Do you want your picture to show exactly what we do in our project?

Julia: That's right.

Patrick: Well then, you can't have a picture of the moth at the end.

Julia: Why not?

Patrick: Didn't you read the book I gave you? If we're going to get silk from the cocoons, we'll have to kill the creatures inside.

Julia: Kill them?

Patrick: Yes, or they'll destroy the silk.

Julia: Oh, no. But kill them? That's terrible!

COMPREHENSION

 **Workbook** Page 5

▲ Silkworm moths resting on cocoons

Right There

1. Why is Patrick videotaping the caterpillars?

2. What is the cocoon made of?

Think and Search

3. Describe the project Julia wants to embroider.

4. Why aren't there going to be any live moths at the end of Julia and Patrick's project?

Author and You

5. Does the author think Julia and Patrick work well together?

6. How does Julia feel about killing the silkworms?

On Your Own

7. What steps would you take to begin a research project?

8. Did you ever work with a partner on a project? Explain.

DISCUSSION

Speaking TIP

Speak slowly and clearly.

Discuss in pairs or small groups.

1. What did Julia do well for her project? What did Julia do poorly?
2. What do you think will happen next in *Project Mulberry*?
3. Have you ever had any problems with an activity or project? What was one of your problems? How did you solve it?

Q **How does the natural world affect us?** Do you think people have a responsibility to animals? Why or why not?

RESPONSE TO LITERATURE

Workbook
Page 5

Have you ever done an activity or worked on a project that taught you something about nature? Did you learn anything that surprised you? Did you have any problems? Compare your activity or project to Julia's project. Copy the chart below into your notebook. Share your chart in a small group.

	Julia's Project	My Project
Project:	Study the life cycle of a silkworm moth	
Facts learned:	How silkworms spin silk How people get silk thread from cocoons How a silkworm turns into a moth	
Surprising facts:	People have to kill the moths in order to get silk from the cocoons.	
Problem:	The picture of the project can't show the entire life cycle.	

Grammar and Writing

Order of Adjectives

There are different kinds of adjectives. An adjective such as *funny* tells an opinion, *short* describes size, and *red* and *blue* are colors. Adjectives such as *wooden* and *paper* describe the material something is made of.

When you use more than one adjective before a noun, place them in the order shown in the chart (from left to right):

Adjectives				Noun
Opinion	**Size**	**Color**	**Material**	
interesting			glass	jewelry
	narrow	blue	silk	ribbon
beautiful		orange		butterfly
	tiny		gold	key

Wrong	Right
She makes **glass interesting** jewelry.	She makes **interesting glass** jewelry.
I bought a **silk blue narrow** ribbon.	I bought a **narrow blue silk** ribbon.
That is an **orange beautiful** butterfly.	That is a **beautiful orange** butterfly.
The box came with a **gold tiny** key.	The box came with a **tiny gold** key.

Practice

**Workbook
Page 6**

Work with a partner. Take turns role-playing Julia and Patrick having a conversation. Put the adjectives in parentheses in the correct order. Write the dialogue in your notebook.

Patrick: Julia, what are you doing with that _____ _____ cloth? (cotton, large)

Julia: I'm going to use _____ _____ thread to make the egg and the worm. (cotton, bright)

Patrick: That *is* a great idea. And I'll ask my mom if I can bring in her _____ _____ scarf as part of our exhibit. (silk, fancy)

Julia: Silk is so amazing. Who would believe that it comes from these _____ _____ cocoons? (white, little)

14

WRITING A DESCRIPTIVE PARAGRAPH

Describe an Object

Before you write a descriptive essay, you'll need to learn about descriptive writing. When you describe something, you use sensory details. Sensory details help the reader see, hear, smell, taste, or feel what you are describing. They appeal to the reader's five senses. For example, to describe a caterpillar, you might use the word *fuzzy*. *Fuzzy* appeals to the sense of touch. You might also say the caterpillar has *black and yellow stripes*. These words appeal to the sense of sight.

Here is a model of a descriptive paragraph. Notice the sensory details that the writer included. Before writing he listed his ideas in a word web.

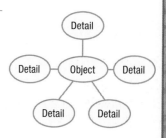

Andrew Tilley

The Butterfly

The butterfly is a beautiful and delicate insect. It often sits on gorgeous, tall, red flowers. It has delicate, black wings with a beautiful white and orange pattern. If you were to hold it in your hand, it would feel like you were holding fluttering cotton balls. It has soft silky wings and six long, skinny, black legs. The insect's abdomen has polka-dots between two solid lines that create a pattern. The butterfly's two thin antennae are attached to a head with white lines and two big red eyes. The butterfly seems so peaceful and mellow. Some insects might be ugly and hard, but I'm sure you'll agree that the butterfly is beautiful and delicate.

Practice  Workbook Page 7

Write a paragraph describing a living thing you have observed in nature, such as a beautiful flower, bird, or tree. Use sensory details to help the reader see, hear, smell, taste, or feel what you are describing. Use a graphic organizer like the one above. Be sure to use adjectives in the correct order.

Writing Checklist

WORD CHOICE:
☑ I chose words carefully to create vivid sensory details.

ORGANIZATION:
☑ I included details to support the main idea.

Prepare to Read

What You Will Learn

Reading

■ Vocabulary building:
Context, dictionary skills, word study

■ Reading strategy:
Preview

■ Text type:
Informational text (science)

Grammar, Usage, and Mechanics
Comparison structures

Writing
Describe a place

THE BIG QUESTION

How does the natural world affect us? Have you ever been to a forest? A desert? A beach? What living and nonliving things did you see there? Work with a partner. Copy the chart below into your notebook. List facts you know about each place. Then share what you know with the class.

Tropical Rain Forest	Desert	Ocean
	sand	whales

BUILD BACKGROUND

"Ecosystems: The Systems of Nature" is a science article. It tells important facts about the world around us. The world is made up of different kinds of habitats, populations, communities, and ecosystems. Ecosystems consist of living things, such as plants, animals, and tiny organisms, and nonliving things, such as rocks and water. An ecosystem can be a forest, a desert, or even your own backyard. The living things depend on each other and on the nonliving things in the ecosystem for survival.

◀ Tropical rain forest ▶

◀ Tundra with ice

Savannah (grassland) ▶

◀ Ocean

VOCABULARY

Learn Key Words

Read these sentences. Use the context to figure out the meaning of the red words. Use a dictionary to check your answers. Then write each word and its meaning in your notebook.

Key Words

nonliving
nutrients
organism
photosynthesis
reproduce
species

1. Animals and plants are living things. Air, water, and rocks are nonliving things.

2. Nutrients are found in the soil and are needed for all plants, animals, and people to live and grow.

3. You are an organism because you are alive.

4. During photosynthesis, plants make food using sunlight.

5. Animals must reproduce to have offspring, or babies.

6. House cats are a species of animal. They are alike in many ways and can have babies together.

Practice  Workbook Page 8

Write the sentences in your notebook. Choose a red word from the box above to complete each sentence. Then take turns reading the sentences aloud with a partner.

1. Dogs can have puppies together because they are the same _____.

2. The natural world is made up of both living and _____ things.

3. A whale, like an ant, is an _____, or living thing.

4. The _____ in the soil help plants grow.

5. Plants make food by a process called _____.

6. Rabbits and squirrels cannot _____ together because they belong to different species.

◀ A whale

17

Learn Academic Words

Study the **red** words and their meanings. You will find these words useful when talking and writing about informational texts. Write each word and its meaning in your notebook. After you read "Ecosystems: The Systems of Nature," try to use these words to respond to the text.

consume = eat or use something	➡	Cows **consume** tons of grass each year.
environment = the world of land, sea, and air that we live in	➡	Trees, air, soil, and water are parts of the natural **environment**.
interact = have an effect on each other	➡	Different kinds of animals **interact** in a forest.
similar = almost the same, but not exactly the same	➡	Dogs are **similar** to wolves in many ways.
survive = continue to live	➡	All animals need food to **survive**.

Practice  **Workbook Page 9**

Work with a partner to answer these questions. Try to include the **red** word in your answer. Write the sentences in your notebook.

1. What kind of food does a bird **consume**?
2. What can people do to protect the **environment**?
3. How do dogs **interact** with humans?
4. How are lions and tigers **similar**?
5. What does a plant or animal need to **survive** in the desert?

A tiger ▶

A lion ▶

18

Word Study: Spelling Regular Plurals

To make most nouns plural, add -s to the end of the word.

Singular	Plural with -s
animal	animal**s**
lake	lake**s**

Add -es to singular nouns that end in s, z, x, sh, or ch.

Singular	Plural with -es
virus	virus**es**
fox	fox**es**

If the noun ends with a consonant + y, change y to i, and add -es.

baby	bab**ies**

If the noun ends with a vowel + y, add -s.

monkey	monkey**s**

Practice

Work with a partner. Look at the words in the box. Write the plural form of each noun in your notebook.

brush   carnivore   city   class   community   donkey   forest   lynx   whale

▲ A monkey

READING STRATEGY PREVIEW

Previewing a text helps you understand the content more quickly. When you preview a text, you prepare yourself for the information you are about to learn. To preview, follow these steps:

- Look at the title, headings, and visuals. Read the captions or labels.
- Think about what you already know about the subject.
- Think about your purpose for reading the text.

Before you read "Ecosystems: The Systems of Nature," look at the title, visuals, and captions. Think about what you already know about this subject. What more would you like to know?

Set a purpose for reading How do living and nonliving things in the natural word depend on each other?

Ecosystems
THE SYSTEMS OF NATURE

Organisms and Species

An organism is a living thing. A huge redwood tree is an organism. A small mouse is an organism. A tiny insect is an organism. A human is an organism, too. Some organisms, such as bacteria, are so small that you cannot see them.

A group of very similar organisms is a species. The organisms in a species are so similar that they can reproduce—that is, have offspring, or babies—together, and their offspring can reproduce, too. Horses and cows, for example, cannot have offspring together because they are different species.

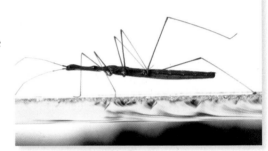

▲ An insect (water strider)

▲ A cat and its offspring

▲ Birds tend their nest.

Habitats

A habitat is the place where an organism lives—its surroundings, or environment. A habitat provides the things an organism needs to survive, such as food, water, a livable temperature, and shelter. A habitat can be as large as an ocean or as small as a drop of water. It can be a forest or one tree. Several species may live in the same habitat, such as a river.

Different organisms live in different habitats because they have different requirements for survival. For example, a river or lake can be the habitat of some species of freshwater fish, such as trout. Freshwater trout cannot survive in the ocean, which contains salt water. An ocean and a lake are very different habitats. Similarly, the desert in the southwestern United States and northern Mexico is the habitat of the saguaro cactus. The saguaro cactus cannot survive in a tropical rain forest.

▲ Saguaro cactuses

Sometimes animals move to different places within their habitats. For example, many kinds of frogs are born in water. However, they live mostly on land when they grow up. During very cold weather, some frogs go under the ground or bury themselves in mud at the bottom of ponds to stay warm.

---

shelter, place that protects you from bad weather or danger
requirements, needs
tropical, hot and wet
ponds, small lakes

BEFORE YOU GO ON

1 What is an organism? Give an example.

2 What is a species? Give an example.

On Your Own
What is your habitat?

21

Populations and Communities

All the members of one species in the same area are a population. For example, all the frogs in a lake are a population. All the pine trees in a forest are a population. All the people in a city, state, or country are a population. Some populations do not stay in one place. Monarch butterflies travel south each year from parts of western Canada and the United States to Mexico. Some species of whales travel around many oceans.

A community is all the populations that live together in one place, such as all the plants and animals in a desert. In a community, the different populations live close together, so they interact with one another. One way populations interact in a community is by using the same resources, such as food and shelter. In a desert, for example, snakes, lizards, and spiders may all use rocks and holes for shelter. They may eat insects, other animals, or their own kind of food.

▲ A population of pine trees

▲ American toads

22

The Parts of an Ecosystem

An ecosystem is made up of both the living and nonliving things in an area. Nonliving things include air, sunlight, water, rocks, and soil. All parts of an ecosystem, living and nonliving, interact. Plants take water from the soil, and they produce oxygen. Animals breathe in oxygen from the air. They eat plants and other animals.

soil, top layer of earth
oxygen, gas in the air that all plants and animals need to live
breathe, take in air through the nose and mouth

▲ An oak tree ecosystem

BEFORE YOU GO ON

1 What is a population?

2 What is an ecosystem?

On Your Own
What parts of the ecosystem do you interact with?

23

▲ A vulture (scavenger)

▲ A bear (omnivore)

Three Kinds of Organisms

In an ecosystem, there are three kinds of organisms: producers, consumers, and decomposers. Each kind of organism is important.

Most producers are plants. They use energy from sunlight to make their own food from water and carbon dioxide. (Carbon dioxide is a gas in the air. People and animals breathe it out.) This process of making food is called photosynthesis.

Consumers cannot make their own food. They eat, or consume, other organisms. All animals are consumers. Consumers are classified by what they eat.

- **Herbivores,** such as deer, horses, and many birds, eat only plants.
- **Carnivores**, such as lions, spiders, and snakes, eat only animals. Some carnivores are scavengers. A scavenger eats dead organisms. Scavengers include vultures and catfish.
- **Omnivores**, such as crows and bears, eat plants *and* animals.

Some consumers are also decomposers. Decomposers break down dead plants and animals. The dead plants and animals are changed into nutrients, which go back into the soil. Producers—plants—consume these nutrients. Decomposers are very important in the ecosystem because plants need nutrients to grow.

The two main kinds of decomposers are bacteria and fungi. Bacteria are very small living things. We cannot see bacteria, but they live in soil, air, and water and on other organisms. A fungus is a plantlike organism without leaves that grows in dark, warm, wet places. Mushrooms are one kind of fungus.

▲ A fungus
(a decomposer)

---

energy, power that produces heat
classified, put into groups

24

▲ A food chain of grass (a producer), a mouse (a small consumer), and a hawk (a larger consumer)

Food Chains

The movement of food through a community is called a food chain. A food chain always begins with producers—plants. In the ocean, a food chain begins with algae, which are very small plantlike organisms. Small fish eat the algae. Medium-size fish eat the small fish. Big fish eat the medium-size fish.

On land, a food chain is similar. It begins with a plant. A consumer, such as an insect, eats the plant. Then another consumer, such as a bat, eats the insect. Next, a bigger consumer, such as an owl, eats the bat. Finally, the owl dies, and decomposers break it down into nutrients.

Every part of the food chain is necessary to every other part. Without water, plants die. Without plants, animals cannot live.

BEFORE YOU GO ON

1 Name three kinds of organisms in an ecosystem.

2 What are three kinds of consumers?

On Your Own
Describe how living and nonliving things are important to the natural world.

25

COMPREHENSION
Workbook
Page 12

Right There

1. What does a habitat provide for living things?
2. Name two main kinds of decomposers.

Think and Search

3. Compare and contrast a community and an ecosystem.
4. Describe how the different organisms interact in a food chain.

Author and You

5. What is one interesting fact you learned about ecosystems?
6. Do you think the author would agree with this statement: "All living things depend on nonliving things"? Explain.

On Your Own

7. Why do you think humans can live in many different kinds of places?
8. Do you think it is important for humans to protect nature? Why?

IN YOUR OWN WORDS

Summarize the reading. Use the words from the chart to tell a partner about ecosystems.

Organisms and Species	➡	similar, reproduce
Habitats	➡	species, organisms, interact, resources
Populations and Communities	➡	organisms, survive, environment
The Parts of an Ecosystem	➡	living, nonliving, interact
Producers, Consumers, and Decomposers	➡	process, carnivores, omnivores, herbivores
Food Chains	➡	producer, consumer, decomposer

DISCUSSION

Discuss in pairs or small groups.

1. Why do different organisms live in different habitats? Give examples.

2. What would happen to a forest ecosystem if someone cut down all the trees?

3. If you could choose, what type of habitat would you prefer to live in? Why?

Q How does the natural world affect us? How do the organisms in your community interact with each other?

»)⌒ Listening TIP

Listen carefully to other people's ideas.

READ FOR FLUENCY

It is often easier to read a text if you understand the difficult words and phrases. Work with a partner. Choose a paragraph from the reading. Identify the words and phrases you do not know or have trouble pronouncing. Look up the difficult words in a dictionary.

Take turns pronouncing the words and phrases with your partner. If necessary, ask your teacher to model the correct pronunciation. Then take turns reading the paragraph aloud. Give each other feedback on your reading.

EXTENSION  Workbook Page 12

Explore the community that you live in. Find out which plants and types of animal consumers live there. Then copy and complete the chart below.

In My Ecosystem
Carnivores:
Herbivores:
Omnivores:
Plants:

▲ A park in a community

Grammar and Writing

Comparison Structures

You can use *as _____ as, so _____ that,* or *similarly* to describe something by comparing it to something else. For example, you can say:

> Each part of a food chain is **as** necessary **as** every other part.

You could also say, *Each part of a food chain is necessary.* However, using the comparison structure *as _____ as* adds to your description and makes it clearer.

A habitat can be large. An ocean is large.	*as _____ as*	A habitat can be **as** large **as** an ocean.
Bacteria are small. You cannot see them.	*so _____ that*	Bacteria are **so** small **that** you cannot see them.
The food chain in the ocean begins with algae. The food chain on land begins with plants.	*similarly*	The food chain in the ocean begins with algae. **Similarly**, the food chain on land begins with plants.

Practice  **Workbook** Page 13

Work with a partner. Look at the chart below. Combine each sentence or phrase in column A with the one in column B to make a new sentence using one of the comparison structures.

Column A	Column B
A habitat can be small.	A drop of water can be small.
All the frogs in a lake are a population.	All the trees in a forest are a population.
The organisms in a species are similar.	They can reproduce.
A consumer, such as a bat, eats insects.	A larger consumer, such as an owl, eats bats.
Decomposers are important.	Producers and consumers are important.
Plants are important.	Animals could not live without them.

WRITING A DESCRIPTIVE PARAGRAPH

Describe a Place

You have learned to use sensory details when describing an object. When you describe a place, it's important to arrange the details in the order that makes sense for the place you're describing. For example, to describe a rain forest, you might start from the treetops and end with the forest floor. To describe a garden, you might start from the front and end with the back. When you describe a place according to the position of the things in it, you are using spatial order.

Here is a paragraph describing a place. This writer has arranged the sensory details using spatial order. She listed her ideas in a graphic organizer.

On the porch
↓
On the patch of grass
↓
In the garden

Muniphe Green

My Backyard

One of my favorite places in the world is the backyard. We have a small porch with a chair where you can sit for hours, reading or just taking in the sights, sounds, and smells. The sound of the birds chirping is so calming, and I love the fresh smell of the trees and grass. You step off the porch into a patch of grass so soft that I sometimes lie down on it and watch the trees from below. When I do this I can see the birds twittering and the squirrels racing around. Once I saw our neighbor's cat up in the branches. Another thing I like to do is to check out my mother's garden. She put it right behind the patch of grass, where the trees don't block the sunlight. Mom usually plants vegetables, and I like to check on their progress. Sometimes I help her with the weeding or the watering. It's so great to have a little bit of nature to hang out in.

Practice

Workbook Page 14

Write a paragraph describing a place where you can enjoy the sights, sounds, and smells of the natural world, such as a park, a beach, a pond, or a nature preserve. Arrange your details using the type of spatial order that makes sense for your topic. Use a graphic organizer like the one above. Be sure to use comparison structures correctly.

Writing Checklist

ORGANIZATION:
☑ I organized my ideas using the type of spatial order that suits my subject matter.

CONVENTIONS:
☑ I used comparison structures correctly.

29

Prepare to Read

What You Will Learn

Reading
- Vocabulary building: *Literary terms, word study*
- Reading strategy: *Visualize*
- Text type: *Literature (short story, poetry)*

Grammar, Usage, and Mechanics
Simple and compound sentences

Writing
Describe a person

THE BIG QUESTION

How does the natural world affect us? Have you ever been to a desert or seen pictures of a desert? Discuss with a partner what you know about deserts. List your ideas in your notebook. As you read the story and the poem, add new facts that you learn about deserts.

BUILD BACKGROUND

The short story **"Ali, Child of the Desert"** and the poem **"Desert Women"** are set in a particular part of the natural world—the desert. About one-fifth of the earth is made up of deserts. Deserts are found on every continent except Europe. There are two different kinds of deserts: hot and dry (such as the Arabian and Sahara deserts), and cold and dry (such as Antarctica and the Gobi Desert). Few plants and animals live in the desert because of the lack of water and intense heat or cold. Some animals have adapted to the desert heat, such as snakes and lizards. Another famous desert animal is the camel, which can survive for days without food—living off the fat stored in its hump.

The short story takes place in Morocco, a country in North Africa. In Morocco, it is common for people to make long and difficult journeys through the desert to buy and trade goods. As you read the story and poem, look for words that tell you how the authors and characters feel about life in the desert.

▼ Camels in the Sahara Desert

VOCABULARY

Learn Literary Words

Figurative language is writing or speech that is not meant to be read as fact. Figurative language creates vivid images by comparing two different things. **Personification** is a type of figurative language. Personification gives human qualities to nonhuman things. Here is an example:

> The violets whisper from the shade
> Which their own leaves have made.
> —*Christina Rossetti*

The poet is giving violets a human quality by calling the sound their leaves make "whispering."

Setting is the time and place of a story's action. The time might be the year, the season, the day, or the hour. The place might be a city, a forest, a garden, or a kitchen. Read the following sentence. What does it tell you about the setting? (Note: A fist is a closed hand.)

> The sun was only two fists high in the sky, but already it was hot.

Practice

Work with a partner. Take turns reading these examples of personification. Identify the words that give human qualities to nonhuman things.

> The wind is singing to me.
> The sled danced across the icy pond.
> The stars watched us with cold eyes.
> Waves were licking our toes.
> The old door screamed when it opened.

▲ The Sahara Desert at sunrise

Create two examples of personification. Write about two nonhuman things—such as a tree, a door, or waves—as if they were human. Have each thing make a sound or motion, or express an idea as only a human would do.

31

Learn Academic Words

Study the **red** words and their meanings. You will find these words useful when talking and writing about literature. Write each word and its meaning in your notebook. After you read "Ali, Child of the Desert" and "Desert Women," try to use these words to respond to the text.

Academic Words

adapt
capable
concluded
rely
route

adapt = change something so that it is suitable for a new situation	➡	Desert animals **adapt** to life in a hot, dry climate.
capable = able to do something	➡	Camels are **capable** of carrying heavy loads.
concluded = made a decision based on evidence	➡	The land was dry and dusty. We **concluded** it hadn't rained in a long time.
rely = trust someone or something	➡	You should have a guide to **rely** on when you travel in the desert.
route = way from one place to another	➡	The long **route** through the desert made the journey slow and difficult.

Practice

Workbook Page 16

Write the sentences in your notebook. Choose a **red** word from the box above to complete each sentence. Then take turns reading the sentences aloud with a partner.

1. The scientists _____ that they needed to test the water before drinking it.

2. The boy and his grandfather took the same _____ from north to south every year.

3. When an animal starts to live in a new ecosystem, it has to _____ to the change in climate.

4. The snake is _____ of surviving in a hot and dry desert.

5. The children have to _____ on their family for food and protection.

A camel carrying crates of oranges ▶

Word Study: Compound Nouns

A compound noun is made up of more than one word. Sometimes compound nouns are written as one word. Sometimes they are written as two separate words, and sometimes the words are separated with a hyphen.

One Word	Two Words	Hyphenated Words
grandmother	folk music	son-in-law
goatherd	vice president	well-being
rattlesnake	high school	high-rise

Practice

Work with a partner. Look at the charts below. Combine the words in each row to form a compound word. Then check a dictionary to see if the compound word is written as one word, separated as two words, or hyphenated. Write the compound words in your notebook.

grand	father
tall	tale
over	head
deep	set

sun	rise
camp	fire
good	night
wind	mill

▲ A diamondback rattlesnake

READING STRATEGY | VISUALIZE

Visualizing helps you make pictures in your mind of what you are reading. To visualize, follow these steps.

- Read this sentence:

  The desert rolled beneath Ali, its sharp, delicate ridges reflecting the heat.

- Now close your eyes and visualize the sentence. What do you see?
- As you read, pay attention to descriptive words and figurative language. Visualize the characters, places, and events.

Read the story "Ali, Child of the Desert." As you read, ask yourself, "What language is the author using to create a picture of the characters, setting, and events?"

Set a purpose for reading How are the people who live in the desert affected by the natural world?

Ali, Child of the Desert

Jonathan London

The sun was only two fists high in the sky, but already it was hot. The desert rolled beneath Ali, its sharp, delicate ridges reflecting the heat. Three days' ride ahead lay the Moroccan market town of Rissani, at the edge of the Great Sahara.

Until now, Ali had been too young to go on the yearly journey to the market. But this year, at last, he could show his father that he was ready to be a man.

Ali rode at the rear of the herd, his father at the head. When they sold the camels, they would have money to buy cloth, a copper kettle, sugar for their tea, new knives and gold coins and hard candy.

For now, though, there was only the slow, steady sway of Jabad over the rippling dunes. It seemed to Ali that he had been sitting atop his camel for weeks. But he had not spoken of the heat, his thirst, his sore rump. Only a child would complain of his discomfort.

> ✔ **LITERARY CHECK**
> *What is the **setting** of this story?*

Suddenly, out of nowhere, the wind came howling like a pack of wild dogs. Ali heard his father's voice calling, "Ali! Come here! Stay close behind me!" Then he heard nothing but the whirling sand. It swallowed the sun, and the herd—and his father.

Ali jerked up the hood of his *djellaba* and kicked hard at Jabad's sides. Jabad roared, then broke into a gallop. Ali's heart pounded like a drum.

Finally, blinded by the needle-sharp sand, he brought Jabad to a halt and commanded him to kneel. He climbed down and sat leaning against Jabad's flank. He knew he musn't lie down, or he could be buried alive by the sand. He squeezed his eyes shut and pulled the hood close around his face. Alone in the vast Sahara, he waited.

At last, the wind no longer screamed. Ali slowly lifted his head. His eyes and ears were packed with sand. His teeth were gritty. He spit on his sleeve and wiped his eyes.

The sun was sinking. A white vulture circled overhead. Puff adders and cobras would soon slide out into the cool of the evening. The jackals and hyenas would be hungry after the storm. Ali must find his father before it became dark. He climbed onto Jabad's back and headed toward the west—and Rissani.

After a time, Ali heard the jangle of bells from somewhere over the dunes. He turned Jabad toward the sound and spurred him on. Soon he saw the silhouettes of a goatherd and his flock, black against the blazing sky, and his heart leaped.

"*Asalaam-o-Aleikum!*" called Ali as he neared the herd.

"*Aleikum-o-Asalaam!*" replied the old Berber. His face was crinkled and browned from the sun and wind. His deep-set eyes were dark beneath his hood. Beside him a boy, younger than Ali, stared, his big black eyes wide with curiosity.

With a grunt, Jabad folded his long, knobby legs. Ali stepped into the strong U of his neck and onto the ground.

djellaba
(jih-LAH-bah): long, loose, hooded robe with full sleeves

Asalaam-o-Aleikum
(ah-sah-LAY-moo ah-LAY-kuhm): Peace be with you (formal greeting)

Aleikum-o-Asalaam
(ah-LAY-kuh-moo sah-LAHM): Peace be with you (polite reply)

---

whirling, spinning around very fast
flank, side of an animal's body
spurred, urged; pushed forward
silhouettes, dark shapes against a light background

BEFORE YOU GO ON

1 Where were Ali and his father going? Why?

2 Where did Ali hide during the sandstorm?

On Your Own
Have you ever been in a bad storm? What was it like?

35

When he and the herdsman had touched fingertips and told each other their names, Abdul invited Ali to share tea. With a nod of gratitude, Ali took up Jabad's goat-hair reins and commanded him to stand. They followed Abdul and his grandson to a dwelling half-sunk in the sand.

Abdul ducked into the one-room adobe hut where he and the boy, Youssef, had wintered with their goats. With a red woolen rug under his arm, he stepped back outside, then unrolled the rug on the sand before the door. While Abdul built a fire beside the rug, Youssef fetched water from the well. Soon, flames licked the cool night air.

Setting the water to boil, Abdul asked, "How do you come to be here alone, boy?"

Ali tried to sound brave as he told about the *cherqui*—the sandstorm—and about his father and their camels.

"Our small oasis is on the route to Rissani," said Abdul as he buried a round of bread dough in the coals at the edge of the fire. "In the morning, if God so wills it, your father shall find you. If not, you are welcome to come with us to the mountains. Now the goats have eaten almost all the dates, and they are hungry. We must leave early tomorrow to herd them to the high pastures."

Ali had heard of bandits who lived in the caves on the slopes, raiding goatherds and travelers. He licked his lips. His mouth was as dry as the desert sands.

The kettle came to a boil, and Youssef dropped in a rock of sugar. Abdul poured the bubbling water into three tall glasses stuffed with sprigs of wild peppermint and let it steep. Then he reached into the coals for the loaf of *kesrah*.

He dusted off the ashes, broke the pocket bread into three, and handed out the pieces. Its warmth filled Ali's palms as Abdul murmured a blessing. To Ali, the warm bread and the sweet mint tea seemed like a feast!

Youssef fiddled with the knobs of a tiny transistor radio, but only static came through. "Grandfather?" he asked. "Would you tell us a story?"

Abdul gazed into the glowing coals. Then his quiet, rumbly voice filled the night, just as Grandmother's did when she told Ali and his sisters stories around their campfire. "When I was a young man, little more than a boy . . ." Abdul told a tale about the warrior-tribesmen of the Berber.

---

oasis, place in the desert with water and trees
pastures, land covered with grass
sprigs, small branches
transistor radio, older style portable radio
static, noise caused by electricity

✔ LITERARY CHECK

What type of figurative language does the author use to describe the flames?

cherqui
(SHAIR-kyah): eastern wind, sandstorm

kesrah
(KEE-srah): flat pocket bread

BEFORE YOU GO ON

1 What was Abdul's dwelling like?

2 Why were Abdul and his grandson going to the mountains?

💡On Your Own
What are some good stories to tell around the campfire?

37

Ali pictured the charge of the horsemen into battle, their white turbans and bandoliers flashing in the sunlight. He could almost hear the thunder of hooves and the clash of swords, the boom of muskets ripping the air.

"In those days," Abdul concluded, "warriors shaved their heads, except for a single lock of hair." He pushed back his hood, revealing a white turban. "When a warrior dies, Allah grabs him by the lock of hair and pulls him into heaven." Abdul unwound his turban. His bald skull gleamed in the firelight. A single lock of white hair hung from the crown of his head.

Ali's scalp prickled. He brushed his own black, short-cropped hair, picturing Abdul as a young warrior, sitting tall atop his prancing stallion, ready for battle.

They sat in silence for a moment. Then Abdul and Youssef said good night and went inside the hut. As Ali bundled the rug around him and lay down, a thousand stars stared down at him from the cold Saharan night. By morning, he must decide whether to wait for his father to find him, or go with Abdul to the mountains. If he left with the goatherd, would he ever see his family again?

Ali sat up and stoked the fire. He would keep it burning, so his father could see it in the dark. He would sit tall, like a warrior, and wait. The fire would keep away the striped hyenas. Ali wondered what he would find to eat if he stayed in the desert. What if his father didn't come? Ali's mind ran through the night as the flames danced and dwindled, taking on the shapes of dreams.

✔ LITERARY CHECK
*How does the author use **personification** to describe the fire?*

Ka-*pow!* Ali awoke trembling. *Bandits!* he thought. Abdul stood outside the hut, holding his musket. "If your father is near," he said, "perhaps he'll hear this." Then he ducked inside to pack his few belongings.

Ali breathed deep. Then, facing east, he bowed in morning prayer.

When Abdul reappeared, the sun was a fist high in the east. "Your father hasn't come. If we don't head for summer pastures now, the goats will starve. What have you decided? Will you come with us, or stay?"

If he stayed, would there be anything for him in the desert but jackals and cobras, sizzling sun and burning hunger? Ali thought of something his father had said that had always puzzled him: "In the desert there is nothing. Or everything. It depends how you look at it, how you live."

"I will wait here," he said.

---

turbans, long pieces of cloth that are wrapped around the head
bandoliers, belts fitted with small pockets for carrying bullets
muskets, old types of guns
stoked, added more wood or fuel
dwindled, got smaller

Abdul handed Ali his musket. "Although you are young," he said, "you have the heart of a warrior. Fire the musket every time the sun moves a hand's width across the sky."

"*Shoukran!*" said Ali, bowing his head in thanks. "And I'll keep a fire burning, smoky during the day, bright at night, to help God guide my father to me."

By the time Abdul and Youssef departed, the sun had risen another hand's width. Ali loaded the musket, as Abdul had taught him, and fired into the air. The blast knocked him to the ground. He rubbed his shoulder and his rump, and got back up.

He continued to tend the fire and shoot when it was time. By midday he was very hungry. The pile of dates Abdul had left for him and Jabad was already dwindling, so Ali tried to fill his belly with more water from the well.

Ali had stayed awake most of the night. Now the heat made him sleepy. His mind started drifting, drifting. . . .

Ali awoke with a start. The sun was almost down. It would soon turn dark. He had little firewood left. He reached for the shot bag. The ammunition was running low. He rammed a ball into the barrel of the musket, then ran his fingers through his bristly hair. Perhaps he should shave his head smooth like a warrior's, leaving just one lock for Allah to grab if he died.

Shoukran
_____
(SHUHK-rahn): Thank you

BEFORE YOU GO ON

1 Why did warriors shave their heads in Abdul's time?

2 What food did Abdul leave for Ali and Jabad?

On Your Own
Have you ever slept outside at night? If so, what was it like? If not, would you like to?

39

He hoisted the heavy musket, aimed into the endless purple of the sky, and fired. Ka-pow! . . . Ka-pow! Had he heard an echo, or . . .

Ali looked around. Behind him was a cloud of dust, moving rapidly toward him. Soon he heard the thunder of hooves. Then he saw a camel and a rider.

"Ali!" It was his father! Jerking his camel to a halt, he slid off and swept Ali into his arms. Jabad joyously bellowed and trotted to his own father, Jebel.

"I waited for you," said Ali.

His eyes fell on the small pile of dates near the well. Abdul and Youssef had so little, but they had given so much. This time, in the desert there had been everything.

ABOUT THE **AUTHOR**

Jonathan London is a popular children's author who has written numerous books, including *Where's Home?* and *The Owl Who Became the Moon.* He has a great love for the outdoors. It's no surprise that nature and animals are the most popular subjects in his books. London lives in northern California, where he enjoys backpacking through the woods and playing in the snow with his wife and two sons.

Desert Women

Desert women know
about survival.
Fierce heat and cold
have burned and thickened
our skin. Like cactus
we've learned to hoard,
to sprout deep roots,
to seem asleep, yet wake
at the scent of softness
in the air, to hide
pain and loss by silence,
no branches wail
or whisper our sad songs
safe behind our thorns.

Don't be deceived.
When we bloom, we stun.

—*Pat Mora*

---

hoard, collect and hide things
deceived, made to believe
   something that is not true

ABOUT THE POET

Pat Mora grew up speaking Spanish and English in El Paso, Texas. She has written more than twenty-five children's books, including *A Birthday Basket for Tia* and *Pablo's Tree.* In 2006 she received the National Hispanic Cultural Center Literary Award. Mora currently splits her time between Kentucky and the southwestern United States.

BEFORE YOU GO ON

1 How did Ali first see his father?

2 In the poem, how are women like cactuses?

On Your Own
Describe some living and nonliving things in the desert.

41

READER'S THEATER

Act out the following scene between Ali and Abdul when they meet in the desert.

Ali: Hello! Can you hear me? I'm lost!

Abdul: Hello! Yes, I can hear you, boy. My name is Abdul. Come with me and have some tea. Youssef, my grandson, will bring us water for the teapot. Why are you all alone out here?

Ali: My father and I were on our way to the market when the sandstorm came. The wind was so strong, and sand was everywhere. I had to hide behind my camel for shelter. When the storm stopped, I was alone.

Abdul: Don't worry, my boy. You can come with us to the mountains. We must go tomorrow to take the goats to the grasslands. They've eaten everything here.

Ali: That is very kind of you. But, if I go . . . how will I ever find my father?

COMPREHENSION

**Workbook
Page 19**

Right There

1. What did Ali and his father want to buy at the market?
2. How did Ali and Abdul first greet each other?

Think and Search

3. What things did Abdul leave for Ali?
4. Why didn't Ali leave with Abdul and go to the mountains?

Author and You

5. Did Ali make the right decision to stay and wait for his father? Why?
6. How do you think the author of the poem feels about the desert?

On Your Own

7. What would you do if you were lost? Explain.
8. Describe something that you accomplished on your own. How did it make you feel?

DISCUSSION

Listening TIP

Look at the speaker as he or she speaks.

Discuss in pairs or small groups.

1. Do you think Ali was right to rely on Abdul? Have you ever had to rely on someone's help?

2. What might have happened to Ali if his father had not found him? Do you think Ali would have been capable of surviving?

3. The poem "Desert Women" compares women to plant life in the desert. Is this an effective way to show personification? Explain.

Q **How does the natural world affect us?** Do you think living in the desert would be difficult? Explain.

RESPONSE TO LITERATURE

Workbook
Page 19

Write a thank-you letter from Ali to Abdul and his grandson. Give details about all the help that Abdul gave to Ali. Explain what Ali learned from his experience. Then share your letter in a small group.

▲ An oasis in the desert

Grammar and Writing

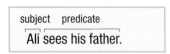

GRAMMAR, USAGE, AND MECHANICS

Simple and Compound Sentences

A sentence is a group of words that expresses a complete thought. It has a subject (noun) and a predicate (phrase that includes a verb).
The predicate tells what the subject does.

> subject   predicate
> Ali sees his father.

A subject may be omitted but understood.

> Come! (The subject is *you*.)

A simple sentence is made up of a main clause with one subject and one predicate.

> subject predicate
> Ali meets Abdul.

A compound sentence has two or more main clauses. Each clause has its own subject and predicate. The clauses are usually joined by a comma and a conjunction, such as *and* or *but*.

> subject   predicate   subject   predicate
> Abdul had so little, but he gave so much.
>   clause   clause

Practice  **Workbook** Page 20

Work with a partner. Look at the sentences below and discuss whether each is simple or compound. Then write a simple sentence and compound sentence of your own.

1. Most deserts are hot during the day, but they are cold at night.

2. Deserts cover at least 20 percent of the earth.

3. Deserts are hot, and they are sometimes dangerous.

44

WRITING A DESCRIPTIVE PARAGRAPH

Describe a Person

To describe a person, you need to describe physical traits and character traits. Physical traits are details telling how the person looks. For example, Abdul's face is "crinkled and browned from the sun and wind." Character traits tell how the person thinks and behaves. For example, "Ali tried to sound brave as he told about the sandstorm."

Here is a model of a paragraph that describes a person. This writer has described the person's physical traits and character traits. Before writing, he used a T-chart to organize his ideas.

Physical traits	Character traits

Caleb Robinson

Hamid

My friend Hamid lives in Lebanon. He is 5 foot 4 inches tall and he weighs about 110 pounds. He has jet black hair, and he has brown eyes. Hamid has a father and three brothers. His father owns a goat farm, and Hamid and his three brothers each have their own pet goat. Hamid's pet goat is very fuzzy, and his name is Omar. Hamid loves his goat as much as I love my pets. He treats it like a part of his family. Hamid is very athletic, and he is a great soccer player. He likes to practice all day and all night. However, Hamid's father is strict and doesn't let him go out past dark because there is a lot of crime in his city. Even though Hamid's city and pets are different from mine, our lives are very similar.

Practice

Workbook Page 21

Write a paragraph describing a person you know well, such as a family member, teacher, friend, or classmate. Include both physical traits and character traits. Use a graphic organizer like the one above. Be sure to use simple and compound sentences correctly.

 Writing Checklist

IDEAS:

☑ I included physical traits and character traits.

SENTENCE FLUENCY:

☑ I used simple and compound sentences.

What You Will Learn

Reading

■ Vocabulary building: *Context, dictionary skills, word study*

■ Reading strategy: *Identify main idea and details*

■ Text type: *Informational text (science)*

Grammar, Usage, and Mechanics
Subject/verb agreement: simple present

Writing
Describe an event or experience

THE BIG QUESTION

How does the natural world affect us? What do you know about water? How is water important to you? How is it important to plants and animals? In your notebook, make a K-W-L-H chart like the one below. In small groups, complete the first and second columns. When you have finished reading the article, complete the third and fourth columns.

K What do I **know**?	W What do I **want** to know?	L What did I **learn**?	H **How** did I learn it?

BUILD BACKGROUND

"Water and Living Things" is a science article that explains why water is so important to animals and plants. It also describes the water cycle—how water changes through the processes of evaporation, condensation, and precipitation. Water changes form from clouds to raindrops, but the amount of water stays the same. The water that was on Earth millions of years ago is the same water on Earth today.

A waterfall ▶

▼ A glacier

◀ Clouds

Learn Key Words

Read these sentences. Use the context to figure out the meaning of the red words. Use a dictionary to check your answers. Then write each word and its meaning in your notebook.

Key Words
atmosphere
condensation
evaporation
precipitation
vapor
water cycle

1. The **atmosphere** surrounds the earth. It is made up of oxygen and other gases.

2. A gas called water vapor cools and changes into drops of liquid water during **condensation**.

3. When the sun heats water, **evaporation** occurs. Water turns into water vapor that rises into the air.

4. Rain, snow, sleet, and hail fall from clouds to the earth as **precipitation**.

5. Water **vapor** forms when water evaporates and changes into gas.

6. The **water cycle** includes evaporation, condensation, and precipitation.

Practice  **Workbook Page 22**

Write the sentences in your notebook. Choose a key word to complete each sentence. Then take turns reading the sentences aloud with a partner.

1. Rain and snow are two types of _____.

   a. condensation   **b.** evaporation   **c.** precipitation

2. Water _____ is the gas that forms when water evaporates.

   a. precipitation   **b.** atmosphere   **c.** vapor

3. Evaporation, condensation, and precipitation are all parts of the _____.

   a. water cycle   **b.** vapors   **c.** atmosphere

4. Small drops of water that form on a window are an example of _____.

   a. evaporation   **b.** precipitation   **c.** condensation

5. Heat from the sun causes _____ of water.

   a. precipitation   **b.** evaporation   **c.** condensation

6. The air around the earth is called the _____.

   a. vapors   **b.** atmosphere   **c.** water cycle

▲ Drops of water on a blade of grass

Learn Academic Words

Study the **red** words and their meanings. You will find these words useful when talking and writing about informational texts. Write each word and its meaning in your notebook. After you read "Water and Living Things," try to use these words to respond to the text.

Academic Words

available
consist
create
process
reverse
source

available = able to be used or seen	➡	In hundreds of years, there may not be enough water **available** on the earth to drink.
consist = be made up of	➡	Clouds **consist** of water vapor.
create = make something new	➡	To **create** its own food, a plant uses the light of the sun.
process = series of actions	➡	Plants make food by a **process** that requires sunlight, water, and carbon dioxide.
reverse = change something so that it is the opposite of what it was before	➡	We need to **reverse** the damage that pollution has done to the environment.
source = person, place, or thing that something comes from	➡	Rivers are a **source** of drinking water for many animals.

Practice

Workbook
Page 23

Work with a partner to answer these questions. Try to include the **red** word in your answer. Write the sentences in your notebook.

1. What sources of water are **available** to animals in the forest?
2. What does an ice cube **consist** of?
3. What kinds of problems does bad weather **create**?
4. What is the daily **process** you go through to get ready for school in the morning?
5. Do you think it is possible to **reverse** pollution? Explain.
6. What **source** of energy does a waterwheel use?

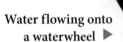

Water flowing onto
a waterwheel ▶

Word Study: Spelling Long *a*

The letter *a* stands for different sounds. Short *a* is usually spelled *a*. Long *a* has several different spellings; *a_e*, *ay*, and *ai*. Read the examples of each long *a* sound-spelling in the chart below.

a_e	ay	ai
make	day	rain
space	may	wait
lake	lay	air

Practice

Work with a partner. Copy the sentences below into your notebook. Take turns reading the sentences. Then circle each word that has a long *a*.

1. In some seasons there may be days without rain.
2. Which kind of whale did you see?
3. Dave stayed with his friends after he got off the train.
4. Who sailed in the main boat in the race?
5. We can't wait to get paid for the bait.

READING STRATEGY	IDENTIFY MAIN IDEA AND DETAILS

Identifying the main idea and details in a reading helps you see the key points the author is making. The main idea is the most important idea in the text. The details are small pieces of information that support the main idea. To identify the main idea and details, follow these steps.

- Look at the title. What do you think the text will be about?
- Read the first paragraph. What do you think is the most important idea in the text?
- Read the whole text. Look for examples, facts, dates, and sentences that tell more about the main idea. These are the details.
- Use a graphic organizer to help you list the details.

As you read "Water and Living Things," identify the main idea of each paragraph, and of the whole article. Then find the details that support the main idea.

Set a purpose for reading What is the importance of water to the natural world and all living things?

Water and Living Things

Distribution of Water on Earth

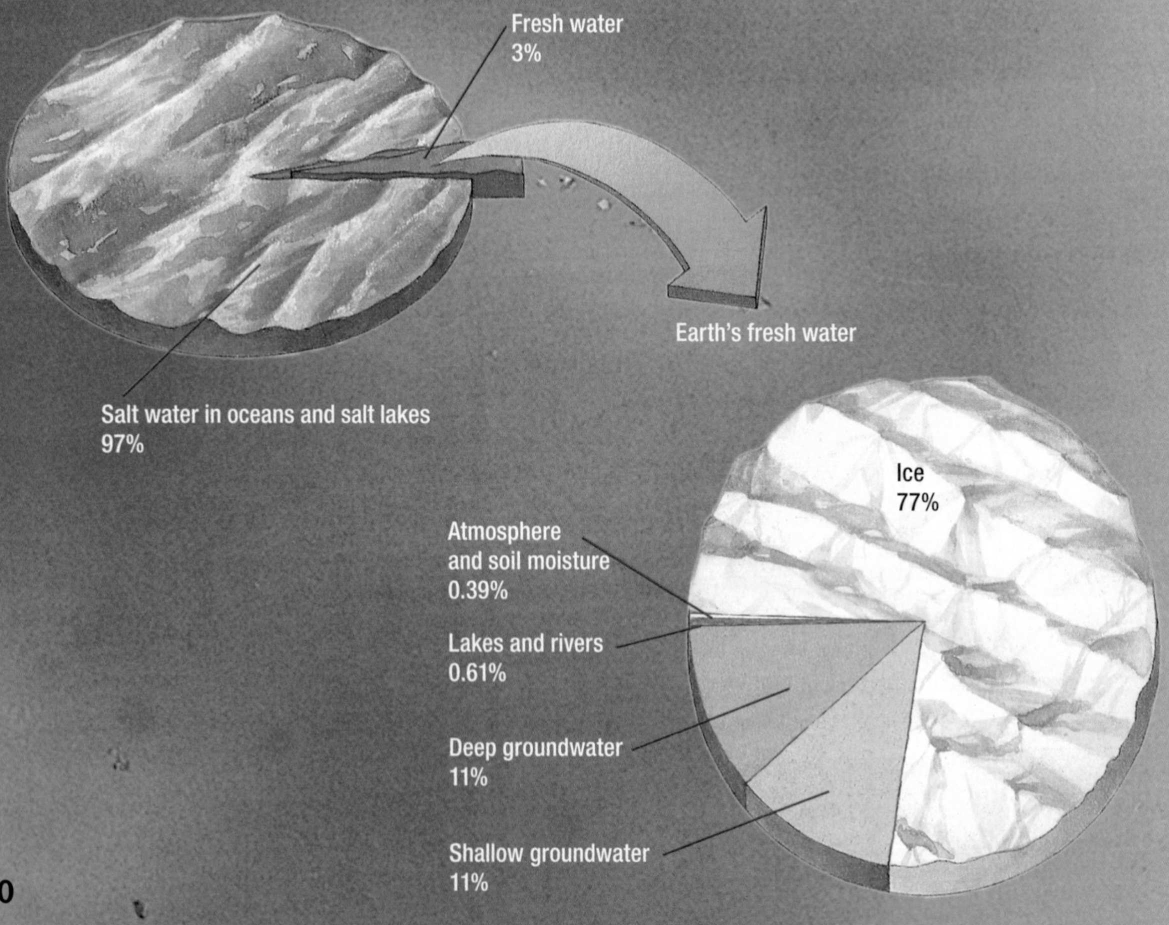

Fresh water
3%

Earth's fresh water

Salt water in oceans and salt lakes
97%

Ice
77%

Atmosphere
and soil moisture
0.39%

Lakes and rivers
0.61%

Deep groundwater
11%

Shallow groundwater
11%

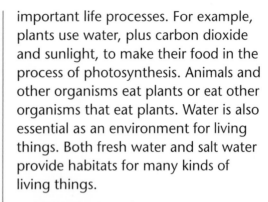

What do Earth's surface and human beings have in common? Answer: They both consist mostly of water. Water covers about three-quarters of Earth's surface. Water makes up about two-thirds of the human body. In fact, water is a large part of *every* living thing.

Water is essential for living things to grow, reproduce, and carry out other

---

human beings, people
carry out, complete

important life processes. For example, plants use water, plus carbon dioxide and sunlight, to make their food in the process of photosynthesis. Animals and other organisms eat plants or eat other organisms that eat plants. Water is also essential as an environment for living things. Both fresh water and salt water provide habitats for many kinds of living things.

Water on Earth

Although Earth has lots of water, the amount of water that humans can use is very small. About 97 percent of Earth's water is the salt water found in the ocean. People have named different parts of the ocean, but in fact these parts are all connected, so they really form a single world ocean.

Only about 3 percent of Earth's water is fresh water. Most of that fresh water is found in the huge masses of ice near the North and South poles. Less than 1 percent of the water on Earth is available for humans to use. Some of this available fresh water is found in lakes, rivers, and streams. Other fresh water is located under the ground. This underground water is called groundwater. It fills the small cracks and spaces between underground soil and rocks.

---

masses, amounts

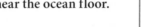

◀ A tropical fish swims past rocks near the ocean floor.

BEFORE YOU GO ON

1 What do Earth's surface and human beings have in common?

2 Why is water essential for living things?

On Your Own
What are two ways that you use fresh water?

51

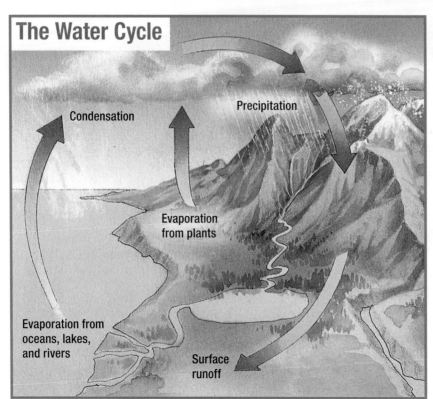

The Water Cycle

Condensation

Precipitation

Evaporation from plants

Evaporation from oceans, lakes, and rivers

Surface runoff

Evaporation
Most evaporation happens over oceans, lakes, and rivers. During evaporation, the sun heats the water and changes it to water vapor.

Condensation
Clouds form as the water vapor cools. The cool vapor changes to very small water drops.

Precipitation
When drops of water in clouds become larger and heavier, they fall back to Earth.

The Water Cycle

Water is always moving from one place to another. The continuous process by which water moves through the living and nonliving parts of the environment is called the water cycle. In the water cycle, water moves from bodies of water (such as oceans, rivers, lakes, and streams), land, and living things on Earth's surface to the atmosphere and back to Earth's surface.

The sun is the source of energy that creates the water cycle. The sun's energy warms water in oceans, rivers, and lakes. Some of this water evaporates—changes into a gas called water vapor. Smaller amounts of water evaporate from the soil,

from plants, and from animals (through their skin or breath). Water vapor rises in the air and forms clouds. As water vapor cools in the clouds, it condenses, or changes, into liquid water drops. When water drops in the clouds become heavy, they fall back to Earth as precipitation—rain, snow, sleet, or hail.

Precipitation is the source of all fresh water on or under Earth's surface. The water cycle renews the supply of usable fresh water on Earth.

---

clouds, tiny drops of water that collect in the air
usable, able to be used

---

continuous, without stopping

Case Study: China's Water Challenge

China has serious environmental problems. It has recently built many factories in an effort to become an industrial power. This rapid industrial growth, along with changes in Earth's climate, have led to polluted air and rivers. Drought has made the problems even worse. China is struggling to fix these problems.

---

drought, a time when no rain falls and the land becomes very dry

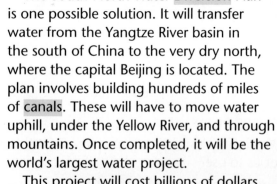

The South-North Water Diversion Plan is one possible solution. It will transfer water from the Yangtze River basin in the south of China to the very dry north, where the capital Beijing is located. The plan involves building hundreds of miles of canals. These will have to move water uphill, under the Yellow River, and through mountains. Once completed, it will be the world's largest water project.

This project will cost billions of dollars. Large areas of land will need to be flooded to create reservoirs. Over 300,000 people who live on the land will be forced to move and settle in other areas.

Some critics believe that this project is a waste of money. Water pipes often leak, and 40 percent of the water could be lost. It could also increase water pollution. But the Chinese government is determined to move forward with this project.

---

diversion, change in direction
canals, long, narrow waterways
reservoirs, places where a lot of water is stored

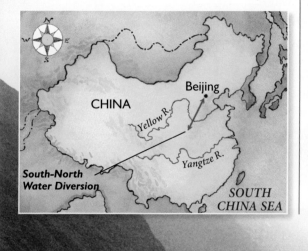

BEFORE YOU GO ON

1 What is the water cycle?

2 What is the purpose of the South-North Water Diversion Plan?

On Your Own
Why is fresh water important to the natural world?

53

Review and Practice

Right There

1. How much of the human body consists of water?

2. Where do you find groundwater?

Think and Search

3. Why is only less than one percent of Earth's water available for us to use?

4. Explain the importance of the sun in the water cycle.

Author and You

5. What is one interesting fact you learned about water?

6. Do you think the author believes that the South-North Water Diversion Plan will solve China's water problems?

On Your Own

7. In your opinion, will humans ever be able to use the oceans for drinking water?

8. How do you feel if you haven't had enough water to drink? How much water do you think we should drink each day?

IN YOUR OWN WORDS

Imagine you are teaching a class about the importance of water. Tell five facts about water that you learned from "Water and Living Things." Then write one or two sentences in your notebook summing up why water is necessary for life on Earth.

▲ All life needs water to survive. This giraffe is drinking from a lake.

DISCUSSION

Discuss in pairs or small groups.

1. What are the steps in the water cycle? Why is each step in this process important?

2. Find Beijing on the map of China on page 53. Do you think the location of Beijing influenced the South-North Water Diversion Plan? Why or why not?

Q **How does the natural world affect us?** How would a shortage of fresh water affect the natural world?

READ FOR FLUENCY

When we read aloud to communicate meaning, we group words into phrases, pause or slow down to make important points, and emphasize important words. Pause for a short time when you reach a comma and for a longer time when you reach a period. Pay attention to rising and falling intonation at the end of sentences.

Work with a partner. Choose a paragraph from the reading. Discuss which words seem important for communicating meaning. Practice pronouncing difficult words. Take turns reading the paragraph aloud and give each other feedback.

EXTENSION

▲ A dry river bed

Use the Internet or go to the library to find information on how problems with water—such as floods, drought, or pollution—can affect the lives of plants, animals, and human beings. Choose one problem and summarize your findings in a cause-and-effect chart like the one below.

Cause		Effects
too little rainfall	➡	streams dry up fish die larger animals lose food source

Grammar and Writing

GRAMMAR, USAGE, AND MECHANICS

Subject-Verb Agreement: Simple Present

In every sentence you write, the subject and the verb must agree in number. A singular subject takes a singular verb. A plural subject takes a plural verb.

Add -s or -es to a verb if the subject is a singular noun or is one of these pronouns: *he, she,* or *it.*

The sun **rises** in the east.
A scavenger **eats** dead organisms.
He **lives** near the water.
She **catches** fish in fresh water.

Do not add -s or -es to verbs if the subject is a plural noun or is one of these pronouns: *I, we, you,* or *they.*

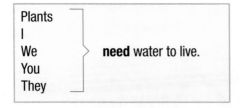

Plants
I
We } **need** water to live.
You
They

Practice  Workbook Page 27

Work with a partner. Choose verbs that agree with their subjects to make correct sentences. Write the sentences in your notebook.

Subject	Verb	Sentence Ending
Human beings	need / needs	water.
Frogs	live / lives	in fresh and salt water.
The sun	warm / warms	the earth's surface.
He	test / tests	the drinking water.
We	like / likes	living near the ocean.
Animals	move / moves	to different places.

WRITING A DESCRIPTIVE PARAGRAPH

Describe an Event or Experience

You have written descriptive paragraphs about an object, a place, and a person. Now you will describe an event or an experience. Remember that you want to describe the event or experience in the order in which it happened. Use sequence words such as *first*, *second*, *next*, *then*, and *finally* to make the order clear. When you describe an event or experience in the order that it happened, you are using chronological order.

Here is a model of a descriptive paragraph. This writer has organized the paragraph in chronological order using a sequence chart.

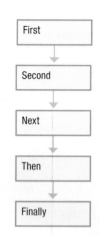

First
Second
Next
Then
Finally

Valeria Morales

The Big Storm

Storms can be scarier than you think. Once I was sleeping at a friend's house when there was a big storm. We were playing outside. First, the wind began blowing really hard, and it started to pour. We ran inside. Second, the lights went off. There was no electricity or phone. We were really scared. We went into the kitchen for a snack. When we returned to the den about thirty minutes later, there was water all over the floor. Their house was only one floor, so we had to climb on the furniture to stay dry. An hour later, the water was as high as the coffee table. Then when I looked outside, I could see a car floating down the street. Finally, several hours later, the rain stopped. All I could think about was my home and my family. When the phone worked again, I rushed to call them, and they were fine. That was the scariest day of my life.

Practice

Workbook
Page 28

Write a paragraph describing an important event or experience you have had in your life, such as a birthday, an award ceremony, or a sporting event. Describe the details in chronological order. Use a graphic organizer like the one above. Be sure the subjects and verbs in your sentences agree.

Writing Checklist

IDEAS:
☑ My topic is clear.

ORGANIZATION:
☑ I described an event clearly using chronological order.

57

Link the Readings

Critical Thinking

Look back at the readings in this unit. Think about what they have in common. They all tell about nature. Yet they do not all have the same purpose. The purpose of one reading might be to inform, while the purpose of another might be to entertain or persuade. In addition, the content of each reading relates to nature differently. Now copy the chart below into your notebook and complete it.

Title of Reading	Purpose	Big Question Link
From *Project Mulberry*	*to entertain*	
"Ecosystems: The Systems of Nature"		
"Ali, Child of the Desert" "Desert Women"		*The setting is a desert, which is part of the natural world.*
"Water and Living Things"		

Discussion

Discuss in pairs or small groups.

- How does the purpose of the article "Water and Living Things" differ from the purpose of "Ali, Child of the Desert"? What does the story include that the article does not?

- **Q** **How does the natural world affect us?** Think about the readings. How did learning about silkworms affect Julia? What parts of the natural world affect your life? How are the living and nonliving things in the desert affected by the desert environment? How are all living things affected by water?

Fluency Check

Work with a partner. Choose a paragraph from one of the readings. Take turns reading it for one minute. Count the total number of words you read. Practice saying the words you had trouble reading. Take turns reading the paragraph three more times. Did you read more words each time? Copy the chart below into your notebook and record your speeds.

	1st Speed	2nd Speed	3rd Speed	4th Speed
Words Per Minute				

Projects

Work in pairs or small groups. Choose one of these projects:

1 Write a poem about a living or nonliving thing. Use personification. Then read your poem to the class.

2 List the living and nonliving things around you. Take photos or draw pictures. Make a poster to show how things interact. Then share your poster with the class.

3 Do you think Julia and Patrick will win the contest at the state fair? Write a detailed plan and make a drawing for a different project.

4 Write a diary excerpt from Ali's perspective about his journey in the desert. Include details about the desert and the people that he met. Then read it aloud to the class.

5 Research facts about a river, lake, or ocean near you. Find pictures or make drawings; and include bar graphs and charts. Create a poster of the information you researched.

Further Reading

To find out more about the theme of this unit, choose from these reading suggestions.

White Fang, Jack London
In this Penguin Reader® adaptation of the classic story, White Fang is a young wolf born in northwest Canada. One day, he is taken to an Indian camp. In his new life, he must learn the ways of men and dogs.

The Yearling, Marjorie Kinnan Rawlings
Jody Baxter lives on a lonely farm with his poor, hardworking family. When a young deer loses its mother, Jody takes it home. Set in Florida, this story has wonderful descriptions of the natural world.

Everglades Forever: Restoring America's Great Wetland, Trish Marx
Follow a group of friends from Homestead, Florida, as they explore the natural history and environment of the Everglades National Park and nearby Miccosukee Reservation.

Put It All Together

LISTENING & SPEAKING WORKSHOP

Presentation

You will give a presentation that explains a process.

1 **THINK ABOUT IT** Look back over the readings in this unit. Talk in small groups about the natural world. Think of natural processes and nature-related activites that take time to complete. Write down your ideas.

Work together to develop a list of processes you know something about, for example:

- how to make a birdhouse
- how a seed becomes a flower
- how caves are formed

2 **GATHER AND ORGANIZE INFORMATION** Choose a process from your group's list. Write down the steps in the process. Also write any questions you have about it.

Research Go to the Internet or the library to get information. Take notes on what you find. Make sure you understand each step in your process.

Order Your Notes Make a numbered list of simple steps to explain the process you have researched.

Use Visuals Make a poster of drawings and diagrams that illustrate the steps in your process. Use numbers or arrows to show the order of your pictures.

A birdhouse ▶

3 **PRACTICE AND PRESENT** Use your list of steps as the written outline for your presentation. Keep your outline nearby, but practice explaining the steps in your process without reading them word-for-word. You may want to look in a mirror as you talk. Give your presentation to a friend or family member. Ask if any steps are unclear. Change your outline and visuals as needed to clarify your process. Keep practicing until you know your presentation well.

Deliver Your Presentation Look at your audience as you speak. Emphasize key ideas by pointing to a graphic. Slow down when you come to the most important steps, or restate them at the end of your talk. If you explained how to make something, like a birdhouse, show an example of it to the class if possible.

4 **EVALUATE THE PRESENTATION** You will improve your skills as a speaker and a listener by evaluating each presentation you give and hear. Use this checklist to help you judge your presentation and the presentations of your classmates.

- ☑ Did the speaker clearly identify the steps in the process?
- ☑ Were the steps in the process well explained and illustrated?
- ☑ Could you understand the speaker's words?
- ☑ Did the speaker know the process well?
- ☑ What suggestions do you have for improving the presentation?

Speaking TIPS

Be sure you are speaking slowly and clearly. Ask your listeners for feedback. Can they hear and understand all of your words? Keep practicing until you are relaxed and confident.

You may want to use words like *first*, *next*, *then*, and *last* to help your listeners follow the steps in the process.

Listening TIPS

Take notes or make drawings as you listen.

Think about what you are hearing. Does it make sense? Write down questions and ask them at the end of the presentation.

WRITING WORKSHOP
Descriptive Essay

In this workshop you will write a descriptive essay. An essay is a piece of writing that develops a specific idea. Most essays begin with an introduction, include one or more body paragraphs, and end with a conclusion. In a descriptive essay, you use descriptive language to convey an impression about a person, place, thing, event, or experience.

Your writing assignment for this workshop is to describe a place that is special to you.

1 PREWRITE Brainstorm a list of possible topics for your essay in your notebook. Choose a topic that offers opportunities to describe sensory experiences. You might want to describe a city street, waves crashing on a beach, or birds singing in a garden. Or you might want to describe a visit to an amusement park, a museum, or a zoo.

List and Organize Ideas and Details After you choose a topic, list ideas for your essay in a sensory details chart. A student named Lukas listed his ideas in the sensory details chart below:

2 DRAFT Use the model on page 65 and your sensory details chart to help you write a first draft. Remember to include an introductory paragraph, three body paragraphs, and a concluding paragraph.

3 REVISE Read over your draft. As you do so, ask yourself the questions in the writing checklist. Use the questions to help you revise your essay.

SIX TRAITS OF WRITING CHECKLIST

☑ **IDEAS:** Are my main ideas clear?

☑ **ORGANIZATION:** Are my ideas presented in an order that makes sense?

☑ **VOICE:** Does my writing express who I am?

☑ **WORD CHOICE:** Did I include vivid sensory details?

☑ **SENTENCE FLUENCY:** Do my sentences flow smoothly?

☑ **CONVENTIONS:** Does my writing follow the rules of grammar, usage, and mechanics?

Here are the changes Lukas plans to make when he revises his first draft:

My Favorite Place

Every day, I wish I could wake up in Texas, Yes, my favorite place is Texas. We go there every spring break, for a week. ~Sometimes~ We also go for Thanksgiving break, for just a few days. The main reason we go to Texas is to visit my grandma. Grandma, and some dogs.

Daisy, Ernie, and Bear are the dogs' names, and what is really great is that they live right down the road ~to my~ *from* grandma's house. Daisy and Ernie are Labradors, while Bear is a cross between a Husky and a Golden Retriever. The advantage of having the dogs ~there~ *nearby* is that I always have someone to play with. They're a big black and white bundle of *hair, brains, bones, play, and a whole lot of* love. They always greet me with happy, noisy barks.

because
Texas is also my favorite place ~~for another reason~~. The scenery is

truly something to behold. The warm yet breezy air wraps around

as softly as a cozy blanket
you. The sun shines its rays hazily over the green dark grass and into

your heart. The sky in the morning is a light, calm blue.

s
In my opinion, the scenery become even more beautiful in the

on
evening. At twilight, a haze of orange and red ~~at~~ the horizon dances

in the distance and over your head. As the haze vanishes, out comes

bright,
the twinkling stars in the night sky.

I'm not sure what else to say to help you understand why Texas is

my favorite place. A visit there is basically a trip to paradise for five

days—no work, no stress, just a chance to relax with a dark orange

sun and with a couple of dogs with a playful attitude. What more

could you ask for? The only way it could be better would be if it

lasted longer.

4 EDIT AND PROOFREAD

Workbook
Page 29

Copy your revised draft onto a clean sheet of paper. Read it again. Correct
any errors in grammar, word usage, mechanics, and spelling. Here are the
additional changes Lukas plans to make when he prepares his final draft.

Lukas Arbogast

My Favorite Place

Every day, I wish I could wake up in Texas. Yes, my favorite place is Texas. We go there every spring break, for a week. Sometimes we also go for Thanksgiving break, for just a few days. The main reason we go to Texas is to visit my grandma. Grandma, and some dogs.

Daisy, Ernie, and Bear are the dogs' names, and what is really great is that they live right down the road from my grandma's house. Daisy and Ernie are Labradors, while Bear is a cross between a Husky and a Golden Retriever. The advantage of having the dogs nearby is that I always have someone to play with. They're a big black and white bundle of hair, brains, bones, play, and a whole lot of love. They always greet me with happy, noisy barks.

Texas is also my favorite place because the scenery is truly something to behold. The warm yet breezy air wraps around you as softly as a cozy blanket. The sun shines its rays hazily over the dark green grass and into your heart. The sky in the morning is a light, calm blue.

In my opinion, the scenery becomes even more beautiful in the evening. At twilight, a haze of orange and red on the horizon dances in the distance and over your heads. As the drifting haze vanishes, out comes bright, twinkling, moonlit stars in the night sky.

I'm not sure what else to say to help you understand why Texas is my favorite place. A visit there is basically a five-day trip to paradise—no work, no stress, just a chance to relax under with a dark orange sun and with a couple of dogs with a playful attitude. What more could you ask for? The only way it could be better would be if it lasted longer.

5 PUBLISH Prepare your final draft. Share your essay with your teacher and classmates.

Workbook
Page 30

65

Painting the American Landscape

*B*efore television, movies, and photographs, if someone had never seen a bear, they could only imagine what it looked like. In the 1800s, many American painters wanted to change this. They wanted to show people what animals like bears and mountain lions looked like. They also wanted to show people the natural world—lakes, rivers, and trees. So artists like Albert Bierstadt painted these kinds of scenes. He and other painters used bright colors. They put many details in their paintings. For the first time, a person who lived in a city could see what a bear looked like!

Albert Bierstadt, *Among the Sierra Nevada, California* (1868)

Albert Bierstadt liked to put on a show. When he finished one of his paintings, he would put it in a fancy frame. Then he would hide the painting behind curtains in a dark room. Bierstadt would have someone pull the curtains back. Then he would turn on the lights. People would gasp when they saw the painting. Most of them had never seen mountains out West. They had never seen huge open spaces. They had never seen animals such as deer. It made them feel as though a wonderland was beyond the Mississippi River.

It was very difficult to travel anywhere in the United States in the early 1800s. Bierstadt was the first serious artist to travel west of the Mississippi River. He painted some of the nation's most famous natural wonders. These include the Sierra Nevada Mountains and the Rocky Mountains. But Bierstadt also realized he was putting on a show in his paintings.

▲ Albert Bierstadt, *Among the Sierra Nevada, California,* 1868, oil, 72 x 120⅛ in., Smithsonian American Art Museum

In this painting, Bierstadt made the Sierra Nevada Mountains a little higher than they really are. He actually painted the mountains while he was living in London, England! Bierstadt used sketches he had made during visits to the American West. He also used memories he had of the Alps in Switzerland.

Until photography became more popular, paintings like this one were often the only way many Americans could see what the wilderness looked like. If viewers get up close, they can see a trout jumping in the left corner of the painting, deer moving toward the lake in the bottom center, and ducks feeding on the water. Even today, with all of our movies and television shows, we think of the American West the way artists like Bierstadt wanted us to see it. It is wild and filled with animals. There are very few people. Of course this is hardly the case today, even in the biggest national parks. But sometimes an idea can be more powerful than what is real.

Apply What You Learned

1 Why did so few artists travel west to paint the mountains and other landmarks in the nineteenth century?

2 Do you think Bierstadt's paintings might have influenced more people to move west? Why or why not?

Big Question

How did the natural world influence the painter Albert Bierstadt?

Workbook
Pages 31–32

Where can a journey take you?

This unit is about journeys. You will read literature, science, and social studies texts about exploring, migrating, leaving home, and trying to return home. Learning about these topics will help you become a better student. It will also help you practice the language you need to use in school.

READING 1: Myth
- From *Tales from the Odyssey,* retold by Mary Pope Osborne

READING 2: Social Studies Article
- "Early Explorers"

READING 3: Science Articles
- "Migrating Caribou"
- "Magnets in Animals" by Darlene R. Stille

READING 4: Novel Excerpt
- From *The Journal of Wong Ming-Chung* by Laurence Yep

Listening and Speaking

At the end of this unit, you will relate a **personal narrative**. In your personal narrative you will tell about a journey you took.

Writing

In this unit you will practice **narrative writing**. This type of writing tells a story. After each reading you will learn a skill to help you write a narrative paragraph. At the end of the unit, you will use these skills to help you write a fictional narrative.

QuickWrite
Make a list of places you have been to or places you would like to visit.

Prepare to Read

What You Will Learn

Reading

■ Vocabulary building:
Literary terms, phonics

■ Reading strategy:
Identify problems and solutions

■ Text type: *Literature (myth)*

Grammar, Usage, and Mechanics
Simple past: regular and irregular

Writing
Write a story from a different point of view

 THE BIG QUESTION

Where can a journey take you? Have you been on a journey or a long trip? How did you get there? What interesting events occurred on the way or once you arrived? Many exciting things can happen to you when you travel. Describe something that happened during a trip or a vacation.

BUILD BACKGROUND

You will read a story from a famous myth written a long time ago. Myths are very old stories. The ancient Greeks believed that gods and goddesses ruled the world. The Greeks created myths about the gods to help explain the world around them. For example, they believed that thunder and lightning were signs that the gods were angry.

Tales from the Odyssey are retold myths from a book called *The Odyssey* by Homer, an ancient Greek storyteller. An odyssey is a long journey full of many adventures. This story tells about a king, Odysseus. After fighting for many years in the Trojan War, Odysseus wanted to return to his kingdom and his family. But he and his men angered the gods, so they suffered a very long and difficult journey home.

Odysseus and his men ▶

Learn Literary Words

A **plot** is a sequence of connected events in a story. In most stories, the plot has a main problem, or a conflict. The conflict sets the plot in motion and moves the story forward.

A **character** is a person who takes part in the action of a story. A plot can have many characters or just one or two.

Writers often use a narrator, or speaker, to describe the events in a story. The narrator might be a character in the story or someone outside the story. When a character tells the story, the writer often uses the first-person **point of view**. The reader sees only what the character sees. The writer uses the words *I* and *my*.

> **First-person point of view:**
> I explored the island alone and left my men aboard the ship.

Sometimes writers tell a story using the third-person point of view. The narrator is either a character in the story or someone outside the story. The reader sees the story through one character's point of view or many characters' points of view. The writer uses the words *he, she, his,* and *her*.

> **Third-person point of view:**
> For many days, Odysseus and his men fought the wind and waves.

Practice

Workbook
Page 33

Think of a time you had an argument or disagreement with a friend or family member. Work with a partner. Take turns telling about the argument. Then pretend you are the person that you were disagreeing with. Tell your partner the same story but from the other person's point of view. Talk about how the two stories are similar and different.

▲ Students disagreeing

Learn Academic Words

Study the **red** words and their meanings. You will find these words useful when talking and writing about literature. Write each word and its meaning in your notebook. After you read the excerpt from *Tales from the Odyssey*, try to use these words to respond to the text.

abandon = leave someone or something that you are responsible for	➡	A good captain will never **abandon** his ship or leave his men to save himself.
collapse = fall down suddenly	➡	We were afraid the bridge would **collapse** because there was a flood.
finally = after a long time	➡	The train **finally** left the station, one hour late.
investigate = search for information by looking or asking questions	➡	She had to **investigate** in order to find out what happened to her lost package.
react = behave in a certain way because of what someone has done or said to you	➡	Meercats **react** quickly when they sense danger.
strategy = set of plans and skills to gain success	➡	His **strategy** to pass the science test was to study every night for two hours.

Practice

Workbook Page 34

Work with a partner to answer these questions. Try to include the **red** word in your answer. Write the sentences in your notebook.

1. What would be a good reason for people to **abandon** a ship?

2. Have you ever seen a runner **collapse** at the end of a race?

3. After a long trip, how do you feel when you **finally** get home?

4. Have you ever had to **investigate** something? Tell about it.

5. How do you usually **react** to good news?

6. What is a good **strategy** for getting people to help you do something?

Meercats ▶

Word Study: Roots *vict, laps, vis, mem, mand*

Many English words come from Greek or Latin and still keep parts of the words from which they came. These word parts are called roots. Learning word roots can help you understand the meaning of many words. The chart below shows some roots, their meanings, their origins, and some English words that contain them.

Root	Meaning	Origin	English Word
vict	conquer	Latin	victory
laps	slip	Latin	collapsed
vis	see	Latin	provisions
mem	mind	Latin	memories
mand	order	Latin	commanded

Practice

Workbook
Page 35

Work with a partner. Look through the excerpt from *Tales from the Odyssey* to find each of the English words in the chart above. Copy each sentence in which you find a word into your notebook. Talk about what the word means. Then write a definition of the word under the sentence.

READING STRATEGY | IDENTIFY PROBLEMS AND SOLUTIONS

Identifying problems and solutions helps you better understand the text. Many texts include a problem that a person or character has to solve (or find a solution to). To identify problems and solutions, follow these steps:

- What problem or problems does the person have?
- Think about your own experience and what you would do about that problem.
- Think about the person. What do you think the solution will be?
- What does each character try to do to solve his or her problem?
- Read to find out how the person solves or tries to solve the problem.

As you read the excerpt from *Tales from the Odyssey*, ask yourself what big problem or problems Odysseus has. How does Odysseus try to solve his problems? Does he find solutions, or not?

Workbook
Page 36

Set a purpose for reading Where is Odysseus going?
Look for specific challenges he faces on his journey.

from

TALES *from* the ODYSSEY

retold by Mary Pope Osborne

Prologue

In the early morning of time, there existed a mysterious world called Mount Olympus. Hidden behind a veil *of clouds, this world was never swept by winds, nor washed by rains. Those who lived on Mount Olympus never grew old; they never died. They were not humans. They were the mighty gods and goddesses of ancient Greece.*

The Olympian gods and goddesses had great power over the lives of the humans who lived on earth below. Their anger once caused a man named Odysseus to wander the seas for many long years, trying to find his way home.

Almost 3,000 years ago, a Greek poet named Homer first told the story of Odysseus's journey. Since that time, storytellers have told the strange and wondrous tale again and again. We call that story the Odyssey.

The Odyssey Begins

Soon after the Greek ships left Troy, the skies began to blacken. Lightning zigzagged above the foamy sea. Thunder shook the heavens.

Mighty winds stirred the water. The waves grew higher and higher, until they were rolling over the bows of the ships.

"The gods are punishing us!" the Greek warriors shouted. "We shall all drown!"

---

veil, covering
zigzagged, moved in a pattern like a line of *Z*'s

As his men **frantically** fought the storm, Odysseus felt bewildered. Why was Zeus, god of the skies, **hurling** his thunderbolts at them? Why was Poseidon, lord of the seas, sending great waves over the waters?

Odysseus turned to his men. "What has happened to anger the gods?" he shouted. "Tell me!"

"Before we left Troy, Greek warriors invaded Athena's temple!" said one of his men. "They were violent and disrespectful."

Odysseus was stunned. The Greeks had offended the goddess who had helped them to victory! And now her anger might drown them all.

The wind grew stronger. It whipped the sails of the Greek ships and slashed them to rags. "Lift your oars!" Odysseus shouted to his men. "Row! Row to shore!"

The Greeks struggled **valiantly** against the mighty wind and waves. Fighting for their lives, they finally rowed their battered ships to a strange shore. There they found shelter in a rocky cave.

The storm raged for two more days and nights. Then, on the third day, a fair wind blew, the sun came out, and the wine-dark sea was calm at last.

"Now we can continue on our way," Odysseus said to his men. "Athena is no longer angry." In the rosy dawn, he ordered them to raise their tattered sails and set off again for Ithaca.

But, **alas**, the **wrath** of Athena had not been fully spent. Hardly had Odysseus reached the open sea when another gale began to blow.

---

frantically, anxiously
hurling, throwing
valiantly, bravely
alas, sadly
wrath, great anger

✔ **LITERARY CHECK**

*From which **character's point of view** is this story told?*

BEFORE YOU GO ON

1 Where do the gods and goddesses of ancient Greece live?

2 According to Odysseus who is responsible for the thunderbolts?

🔦**On Your Own**
Why do you think Odysseus should continue his journey?

75

For many days, Odysseus and his men fought the wind and the waves, refusing to surrender to the storm. Finally, on the tenth day, there was sudden calm.

Odysseus ordered his fleet to sail into the cove of a leafy green island. There he hoped to find food and drink for his hungry, weary men.

The Greeks dropped anchor. Then they dragged themselves ashore. They drank cool, fresh water from a spring and collapsed onto the sand.

As Odysseus rested, he ordered three of his men to explore the island and look for provisions.

When the three had not returned by late afternoon, Odysseus grew angry. Why did they tarry? He wondered.

Odysseus set out in search of the men. He moved through the brush and brambles, calling their names.

He had not gone far when he came upon a group of peaceful islanders. They greeted him with warm, friendly smiles. And they offered him their food—lovely bright flowers.

Odysseus was famished. But just as he was about to eat the flowers, he caught sight of his missing men. The three were lying on the ground with dreamy smiles on their faces.

Odysseus called each man by name, but none of them answered. They did not even look at him.

"What have you done to them?" he asked the islanders.

"We have given them our flowers to eat," an islander answered. "This is our greatest gift. The gods would be angry if we did not offer to feed our guests."

"What sort of flowers are these?" Odysseus asked.

"They come from the lotus tree," the islander said. "They have the magical power of forgetfulness. They make a man forget the past."

---

provisions, food and supplies
tarry, delay
famished, very hungry

"Forget his memories of home?" asked Odysseus. "And his memories of his family and friends?"

The lotus-eaters only smiled. They again offered Odysseus their sweet, lovely flowers. But he roughly brushed them away. He pulled his three men to their feet and commanded them all to return to their ships at once.

The men began to weep. They begged to be left behind so they could stay on the island and eat lotus flowers forever.

Odysseus angrily herded the men back to the ships. As they drew near the shore, the three tried to escape. Odysseus called for help.

"Tie their hands and feet!" he shouted to his crew. "Make haste! Before others eat the magic flowers and forget their homes, too!"

The three flailing men were hauled aboard and tied to rowing benches. Then Odysseus ordered the twelve ships to push off from shore.

Once more, the Greeks set sail for Ithaca, sweeping the gray sea with their long oars. As they rowed past dark islands with jagged rocks and shadowy coves, Odysseus felt troubled and anxious. What other strange wonders lurked on these dark, unknown shores?

---

make haste, move quickly or hurry up
flailing, waving arms and legs in an uncontrolled way

ABOUT THE AUTHOR

Mary Pope Osborne grew up in a typical military family and was always moving. As a child, she lived in Oklahoma, Florida, North Carolina, Virginia, and Austria. Her books include *Blizzard of the Blue Moon* and *Night of the New Magicians*. Mary Pope Osborne currently lives in New York City with her husband, Will, and their terrier, Bailey.

BEFORE YOU GO ON

1 How do the islanders first greet Odysseus?

2 What magical powers do the lotus flowers have?

On Your Own
Would you have preferred to stay on the island?

77

Review and Practice

READER'S THEATER

Speaking TIP

Speak clearly and slowly. Use gestures to emphasize important ideas.

Act out this scene between Odysseus and one of the islanders.

Odysseus: Aha, my men, there you are! I finally found you. What is wrong? Why aren't you looking at me? Islander, what have you done to my men?

Islander: We have done nothing to your men. We only gave them a gift of our flowers to eat.

Odysseus: Flowers? What kind of flowers?

Islander: We fed them our special, sweet flowers from our lotus tree. These flowers are able to take away the memories of all problems and worries.

Odysseus: But these flowers made my men forget everything! They cannot remember their names. They cannot remember their homes.

Islander: Here, try some. Have some of our lotus flowers. They will make you as happy and peaceful as your men.

Odysseus: I do not want to forget my people or my home! I am not going to abandon my men here. I am taking them back to our ship!

COMPREHENSION  Workbook Page 37

Right There

1. Which gods do the Greeks believe they have upset, and why?

2. What does Odysseus hope to find on the island?

Think and Search

3. Why does Odysseus believe that Athena is no longer angry?

4. How do the islanders react to Odysseus?

Author and You

5. What does the author suggest about the relationship between the gods and humans?

6. Does this myth show Odysseus as a hero? If so, in what ways?

On Your Own

7. Who do you consider to be heroes today?

8. In your opinion, how do you think Odysseus felt about his men?

DISCUSSION

Discuss in pairs or small groups.

1. Explain how Odysseus realized there were problems on the island.

2. Have you ever visited a place so special or exciting that you wanted to stay? Tell about it.

Q Where can a journey take you? Do some journeys take you to unexpected places?

»❩ **Listening TIP**

If you can't hear the speaker, you may say, "Excuse me, could you speak louder, please?"

RESPONSE TO LITERATURE

Workbook
Page 37

Use the Internet or library to find out about some Greek gods or goddesses. In your notebook, make a chart like the one below. Write the information you discover. Then find a myth about one of the gods or goddesses you researched. Retell it to the class in your own words.

Name of God or Goddess		Role of God or Goddess
Zeus	➡	king of the gods, god of thunder
Athena	➡	daughter of Zeus, goddess of wisdom, war, and arts and crafts

◀ Zeus and the birth of Athena

79

Grammar and Writing

Simple Past: Regular and Irregular Verbs

We use the simple past to talk about actions, states, or situations that happened in the past and are finished. The simple past of regular verbs is formed by adding *-d* or *-ed* to the base form of the verb. If the verb ends in a *y*, change the *y* to an *i* and add *-ed*.

Base Form	Simple Past	Base Form	Simple Past
live	live**d**	shout	shout**ed**
die	die**d**	cry	cr**ied**
hope	hope**d**	try	tr**ied**

Many common verbs are irregular. Their past is not formed by adding *-d* or *-ed*.

Base Form	Simple Past	Base Form	Simple Past
be	was / were	have	had
get	got	tell	told
go	went	grow	grew

Form questions and negatives of regular and irregular verbs with the auxiliary verb *did (not)* and the base form.

| Why **did** they **eat** the flowers? | They **did not answer**. |

Practice  Workbook Page 38

Work with a partner. Copy the sentences below into your notebook. Circle the verb in each sentence and write the sentences in the simple past.

1. That story is a myth.
2. He lives in Greece.
3. The men go to the island.
4. They tell an amazing story.
5. I call him by his last name.
6. They have a lot of interesting things on the ship.

WRITING A NARRATIVE PARAGRAPH

Write a Story from a Different Point of View

At the end of this unit you will write a fictional narrative. To do this, you'll need to learn some of the skills writers use to write narratives. When you write a narrative, you can write it from any character's point of view. For example, the story you just read is told from Odysseus's point of view. The reader learns how Odysseus reacts to the other characters and the events. But what if the story focused on one of the people who live on the island? The narrative would be told from that person's point of view. How would it be different?

Here is a model of a narrative paragraph written from the point of view of one of the island dwellers. Notice how changing the point of view changes the story. The writer used a T-chart to organize his ideas.

Odysseus	Islanders

Ben Berman

Greek Guests

It seemed like it was going to be a normal day on our island with my fellow islanders. But around noon, three Greek warriors met us. It was a bit surprising, because we rarely had visitors. The three Greeks looked fatigued, probably due to the storm. We offered them some lotus flowers. The men gratefully accepted and ate them. They immediately fell to the ground. Lotus flowers make people forget the past. But sometime later, another warrior found us. This one seemed much stronger. We tried to offer him our lotus flowers, but he refused. Then he saw the other three Greeks. The man seemed to think that forgetfulness was a curse! He harshly grabbed his men and left, without a single word or wave. How rude and ungrateful he was.

Practice

Workbook
Page 39

Write a narrative paragraph from the point of view of one of Odysseus's crew members. Think about the way the character would react to the events. Use a graphic organizer like the one above. Be sure to use the simple past of both regular and irregular verbs correctly.

Writing Checklist

IDEAS:
☑ I changed the story based on the shift in point of view.

CONVENTIONS:
☑ I used the simple past of regular and irregular verbs correctly.

81

Prepare to Read

What You Will Learn

Reading

- Vocabulary building: *Context, dictionary skills, word analysis*
- Reading strategy: *Use visuals*
- Text type: *Informational text (social studies)*

Grammar, Usage, and Mechanics
Passive voice: omitting the *by*-phrase

Writing
Write a personal narrative

THE BIG QUESTION

Where can a journey take you? Why do you think people have the desire to explore the unknown? How can explorers and their discoveries change the world? Which explorers to you know about? Make a chart like the one below and fill in information that you know about explorers.

Explorer	Where They Were From	Where They Went
Marco Polo	Italy	China

BUILD BACKGROUND

"Early Explorers" is a social studies article about some important explorers. Some explorers were searching for new goods to trade, like gold, spices, silk, and foods such as pineapples and sweet potatoes. Some were looking for new markets to trade in. Some people explored the world to spread their religion or to worship freely. And others wanted new land where they could settle.

When people first started exploring by sea, they stayed close to the coastline so they wouldn't get lost. Then explorers used the sun and stars to guide them. Later, they invented instruments to tell them where they were and where they were going.

▲ A compass points to the magnetic north.

A telescope helps us see land that is far away. ▶

▲ An astrolabe locates the position of the sun, moon, planets, and stars.

◀ A sextant is a measuring tool used to find latitude.

VOCABULARY

Learn Key Words

Read these sentences. Use the context to figure out the meaning of the **red** words. Use a dictionary to check your answers. Then write each word and its meaning in your notebook.

Key Words

civilizations
expeditions
exploration
markets
navigator
trade

1. The explorers were surprised to find large cities, or **civilizations**, in the New World.

2. Many **expeditions** to faraway places were long and difficult; explorers sometimes died along the way.

3. During the **exploration** of the new land, the men discovered gold.

4. Early explorers searched for new **markets** where they could buy tea and spices.

5. A **navigator** uses maps, compasses, and sometimes the stars to find the right direction.

6. The explorer wanted to **trade** with another country. He wanted to buy silk and sell his goods.

Practice

Workbook Page 40

Write the sentences in your notebook. Choose a **red** word from the box above to complete each sentence. Then take turns reading the sentences aloud with a partner.

1. The explorers found new _____ where they could buy and sell their goods.

2. There were many ancient _____ in South America before the explorers arrived.

3. The men discovered amazing things during the _____ of the new land.

4. Some explorers made many _____ to find a more direct route.

5. The explorers wanted to _____ their goods for pineapples and sweet potatoes.

6. The _____ of the ship used an astrolabe to help find the way home.

▲ A pineapple and sweet potatoes

Learn Academic Words

Study the red words and their meanings. You will find these words useful when talking and writing about informational texts. Write each word and its meaning in your notebook. After you read "Early Explorers," try to use these words to respond to the text.

Academic Words

conducted
established
financed
region
varied

conducted = led or guided	➡	She **conducted** an expedition along the Amazon River in South America.
established = started something new	➡	Some explorers settled in new lands and **established** towns and cities.
financed = gave money for something	➡	The queen gave the explorer money and **financed** the voyage to the new continent.
region = large area	➡	The Americas was a **region** of the world that the early explorers didn't know existed.
varied = consisting of many different kinds of things	➡	The museum had a **varied** collection from South America. It included everything from Aztec art to modern paintings.

Practice

Workbook
Page 41

Work with a partner to answer these questions. Try to include the red word in your answer. Write the sentences in your notebook.

1. Have you ever **conducted** a tour around your school or home?

2. Have any new clubs or activities been **established** at your school?

3. Who **financed** the clubs at your school?

4. Which **region** of the world would you most like to visit?

5. Do you eat a healthy and **varied** diet? What does it consist of?

An Aztec gold pendant ▶

Word Study: Suffixes *-er* / *-or*

A suffix is a letter or group of letters added to the end of a word to form a new word. When you add a suffix to a word, the meaning changes. The suffix *-er* or *-or* at the end of a verb creates a noun that means "someone or something that does" the action of the verb. (Note: If the verb ends with *e*, drop the *e*. dance—danc**er**)

Verb	Suffix	New Word	Definition
build	-er	build**er**	someone who builds
produce	-er	produc**er**	someone who produces
inspect	-or	inspect**or**	someone who inspects
create	-or	creat**or**	someone who creates

Practice

Work with a partner. Copy the chart below into your notebook. Add the suffix *-er* or *-or* to the end of the word to create a word meaning someone who performs this action. Check a dictionary to make sure that you have selected the correct spelling.

Verb	Suffix *-er* / *-or*
explore	
farm	
navigate	
sail	

READING STRATEGY | USE VISUALS

Using visuals helps you understand the text better. Visuals are art, photographs, diagrams, charts, maps, etc. Many informational texts include visuals. To use visuals, follow these steps:

- Look at the visual. Ask yourself, "What does the visual show? How does it help me understand the reading?"
- Read the titles, headings, labels, or captions carefully.
- Review the visuals as you read each section.

As you read "Early Explorers," look at the photos and maps. What do they tell you about life at the time of the early explorers?

Set a purpose for reading Why do explorers take journeys? What motivates them to go?

EARLY EXPLORERS

The Phoenicians

Six thousand years ago people grew their own food and made everything they needed. They did not travel far. They did not know what lay beyond a few days' journey from their homes.

However, as civilizations developed, people saw and wanted new products. So the idea of trading goods evolved. One of the earliest peoples to begin trading were the Phoenicians. They lived on the Mediterranean coast of modern-day Israel and Lebanon. The Phoenicians were expert shipbuilders, able to sail great distances. They understood that they could make money by trading.

Between about 700 B.C.E. and 100 B.C.E., Phoenician ships explored the lands that border the Mediterranean Sea. They searched for new markets. They established colonies. They even sailed through the Strait of Gibraltar to the Atlantic, reaching Britain and West Africa.

▲ A silver coin showing a Phoenician ship

---

evolved, developed slowly

◄ An early map of the Mediterranean Sea

◄ A Viking longship

▲ A Viking helmet

▲ Chinese silk

Viking Voyages

The Vikings were from Scandinavia, a region in northern Europe. From the eighth to the twelfth century, Vikings built magnificent sailing vessels and set out from their homeland on voyages of exploration.

During the early Middle Ages, Viking raiders invaded many other parts of Europe. The reasons for these journeys were varied. Some Vikings were interested only in stealing treasure and capturing slaves. They plundered the unlucky communities they found in Britain and the Mediterranean. Other Vikings were in search of new lands across the Atlantic. Viking farmers needed new places to settle, as farmland in Scandinavia was scarce and poor. The Swedish Vikings set their sights on the lands of Eastern Europe and Asia. Mainly traders, these Vikings hoped to develop new markets for exchanging goods. By 1000, the Vikings had also reached North America.

After about 1200, the Vikings became more settled. Their long voyages of discovery ceased.

The Silk Road

Not all exploration took place over rolling seas. The Silk Road was a land route between Europe and Asia. It was used from around 500 B.C.E. until sea routes to China were opened up in about 1650. The most important product traded along the Silk Road was silk. For centuries the Chinese kept the secret of how to make silk from other nations.

Along this road, trade was conducted between China and Europe. Chinese merchants sent silk and spices to Europe over the mountains and deserts of Asia. In return, gold, silver, and horses were imported to China. The road was about 7,000 kilometers (4,300 mi.) long and very dangerous.

---

voyages, long trips
plundered, stole money or property
scarce, not enough
ceased, stopped

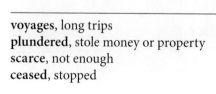

BEFORE YOU GO ON

1 Why did the Phoenicians explore new lands?

2 Where were the Vikings from?

On Your Own
Why is finding markets in different regions important?

87

It passed through numerous kingdoms where rulers demanded gifts from travelers. In addition, bandits would often pillage a traveling camel train. Because of these dangers, the goods were passed from one merchant to another, with no trader traveling for more than a few hundred miles at a time.

Marco Polo was a trader and great storyteller from Venice, Italy. He was the first European explorer to travel the entire length of the Silk Road in the thirteenth century. It took him four years, and he wrote about his travels. The Silk Road became less important after European ships began regular trade with China around the southern tip of Africa.

▲ The Silk Road

▲ Marco Polo (1254–1324)

The Age of Exploration

The Age of Exploration began in fifteenth-century Portugal. In 1415, Prince Henry of Portugal, known as Henry the Navigator, took command of a port in northern Morocco. Henry sent out his ships to explore the west coast of Africa. He paid for many expeditions that eventually reached Sierra Leone on Africa's west coast. Later kings of Portugal financed expeditions that sailed around the Cape of Good Hope at the southern tip of Africa. This opened up trade routes to India, China, and the Indonesian and Philippine Islands (called the Spice Islands). Portugal became rich and powerful through its control of trade in this area.

---

bandits, people who rob or attack
pillage, steal things using violence, especially during war

Henry the Navigator (1394–1460)
and his men ▶

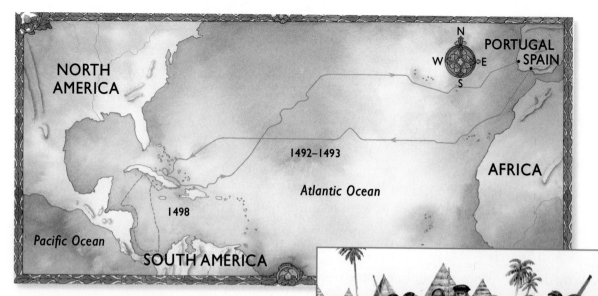

▲ Columbus's voyages of exploration

1492–1493

1498

NORTH AMERICA

SOUTH AMERICA

AFRICA

PORTUGAL

SPAIN

Atlantic Ocean

Pacific Ocean

▲ Columbus meeting the Taino people

The New World

In the late fifteenth century, even the most educated Europeans knew little about the world outside Europe. The stories travelers brought back were so amazing that few people believed them. Thick jungles stretched south of the Sahara Desert. To the west lay the vast Atlantic Ocean. Nobody knew how wide the Atlantic was, nor what lay on the other side.

Then, in 1480, Italian navigator Christopher Columbus announced that, by his calculations, the East Indies lay only 4,500 kilometers (2,795 mi.) to the west.

Few experts agreed with him. Indeed, he was later proved wrong. Nevertheless, the Spanish king and queen paid for his expedition. Columbus landed on islands in the Caribbean Sea. People called the Tainos were living on these islands. Columbus thought he had landed in India, so he called the Tainos *Indians*. When Columbus returned to Spain, he brought back gold, pearls, parrots, and some Taino people.

The Spanish made the islands a colony, and the Tainos became slaves. The Spanish brought diseases to the islands, and many Taino people died.

This voyage to the Americas was one of the most important that took place during the Age of Exploration. It opened up the New World to Europe.

---

calculations, ways of using numbers to find an answer

BEFORE YOU GO ON

1 Where was Marco Polo from? Where did he travel?

2 What country financed Prince Henry's trip around Africa?

On Your Own
Why are the early journeys of exploration important?

COMPREHENSION  Workbook Page 44

Right There

1. Where did the Phoenicians live? Where did they explore?

2. Where did Christopher Columbus want to go? Where did he land instead?

Think and Search

3. Why did the Vikings set out to explore new regions? Where did they go?

4. What was the purpose of the Silk Road?

Author and You

5. Why do you think that the Chinese kept the secret of silk to themselves?

6. Why do you think Columbus took some Taino people back to Spain?

On Your Own

7. In what ways are long journeys easier now than they were hundreds of years ago?

8. If you were an explorer, where would you go?

IN YOUR OWN WORDS

Use the words in the chart below to tell a partner about early explorers.

Voyages	➡	expeditions, trade, markets
Explorers	➡	established, trade routes
Vikings	➡	pillaged, plundered, ceased
Exploration	➡	expeditions, civilizations, markets, trade

DISCUSSION

Discuss in pairs or small groups.

1. What did all of the explorers have in common?

2. What were the positive effects of exploration in the fifteenth century? What were the negative effects of exploration?

3. How did the Europeans' journeys change the lives of people they encountered?

Q **Where can a journey take you?** Are there any places left to explore today? If so, where?

»)) Listening TIP

Do not interrupt the speaker. Save your comments until the speaker is finished.

READ FOR FLUENCY

It is often easier to read a text if you understand the difficult words and phrases. Work with a partner. Choose a paragraph from the reading. Identify the words and phrases you do not know or have trouble pronouncing. Look up the difficult words in a dictionary.

Take turns pronouncing the words and phrases with your partner. If necessary, ask your teacher to model the correct pronunciation. Then take turns reading the paragraph aloud. Give each other feedback on your reading.

EXTENSION  **Workbook** Page 44

During the Age of Exploration, many explorers faced great dangers and difficulties on their expeditions. Men died and ships sank. Others fought with the people and civilizations they encountered. Choose one of the explorers from this reading and use the Internet or the library to find information about what happened during one of his expeditions.

Write a paragraph in which you explain to readers the events of one explorer's expedition. Share your paragraph with the class.

Spanish
silver coins ▶

91

Grammar and Writing

Passive Voice: Omitting the *by*-Phrase

A sentence can be in the active or passive voice. Use the active voice when the focus is on who or what does the action, also called the performer. Use the passive voice when the focus is on the receiver of the action. Form the passive voice with the verb *be* + the past participle. A *by*-phrase identifies the performer.

Active Voice	Passive Voice
The Phoenicians **explored** the lands that bordered the Mediterranean. [focus is on the Phoenicians]	The lands that bordered the Mediterranean **were explored by** the Phoenicians. [focus is on the land]

Often the *by*-phrase identifying the performer is omitted. Sometimes the performer of the action is unknown or not as important as the receiver of the action.

Gold, silver, and horses	**were imported** to China.
The goods	**were traded** at the market.

Practice

Work with a partner. Copy the sentences below into your notebook, rewriting each in the passive voice. Then take turns reading the sentences aloud. Decide whether each sentence sounds better with or without the *by*-phrase.

1. The farmers planted their crops.
2. The Chinese traded silk.
3. Prince Henry paid for many expeditions.
4. Travelers brought back amazing stories.
5. The Vikings built the ship.

▲ A Phoenician necklace

92

WRITING A NARRATIVE PARAGRAPH

Write a Personal Narrative

In the previous writing assignment, you wrote a short narrative from a particular character's point of view. Now you will write a narrative from your own point of view. When you write a personal narrative, you tell about a real event in your life. Your narrative should show the reader your personality by including character traits such as courage, humor, creativity, or leadership.

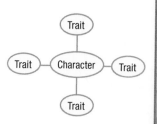

Here is a model of a personal narrative. Notice that the writer's actions give you information about his personality. He used a word web to organize his ideas.

Sebastian Z. Mitchell

Snorkeling at Hanauma Bay

Hanauma Bay is a great snorkeling spot in Hawaii, full of tropical fish and marine life. I went there with my mom on vacation, and I have to say it was one of the best times in my life. At first I was frightened by the idea of diving into such deep water. But I like to try new things so I jumped in anyway. The instant I entered the water I felt better. The coral reef was a fascinating place to explore. I saw schools of bright yellow fish and clumps of red coral. Strangely, the fish weren't scared of me. But then, out of the corner of my eye, I saw an octopus. My curiosity got the better of me, and I decided to follow it. I soon found its home, which was a hole in the side of a rock. Just then my mom caught up with me and we had to leave, but that experience will stay with me forever.

Practice

Workbook
Page 46

Write a paragraph about a real event in your life, such as a travel adventure or a meeting with an interesting person. Tell the reader about your personality by including descriptive words that show your character traits. Use a graphic organizer like the one above. Be sure to use the passive voice correctly.

Writing Checklist

IDEAS:
☑ I included information about my personality.

WORD CHOICE:
☑ I used descriptive words and vivid details.

93

What You Will Learn

Reading

- Vocabulary building: *Context, dictionary skills, phonics*

- Reading strategy: *Recognize cause and effect*

- Text type: *Informational text (science)*

Grammar, Usage, and Mechanics
Prenominal and postnominal adjectives

Writing
Write a story with a story starter

THE BIG QUESTION

Where can a journey take you? What do you know about migrating animals—animals that travel from one place to another? Have you ever seen animals migrate? Where are they going? Why do you think some animals migrate? Share your ideas with the class.

BUILD BACKGROUND

You will read two science articles about animal migration. **"Migrating Caribou"** tells about the difficult journey caribou make as the cold winter approaches. The caribou are members of the deer family. They are herd animals and are always on the move. Caribou roam throughout the cold regions of Russia, Alaska, Canada, and Greenland.

"Magnets in Animals" presents an interesting theory about how some animals find their way as they travel thousands of miles.

▼ A caribou

VOCABULARY

Learn Key Words

Read these sentences. Use the context to figure out the meaning of the **red** words. Use a dictionary to check your answers. Then write each word and its meaning in your notebook.

1. **Biologists** study animals to learn about their lives and behavior.

2. The large **herd** of caribou is made up of males, females, and newborn calves.

3. Some geese fly south in the winter—a very long **journey**.

4. The **landscape** at the North Pole is icy and barren, which makes it hard for some animals to live there.

5. Many scientists believe that some animals have material in their bodies that creates an internal compass by sensing Earth's **magnetic** field.

6. If animals cannot find food in winter, they die of **starvation**.

Practice

Workbook
Page 47

Write the sentences in your notebook. Choose a **red** word from the box above to complete each sentence. Then take turns reading the sentences aloud with a partner.

1. Some animals travel for thousands of miles, using Earth's _____ field to help them find their way.

2. A large _____ of buffalo thundered across the plains.

3. _____ study how animals travel so they can learn more about their migration.

4. Many animals die of _____ each winter because there is not enough food to eat.

5. The _____ of the Arctic is white because of the snow and ice.

6. Many animals make a long _____ south each winter.

▲ A herd of buffalo

Learn Academic Words

Study the **red** words and their meanings. You will find these words useful when talking and writing about informational texts. Write each word and its meaning in your notebook. After you read "Migrating Caribou" and "Magnets in Animals," try to use these words to respond to the text.

Academic Words

approaches
migrate
sufficient
transport

approaches = moves closer	→	As winter **approaches**, squirrels start to gather nuts so they will have enough food.
migrate = move from one place to another	→	Some zebras **migrate** over huge stretches of land to find water.
sufficient = as much as one needs; enough	→	There is a **sufficient** amount of food for the animals to survive the long winter.
transport = move or carry goods from one place to another	→	It is not always easy to **transport** large amounts of food to drought-stricken countries.

Practice

Workbook
Page 48

Work with a partner to answer these questions. Try to include the **red** word in your answer. Write the sentences in your notebook.

1. How do you know when summer **approaches**?
2. Why do some animals **migrate**?
3. What must animals do to make sure they have **sufficient** food for winter?
4. How do some animals **transport** their young?

◄ Migrating zebras

96

Word Study: Words as Multiple Parts of Speech

Nouns and adjectives are two basic parts of speech. A noun is a person, place, or thing. An adjective is a word that modifies, or describes, a noun. Sometimes a word that is used as a noun can also be used as an adjective. The words *caribou*, *Arctic*, *migration*, *history*, and *summer* can be used as nouns, but in the sentences below they are used as adjectives to modify nouns.

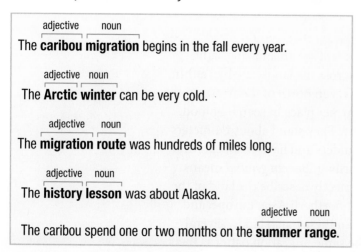

adjective   noun

The **caribou migration** begins in the fall every year.

adjective   noun

The **Arctic winter** can be very cold.

adjective   noun

The **migration route** was hundreds of miles long.

adjective   noun

The **history lesson** was about Alaska.

adjective   noun

The caribou spend one or two months on the **summer range**.

Practice  **Workbook** Page 49

Work with a partner. Take turns reading aloud the sentences above. Copy the sentences into your notebook. Then write a new sentence for each word in bold, changing the word from an adjective to a noun.

READING STRATEGY | RECOGNIZE CAUSE AND EFFECT

Recognizing a cause and an effect helps you understand explanations in texts. It is a useful strategy to know when you are reading informational texts. An effect is "what happened." A cause is "why it happened." To recognize causes and effects, follow these steps:

- As you read, look for events in the text. These are the effects.
- Now look for reasons for what happened. These are the causes.
- Look for words and phrases the author uses to talk about causes and effects. For example: *because, since, so that, therefore, as a result of,* and *therefore.*

As you read "Migrating Caribou," look for the causes and effects of migration. Use a two-column chart to keep track of each cause and effect.

 **Workbook** Page 50

Set a purpose for reading What dangers do animals face on their journeys?

Migrating Caribou

If you fly over the Arctic in the fall, you will see an amazing sight: thousands of migrating caribou flowing across the landscape like a thin, brown river. They are traveling from the frozen north of the Arctic to the forest in the south. They are going to a warmer place in search of food.

Caribou are members of the deer family. They stand about 1½ meters (4–5 ft.) tall from the ground to their shoulders and have small ears and tails. These caribou are barren-ground caribou. *Barren ground* means "lacking plants or crops." These words perfectly describe the land of the Arctic tundra, the cold, treeless regions of northern Asia, Europe, and North America where these caribou live. In these harsh lands, several million barren-ground caribou follow the same migration patterns their ancestors did thousands of years ago.

---

harsh, very uncomfortable
ancestors, family members from the past

▼ Migrating caribou

◀ Caribou roaming on barren ground

Barren-ground caribou are social animals. They travel in large herds made up of thousands. Caribou eat grass, mushrooms, twigs, and shrubs, but their favorite food is lichen. Lichen is a low-growing plant that is common in the Arctic. It grows on rocks and trees. One caribou can eat four kilograms (9 lb.) of lichen a day.

The caribou spend the summer in the northern part of their range. There, they reproduce (have babies) and move from pasture to pasture. On the summer range, the new calves grow healthy and fat. However, the tundra is a harsh and windy place during the long winter. Deep, wind-hardened snow covers the ground. The caribou cannot scrape through the thick ice to reach the food they need. A big snowfall or a rapid drop in temperature inspires the caribou to move south to avoid starvation.

Caribou cover about 20 to 65 kilometers (12–40 mi.) a day while migrating. They are excellent swimmers and can easily cross wide lakes and rivers. Different caribou herds migrate different distances. Large herds usually travel longer distances. The Porcupine caribou herd contains about 125,000 animals. It travels about 650 kilometers (400 mi.). The Central Arctic herd contains about 25,000 animals and migrates about 200 kilometers (125 mi.). However, the herds actually travel much more than this. They wander back and forth, adding many kilometers to their journeys.

The caribou travel for several months. In December, they arrive at their winter range, south of the Arctic tree line, in the forest. North of the tree line, no trees will grow. South of the tree line, the snow remains soft. This makes it easier for the caribou to find lichen to eat.

---

range, area of land
inspires, encourages

BEFORE YOU GO ON

1 Why are some caribou called "barren-ground" caribou?

2 What do barren-ground caribou eat?

💡 **On Your Own**
Would you like to travel to the Arctic tundra? Explain.

99

In April and May, the snow begins to melt. This is a sign for pregnant female caribou, called cows, to leave. The cows begin the long migration to their calving grounds back in the northern Arctic. Why do the caribou travel so far to have their babies? In the north, the young calves are much safer. Predators like wolves and bears are less common there. The best calving grounds also have a lot of new plants, which are high-energy food. This allows the mother caribou to produce rich milk for their calves. And the cool breezes keep away mosquitoes and biting flies. For the caribou, it is worth traveling hundreds of kilometers to reach these special places.

The caribou travel through deep snow and cross ice-filled rivers to reach their destination. After two months and about 1,000 kilometers (600 mi.) of walking, the cows finally reach the northern Arctic. The young are born in early June, almost as soon as their mothers arrive. The other caribou follow several weeks later.

The caribou stay on their summer range for one or two months. At first, they spend their time alone or in small groups. Then the herd begins to gather, and thousands of caribou start to move across the landscape. They begin their long southward journey again, away from the tundra and back across the tree line to the forest.

---

predators, animals that kill and eat other animals
destination, place at the end of a journey

▼ A caribou and her calf

Magnets in Animals

Darlene R. Stille

Every year, many animals migrate, or travel, from one place to another. Some animals go north for summer and south for winter. They may make round trips that cover thousands of miles. Swarms of monarch butterflies travel from Canada and the northern United States to spend the winter in places as far south as Mexico.

Some whales and fish swim across the open sea. One kind of sea turtle finds its way between South America and a tiny island in the middle of the Atlantic Ocean.

Every autumn, flocks of ducks and geese fly overhead. They travel south for the winter. Some are making a journey of thousands of miles.

Arctic terns are migrating birds that cover up to 22,000 miles (35,400 kilometers) every year.

How do animals find their way? Biologists think that some animals use the position of the sun and the stars to help tell where they are going. Some animals may see or even smell landmarks to find their way.

Many biologists now think that some animals have a built-in compass. They think that certain birds, insects, fish, and other sea animals have tiny bits of magnetic material in their bodies. The tiny magnets line up along Earth's magnetic field. Somehow the animals use these compasses inside their bodies to find their way over thousands of miles.

▼ **Monarch butterflies migrating**

---

swarms, large groups of insects that move together
flocks, groups

BEFORE YOU GO ON

1 How long does it take for the caribou herd to reach the northern Arctic?

2 Where do the monarch butterflies spend the winter?

On Your Own
Why do some animals need to make long journeys?

101

Review and Practice

COMPREHENSION

Workbook
Page 51

Right There

1. Where is the Arctic tundra?

2. What happens when caribou sense that winter is approaching?

Think and Search

3. Describe life for the caribou on the tundra in the summer.

4. Why do the caribou go back to the northern Arctic to have their babies?

Author and You

5. Why do you think the caribou stay together in such large herds?

6. What are some explanations for how animals find their way?

On Your Own

7. Do you know of any other migrating animals? Have you ever seen any?

8. Do you think people have built-in compasses? Why or why not?

IN YOUR OWN WORDS

Use the words in the chart below to make sentences about migration.

approaching	➡	starvation, migrate, swarms, herd
migrate	➡	dangerous, journey, flocks
tundra	➡	landscape, barren
sufficient	➡	starvation
caribou	➡	deer, calves
biologists	➡	mystery, magnetic, journey

DISCUSSION

Discuss in pairs or small groups.

1. Why do you think the caribou spend their time alone or in small groups in the summer?

2. Where do the caribou go on their journey? Why?

Q **Where can a journey take you?** What are some reasons that people migrate from one place to another?

 *Speaking* TIP

Speak naturally and with feeling.

READ FOR FLUENCY

When we read aloud to communicate meaning, we group words into phrases, pause or slow down to make important points, and emphasize important words. Pause for a short time when you reach a comma and for a longer time when you reach a period. Pay attention to rising and falling intonation at the end of sentences.

Work with a partner. Choose a paragraph from the reading. Discuss which words seem important for communicating meaning. Practice pronouncing difficult words. Take turns reading the paragraph aloud and give each other feedback.

EXTENSION

Workbook
Page 51

Animals behave the way they do for many reasons. Copy the chart below into your notebook. Read the causes. Write one effect for each cause.

▲ Migrating salmon

Cause	Effect
winter is approaching	birds fly south
lack of sufficient food	
magnetic materials in their bodies	
animals see or smell landmarks	
spring is approaching	

Grammar and Writing

GRAMMAR, USAGE, AND MECHANICS

Prenominal and Postnominal Adjectives

A prenominal adjective precedes, or appears before, the noun it modifies. In English, most adjectives are prenominal.

>   adjective   noun   adjective noun
>
> In winter, **terrible storms** blow across the tundra, making **deep layers** of ice.

A postnominal adjective appears after the noun. Postnominal adjectives modify indefinite pronouns such as *something, anybody, everyone,* and *nothing*.

>   noun   adjective
>
> I recently read **something fascinating** about caribou.
>
>   noun   adjective
>
> There was **nothing unusual** about that winter.

Practice  **Workbook Page 52**

Work with a partner. Copy the sentences below into your notebook. Complete the sentences with the adjectives in the box. Then circle the nouns that the adjectives modify. Decide whether the adjectives are prenominal or postnominal.

barren	cold	interesting	safe	terrible	younger

1. There is nothing _____ about wolves eating caribou—it is simply part of nature.
2. The _____ caribou travel in the back of the herd.
3. Every September, with the approaching _____ weather, the caribou search for each other.
4. Tell me something _____ about the migration of caribou.
5. The caribou are looking for someplace _____ to spend the winter.
6. In summer, the caribou go back to the _____ tundra.

WRITING A NARRATIVE PARAGRAPH

Write a Story with a Starter

At the end of this unit, you will write a fictional narrative. To do this, you'll need to learn some of the skills writers use to write narratives. One important part of writing a narrative is establishing a setting. The setting is where and when the story takes place. To establish a setting, you need to include vivid details about the time or place of the story's action. For example, *Tales from the Odyssey* begins: "Soon after the Greek ships left Troy, the skies began to blacken. Lightning zigzagged above the foamy sea. Thunder shook the heavens."

Here is a model of an opening paragraph. The writer began his story with this starter: *Little did I know that my incredible adventure was about to begin.* Notice how the writer uses details to establish the setting and a details chart to help organize his ideas.

Emanuel Bonilla

Birds Migrating

Little did I know that my incredible adventure was about to begin. That school day seemed to go on forever. There was nothing unusual about that day, but when the final bell rang, I felt like I was free. When I got off the bus, I could see a lot of birds. They were forming a triangle. It was just the beginning of winter. I remembered that birds migrated to the south for the winter and then came back north for the summer. I thought flying was an amazing way to travel, and there was something fascinating about how these birds travel. I couldn't keep my eyes off of how they stayed in such an interesting formation. They did not get out of their place, and they were all working together. Then, I finally saw the birds fading away as they continued south.

Practice

Workbook Page 53

Write a story using this story starter: *I arrived at the most amazing place.* The setting could be a beach, a mountain peak, a desert, or a forest. Include vivid details about the time and place of the story's action. Use a graphic organizer like the one above. Be sure to use prenominal and postnominal adjectives correctly.

Writing Checklist

WORD CHOICE:
☑ I included vivid details to establish setting.

CONVENTIONS:
☑ I used prenominal and postnominal adjectives correctly.

What You Will Learn

Reading

■ Vocabulary building: *Literary terms, spelling*

■ Reading strategy: *Make inferences*

■ Text type: *Literature (novel excerpt)*

Grammar, Usage, and Mechanics
Adverb clauses of time

Writing
Write a personal letter

THE BIG QUESTION

Where can a journey take you? Why do you think people keep journals when they travel? How is writing in a journal different from other kinds of writing? Have you ever kept a journal?

BUILD BACKGROUND

You will read an excerpt from the novel ***The Journal of Wong Ming-Chung.*** The story takes place in the 1850s during the California gold rush. People came from all over the United States and other countries to dig for gold. These people, called miners, all wanted to find gold and make money. Wong Ming-Chung, the boy in the story, comes to America from China to help his uncle search for gold. The story is told from Wong Ming-Chung's point of view. Presenting the story as a journal allows the author to share the private thoughts of the main character. It also allows the reader to learn about history—California in the 1850s—from a personal point of view.

▲ Miners in California in 1852

VOCABULARY

Learn Literary Words

A simile is a figure of speech that writers use to make a comparison between two different things. A simile uses the words *like* or *as* to compare two different things.

Literary Words

simile
metaphor

> He snapped at us **like** a hungry dog.
> Her temper was **as** explosive **as** a volcano.

A metaphor is also a figure of speech that writers use to describe something as if it were something else. A metaphor compares two unlike things without using the words *like* or *as*.

> No man is an island. *(John Donne)*
> The snow was a blanket covering the earth.

Writers use metaphors and similes to help the reader imagine people, places, and things in vivid and interesting ways.

Practice

Workbook
Page 54

Work with a partner. Take turns reading the following metaphors and similes aloud. First, decide if it is a metaphor or simile. Then identify the two things that are being compared.

> Finding my way around the city was like putting together an impossible puzzle.
> All the world's a stage. *(Shakespeare)*
> Life is a journey with many different roads and signposts.
> Her eyes are like the sun.
> Your friend is your needs answered. *(Khalil Gibran)*

Create a metaphor of your own that compares a person, place, or thing to something else. Write the metaphor in your notebook.

Learn Academic Words

Study the **red** words and their meanings. You will find these words useful when talking and writing about literature. Write each word and its meaning in your notebook. After you read the excerpt from the novel *The Journal of Wong Ming-Chung*, try to use these words to respond to the text.

adjust = make a change in something to make it better	➡	When we moved, we had to **adjust** to life in the city.
emphasize = show that something is important	➡	Most schools **emphasize** the rules that students must obey, such as being on time for class.
expand = become larger	➡	The human population will continue to **expand** as people live longer.
immigration = the act of going to live in another country	➡	There were great waves of **immigration** in the late 1800s. Many people left Europe and moved to America.
temporary = existing or happening for a short time only	➡	The government gave families a **temporary** shelter until they could find a permanent place to live.

Practice  Workbook Page 55

Work with a partner to answer these questions. Try to include the **red** word in your answer. Write the sentences in your notebook.

1. How can people make it easier to **adjust** to a new place?

2. What would you **emphasize** to a new student about your school's rules?

3. What are two reasons the population of a city might **expand**?

4. Do you think there is still a lot of **immigration** to the United States?

5. What is an example of a **temporary** place to live?

▲ More than 12 million immigrants passed through the doors to Ellis Island in New York Harbor.

Word Study: Words Ending in *y*

When changing the spelling of certain words that end in consonant *y*, change *y* to *i* and add -*es*.

Singular Noun	Plural Noun
body	bod**ies**
story	stor**ies**
company	compan**ies**

Verb	Third-Person Singular Verb
marry	marr**ies**
try	tr**ies**

When using comparative and superlative adjectives ending in *y*, change the *y* to *i* and add -*er* or -*est*.

Adjective	Comparative	Superlative
scary	scar**ier**	scar**iest**
dirty	dirt**ier**	dirt**iest**

Practice

Look at the chart to the right. Write the correct spelling in your notebook. If you are unsure about the part of speech, check a dictionary.

hungry	➡	comparative: superlative:
city	➡	plural noun:
cry	➡	third person singular:

READING STRATEGY   MAKE INFERENCES

Making inferences helps you figure out the information that authors do not always give directly. When you make inferences (or infer), you are figuring out what the author means. To make inferences, follow these steps. Read these sentences:

Wong Ming-Chung is far from home. He is homesick.

- Think about your own experiences. Have you ever felt homesick?
- Now use the information in the text and your own experiences to make inferences. You can figure out that Wong Ming-Chung does not feel comfortable in his new home yet, even though the writer does not say this.

As you read *The Journal of Wong Ming-Chung*, think about what the author means but does not say directly. What inferences can you make?

109

Set a purpose for reading How did Wong Ming-Chung's life change on his journey to the United States?

from # The Journal of Wong Ming-Chung

Laurence Yep

After a dangerous journey from China, Wong Ming-Chung, a twelve-year-old boy, arrives in San Francisco in 1852. He is on his way to help his uncle in the gold mines. This excerpt is from his diary.

June 18 San Francisco, or First City

The Golden Mountain is stranger, scarier, funnier, sadder and more wonderful than I ever imagined. Now that I am here I will use only the American calendar.

When we got off the ship, I thought I was in the middle of a forest. Except I could hear the ocean. Then I realized the tall poles were the masts of ships. I was surrounded by hundreds of empty boats. They jam the harbor like fish in my village pond. I bet I could have walked from one deck to another across the bay.

I didn't see any sailors. Instead, I saw laundry hanging from lines as if people were using the boats as houses. Then I saw one ship that literally had a house built on top of it. Maybe all the sailors had left their ships to find gold too.

Big, loud machines were pounding logs vertically into the mud a half-kilometer from shore. Real houses perched on top of logs that had already been driven in.

Men and machines were filling in the shoreline to make more space. In some places, they weren't even bothering to move the ship, but were just filling the dirt around it. Blessing [Wong's brother] would have loved the machines.

> ✔ LITERARY CHECK
> *What is the simile in this paragraph?*

---

masts, poles on which the sails are hung
vertically, pointing straight up
perched, sat on a high spot

First City nestles at the foot of steep hills between the shore and the hillsides. A few houses lie scattered on the slopes. Instead of building on the hills, they're expanding into the water.

Though it's summer, the air is as chilly here as winter back at home.

I have to stop now. They're calling for us to register.

Later

Just got back. I don't want to forget a thing, so I'm going to write it all down. But there's so much.

After all these months at sea my legs are used to the motion of the waves. It was strange to stand on solid ground. My legs kept wanting to adjust for a moving platform. They still are.

On shore, there was a Chinese man shouting for people from the Four Districts to come over to him. Another was ordering Three Districts people to gather around him.

---

nestles, sits comfortably
register, put a name on an official list
districts, particular areas of a city

BEFORE YOU GO ON

1 Why did the narrator think he was standing "in the middle of a forest"?

2 What is summer like in San Francisco?

On Your Own
Have you ever been on a boat? What was it like?

111

Gem, Melon, Squash-Nose, and I stuck together as a group. Our own district belongs to the area known as the Four Districts. We tried to ask the clerk what he wanted, but he looked impatient and bored. He snapped at us to wait and then went back to bawling out his call over and over.

When all the Chinese had left the ship, he mechanically began to recite a speech he must have given a hundred times.

It seems that the Chinese in the land of the Golden Mountain have grouped together by areas and family clans. But primarily by areas. His headquarters will act as our clearinghouse for everything—temporary shelter, jobs, and transportation to the gold fields. I was grateful to hear that.

The headquarters will also send our money and letters back home.

He emphasized that we will not be allowed to go home until we have paid back everything that we owe. If we die before then, they will see to it that our bones are shipped back for burial.

I felt a little trapped. It sounds as if the only way out of here is to die. But then I reminded myself that Uncle is doing well. He will watch over me.

---

bawling, yelling loudly
clans, groups of families
headquarters, centers of organizations
clearinghouse, central place for information

Still later

Finally, real food! Rice, vegetables, and meat! At first, I wondered if I had lost track of time. Maybe it was a feast day. However, the people at the headquarters act like they have it all the time. At home only rich people can feast like this every day.

To get to Chinatown we had to pass through the American part of the city. San Francisco is like a big pot of stew with everything mixed in.

People seem to live in anything they can. In many places, I saw tents of dirty canvas. Other buildings were wooden fronts with canvas sides and roofs that flapped up and down. The first good wind ought to blow most of them away. When I asked the clerk, he explained that in the past three years, six fires had destroyed the city. The latest was just a year ago.

Then I saw some little cottages built out of iron. The clerk said that there used to be a lot more. However, in the last fire, many people had stayed inside them, thinking they were safe. Unfortunately, the flames turned the iron cottages into huge stoves. When the unlucky people tried to escape, they found the doors and windows had sealed tight and they were trapped. Most of them died.

Finally, we came to an area that the fire must have skipped. Tall buildings of brick or wood rose several stories high. Through the open windows and doorways came the sound of loud laughter. Gem tried to peek inside one place and got a hard-boiled egg in the face. He said they were playing cards inside.

Other wooden buildings were so new that their lumber smelled of freshly planed wood and shone like pale gold. Still others had already weathered gray while a few had been painted white, the color of death. At first I thought they were mausoleums for the dead. But as I passed I saw they were stores. All of them were crammed with goods. In fact, the goods spilled out of some of them and were piled on the sidewalk.

Then I saw tall stone walls rising from the dirt. Chinese were on scaffolding building the walls, so I thought we were in Chinatown. However, when we just kept on walking, I asked the clerk.

He said it is an American building, but that tall mountains shut off this province from the rest of the country. It had been cheaper to bring the stones from China. Unfortunately, the assembly instructions had been written in Chinese, so the American owner had hired a boatload of Chinese stone masons to put it together. It is to be the First City's first building of stone. I feel proud that it is Chinese who are doing that.

Have to go. Gem and Melon need help reading the employment notices.

---

planed, smoothed
mausoleums, large stone buildings containing graves
scaffolding, boards for people to stand on
province, large area in a country
masons, people who cut stones into pieces

BEFORE YOU GO ON

1 How did the Chinese group together when they first arrived?

2 Why were many people living in tents in San Francisco?

On Your Own
When you go to a new place, what kinds of things do you first notice?

113

Evening

San Francisco is also a big stew of people. Every country in the world has dumped someone into the pot. And most of us are hurrying to the Golden Mountain.

I've seen hair of almost every color, and faces and bodies stranger than the British man in Hong Kong. Many of them are Americans, but many others speak languages that don't sound like English. They wear every type of costume from elegant to cheap and plain.

I also see people with skin the same color as mine. However, when I try to greet them, they don't understand me. I don't think they are speaking English, either.

Most of them are miners and look as eager and new as us.

The air is crackling with energy. I wish I could bottle it and sell it as a tonic.

Two things worry me, though. Even if the Golden Mountain is pure gold, can there really be enough for all the miners I see?

Almost all of them are armed with at least a pistol and a knife, too. Why do they need so much protection? And from what?

✔ LITERARY CHECK
What does the author compare San Francisco to in this metaphor? Why?

114

Could the Golden Mountain be even more dangerous than the sea voyage here? I don't see how. And yet . . .

The others want to turn off the light so they can sleep. Another wonder. The light is inside glass. The Americans call it kerosene.

I don't see how they can sleep. I know I won't.

June 19

Another big meal. It was rice porridge and fried crullers like at home. But the porridge had big chunks of pork and preserved eggs. I've never eaten so well. Blessing would definitely have liked this part of the trip.

The Chinese live in an area on a steep hill of San Francisco. The clerk was careful to tell us the Chinese and American names in case we get lost. In Chinese, it's the street of the people of T'ang. The T'ang was a famous dynasty back in China a thousand years ago. In English, it is called Sacramento Street.

However, since there are thousands of Chinese living here now, Chinatown has begun to spill over onto other streets, especially Dupont.

Like the American town, Chinatown is a mixture of wooden buildings and tents. The buildings are American-style but wooden carvings and signboards in Chinese mark their owners.

Above Chinatown, on an American street called Stockton, are a few wooden mansions where the richer Americans live.

Our group is luckier than some of the Chinese who have to stay in tents. We're inside the headquarters itself. The smells make me feel right at home. Altar incense mixes with the smell of cooking.

We are crowded into a room on the second floor. Though we are packed side to side, it seems spacious after the *Excalibur*.

---

kerosene, oil that is burned for heat and light

ABOUT THE **AUTHOR**

Laurence Yep writes stories for children and adults. He was born in San Francisco, California, in 1948 and lives there with his wife, Joanne, who is also a writer. Yep's books *Dragonwings* and *Dragon's Gate* are Newbery Honor winners. In addition to writing books, Yep has also taught creative writing and Asian-American studies at various universities.

BEFORE YOU GO ON

1 What two things worry Wong Ming-Chung?

2 Where are the wooden mansions located?

On Your Own
What is Wong Ming-Chung's next journey? Where is he going?

115

Review and Practice

DRAMATIC READING

Reading a narrative aloud can help to make the characters seem more real. With a partner, read aloud the excerpt from *The Journal of Wong Ming-Chung*. Stop occasionally to comment on how you think the narrator probably feels in the different entries. Is he nervous, homesick, or hopeful? Try to emphasize the words that give feeling to his journal entries. Ask your teacher for help with pronunciation, if necessary. Practice reading one section silently, and then read it aloud for the whole class.

Speaking TIP

Speak clearly and loudly enough for everyone to hear.

COMPREHENSION

Workbook Page 58

Right There

1. What is the setting of the story?
2. What district in China is Wong Ming-Chung from?

Think and Search

3. What food is served to Wong Ming-Chung? How does he feel about it?
4. Why were Chinese masons working on the first stone building in San Francisco?

Author and You

5. The author writes from Wong Ming-Chung's point of view. Do you think his account of life in California in the 1850s is realistic?
6. How do you think the author feels about San Francisco?

On Your Own

7. Is the journal style an effective way to write a personal story? Why or why not?
8. Is life easier now for immigrants than it was 150 years ago? Explain why or why not.

▲ A miner panning for gold

DISCUSSION

Discuss in pairs or small groups.

1. Why did Wong Ming-Chung want to write everything down in his journal?

2. What do you think will happen next to Wong Ming-Chung?

3. Do you think you can learn more about life through traveling? What do you think Wong Ming-Chung learned on his journey?

Q **Where can a journey take you?** Think of a time when you went to a new place. What was your first impression?

Listening TIP

Respect each speaker. Listen politely, even if you disagree with the speaker's ideas.

RESPONSE TO LITERATURE

Workbook Page 58

Did you or any of your family members immigrate to the United States? If not, can you imagine making a long journey to a new country? Compare your experience to Wong Ming-Chung's. Copy the chart below into your notebook. Then complete the right column with information about your real or imagined experience. Share your chart in a small group.

Experience	Wong Ming-Chung	Me
The journey:	had trouble adjusting to movement of waves	
Reason for leaving home:	opportunity	
Reaction to America:	strange, scary, funny, and wonderful	
Reaction to food:	feels like a feast day	
Shelter:	crowded into temporary homes	

Grammar and Writing

Adverb Clauses of Time

Adverb clauses of time express *when*. An adverb clause of time begins with a time expression, such as *after, before, when, until, while, since,* or *whenever*. When an adverb clause begins the sentence, use a comma. When an adverb clause finishes the sentence, there is no need for a comma.

Adverb Clause at the Beginning	Adverb Clause at the End
When all the Chinese had left the ship, he began to recite a speech.	He began to recite a speech **when all the Chinese had left the ship.**
Until we pay back everything, we will not be able to go back home.	We will not be able to go back home **until we pay back everything.**

In the chart above, the words *when* and *until* are time expressions.

Practice

Work with a partner. Copy the sentences below into your notebook. Circle the time expressions and underline the adverb clauses.

1. They will register after they arrive in the city.
2. Before we leave, I'll write my father a letter.
3. While I was walking, I noticed the houses around me.
4. I haven't seen him since he left this morning.
5. Whenever I remember that time, I feel happy.
6. We stayed there until we had to board the ship.
7. When we arrived, we looked for a place to live.
8. When the boat docked, we got off.

▲ An immigrant family looking at New York City before they finally arrive

WRITING A NARRATIVE PARAGRAPH

Write a Personal Letter

In this unit, you have written three different kinds of narrative paragraphs. Now you will write a personal letter. In a personal letter, you tell the reader about something you did or something that happened to you. It is important to present the events in the order in which they happened. This is called chronological order. Transition words such as *first, next, then,* and *finally* help the reader follow the sequence of events.

Here is a model of a personal letter, written by a student named Lukas Arbogast. The events are in chronological order and the writer used transition words. Notice the structure of the letter. It includes a date, salutation (or greeting), body, closing, and signature. The writer used a graphic organizer to put his letter in the correct format.

Salutation (or greeting)	Date
Body	
	Closing, Signature

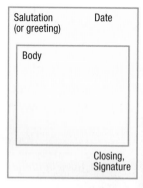

April 16, 2009

Dear Danielle,

Last weekend I visited my grandma, who lives on a small farm in Texas. Whenever we go there, we have such a great time. The first thing my brother and I did was to call over the neighbor's dogs. After all, we only go to Texas once a year, so we wanted to spend as much time with them as possible. On the farm, there is always something to do, like making a scary movie in the old abandoned house next door, or climbing the haystacks in the neighbor's field. Climbing the haystacks is like climbing little mountains. Before we knew it, the weekend was over. Leaving Texas was hard. Even though it is hundreds of miles away, it feels like home.

From,
Lukas

Practice

Workbook
Page 60

Write a personal letter. Tell about a class trip, a visit to a relative's house, or a weekend away from home. List your events in chronological order and use transition words. Use a graphic organizer like the one above. Be sure to use adverb clauses of time correctly.

Writing Checklist

ORGANIZATION:
☑ I told the events in chronological order.

SENTENCE FLUENCY:
☑ I used adverb clauses correctly.

Link the Readings

Critical Thinking

Look back at the readings in this unit. Think about what they have in common. They all tell about journeys. Yet they do not all have the same purpose. The purpose of one reading might be to inform, while the purpose of another might be to entertain or persuade. In addition, the content of each reading relates to journeys differently. Now copy the chart below into your notebook and complete it.

Title of Reading	Purpose	Big Question Link
From *Tales from the Odyssey*		
"Early Explorers"	*to inform*	
"Migrating Caribou" and "Magnets in Animals"		
From *The Journal of Wong Ming-Chung*		*Wong Ming-Chung has completed a journey from China to San Francisco.*

Discussion

Discuss in pairs or small groups.

● How does the purpose of *Tales from the Odyssey* differ from the purpose of "Early Explorers"? What does the story tell that the article does not?

Q **Where can a journey take you?** Think about the readings. Why was Odysseus's journey so long and difficult? Where did the early explorers' journeys take them? Why do migrating animals have to make journeys? How did Wong Ming-Chung change during his journey?

Fluency Check

Work with a partner. Choose a paragraph from one of the readings. Take turns reading it for one minute. Count the total number of words you read. Practice saying the words you had trouble reading. Take turns reading the paragraph three more times. Did you read more words each time? Copy the chart below into your notebook and record your speeds.

	1st Speed	2nd Speed	3rd Speed	4th Speed
Words Per Minute				

Projects

Work in pairs or small groups. Choose one of these projects.

1 Write a journal entry about taking a trip. Describe the setting in an interesting way by using similes and metaphors. Then read your journal entry to the class.

2 What do you think happens next to Odysseus and his men? What will they discuss when they return to their ship? Write a dialogue and practice it. Then perform it for the class or make a video.

3 Make a travel brochure about a particular place or landscape. Take photographs, cut out pictures from magazines, or make drawings of the place. Include animals that might live there or migrate to that landscape. Write a few descriptive sentences about the place. Present it to the class.

4 What are some problems that early explorers faced? Make a poster with a cause-and-effect chart. Show the problems and the reasons for them. Present your poster to the class.

Further Reading

To find out more about the theme of this unit, choose from these reading suggestions.

Apollo 13, Dina Anastasio
The exciting story of the incredible Apollo 13 mission is told in this Penguin Reader® adaptation. When something goes terribly wrong in space, the Apollo 13 crew has to find a way to return to Earth. It's a race against time.

Girl of the Shining Mountains: Sacagawea's Story,
Peter and Connie Roop
Sacagawea joins the Lewis and Clark expedition as it searches for a water route to the Pacific Ocean. Kidnapped years earlier, Sacagawea is hoping to find her own people as she guides the expedition.

The Wanderer, Sharon Creech
This is a story about Sophie, a thirteen-year-old girl who makes a journey across the Atlantic Ocean on a sailboat. She faces difficult challenges at sea. But her true journey involves discovering more about herself and what it means to belong to a family.

Put It All Together

LISTENING & SPEAKING WORKSHOP

Personal Narrative

A personal narrative is a story about events in your life. You will present an oral personal narrative related to a journey you have taken.

1 **THINK ABOUT IT** Look back over the readings in this unit. Talk in small groups about journeys. Describe some journeys you have taken.

Work together to develop a list of journey-related topics you could tell about in a personal narrative, for example:

- how I felt when I had to move to a new place
- how I felt when I went on a trip
- how I made a new friend
- how I tried a new activity or sport

2 **GATHER AND ORGANIZE INFORMATION** Choose a topic from your group's list. Think about the setting and plot of your personal narrative. Write down the sequence of events in the plot. List the characters involved in your story.

Reflect Make an idea web or take notes on the important points you want to communicate. Include many specific details.

Order Your Notes Make a numbered list of the events you want to tell about.

Use Visuals Make a poster that illustrates the events in your story. Point to the poster as you tell your story. Be ready to answer questions.

One way to take a journey—
by high-speed train ▶

3 **PRACTICE AND PRESENT** Use your list of events in the plot as the written outline for your presentation. Keep your outline nearby, but practice talking to your audience without reading. If possible, use a tape recorder to record your storytelling. Then play back your recording and listen to yourself. Keep practicing until you are happy with the pace of your presentation.

Deliver Your Personal Narrative Look at your audience as you speak. Emphasize key words and ideas with your voice and actions. If you talk about visiting a new place, for example, you may want to speak more slowly, emphasize the adjectives you use to describe that place, and point to a picture of it on your poster.

4 **EVALUATE THE PRESENTATION** You will improve your skills as a speaker and a listener by evaluating each presentation you give and hear. Use this checklist to help you judge your presentation and the presentations of your classmates.

- ☑ Did the speaker clearly identify the event(s) he or she was telling about?
- ☑ Was the setting clear?
- ☑ Did the speaker emphasize important ideas or words?
- ☑ Did the speaker answer your questions?
- ☑ What suggestions do you have for improving the presentation?

Speaking TIPS

Be sure you emphasize key words and ideas. Ask your listeners for feedback. Did they understand which ideas were especially important?

Use facial expressions and gestures to show the feelings you had during the story events.

Listening TIPS

Jot down key words and ideas as you listen. Try to picture the events in your mind.

What else would you like to know about these events? Write down questions and ask them at the end of the presentation.

WRITING WORKSHOP
Fictional Narrative

In this workshop you will write a fictional narrative. A fictional narrative is a story that the writer invents. It includes characters created from the writer's imagination and a setting, or a specific time and place, in which the story's events happen. These events, called the *plot*, usually focus on a problem to be solved. The plot opens with an introduction, includes rising action as events build to a climax, and ends with a resolution of the problem. Another feature of a fictional narrative is dialogue, the words characters say. Dialogue brings the characters to life.

Your writing assignment for this workshop is to write a fictional narrative about a character's short trip or weekend visit.

1 **PREWRITE** Brainstorm a list of possible characters for your fictional narrative in your notebook. Then think about the point of view from which your story will be told. Will it be told from the point of view of the main character going on the trip? Think about that character's traits. Is he or she someone like you or different from you? Also brainstorm a list of ideas for your setting. Where is your character going? What is the purpose of your character's visit?

List and Organize Ideas and Details Use a story chart to organize ideas for your fictional narrative. A student named Ben listed his ideas on the story chart below:

Main Character	Setting
Jonathan—my age	Venice, Italy
Very excited about trip!	Last summer
Worried about his stuff!	
Problem	**Resolution**
Lost luggage!	Luggage found
	Great time!

2 **DRAFT** Use the model on page 127 and your story chart to help you write your first draft. Remember to tell events in a logical order and to use time expressions to help readers follow your narrative.

3 **REVISE** Read over your draft. As you do so, ask yourself the questions in the writing checklist. Use the questons to help you revise your fictional narrative.

SIX TRAITS OF WRITING CHECKLIST

☑ **IDEAS:** Does my plot have an introduction, rising action, a climax, and resolution?

☑ **ORGANIZATION:** Are events presented in an order that makes sense?

☑ **VOICE:** Does my writing express my main character's point of view?

☑ **WORD CHOICE:** Does my dialogue bring the characters to life?

☑ **SENTENCE FLUENCY:** Do my sentences vary in length?

☑ **CONVENTIONS:** Does my writing follow the rules of grammar, usage, and mechanics?

Here are the changes Ben plans to make when he revises his first draft:

Jonathan's Trip to Italy

"This is flight 137, nonstop service from Newark to Venice. We will be landing in 10 minutes." As Jonathan listened to the announcement. He was on his way to visit relatives who lived in Venice, Italy. He had never traveled to Italy or met these family members before. His heart raced with excitement.

When Jonathan got off the plane, he looked around. Then He waited. And waited. There wasn't any sign either of his family or his suitcase. He was really starting to get nervous, when he heard a voice calling his name. He saw three people heading towards him--a short woman with blonde hair, a tall man with a thick beard and glasses, and a boy about his own age.

125

"I'm your Aunt Mary, and this is your Uncle Andrew," said the woman, giving Jonathan a hug. "This is Sam." The boy grinned shyly.

"Where's your luggage?" Aunt Mary asked.

"It hasn't shown up, replied Jonathan.

The four of them ~~hurryed~~ hurried over to the Baggage Claim Desk. Aunt Mary spoke to the attendant in italian.

"The luggage may have been sent on another plane by mistake," she reported. "They'll give us a call as soon as possible."

Outside, Jonathan noticed that there weren't many cars in Venice. Instead, there were boats on canals. They boarded a boat that stopped a few minutes later at the edge of the city, where they got off. They walked to a nearby house.

"Hey, we have to take you to St. Mark's Square! It's one of the most famous places in Venice" piped up Sam.

Jonathan's stay went by too quickly. By the time he left, he had seen St. Mark's Square, met his cousin's friends, and even got his luggage. Best of all, he had gotten to know the wonderful relatives he had never met before. ~~Familys~~ Families, he decided, are special. He felt very lucky as he waved good-bye at the airport.

4 EDIT AND PROOFREAD

Workbook Page 61

Copy your revised draft onto a clean sheet of paper. Read it again. Correct any errors in grammar, word usage, mechanics, and spelling. Here are the additional changes Ben plans to make when he prepares his final draft.

Ben Berman

Jonathan's Trip to Italy

"This is flight 137, nonstop service from Newark to Venice. We will be landing in 10 minutes." As Jonathan listened to the announcement, his heart raced with excitement. He was on his way to visit relatives who lived in Venice, Italy. He had never traveled to Italy or met these family members before.

When Jonathan got off the plane, he looked around. Then he waited. And waited. There wasn't any sign either of his family or his suitcase. He was really starting to get nervous when he heard a voice calling his name. He saw three people heading towards him--a short woman with blonde hair, a tall man with a thick beard and glasses, and a boy about his own age.

"I'm your Aunt Mary, and this is your Uncle Andrew," said the woman, giving Jonathan a hug. "This is Sam." The boy grinned shyly.

"Where's your luggage?" Aunt Mary asked.

"It hasn't shown up," replied Jonathan.

The four of them hurried over to the Baggage Claim Desk. Aunt Mary spoke to the attendant in italian.

"The luggage may have been sent on another plane by mistake," she reported. "They'll give us a call as soon as possible."

Outside, Jonathan noticed that there weren't many cars in Venice. Instead, there were boats on canals. They boarded a boat that stopped a few minutes later at the edge of the city, where they got off. They walked to a nearby house.

"Hey, we have to take you to St. Mark's Square! It's one of the most famous places in Venice," piped up Sam.

Jonathan's stay went by too quickly. By the time he left, he had seen St. Mark's Square, met his cousin's friends, and even got his luggage. Best of all, he had gotten to know the wonderful relatives he had never met before. Families, he decided, are special. He felt very lucky as he waved good-bye at the airport.

5 **PUBLISH** Prepare your final draft. Share your fictional narrative with your teacher and classmates.

Traveling The Electronic Superhighway

Have you ever taken a journey? A trip is one kind of journey. You get in a car or a plane and go somewhere. Maybe you are going to visit friends or family. You might want to see some place special, like a big city. But there are other kinds of journeys, too. For example, growing up is a kind of journey. You move from childhood to your teenage years. From there, you continue to grow until you become an adult. As you take this journey, your ideas about life change. You develop new interests. American artists have explored both of these kinds of journeys. Sometimes their art shows connections between them.

Nam June Paik, *Electronic Superhighway: Continental U.S., Alaska, Hawaii* (1995)

Electronic Superhighway: Continental U.S., Alaska, Hawaii by Nam June Paik is a very large work of art. It looks like a giant map. Paik uses 336 televisions, 50 DVDs, and 175 meters (575 ft.) of neon tubing, twisted into different shapes. When you look at the whole map from across a room, all of the TV screens seem to have different pictures. You hear a lot of different voices and noises. It is very loud!

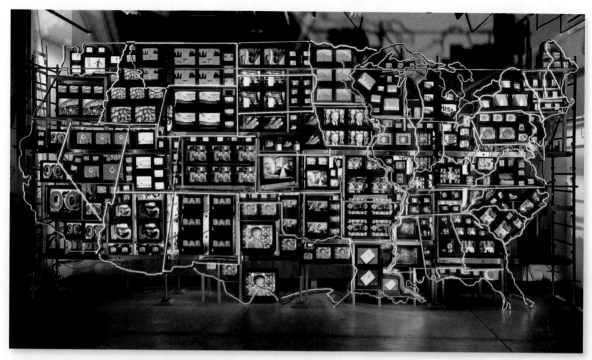

▲ Nam June Paik, *Electronic Superhighway: Continental U.S., Alaska, Hawaii*, 1995, closed-circuit video, approx. 15 x 40 x 4 ft., Smithsonian American Art Museum

But if you move a little closer, you can see that each state has its own story to tell. Paik was one of the first artists to use video in his artwork. He picked out special video or images for each state. These images have something to say about that state's special culture. For example, for the state of Kansas, Paik chose scenes from a movie called *The Wizard of Oz*. In this movie, a girl named Dorothy has taken a journey to a magical place called Oz, but she wants to go home to Kansas.

Paik made his own journey when he was nine years old. He moved from South Korea to the United States. As a boy, Paik loved the big highways in the United States. He could feel the freedom that those open roads promised to people like his family. When he made *Electronic Superhighway*, he wanted to show how big and open the United States is. He also wanted to show how electronic connections, like computers and television, bring the country together. At one time, people could take a trip only by driving on a regular highway. Today, they can turn on a computer and take a trip on an electronic highway called the Internet.

Apply What You Learned

1 In what ways are the open highway and the electronic highway the same? How are they different?

2 What kind of video would you choose for your state? Why?

Big Question
Would you rather take a journey on the electronic superhighway, or on an open highway in a car or a truck? Explain your answer.

Workbook
Pages 63–64

129

THE BIG Q QUESTION

What defines success?

This unit is about people who have achieved success in different ways. You'll find out about people who have overcome hardships, helped others, and worked hard to achieve success. Reading, writing, and talking about these ideas will give you practice using academic language and help you become a better student.

READING 1: Social Studies Article

- "Success Stories"

READING 2: Interview and Poetry

- "An Interview with Naomi Shihab Nye" by Rachel Barenblat
- "Making a Mosaic" by Naomi Shihab Nye

READING 3: Short Story

- "The Marble Champ" by Gary Soto

READING 4: Science Article

- "Students Win Robotics Competition" by Karina Bland

Listening and Speaking

At the end of this unit, you will choose a topic and conduct an **interview**.

Writing

In this unit, you will practice **expository writing**. Expository writing explains or describes something. After each reading, you will learn a skill to help you write an expository paragraph. At the end of the unit, you will use these skills to write an expository essay in the form of a news article.

QuickWrite
Think of a successful person you know or have read about. Write a sentence about his or her accomplishments.

Prepare to Read

What You Will Learn

Reading

■ Vocabulary building: *Context, dictionary skills, word study*

■ Reading strategy: *Connect ideas*

■ Text type: *Informational text (social studies)*

Grammar, Usage, and Mechanics
Independent and dependent clauses

Writing
Write to compare and contrast

THE BIG QUESTION

What defines success? Success can mean different things to different people. In your view, what contributes to a person's success? Read the statements below. Do you agree or disagree with them? Discuss with a partner.

- Success means doing something no one else has ever done.
- To be successful, you have to make a lot of money.
- Being successful depends on what others think of you.
- You have to be smart to be successful.

BUILD BACKGROUND

In the article **"Success Stories,"** you will read short biographies about four successful people. A biography is the story of a person's life. Each person you will read about works in a different field: Frida Kahlo was an artist, Bill Gates is a businessman, Muhammad Yunus is a banker, and Mae Jemison is an astronaut. These people achieved great success in their lives because they had talent and a goal. Each one worked hard to achieve his or her goal. Their success changed their lives and the lives of many others.

▲ *El Camión* (The Bus), 1929, by Frida Kahlo

VOCABULARY

Learn Key Words

Read these sentences. Use the context to figure out the meaning of the **red** words. Use a dictionary to check your answers. Then write each word and its meaning in your notebook.

1. The businessman started a company with a small amount of money and a good idea. His **enterprise** made the company successful.

2. The soccer player trained hard and **excelled** in every game. He won the player-of-the-year award.

3. Floods and droughts often destroy crops and lead to a **famine**. People cannot get enough food, so they starve.

4. The communications company sent a new **satellite** into space to improve their Internet service.

5. Many college students need **scholarships** to help pay for their studies.

6. The artist painted a picture of himself. His **self-portrait** hangs in the local art gallery.

Practice  Workbook Page 65

Write the sentences in your notebook. Choose a **red** word from the box above to complete each sentence. Then take turns reading the sentences aloud with a partner.

1. The student won two _____ for college because of his excellent test results and his hard work throughout high school.

2. The artist sat in front of the mirror and painted a _____.

3. The award-winning scientist worked hard and _____ in her field.

4. Many people suffered during the _____ that began after a hurricane ruined the crops.

5. Television programs are broadcast using a _____ in space.

6. Thanks to the _____ of the women involved, the new project succeeded.

▲ The Skylab satellite orbits Earth.

133

Learn Academic Words

Study the red words and their meanings. You will find these words useful when talking and writing about informational texts. Write each word and its meaning in your notebook. After you read "Success Stories," try to use these words to respond to the text.

Academic Words

aid
commitment
contribution
global
priority

aid = assistance, especially in the form of money, food, equipment	➡	The Red Cross gave **aid** to the people who lost their homes after Hurricane Katrina in New Orleans.
commitment = a promise and a determination to do something	➡	The neighborhood made a **commitment** to help clean up the parks.
contribution = money or help that is offered or given	➡	People from all over the country made a **contribution** of clothes or money to the people in need.
global = affecting or relating to the whole world	➡	Heart disease is a **global** health issue that affects people in every country.
priority = the thing that you think is most important	➡	The doctor's **priority** is to make her patients feel better.

Practice

Workbook
Page 66

Work with a partner to rewrite the sentences. Use the red word in each new sentence. Write the sentences in your notebook.

1. People often need assistance after natural disasters. (**aid**)

2. I made a promise to babysit my little sister every Friday evening during the summer. (**commitment**)

3. I can't give money to the animal hospital, but I can spend two hours on Saturday caring for the animals. (**contribution**)

4. Pollution is an issue that affects every country in the world. (**global**)

5. It is important to our teacher that all of us are prepared for the final exam. (**priority**)

▲ Hurricane Katrina survivors receive aid from Red Cross workers.

134

Word Study: Prefixes *under-*, *re-*, *multi-*, *inter-*

A prefix is a group of letters added to the beginning of a word to change its meaning. As you read "Success Stories," you will see the prefixes *under-*, *re-*, and *multi-*.

In the chart below are prefixes and their meanings. When you combine the prefixes with base words you make new words.

Prefix	(Meaning)	+ Base Word	= New Word
under-	(below)	developed	underdeveloped
re-	(again)	pay	repay
multi-	(many)	billionaire	multibillionaire
inter-	(between)	national	international

Practice

Look at the chart above. Use a dictionary to find the meaning of each new word. Work with a partner. Write sentences using three of the words and record them in your notebook.

▲ Women repaying their loans to the Grameen Bank

READING STRATEGY | CONNECT IDEAS

Connecting ideas in a text helps you understand what the author wants you to know more easily. When you connect ideas, you look for the most important idea in each paragraph and see how it fits with all of the other ideas. To connect ideas, follow these steps:

- Read the first paragraph. What is the main idea?
- Now read the paragraphs that follow. Make a note of the main ideas.
- Look at the list that you made. How are the ideas similar?

As you read "Success Stories," look for the ideas that are similar to each other. Think about what connects each idea to the next.

Set a purpose for reading As you read the biographies, think about each person's accomplishments. What do you think makes each person a success?

Success Stories

▲ *The Frame*, 1938, a self-portrait by Frida Kahlo

Frida Kahlo

Born in 1907, the extraordinary painter Frida Kahlo grew up in Coyoacán, an area which is now part of Mexico City. When she was six years old, Kahlo got polio, a serious disease that often causes paralysis. As a result of her illness, Kahlo's right leg was always thinner and weaker than her left one. She was also involved in a terrible bus accident when she was in college. Her injuries were so severe she was often hospitalized. It took her many months to recover from this accident. It was during this time that Kahlo began to paint from her bed.

At the age of twenty-one, Kahlo met Diego Rivera, a very famous Mexican painter. They got married in 1929. They shared a love of Mexican art and culture. In some of her self-portraits, Kahlo is wearing traditional Mexican clothing and jewelry. In addition to her many self-portraits, Kahlo painted portraits of friends. She is also famous for her still-life paintings— pictures of arranged objects, such as flowers and fruit.

Frida Kahlo exhibited her work in New York City, Paris, and Mexico City. She died at the young age of forty-seven. Her house in Mexico City, called Casa Azul (Blue House), is now the Frida Kahlo Museum. Her work and her life story continue to inspire people all over the world.

---

paralysis, the loss of the ability to move or feel part of your body
exhibited, showed in public

Bill Gates

As an elementary school student in Seattle, Washington, in the 1960s, Bill Gates excelled in science and mathematics. When he was in eighth grade, his school acquired an early computer. Bill Gates was excused from math class so he could work on a program for the computer. Later, he went to Harvard University, where he spent most of his time in the university's computer center.

In 1975, Bill Gates started the Microsoft Corporation. The company developed Windows, the world's most widely used computer operating system. Bill Gates eventually became a multibillionaire and the richest man in the world.

In 2000, Gates and his wife started the Bill and Melinda Gates Foundation. So far, the foundation has contributed $800 million to the United Nations Global Alliance for Vaccine and Immunization, to fight diseases. One disease, malaria, is spread by mosquitoes. Malaria affects about 500 million people every year and kills as many as 3 million people—mostly African children under five years of age. An easy way to prevent malaria is by using bed nets, which cost very little. But very few families can afford them.

▲ A mosquito

Bill Gates has said: "It just blows my mind how little money has been spent on malaria research. . . . I just keep asking myself, Do we really not care because it doesn't affect us? . . . I refuse to sit there and say, Okay, next problem, this one doesn't bother me. It does bother me. Very much. And the only way for that to change is to stop malaria. So that is what we are going to have to do."

---

program, set of instructions
contributed, given; donated
blows my mind, amazes me

◄ Bill and Melinda Gates at a hospital in Madras, India

BEFORE YOU GO ON

1 What happened to Frida Kahlo when she was in college?

2 What did Bill Gates start in 1975? In 2000?

On Your Own
Why do bed nets prevent malaria?

137

Muhammad Yunus

Muhammad Yunus was born in 1940 in a village in Bangladesh. He obtained a scholarship to study in the United States and earned a doctorate. He returned to Bangladesh in 1972 to teach economics.

In 1974, Bangladesh suffered a terrible famine. Yunus decided that it was not enough to teach economics and read textbooks. He needed to do something practical. What if these people were able to receive tiny loans, or microcredit, to improve their situation? Yunus started his project in a small village. He lent $27 to a group of forty-two villagers. They made bamboo stools and bought a cow. And so the Grameen Bank was born.

The Grameen Bank was very different from other banks. First, it provided very small loans. Second, it focused on women borrowers. Yunus believed that women were better at using and repaying loans. Third, only the very poorest people could obtain loans. The system was based on the trust of the bank and the enterprise of the women borrowers. If the borrowers failed to repay, the bank would fail. But it didn't.

▲ Muhammad Yunus, banker to the poor

In 2006, Muhammad Yunus and the Grameen Bank were awarded the Nobel Peace Prize. The Nobel committee said, "Lasting peace cannot be achieved unless large population groups find ways in which to break out of poverty. Microcredit is one such means . . ."

---

doctorate, university degree of the highest level
economics, the way goods and services are produced and used
practical, relating to actions, not words
borrowers, people who use something and give it back later

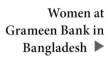

Women at Grameen Bank in Bangladesh ▶

◀ Mae Jemison, first African-American astronaut

▲ Jemison in zero gravity

Mae Jemison

Mae Jemison was born in 1956 in Decatur, Alabama. She grew up in Chicago, Illinois. When she was growing up, Jemison watched spaceflights on television. After college, she went to medical school and also took graduate courses in engineering. What she really wanted, however, was to be a space traveler. In 1987, Dr. Jemison was one of fifteen people, out of almost 2,000 applicants, chosen for NASA's astronaut training program.

On September 12, 1992, Dr. Jemison and six other astronauts went into orbit aboard the space shuttle *Endeavour*. Dr. Jemison was the first African-American female astronaut. During her seven-day flight, she did experiments to understand the effects of weightlessness. She carried with her several small objects from West African countries. She did this to show her belief that space belongs to all nations.

Dr. Jemison is currently a professor of community and family medicine at Dartmouth College, New Hampshire. She is active worldwide in science literacy and sustainable development. She has founded two companies that are devoted to integrating science and technology into society, as well as an annual international science camp.

---

orbit, a circular path
space shuttle, space vehicle that can fly into space and return to Earth
sustainable development, development that meets present needs without
    endangering the needs of people in the future

BEFORE YOU GO ON

1 Why did Muhammad Yunus decide not to teach economics?

2 What did Mae Jemison do after college? What did she really want to do?

On Your Own
Which of these four stories was the most interesting to you? Why?

139

Review and Practice

COMPREHENSION
Workbook
Page 69

Right There

1. What happened to Frida Kahlo when she was six years old?

2. What did the group of villagers do with the $27 Muhammad Yunus lent them?

Think and Search

3. What did Mae Jemison bring with her on the space flight? Why?

4. How is the Grameen Bank different from other banks?

Author and You

5. Why do you think the author talks more about Bill Gates's contributions to the needy than about Gates's business?

6. Why does the author mention that Yunus wanted to do more than teach economics? What does this tell us about Yunus's character?

On Your Own

7. Do you think the people described in these biographies became successful on their own or with the help of others? Explain your answer.

8. Do you think everyone can be successful? Why or why not?

IN YOUR OWN WORDS

Use the words in the chart below to tell a partner about the people described in "Success Stories."

Businessman	➡	excelled, computers, contribution, priority
Painter	➡	accident, self-portrait, exhibited
Banker	➡	suffered, famine, microcredit, enterprise
Astronaut	➡	technology, orbit, satellite-based telecommunications

DISCUSSION

Discuss in pairs or small groups.

- What do you think the success of the Grameen Bank tells us about the people it serves?

- **Q What defines success?** Name another well-known person who you think is successful. How would you define his or her success?

»)ᗡ Listening TIP

Think about the points others are making. Try to relate their ideas to ideas of your own.

READ FOR FLUENCY

It is often easier to read a text if you understand the difficult words and phrases. Work with a partner. Choose a paragraph from the reading. Identify the words and phrases you do not know or have trouble pronouncing. Look up the difficult words in a dictionary.

Take turns pronouncing the words and phrases with your partner. If necessary, ask your teacher to model the correct pronunciation. Then take turns reading the paragraph aloud. Give each other feedback on your reading.

▲ Frida Kahlo in her studio

EXTENSION

Workbook
Page 69

The four people in "Success Stories" came from different backgrounds and succeeded in different ways. Copy the chart below into your notebook. Describe each person's background and achievements. Then research two more people you think are successful.

Successful People	Background	Achievements
1. Frida Kahlo	suffered from polio and from serious injuries	became a world-famous painter
2. Bill Gates		
3. Muhammad Yunus		
4. Dr. Mae Jemison		
5.		
6.		

Grammar and Writing

Independent and Dependent Clauses

A clause is a group of words with a subject and a verb. An independent clause is a complete sentence. A dependent clause is not a complete sentence and must be connected to an independent clause by a relative pronoun. A relative pronoun *relates* the dependent clause to a noun in the independent clause. Some relative pronouns are *that* and *who*. When referring to things, use *that*. When referring to people, use *who* or *that*.

---

independent clause	independent clause
Frida Kahlo painted many portraits.	The portraits were of herself.

relative pronoun

independent clause	dependent clause
Frida Kahlo painted many portraits that	were of herself.

---

independent clause	independent clause
The bank lent money mainly to women.	The women were very poor.

relative pronoun

independent clause	dependent clause
The bank lent money mainly to women who	were very poor.

Practice  Workbook Page 70

Work with a partner. Decide which column has independent clauses and which has dependent clauses. Then combine the clauses to make full sentences. Write the sentences in your notebook.

Frida Kahlo was in an accident	who teaches at Dartmouth College.
Bill Gates set up a fund	who were suffering from famine.
Mae Jemison is a professor	that helps fight diseases in Africa.
Muhammad Yunus gave $27 to villagers	that left her seriously injured.

WRITING AN EXPOSITORY PARAGRAPH

Write to Compare and Contrast

At the end of this unit, you will write an expository essay. Expository writing involves explaining something. In an expository essay, a writer presents facts, discusses ideas, or explains a process.

Often, expository writing involves explaining or describing how things are alike or how they are different. For example, a writer might compare and contrast two friends or family members. To do this, the writer first provides details explaining how the two people are alike. Then the writer describes how they are different.

Here is a model in which a student wrote about two family members. She used a Venn diagram to organize her ideas.

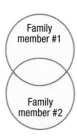

Family member #1

Family member #2

> *Justine Kefauver*
>
> ### Two Very Different People
>
> The members of my family are very different from each other. A good example is my brother and my cousin. My brother is in high school and lives in New York. My cousin is older. He just graduated from college and lives in California. They are both very social, but they are interested in completely different things. My brother is into sports. He likes to run, so he plays a lot of team sports that involve running, like soccer and football. My cousin, on the other hand, is really into music. He plays guitar in a band with his friends. Although they are different ages, they live in different places, and they do different things, my brother and my cousin do have some things in common: they are both very cool people who are fun to be with.

Practice

Workbook
Page 71

Write a paragraph comparing and contrasting two people or two places you have visited. Provide details to explain how they are alike and how they are different. Use a graphic organizer like the one above to organize your ideas. Be sure to use independent and dependent clauses correctly.

Writing Checklist

IDEAS:
- ☑ I fully described differences.

WORD CHOICE:
- ☑ I chose descriptive words.

143

Prepare to Read

What You Will Learn

Reading

- Vocabulary building:
  Literary terms, word study

- Reading strategy:
  Distinguish fact from opinion

- Text type:
  Literature (interview and poetry)

Grammar, Usage, and Mechanics
Gerunds as subject or object

Writing
Write a problem-and-solution paragraph

THE BIG QUESTION

What defines success? Sometimes we succeed at something all on our own—without help from anyone else. But there are times when people or experiences contribute to our success. Think of a time when someone helped you to succeed at something. Tell your partner about that experience.

BUILD BACKGROUND

In this section, you will read **"An Interview with Naomi Shihab Nye."** Then you will read one of her poems, **"Making a Mosaic."** Sometimes knowing about a poet's life helps you understand her writing better. Naomi Shihab Nye's parents are from two different cultures—her mother is American and her father is Palestinian. She lived in three different places growing up. She has always loved to write. As you read the poem, think about how her background is reflected in her work.

▼ San Antonio

▲ Jerusalem

▲ St. Louis

VOCABULARY

Learn Literary Words

You have learned that a metaphor is a figure of speech in which one thing is spoken of as though it were something else. An **extended metaphor** continues the comparison for several lines or for an entire poem.

> All the world's a stage,
> And all the men and women merely players
> They have their exits and their entrances;
> —*William Shakespeare*

Repetition means saying something again and again. Writers use repetition of words, phrases, or sentences to emphasize their ideas.

> "I am your father!" he cried. "Young Rip Van Winkle once; old Rip Van Winkle now! Does anybody know poor Rip Van Winkle?"
> —*Washington Irving*

A **stanza** is a group of lines in a poem. A stanza may have only a few lines, or it may have many lines. The stanzas in a poem may all be the same length, or they may be different lengths.

Practice
Workbook Page 72

Read the following poem. How many stanzas does it have? What is the extended metaphor?

> My mother is the sun.
> She gives light to the world.
> She gives life to all.
>
> In the early morning, my
> mother is warm and welcoming.
> She breathes life into the day.
>
> In the evening, my mother
> tires. A hard day's work is done.
> She slips down behind the mountains and sleeps.

Write a short poem in your notebook using an extended metaphor.

Learn Academic Words

Study the **red** words and their meanings. You will find these words useful when talking and writing about literature. Write each word and its meaning in your notebook. After you read "An Interview with Naomi Shihab Nye" and the poem "Making a Mosaic," try to use these words to respond to the text.

cultural = related to a particular society and its way of life (arts, language, etc.)	➡	The family had many traditional celebrations. The children grew up with a rich **cultural** background.
distinctive = clearly marking a person or thing as different from others	➡	San Francisco's **distinctive** architecture includes many colorful houses built on steep hills.
interpret = explain or translate	➡	Poems are sometimes difficult to **interpret** because their meaning is unclear at first.
precise = exact and correct in every detail	➡	It is often hard to find the **precise** words to say when you are very excited or nervous.
pursue = continue doing an activity or trying to achieve something	➡	She wants to go to California so she can **pursue** her dream of becoming an actress.

Practice

Workbook Page 73

Work with a partner to answer these questions. Try to include the **red** word in your answer. Write the sentences in your notebook.

1. What **cultural** activities do you and your family take part in?

2. What makes your city **distinctive** from other cities?

3. How would you **interpret** the following metaphor: "She was the sunshine of his life"?

4. Why do you think it is important to give **precise** directions to someone who is lost?

5. What career path do you want to **pursue**?

▲ San Francisco's distinctive architecture

146

Word Study: Homophones

A homophone is a word that sounds the same as another word but has a different meaning and usually a different spelling. Words such as *sea* and *see* are examples of homophones. The word *sea* means "a body of water." The word *see* means "to use your eyes." To figure out which meaning is being used, check the spelling. If you still do not know which meaning is correct, check a dictionary.

Homophone and Definition	Sentence Using the Word
tale (a story) tail (the end of an animal)	The author told an interesting **tale**. The dog had a long **tail**.
write (to put into words) right (correct)	She always wanted to **write** stories. She got everything **right** on her test.

Practice

Work with a partner. Define the homophones in the box below. Write them in your notebook. Then use each word in a sentence to show its meaning. Check your answers in a dictionary.

blew/blue	one/won	rose/rows	wear/where
made/maid	peace/piece	some/sum	wood/would

READING STRATEGY | **DISTINGUISH FACT FROM OPINION**

Distinguishing a fact from an opinion will help you form ideas about what you read. A fact is something that can be proven (or is true). An opinion is what someone believes or thinks. An opinion is not right or wrong, it just cannot be proven. Texts often contain both facts and opinions. To distinguish between facts and opinions, follow these steps:

- As you read, ask yourself whether you can check what you are reading in an encyclopedia, a history book, or some other research material. If you can, it's probably a fact.

- Look for phrases the author uses to give opinions, for example, *I think, I believe, I suppose, personally.*

- Look for adjectives that go with opinions, for example, *best, wonderful, luckiest, horrible, bad.*

   As you read "An Interview with Naomi Shihab Nye," look for facts and opinions.

Set a purpose for reading What advice does Naomi Shihab Nye give to young writers? How does she say they can become successful?

An Interview with Naomi Shihab Nye

Rachel Barenblat

Naomi Shihab Nye is a poet, essayist, songwriter, and author of books for children and young adults. Born in 1952, in St. Louis, Missouri, she is the daughter of an American mother and a Palestinian father. Nye published her first poem when she was seven years old. At age fourteen, she and her family moved to Jerusalem, where she attended high school. A year later, her family moved to San Antonio, Texas. Nye now lives in San Antonio with her husband and son.

Naomi Shihab Nye's writing shows many influences and points of view. She writes about Arab Americans like herself, Mexican Americans who live near her, and other cultures in the United States. Because she is from a multicultural family and a multicultural community, her poetry often explores the similarities and differences between cultures. Her poems often describe ordinary people, events, and objects from a new perspective.

---

essayist, someone who writes short pieces about
   a particular subject
influences, things that have an effect on people
   or things
multicultural, made up of many cultures (people
   from different countries, races, or religions)
perspective, way of seeing something

148

Rachel Barenblat (RB): *When did you start writing? Were you writing poems from the start?*

Naomi Shihab Nye (NSN): I started writing when I was six, immediately after learning *how* to write. Yes, I was writing poems from the start. Somehow—from hearing my mother read to me? from looking at books? from watching Carl Sandburg on 1950s black-and-white TV?—I knew what a poem was. I liked the portable, comfortable shape of poems. I liked the space around them and the way you could hold your words at arm's length and look at them. And especially the way they took you to a deeper, quieter place, almost immediately.

RB: *What did you write about, in the beginning? What provided your first inspiration?*

NSN: I wrote about all the little stuff a kid would write about: amazement over things, cats, wounded squirrels found in the street, my friend who moved away, trees, teachers, my funny grandma. At that time I wrote about my German grandma—I wouldn't meet my Palestinian grandma till I was fourteen.

RB: *Place plays an important role in your writing, especially the places you have lived and the places that hold your roots. Tell me about the places that have been important to you.*

NSN: The three main places I have lived—St. Louis, Jerusalem, San Antonio—are each deeply precious to me indeed, and I often find them weaving in and out of my writing. Each place has such distinctive neighborhoods and flavors. . . .

---

portable, light and easy to carry
inspiration, something that gives you a good idea
amazement, great surprise
roots, connections with a place because you were born there
    or your family lived there
flavors, qualities or features

BEFORE YOU GO ON

1 Where did Naomi Shihab Nye attend high school?

2 What did Naomi Shihab Nye write about when she was a child?

On Your Own
Do you like to write stories or poems? How does writing stories or poems make you feel?

149

RB: *Where do you usually write? Do you have a desk, an office, a favorite chair, a favorite tree?*

NSN: I have a long wooden table where I write. Not a desk, really, as it doesn't have drawers. I wish it had drawers. I can write anywhere. Outside, of course, is always great. I am one of the few people I know who *loves* being in airports. Good thing. I can write and read well in them.

RB: *What is your advice to writers, especially young writers who are just starting out?*

NSN: Number one: Read, read, and then read some more. Always read. Find the voices that speak most to *you*. This is your pleasure and blessing, as well as responsibility!

It is crucial to make one's own writing circle—friends, either close or far, with whom you trade work and discuss it—as a kind of support system, place of conversation and energy. Find those people, even a few, with whom you can share and discuss your works—then do it. Keep the papers flowing among you. Work does not get into the world by itself. We must help it. . . .

✔ **LITERARY CHECK**
*Why does Naomi Shihab Nye use **repetition** here?*

---

blessing, something that is good or helps you
responsibility, something that you must do
crucial, very important

ABOUT THE INTERVIEWER

Rachel Barenblat is an associate editor of *Pif,* an online literary magazine. She has a master of fine arts degree in writing and literature. Her first book of poems, *the skies here,* was published in 1995. She is executive director of Inkberry, a literary arts center in Massachusetts.

▲ **A writing circle**

Making a Mosaic

Some people begin at the center,
others at the outer edge,
pressing down chips
of lovely broken plates and cups.
Is this the story of days?
Arranged, glued down,
without much space between.

Here is the blue flowery fragment
from dinnerware
on a ship
that sank in 1780.
The antique green plate
Louise gave me
when I finished fifth grade.
Side by side,
a nice time, a terrible time.

It's a messy job,
glue stuck to fingertips.
You keep standing back
to see a pattern
emerge.

—Naomi Shihab Nye

✔ **LITERARY CHECK**
What is the
extended metaphor
in this poem?

---

fragment, small piece
antique, old and valuable
pattern, arrangement of shapes,
    lines, or colors

ABOUT THE POET

Naomi Shihab Nye is the author of numerous books of poetry. Her short stories and poems have won awards and have been published in many journals. She has traveled throughout the Middle East and Asia promoting goodwill through the arts.

BEFORE YOU GO ON

1 What is Naomi Shihab Nye's number one piece of advice to young writers?

2 In the poem "Making a Mosaic," why does the author refer to the two fragments as "a nice time, a terrible time"?

On Your Own
Which stanza of this poem is your favorite? How would you interpret it?

151

Review and Practice

DRAMATIC READING

🔊 *Speaking* TIP

Make eye contact with your partner.

One of the best ways to understand the pacing and flow of spoken conversation is to act out or recite an interview. Work with a partner to read "An Interview with Naomi Shihab Nye." Take turns reading the part of Rachel Barenblat, the interviewer, and Naomi Shihab Nye. Work together to interpret any difficult words or phrases.

After you have read and examined the interview carefully, memorize Naomi Shihab Nye's first response on page 149 and recite it for the class. Comment on each other's oral reading and make helpful suggestions for improvement.

COMPREHENSION

Workbook
Page 76

Right There

1. When did Naomi Shihab Nye publish her first poem?

2. Where has Nye lived?

Think and Search

3. What are Nye's influences and points of view in her writing?

4. What does "support system" mean?

Author and You

5. Why do you think Nye places so much emphasis on reading? How is reading a "pleasure and a blessing" for young writers? How is it a "responsibility"?

6. What do you think Nye means by the title "Making a Mosaic"?

On Your Own

7. Are any places "deeply precious" to you? Explain.

8. When you were younger, did you write about any of the things Nye wrote about? Did you write about other things?

DISCUSSION

Discuss in pairs or small groups.

1. Do you have a place where you prefer to write? Do you like to write indoors or outdoors? Alone or with others?

2. What is your interpretation of the following lines from the poem *Making a Mosaic*?

> You keep standing back
> to see a pattern
> emerge.

Q **What defines success?** How do you define "successful writing"? In other words, when you evaluate your own writing, how do you know that it's good? Explain your answer.

>)) *Listening* TIP

If you don't understand someone's answer, ask the speaker to repeat or explain it.

RESPONSE TO LITERATURE

Workbook
Page 76

"Making a Mosaic" is a poem about making something. It also has a deeper meaning that is open to interpretation. Choose something that you know how to do. Make a chart like the one below. List the steps involved in the process. Then say what the object or process reveals about you—your habits, personality traits, or lifestyle. For example, does it reveal that you love the color red, or cats, or chocolate?

Making a _____	
Step 1:	
Step 2:	
Step 3:	
What this shows about the artist (you):	

Write a short poem about the object you made. Include two or three stanzas about the steps involved. In the last stanza, explain what the object reveals about you. Share your poem with the class.

Grammar and Writing

Gerunds as Subject or Object

A gerund is a verb form, ending in *-ing*, that functions as a noun in a sentence. A gerund or gerund phrase can be the subject of a sentence. A gerund or gerund phrase can also be the object of certain verbs, such as *like, dislike, enjoy, prefer, start,* and *finish*.

> **Reading other writers** helps Naomi be a better writer. [gerund phrase as subject]
> Naomi started **writing** when she was six. [gerund as object of verb *started*]

You can also use a possessive noun or pronoun before the gerund. Again, the gerund phrase can be the subject of the sentence or the object of the verb.

> **The poet's reading** of that poem was very nice. [gerund phrase as subject]
> I enjoyed **his reading** of that poem. [gerund as object of verb *enjoyed*]

Practice  **Workbook** Page 77

Work with a partner. Copy the sentences below into your notebook. Circle the gerunds. Write **S** after the sentence if the gerund is the subject of the sentence. Write **O** if the gerund is the object of the verb. Check each other's answers.

1. Reading is important if you want to become a successful writer.
2. My aunt enjoys going to poetry readings, but my uncle prefers going to concerts.
3. My brother's traveling takes him to many interesting parts of the world.
4. Writing poetry is a passion for my father.
5. My cousin Sam likes listening to music, but his brother Rupin enjoys reading.

WRITING AN EXPOSITORY PARAGRAPH

Write a Problem-and-Solution Paragraph

You have learned that expository writing involves presenting facts, discussing ideas, or explaining a process. Expository writing can also focus on problems and solutions. In a problem-and-solution piece, the writer presents a problem and suggests one or more possible solutions. As with all expository writing, it is important to use descriptive details. Sometimes the writer will also use comparisons and contrasts. For example, the writer might compare two ways to solve a problem, and then suggest why one option is better than the other.

Here is a model of a problem-and-solution paragraph. Notice that the writer states the problem clearly and gives possible solutions. He used an idea web to help organize his ideas.

Caleb Robinson

The Carnival Problem

Have you ever had a money problem? I did. I needed to raise money to go to my local carnival. A ticket to the carnival was $25, plus food money. I thought I would need about $50 total. Selling stuff is easy; you can make money from what you no longer want. I could either sell my old baby toys, or I could sell my video games. If I sold my video games, I would miss them, because I still like playing them every weekend. I decided selling my old baby toys was the best choice and I made $37. I was still $13 short. What else could I do? I got it! I enjoy working outside. I started washing cars and charging $3 per car. I did it! I made $24. I had enough money to ride all the rides, buy food, and play in the arcade.

Practice

Workbook Page 78

Write a paragraph about a problem you need to solve. It could be a problem in your school, such as how to raise money for a school trip, or a more personal problem, such as how to break a bad habit. Discuss two or more possible solutions. Use a graphic organizer like the one above to help you organize your ideas. Be sure to use gerunds correctly.

Writing Checklist

IDEAS:
☑ I stated a problem and offered solutions.

ORGANIZATION:
☑ I organized my paragraph with a main idea and supporting details.

155

Prepare to Read

What You Will Learn

Reading

■ Vocabulary building: *Literary terms, word study*

■ Reading strategy: *Predict 2*

■ Text type: *Literature (short story)*

Grammar, Usage, and Mechanics
Infinitives and infinitives of purpose

Writing
Write a critique

🔍 THE BIG QUESTION

What defines success? Have you ever entered a competition such as a spelling bee, a race, a chess tournament, or a science fair? Did you win first place? If you didn't, do you still think you were successful? Why or why not? Discuss with a partner.

BUILD BACKGROUND

You will be reading a short story called **"The Marble Champ."** How much do you know about marbles? Did you know that the game of marbles is more than 3,000 years old? Archaeologists have found clay marbles in Egypt and Italy. They have also found marbles in parts of Mexico and the United States dating back to 100 B.C.E. Marbles were made of clay, bone, polished nuts and stones, and, of course, marble (a hard white rock). Now most marbles are made of glass.

The most popular game of marbles is called Ringer. One player draws a circle on the ground. Then players take turns knocking other players' marbles out of the circle with their own marbles. This is done by "knuckling" the marble, which means that the marble is flicked by the thumb out of the hand.

Playing marbles ▶

VOCABULARY

Learn Literary Words

Character motivation explains why a character does certain things. Motivation is what drives a character's actions. A character may be motivated by many things. A good writer helps the reader understand a character's motivations so the reader can understand a character's actions or behavior. Read the paragraph below.

> Talia used to go right home after school. Now she stays after school for extra help three times a week. Her grades were slipping and her parents wanted her to stop playing softball. Talia loved softball and would do anything to keep playing.

What do you think motivates this character to stay after school for extra help?

Suspense is a feeling of excitement or curiosity about what is going to happen next in a piece of literature. Writers create suspense by hinting at things to come. They also raise questions in the readers' minds. Read the paragraph below.

> The polls had closed and the election was over. However, it was a very close race. A winner could not be predicted. The entire country waited anxiously. Who would win the election? Every ballot needed to be counted. Everyone waited. When would the results finally be announced?

How is suspense shown in this paragraph?

Practice  **Workbook Page 79**

Take turns reading the following example of character motivation with a partner. Discuss what the character wants to do. How will she go about it?

> My sister always does things better than I do. At the concert she played lead solo. I sat in the last row. That will not happen again! I'll practice hard so that next year I'll play the lead.

Create an example of character motivation. Write the example in your notebook.

Learn Academic Words

Study the red words and their meanings. You will find these words useful when talking and writing about literature. Write each word and its meaning in your notebook. After you read "The Marble Champ," try to use these words to respond to the text.

considerable = large enough to be noticed or have an effect	→	She had **considerable** success at school. She got As and Bs and won some writing contests.
displayed = put things where people could see them easily	→	The team proudly **displayed** all of their trophies in a glass case.
objective = goal; something that you are working hard to achieve	→	George worked hard at playing chess. His **objective** was to win the chess match.
participate = be involved in a particular activity	→	Everyone in the class must **participate** in the science fair, so start thinking about your project.
previous = happening before something else	→	The champion of the **previous** year's match was a girl. The champion of this year's match is a boy.

Practice

Workbook
Page 80

Work with a partner to answer these questions. Try to include the red word in your answer. Write the sentences in your notebook.

1. Who would you say has **considerable** athletic talent in your class?

2. What kinds of things are **displayed** on your classroom's walls?

3. What is your math teacher's **objective**?

4. Do you think it is important to **participate** in class discussions? Why or why not?

5. What did you do after school yesterday? What did you do the **previous** day?

Trophies displayed
in a glass case ▶

158

Word Study: Inflections -*ed* and -*ing*

Some words have inflections at the end of them. An inflection adds a different meaning to a base word.

Base word	Inflection -*ed*	Inflection -*ing*
play	play**ed**	play**ing**
kick	kick**ed**	kick**ing**

Sometimes the spelling of the base word changes when you add -*ed* or -*ing*. Read the examples below. When an inflection is added to each base word, the final consonant is doubled. That is because there is a short vowel before the final consonant.

Base word	Inflection -*ed*	Inflection -*ing*
beg	beg**ged**	beg**ging**
slip	slip**ped**	slip**ping**

Practice  Workbook Page 81

Work with a partner. Copy the chart above into your notebook. Add nine blank rows. Then take turns reading the words in the box. Write the base word in the first column and then write the word with the inflections -*ed* and -*ing*.

| clap | enter | hug | learn | lick | pass | rip | roll | stop |

READING STRATEGY | **PREDICT 2**

Predicting helps you better understand and focus on the text. Before you read, predict (or guess) what the story will be about. You can also make new predictions as you're reading. To predict, follow these steps:

- Stop reading from time to time and ask yourself, "What will happen next?"

- Look for clues in the story and illustrations. Think about what you already know. Make a prediction.

- As you read, check to see if your prediction is correct. If it isn't correct, you can change your prediction.

   Read "The Marble Champ." From time to time, stop and check to see if your prediction was correct. Did you learn anything new that made you want to change your prediction? Make a new prediction if necessary.

 Workbook Page 82

159

Set a purpose for reading You are going to read a story about a girl who sets a goal for herself. Where does she find the motivation and encouragement to succeed at her goal?

The Marble Champ

Gary Soto

Lupe Medrano, a shy girl who spoke in whispers, was the school's spelling bee champion, winner of the reading contest at the public library three summers in a row, blue ribbon awardee in the science fair, the top student at her piano recital, and the playground grand champion in chess. She was a straight-A student and—not counting kindergarten, when she had been stung by a wasp—never missed one day of elementary school. She had received a small trophy for this honor and had been congratulated by the mayor.

But though Lupe had a razor-sharp mind, she could not make her body, no matter how much she tried, run as fast as the other girls'. She begged her body to move faster, but could never beat anyone in the fifty-yard dash.

The truth was that Lupe was no good in sports. She could not catch a pop-up or figure out in which direction to kick the soccer ball. One time she kicked the ball at her own goal and scored a point for the other team. She was no good at baseball or basketball either, and even had a hard time making a hula hoop stay on her hips.

---

champion, person who has won a competition
recital, public performance of music or dance
razor-sharp, extremely sharp

160

It wasn't until last year, when she was eleven years old, that she learned how to ride a bike. And even then she had to use training wheels. She could walk in the swimming pool but couldn't swim, and chanced roller skating only when her father held her hand.

"I'll never be good in sports," she fumed one rainy day as she lay on her bed gazing at the shelf her father had made to hold her awards. "I wish I could win something, anything, even marbles."

At the word "marbles," she sat up. "That's it. Maybe I could be good at playing marbles." She hopped out of bed and rummaged through the closet until she found a can full of her brother's marbles. She poured the rich glass treasure on her bed and picked five of the most beautiful marbles.

She smoothed her bedspread and practiced shooting, softly at first so that her aim would be accurate. The marble rolled from her thumb and clicked against the targeted marble. But the target wouldn't budge. She tried again and again. Her aim became accurate, but the power from her thumb made the marble move only an inch or two. Then she realized that the bedspread was slowing the marbles. She also had to admit that her thumb was weaker than the neck of a newborn chick.

She looked out the window. The rain was letting up, but the ground was too muddy to play. She sat cross-legged on the bed, rolling her five marbles between her palms. Yes, she thought, I could play marbles, and marbles is a sport. At that moment she realized that she had only two weeks to practice. The playground championship, the same one her brother had entered the previous year, was coming up. She had a lot to do.

---

fumed, showed anger
rummaged, searched for something by moving things around
accurate, correct or exact

✔ **LITERARY CHECK**
*What **motivates** Lupe to practice playing marbles?*

BEFORE YOU GO ON

1 Why did the mayor congratulate Lupe?

2 How did Lupe score a point for the other team in soccer?

💡**On Your Own**
Have you ever won an award? Explain.

161

To strengthen her wrists, she decided to do twenty push-ups on her fingertips, five at a time. "One, two, three . . ." she groaned. By the end of the first set she was breathing hard, and her muscles burned from exhaustion. She did one more set and decided that was enough push-ups for the first day.

She squeezed a rubber eraser one hundred times, hoping it would strengthen her thumb. This seemed to work because the next day her thumb was sore. She could hardly hold a marble in her hand, let alone send it flying with power. So Lupe rested that day and listened to her brother, who gave her tips on how to shoot: get low, aim with one eye, and place one knuckle on the ground.

"Think 'eye and thumb'—and let it rip!" he said.

After school the next day she left her homework in her backpack and practiced three hours straight, taking time only to eat a candy bar for energy. With a popsicle stick, she drew an odd-shaped circle and tossed in four marbles. She used her shooter, a milky agate with hypnotic swirls, to blast them. Her thumb had become stronger.

After practice, she squeezed the eraser for an hour. She ate dinner with her left hand to spare her shooting hand and said nothing to her parents about her dreams of athletic glory.

Practice, practice, practice. Squeeze, squeeze, squeeze. Lupe got better and beat her brother and Alfonso, a neighbor kid who was supposed to be a champ.

---

milky, white, like milk
agate, hard stone with bands of different colors
hypnotic, fascinating

"Man, she's bad!" Alfonso said. "She can beat the other girls for sure. I think."

The weeks passed quickly. Lupe worked so hard that one day, while she was drying dishes, her mother asked why her thumb was swollen.

"It's muscle," Lupe explained. "I've been practicing for the marbles championship."

"You, honey?" Her mother knew Lupe was no good at sports.

"Yeah. I beat Alfonso, and he's pretty good."

That night, over dinner, Mrs. Medrano said, "Honey, you should see Lupe's thumb."

"Huh?" Mr. Medrano said, wiping his mouth and looking at his daughter.

"Show your father."

"Do I have to?" an embarrassed Lupe asked.

"Go on, show your father."

Reluctantly, Lupe raised her hand and flexed her thumb. You could see the muscle.

The father put down his fork and asked, "What happened?"

"Dad, I've been working out. I've been squeezing an eraser."

"Why?"

"I'm going to enter the marbles championship."

---

reluctantly, unwillingly; slowly

BEFORE YOU GO ON

1 How does Lupe strengthen her wrists?

2 Who does Lupe beat at marbles in her backyard?

On Your Own
Did you ever practice hard to get better at something?

163

Her father looked at her mother and then back at his daughter. "When is it, honey?"

"This Saturday. Can you come?"

The father had been planning to play racquetball with a friend Saturday, but he said he would be there. He knew his daughter thought she was no good at sports and he wanted to encourage her. He even rigged some lights in the backyard so she could practice after dark. He squatted with one knee on the ground, entranced by the sight of his daughter easily beating her brother.

The day of the championship began with a cold blustery sky. The sun was a silvery light behind slate clouds.

"I hope it clears up," her father said, rubbing his hands together as he returned from getting the newspaper. They ate breakfast, paced nervously around the house waiting for 10:00 to arrive, and walked the two blocks to the playground (though Mr. Medrano wanted to drive so Lupe wouldn't get tired). She signed up and was assigned her first match on baseball diamond number three.

Lupe, walking between her brother and her father, shook from the cold, not nerves. She took off her mittens, and everyone stared at her thumb. Someone asked, "How can you play with a broken thumb?" Lupe smiled and said nothing.

✔ **LITERARY CHECK**
*What is Lupe's father's **motivation** to help her?*

---

rigged, put up temporarily

164

She beat her first opponent easily, and felt sorry for the girl because she didn't have anyone to cheer for her. Except for her sack of marbles, she was all alone. Lupe invited the girl, whose name was Rachel, to stay with them. She smiled and said, "OK." The four of them walked to a card table in the middle of the outfield, where Lupe was assigned another opponent.

She also beat this girl, a fifth-grader named Yolanda, and asked her to join their group. They proceeded to more matches and more wins, and soon there was a crowd of people following Lupe to the finals to play a girl in a baseball cap. This girl seemed dead serious. She never even looked at Lupe.

"I don't know, Dad, she looks tough."

Rachel hugged Lupe and said, "Go get her."

---

opponent, person who tries to defeat someone else in a game
assigned, given

BEFORE YOU GO ON

1 What is the weather like on the day of the championship?

2 Who goes with Lupe to the championship?

On Your Own
Do you ever feel sorry for an opponent? Explain.

165

"You can do it," her father encouraged. "Just think of the marbles, not the girl, and let your thumb do the work."

The other girl broke first and earned one marble. She missed her next shot, and Lupe, one eye closed, her thumb quivering with energy, blasted two marbles out of the circle but missed her next shot. Her opponent earned two more before missing. She stamped her foot and said, "Shoot!" The score was three to two in favor of Miss Baseball Cap.

The referee stopped the game. "Back up, please, give them room," he shouted. Onlookers had gathered too tightly around the players.

Lupe then earned three marbles and was set to get her fourth when a gust of wind blew dust in her eyes and she missed badly. Her opponent quickly scored two marbles, tying the game, and moved ahead six to five on a lucky shot. Then she missed, and Lupe, whose eyes felt scratchy when she blinked, relied on instinct and thumb muscle to score the tying point. It was now six to six, with only three marbles left. Lupe blew her nose and studied the angles. She dropped to one knee, steadied her hand, and shot so hard she cracked two marbles from the circle. She was the winner!

✔ LITERARY CHECK
*How does the author build **suspense** in this paragraph?*

"I did it!" Lupe said under her breath. She rose from her knees, which hurt from bending all day, and hugged her father. He hugged her back and smiled.

Everyone clapped, except Miss Baseball Cap, who made a face and stared at the ground. Lupe told her she was a great player, and they shook hands. A newspaper photographer took pictures of the two girls standing shoulder-to-shoulder, with Lupe holding the bigger trophy.

Lupe then played the winner of the boys' division, and after a poor start beat him eleven to four. She blasted the marbles, shattering one into sparkling slivers of glass. Her opponent looked on glumly as Lupe did what she did best—win!

The head referee and the President of the Fresno Marble Association stood with Lupe as she displayed her trophies for the newspaper photographer. Lupe shook hands with everyone, including a dog who had come over to see what the commotion was all about.

That night, the family went out for pizza and set the two trophies on the table for everyone in the restaurant to see. People came up to congratulate Lupe, and she felt a little embarrassed, but her father said the trophies belonged there.

---

quivering, trembling
instinct, natural ability
slivers, small broken pieces
commotion, sudden noisy activity

Back home, in the privacy of her bedroom, she placed the trophies on her shelf and was happy. She had always earned honors because of her brains, but winning in sports was a new experience. She thanked her tired thumb. "You did it, thumb. You made me champion." As its reward, Lupe went to the bathroom, filled the bathroom sink with warm water, and let her thumb swim and splash as it pleased. Then she climbed into bed and drifted into a hard-won sleep.

ABOUT THE **AUTHOR**

Gary Soto was born and raised in Fresno, California. He is the author of many books for adults and children, as well as several poetry collections. He has won numerous awards and medals for literature. Much of his work is based on his own experiences. Soto lives in Berkeley, California.

BEFORE YOU GO ON

1 How does Lupe do in the boys' division?

2 Where do Lupe and her family go to celebrate?

On Your Own
Do you think practice and hard work always lead to success?

167

READER'S THEATER

Speaking TIP

Use facial expressions, gestures, and other movements to show the character's feelings and actions.

Act out the following interview between Lupe and a reporter from her school newspaper.

Reporter: Lupe, congratulations on winning the marble championship. You must feel great!

Lupe: Thank you. Yes, I'm very happy and a little surprised.

Reporter: Surprised? Why is that?

Lupe: Well, I've never won any sports competitions before. I won the school spelling bee and the writing contest, but I've never been very good at sports.

Reporter: You showed considerable talent today! What motivated you to start training for the marble championship?

Lupe: I really wanted to prove to myself that I could win at some sport. My brother plays marbles. He encouraged me a lot, and I made it a priority to win.

Reporter: Well, your determination paid off, didn't it?

Lupe: Yeah, I guess it did. And who knows; maybe next year I'll try another sport!

COMPREHENSION

Workbook
Page 83

Right There

1. What did Lupe's father do to help her practice?

2. Why did Lupe feel sorry for her first opponent?

Think and Search

3. Describe Lupe's successes in school and her lack of athletic ability.

4. What did Lupe do to strengthen her hands?

Author and You

5. What does the author's portrayal of Lupe suggest about her character?

6. How do you think Lupe's father would describe his daughter?

7. Based on your experience, what usually happens after someone practices hard at doing something? Explain.

8. Lupe challenged herself to get better at marbles. What could you challenge yourself to get better at?

▲ Playing chess

DISCUSSION

Discuss in pairs or small groups.

1. How does Lupe react to winning the championship?

2. How did Lupe's family help her succeed? Could she have done as well without their help? Explain.

Q **What defines success?** Why do you think Lupe's father displays her trophies? Why do you think Lupe was embarrassed to display them? Is it important for winners to display the trophies they win? Explain your answers.

RESPONSE TO LITERATURE

Workbook
Page 83

Have you ever entered a competition? If not, can you imagine yourself competing in a sport or club activity? Compare your experiences to Lupe's. Copy the chart below into your notebook. Then complete the right column with information about your experience. Share your chart in a small group.

	Lupe	Me
What's the character's motivation?	to excel at a sport	
What's the character's objective?	to win the marble championship	
What actions are taken to reach the objective?	practicing, squeezing an eraser to build strength	
What was the result?	became champion	

Grammar and Writing

Infinitives and Infinitives of Purpose

An infinitive is formed with *to* + the base form of a verb. An infinitive or an infinitive phrase can be the subject of the sentence or the object of certain verbs. In this case, like gerunds, they function as nouns.

> **To win** the championship was her greatest wish. [infinitive phrase as subject]
> Her father wanted **to encourage** her. [infinitive as object of verb *wanted*]

An infinitive can also follow adjectives.

> Her mother was surprised **to see** Lupe's thumb.
> The girl was disappointed **to lose** the championship.

An infinitive of purpose often answers the question "Why?" The following two sentences have the same meaning.

> She did twenty push-ups **to strengthen** her wrists.
> She did twenty push-ups because she wanted **to strengthen** her wrists.

You can use short answers with infinitives to answer questions.

> Why did Lupe do twenty push-ups on her fingertips? **To strengthen** her wrists.

Practice

Copy the following paragraph into your notebook. Find the infinitives and infinitives of purpose. Underline the infinitives, and circle the infinitives of purpose. Work with a partner. Compare your answers.

> I think Lupe deserved to win the championship. She worked hard every day to get better at shooting marbles. I don't think it was very easy to learn. She practiced three hours straight to strengthen her thumb. I believe she was very brave to compete against that girl. Lupe went to the championship to win, and that's what she did.

WRITING AN EXPOSITORY PARAGRAPH

Write a Critique

A critique is another example of expository writing. In a critique, a writer evaluates or judges something. The writer could be reviewing a book or a movie, or examining an idea, or considering a viewpoint. Whatever the writer is critiquing, he or she provides supporting reasons and examples. You might write a critical paragraph explaining why you don't think playing marbles is a sport. Then you would back up your opinion with examples.

A sport	Not a sport

Here is a model of a critique. Notice that the writer gives reasons to back up her opinion. Also notice that words such as *I think* or *I believe* come before each opinion. The writer used a T-chart to organize her ideas.

> Vanessa Costa
>
> ### Sport or Hobby?
>
> I believe marbles is more of a hobby than a sport. Although it takes skill and coordination to play marbles, it does not require a great amount of physical activity. The most physical activity in marbles is when people use their thumbs to launch their marbles. When I think of sports, the first things that come to my mind are running, exercising, and jumping—in short, activities using your whole body. I think playing marbles involves too little physical activity to be considered a sport.

Practice
Workbook Page 85

Write a paragraph in which you evaluate something. You could write a critique of a story you have read or take a critical look at an issue, such as whether Lupe acts like a real girl in "The Marble Champ." Remember to back up your opinion with reasons and examples and use a graphic organizer like the one above. Be sure to use infinitives and infinitives of purpose correctly.

Writing Checklist

VOICE:
☑ I used a voice that was lively and engaging.

SENTENCE FLUENCY:
☑ I used a variety of sentences.

Prepare to Read

What You Will Learn

Reading

- Vocabulary building: *Context, dictionary skills, word study*
- Reading strategy: *Ask questions*
- Text type: *Informational text (science)*

Grammar, Usage, and Mechanics
Expressions of quantity

Writing
Write a news article

THE BIG QUESTION

What defines success? Can success change people's lives? We often hear of famous people (like athletes and musicians) whose lives change dramatically once they achieve success. But it's not just celebrities who are affected by success. In this reading, you will learn about a group of students who see big changes in their lives all because of a school activity: building robots.

In what ways can success change a person's life? Is the change always positive? Discuss with a partner.

BUILD BACKGROUND

In this section, you will read the news article, **"Students Win Robotics Competition."** A news article is a type of informational text. It gives current information about a news event. News articles answer five questions called "the 5Ws"—Who? Where? When? What? and Why?

This article tells about a struggling inner-city high school in Arizona that wins a national robotics competition. This high school was an underdog team, which means that no one expected it to win, or even to do well. It competed against high schools and famous colleges throughout the United States.

▲ A robot arm on a factory assembly line

Learn Key Words

Read these sentences. Use the context to figure out the meaning of the red words. Use a dictionary to check your answers. Then write each word and its meaning in your notebook.

1. The **corporation** is made up of many different businesses from around the country.
2. The **engineer** designed the plans to build a robot.
3. The cell phone is an example of an **innovation** in technology that changed the way people communicate.
4. A **physicist** is a scientist who studies natural forces such as light, heat, and movement.
5. Students who are interested in **robotics** must study engineering and computer science.
6. There are many **theories** about how to cure the common cold, but none have been proved.

Practice  Workbook Page 86

Write the sentences in your notebook. Choose a red word from the box above to complete each sentence. Then take turns reading the sentences aloud with a partner.

1. Scientists have many _____ about what lies beyond our solar system.
2. The team of experts in _____ built a robot that can explore underwater.
3. A student who wants to design robots must study to be an _____.
4. The _____ allowed its employees to volunteer some of their time to help people in need.
5. A _____ can explain how electricity works.
6. Hybrid cars are a major _____ in automobile technology.

▲ An underwater robot enters the *Titanic*.

173

Learn Academic Words

Study the **red** words and their meanings. You will find these words useful when talking and writing about informational texts. Write each word and its meaning in your notebook. After you read "Students Win Robotics Competition," try to use these words to respond to the text.

affect = influence; produce a change	➡	He wondered if his error would **affect** his chances of winning a trophy.
attain = succeed in getting something you want	➡	Hard work helped the students **attain** their goal and win the grand prize.
awareness = knowledge or understanding	➡	They had a concert to raise **awareness** of poverty throughout the world.
challenge = a difficult task or problem	➡	The robotics competition presented a great **challenge** to all the students.
design = a plan or sketch	➡	The finished robot was very similar to the first **design** the team drew.

Practice  Workbook Page 87

Work with a partner to answer these questions. Try to include the **red** word in your answer. Write the sentences in your notebook.

1. How does studying hard **affect** your test results?

2. What are some important goals that you would like to **attain**?

3. How can we raise **awareness** of the importance of caring for the environment?

4. Have you ever participated in a **challenge**? Explain.

5. Why is it important to have a good **design** before you start building something?

▲ Special Olympics athletes attain their goal.

174

Word Study: Foreign Words

The English language includes many borrowed and foreign words. Some have become so common that we forget where they came from. Look at these examples.

Borrowed Word	Borrowed From
protégé	French
volcano	Italian
zero	Arabic
ecology	German
tea	Chinese
tycoon	Japanese
mammoth	Russian
cafeteria	Spanish
safari	Swahili

Practice

Work with a partner. Look up the words in the box below in a dictionary. Write the definition and where the word comes from.

balcony	brochure	magazine	patio	ranch	vague

READING STRATEGY | ASK QUESTIONS

Asking questions makes you a better reader because you get more information from the text. The five questions you should ask are: *Who? Where? When? What? Why?* These are sometimes called the 5Ws. They focus on people, places, time, events, and reasons. To ask questions, follow these steps:

- Read a paragraph. Stop and ask yourself one of the five questions.
- Now try to answer the question from what you've learned.
- Read on and see if your answer is correct. Then ask more questions.
- Look at any visuals that may help you answer the questions.

As you read "Students Win Robotics Competition," ask yourself the five questions. Make notes about your answers.

Set a purpose for reading Why was winning the robotics competition such a special achievement for this team of students? How did the team's success change the students' lives?

Students Win ROBOTICS COMPETITION

Karina Bland

The Arizona Republic
March 15, 2006

In a stunning upset in the summer of 2004, four inner-city kids from Carl Hayden High won a national robotics competition in California. They beat out high school and university teams from across the country, including the renowned Massachusetts Institute of Technology (MIT).

The school's team of young engineers hasn't done as well since. They came in 26th among 45 teams from across the country, Mexico, and Canada in last weekend's For Inspiration and Recognition of Science and Technology (FIRST) Regional Championship at Veterans Memorial Coliseum in Phoenix.

---

stunning, surprising or shocking
recognition, special attention

▲ Students with their robot, Karen

▲ A model of the playing field

Still, the winning legacy handed to them two years ago lives on.

The Carl Hayden team earned the top award for their work to get other students involved in engineering and science. It is the only Arizona team ever to win, and now it has done it twice.

Only its robot didn't fare as well. It doesn't seem to matter.

For these teens, there's much more at stake in learning about engineering and building robots than just winning. The 2004 win transformed their school and changed the course of their lives.

The team has grown from a dozen kids to 50, attracting students from across campus and in different areas of study. It operates like a little corporation promoting a stand-out athletic team, with some students creating brochures, videotaping practice runs or raising money, while others program, design and build robots. Even the cheerleaders come to matches.

"We used to be known as an underperforming school," said Annalisa Regalado, 17. "Now we're known as the robot school."

And now every senior on the robotics team at Carl Hayden in the past three years—about 25, so far—has gone into the military or college, most on full scholarships. All six of this year's seniors are going to college on full scholarships.

Success Stories

A robotics competition is as raucous as any football game. There are teenagers in matching T-shirts and hollering parents, teammates and coaches.

"It's NASCAR, science fair and the champion [Phoenix] Suns game all rolled into one," said Allan Cameron, one of the Carl Hayden coaches.

This year's challenge was to design, program and build a robot that could shoot soft foam balls through a hole in a clear plastic wall, like a basketball game for machines.

Carl Hayden's blue robot is "Karen," named after Karen Suhm, a team mentor who has a doctorate in physics. The robot shoots balls off a spinning wheel, like a pitching machine.

legacy, result of something that happened earlier
fare, manage; succeed
at stake, to be risked

raucous, noisy and loud
mentor, experienced adviser

BEFORE YOU GO ON

1 Why was the team's 2004 win a "stunning upset"?

2 What did the robot need to be able to do for this year's challenge?

On Your Own
If you could design a robot, what would it do?

177

▲ Robot Karen sprints across the field

On to the Nationals

Last year, the teenagers finished third in the underwater robotics competition but edged out MIT again. In last year's FIRST robotics competition, the Carl Hayden kids placed 53rd out of 85 teams.

This weekend's 26th-place finish didn't seem to concern anyone on the team, either, though they wished they had done better.

"Can't win them all," shrugged Fredi Lajvardi, the team's other coach.

What they do keep winning is the Chairman's Award. This is given to teams that increase awareness for science and technology and encourage more children to become scientists, engineers and physicists. It is FIRST's most prestigious team award.

"A lot of these kids would have been engineers anyway," Cameron said of Carl Hayden's opponents. "Their parents are engineers or scientists or professors."

But students at Carl Hayden sometimes are the first in their families to graduate from high school, let alone go to college. Now they talk of being computer programmers, engineers and scientists.

Luis Gutierrez, 18, the team's captain, thought he might attend community college.

Annalisa had no intention of going to college. She planned to graduate and get a job, any job. But her teachers have encouraged her to continue her education: "I would feel bad if I didn't go and I let them down."

This fall, both Annalisa and Luis will attend Arizona State University on full scholarships and study engineering.

So What Do Engineers Do?

Did you ever wonder what makes a bridge remain standing? Did you ever dream of a car that could run on something other than gasoline? Or ponder how a spacecraft could achieve lift off and then defy gravity and disappear into space? Or wonder how you could actually be safe on a rollercoaster hurtling through space?

These are the kinds of questions engineers ask. They apply theories of science and math to create practical solutions to real world situations. They make things run faster, slower, higher and safer. They also work to make things more environmentally friendly or more economically sound. Engineers make the world a better and safer place. They change our lives through the innovations they create. Engineering is a growing field, open to almost anyone with the passion and stick-to-itiveness to pursue it.

---

prestigious, respected as one of the best
defy, resist or challenge
stick-to-itiveness, ability or desire

Do Robots Really Exist outside of Movies and Competitions?

The answer is yes. However, the robots that exist today tend not to be the sophisticated human-like machines we see in movies. Robots like those created by Carl Hayden High are used in factories to do routine or dangerous activity. They're used in situations that people would find too boring, difficult or dangerous. They disarm bombs, are used in space, explore volcano openings or handle toxic chemicals. Robots will increasingly become more complex.

Robot museum guard ▼

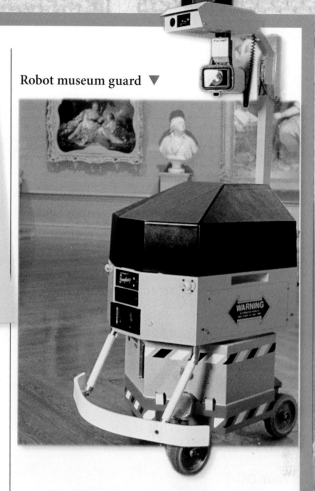

In a year, the students do as many as 45 presentations in schools and to government and community groups. They recently met with Arizona's governor to talk about education policies that could encourage kids to study math and science.

The Carl Hayden kids also mentor kids from 10 junior high schools, helping them build robots and talking about career choices. In December, the students put on the state's annual LEGO competition, recruiting students from the National Honor Society and student government to help.

The robot rests now in a crate, ready to be shipped to Atlanta for the national championship. There, the Carl Hayden kids will face as many as 100 teams with their robot and 30 or so regional Chairman's Award winners for the national title.

Last year, the team placed second in the national competition for the Chairman's Award.

In August, the team's seniors, like Luis and Annalisa, will leave for college, their spots filled by student protégés from the junior high outreach program. They are 15, freshmen and aware of the legacy they will be expected to carry on.

"We know we have to do well," the freshmen said, both in competition and academically. The boys look at each other and nod. "And we will."

recruiting, finding; inviting

protégés, young people who are guided by someone with more experience

BEFORE YOU GO ON

1 What do you have to study to become an engineer?

2 What other activities are the Carl Hayden kids involved with?

On Your Own
Do you think it would be fun to be part of the Carl Hayden team? Why?

179

Review and Practice

COMPREHENSION  Workbook Page 90

Right There

1. What is the name of the team's robot? Why?

2. What are some practical uses for robots today?

Think and Search

3. What award does Carl Hayden High keep winning? What does this award mean?

4. What do engineers do? How do they improve our lives?

Author and You

5. Why does the author say that it doesn't matter how the robot did in the competition?

6. Why is it suggested that the science competition is similar to NASCAR or a basketball game?

On Your Own

7. In your opinion, what makes a good team?

8. Would you like to become an engineer? Why or why not?

IN YOUR OWN WORDS

Use the words in the chart below to tell a partner about the robotics team of Carl Hayden High.

Team	➡	corporation
Robotics competition	➡	raucous, cheering
Challenge	➡	program, build
Engineers	➡	design, complex
Winning legacy	➡	protégés

DISCUSSION

Discuss in pairs or small groups.

1. Why do you think the robotics team at Carl Hayden High has become so popular?

2. How do you think the students' experience in the robotics competition will help them in their future careers?

Q **What defines success?** The team hasn't won first place in a competition for the last several years. But twice they have won an award for inspiring teenagers to consider jobs in science and technology. Knowing this, how would you define the team's success? Explain your answer.

»)⊙ Listening TIP

Be a careful listener so you don't repeat what someone else has already contributed to the discussion.

READ FOR FLUENCY

Reading with feeling helps make what you read more interesting. Work with a partner. Choose a paragraph from the reading. Read the paragraph to yourselves. Ask each other how you felt after reading the paragraph. Did you feel happy or sad?

Take turns reading the paragraph aloud to each other with a tone of voice that represents how you felt when you read it the first time. Take turns reading the paragraph aloud and give each other feedback.

EXTENSION  Workbook Page 90

Reading news articles can be interesting and inspiring. Find an article in a newspaper or magazine about students your age who have done something interesting. Then copy the chart below into your notebook and complete it.

What is the date of the article?	
Who is the story about?	
What did they do?	
When did this happen?	

181

Grammar and Writing

Expressions of Quantity

Certain words and phrases can be used to describe quantity. These expressions are used with either count nouns (nouns that can be counted, such as *robots*), noncount nouns (nouns that cannot be counted, such as *education*), or both.

Every and *one of* are used only with count nouns. *Every* is followed by a singular noun. *One of* is followed by a plural noun.

> **Every** senior on the robotics team has a full scholarship.
> Only **one of** the teams will win first place.

All is used with both count nouns and noncount nouns. *All* is always followed by a noncount noun or a plural count noun.

> **All** seniors are going to college on full scholarships. (count noun *seniors*)
> The team members did **all** the work. (noncount noun *work*)

Several is used only with count nouns and is followed by a plural noun.

> They entered **several** robots into the competition.

Most is used with both count and noncount nouns.

> **Most** students at this school are on scholarships. (count noun *students*)
> **Most** information was available. (noncount noun *information*)

Both is used only with count nouns. *Both* is followed by two nouns or a plural noun in which two nouns are understood.

> **Both** Annalisa and Luis will stay in Arizona. **Both** students will attend the university.

Practice  Workbook Page 91

Work with a partner. Write sentences using each of these expressions of quantity in your notebook.

WRITING AN EXPOSITORY PARAGRAPH

Write a News Article

A news article is another type of expository writing. In fact, it can combine elements of all three kinds of expository writing you have explored: making comparisons, exploring problems and solutions, and offering critiques. A news article reports the most important facts about an event. The article should answer the 5Ws—*Who? Where? When? What?* and *Why?*

Here is a model of a short news article. Notice that the writer answered all of the 5Ws and used a sequence chart to help organize his ideas.

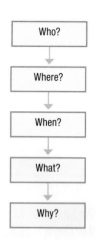

| Who? |
| Where? |
| When? |
| What? |
| Why? |

Sebastian Z. Mitchell

The Renaissance Fair

Students from Mr. Donnelly's seventh-grade history classes invited their families to the annual Renaissance Fair at Crest View Middle School last night. This event showcased student projects relating to the Renaissance, such as paintings from the time period, models of inventions, or student-made movies about that time. Most of the girls did their projects on things such as clothes and art, and most of the boys did their projects on war machines and weapons. All students had researched the significance of their project to the Renaissance and had written a one-page description of the project. The description was displayed next to the project. Later on, several of the students served a large feast of dishes from the Renaissance, such as stew in "bowls" of bread, roasted chicken, and traditional pies and puddings. Everyone had a great time. It was an enjoyable and incredibly educational event.

Practice

 **Workbook Page 92**

Write a short news article reporting on an interesting event, such as a sports contest, a school election, a local fair, or a popular performance. Keep in mind the 5Ws. Use a graphic organizer like the one above to help organize your ideas. Be sure to use expressions of quantity correctly.

Writing Checklist

IDEAS:
☑ I answered the 5Ws.

CONVENTIONS:
☑ I reviewed my writing for grammar, spelling, and punctuation.

183

Link the Readings

Critical Thinking

Look back at the readings in this unit. Think about what they have in common. They all tell about success. Yet they do not all have the same purpose. The purpose of one reading might be to inform, while the purpose of another might be to entertain or persuade. In addition, the content of each reading relates to success differently. Now copy the chart below into your notebook and complete it.

Title of Reading	Purpose	Big Question Link
"Success Stories"	*to inform*	
"An Interview with Naomi Shihab Nye" "Making a Mosaic"		
"The Marble Champ"		
"Students Win Robotics Competition"		*tells how students achieved success*

Discussion

Discuss in pairs or small groups.

- How does the purpose of "Success Stories" differ from the purpose of "The Marble Champ"? What does the informational text tell that the story does not?

- **Q** **What defines success?** Think about the readings. Is success always about winning? What can help a person become successful? How can you strive for success?

Fluency Check

Work with a partner. Choose a paragraph from one of the readings. Take turns reading it for one minute. Count the total number of words you read. Practice saying the words you had trouble reading. Take turns reading the paragraph three more times. Did you read more words each time? Copy the chart below into your notebook and record your speeds.

	1st Speed	2nd Speed	3rd Speed	4th Speed
Words Per Minute				

Projects

Work in pairs or small groups. Choose one of these projects.

1 Write a poem about success. Use repetition or extended metaphor in your poem. Then read your poem to the class.

2 Walk around your school or neighborhood. List the things engineers have designed and made. Make a poster to show how engineers affect our world. Then share your poster with the class.

3 What challenge do you think Lupe in "The Marble Champ" will decide to take on next? Write a speech in which Lupe explains her next challenge. Include a detailed plan and schedule. Practice this speech and perform it for the class.

4 Research a successful person, team, or corporation. Describe their successes and accomplishments. Describe how it all began. Collect photographs, if possible. Make a presentation to the class or videotape it as if it was on a news program on television.

Further Reading

To find out more about the theme of this unit, choose from these reading suggestions.

New York, Vicky Shipton
This Penguin Reader® tells all about New York, one of the most exciting cities in the world. Here, you will read about the people, events, work, and culture that make New York such a special place.

Extraordinary People with Disabilities,
Deborah Kent and Kathryn A. Quinlan
The men and women in this book have earned lasting recognition for their accomplishments. All of them have disabilities. The book tells the stories of people like Louis Braille, who created a reading system for the blind, and Stevie Wonder, a popular musician.

"Born Worker," a short story from Petty Crimes, Gary Soto
People said Jose was a "born worker." But when Jose and his cousin Arnie teamed up to do yard work and other jobs, Jose did most of the work while Arnie sat around and watched. But then something happened that changed Jose's view of himself and others.

Put It All Together

LISTENING & SPEAKING WORKSHOP

Interview

You will conduct an interview with someone you admire. Then, if possible, you will play a recording of your interview for the class.

1 **THINK ABOUT IT** Review "Success Stories" and "An Interview with Naomi Shihab Nye." In small groups, discuss how the people in these texts began their careers and how they became successful.

What do you think helps people succeed? Discuss your ideas. Work together to develop a list of questions you could ask someone who is successful in his or her field. For example:

- Why did you decide to pursue this career or hobby?
- How did you learn to _____?
- What have you done to improve your skills?
- Who or what has helped you become successful?

As a class, make a list of successful people in your community. Your teacher will help you decide which ones might be available for interviews.

2 **GATHER AND ORGANIZE INFORMATION** Choose a person to interview from the class list. Pick someone whose skills you admire or whose job interests you.

Set Up Your Interview Work with your teacher to request an interview with the person you have chosen. Set a convenient place and time to meet. If you have access to a tape recorder or videocamera, ask permission to record the interview so you can present it to the class.

Prepare a Script Prepare a list of questions to ask. Plan how to begin your interview, including introducing yourself and explaining your assignment. Also make notes on how you will end the interview. Remember to say thank you!

Order Your Notes Arrange your questions in a logical order. Write them on separate, numbered note cards. Write the main points of your introduction and conclusion on note cards, too.

3 **PRACTICE AND PRESENT** Follow your script to interview some friends or family members. Practice until you are comfortable using your recording equipment or taking notes on the person's answers.

Conduct Your Interview Take your note cards, recording equipment, paper and pencil, and a camera if available. Remember to get permission before recording the interview or taking photos. Be flexible: If the person begins to talk about something interesting, allow the conversation to follow naturally. Keep your note cards handy, and make sure you have asked all your questions before you finish the interview.

Deliver Your Presentation Tell the class who you interviewed. Explain why you chose that person, and show your pictures of him or her. If you recorded your interview, play the recording for the class. If not, tell some of the questions you asked and the person's answers.

4 **EVALUATE THE INTERVIEW**
You can improve your interviewing skills by evaluating each interview you conduct and hear. Use this checklist to help you judge your interview and the interviews of your classmates.

- ☑ Did the student begin and end the interview in a polite and friendly manner?
- ☑ Were the questions asked in a logical order?
- ☑ Was the interviewer easy to hear and understand?
- ☑ Did the interviewer allow the conversation to progress naturally?
- ☑ What suggestions do you have for improving the interview?

Speaking TIPS

Remember to introduce yourself and explain the assignment first, and to say thank you at the end of your interview.

Be sure you are speaking slowly and clearly. Ask if the person can understand all your words. If necessary, repeat or rephrase what you said in a friendly way.

Listening TIPS

Give the person your full attention. Make frequent eye contact, even if you are taking notes. Avoid fiddling with your recording equipment or note cards.

As you listen, make encouraging comments like "Really?" and "I see." Ask appropriate follow-up questions even if they're not on your list.

WRITING WORKSHOP
Expository Essay

In this workshop you will write an expository essay. An expository essay gives information about a topic. One type of expository essay is a news article. The title of a news article is called a *headline*. A headline is a short phrase that tells what the article is about, and that tries to capture readers' attention. The first paragraph of a news article answers the 5Ws—*Who? Where? When? What? Why?* The writer develops this information in two or more body paragraphs by adding details, quotations, facts, and examples. Information is presented in an order that is easy for readers to follow. A conclusion sums up the important ideas.

Your writing assignment for this workshop is to expand the news paragraph you wrote earlier in this unit into a five-paragraph news article.

1 **PREWRITE** Brainstorm a list of details, facts, and examples that you plan to add when you expand your paragraph into an article. Write them in your notebook. If there are individuals you want to interview, arrange a time and place to talk with them. Create a list of questions to ask them. Take notes on your interviews.

List and Organize Ideas and Details Use a 5Ws chart to organize your ideas for your article. Include some important details that were not in your previous paragraph. A student named Valeria wrote about a school election. Here is the 5Ws chart that she prepared:

Who	Joseph DeCarlo
Where	Ben Franklin Junior High
When	Last Friday
What	Won Election—ran against four others
Why	Best speech, promises of more activities, strong leadership

2 **DRAFT** Use the model on page 191 and your 5Ws chart to help you write a first draft. Remember to write a strong headline that will tell what the article is about and capture readers' attention.

3 **REVISE** Read over your draft. As you do so, ask yourself the questions in the writing checklist. Use the questions to help you revise your article.

SIX TRAITS OF WRITING CHECKLIST

☑ **IDEAS:** Do I answer the 5Ws clearly and completely?

☑ **ORGANIZATION:** Is the information presented in an order that makes sense?

☑ **VOICE:** Does my writing show that I know my subject?

☑ **WORD CHOICE:** Do I use the right words for the subject?

☑ **SENTENCE FLUENCY:** Do my sentences flow smoothly?

☑ **CONVENTIONS:** Does my writing follow the rules of grammar, usage, and mechanics?

Here are the changes Valeria plans to make when she revises her first draft.

DeCarlo Wins!

Last Friday, we elected the next president of our student body. The new president of Ben Franklin Junior High is Joseph DeCarlo, who He defeated four other candidates for the job. DeCarlo had to prove he was a better choice than any of the other candidates in order to win the election.

DeCarlo's strong speech convinced most voters that he would be the best person to represent them. "I belive Joe really thought about what was best for the school and expressed it in his speech," one student explained. DeCarlo promised more school activities such as sports, clubs, and games. He also appealed to other students to tell him their ideas for school projects and to help him understand their needs._∧ *This speech helped to make him the winner.*

Of course, some students did not vote for DeCarlo. Many of them still have mixed feelings on the new president of the school. One disappointed voter complaine that the same key points were also stated in the speech of another candidate. Other voters felt that DeCarlo did not really know what the school needed

However, most student belive he can do the job, as the vote clearly demonstrated. "I wanted to win, but I believe he shows great leadership, commented a former candidate. Even the other candidates had good things to say about Joseph DeCarlo. Although they each wanted to be elected, they are standing by the new president.

Now, it's up to DeCarlo, who takes office next month, to deliver on his promises. Wining is just the begining! Students are looking forward to seeing what he can accomplish. Electing him was a big step. Most students are hopeful, and their message to Decarlo is a positive one. Congratulations and good luck!

4 EDIT AND PROOFREAD  **Workbook Page 93**

Copy your revised draft onto a clean sheet of paper. Read it again. Correct any errors in grammar, word usage, mechanics, and spelling. Here are the additional changes Valeria plans to make when she prepares her final draft.

Valeria Morales

DeCarlo Wins!

Last Friday, we elected the next president of our student body. The new president of Ben Franklin Junior High is Joseph DeCarlo, who defeated four other candidates for the job. DeCarlo had to prove he was a better choice than any of the other candidates in order to win the election.

DeCarlo's strong speech convinced the majority of most voters that he would be the best person to represent them. "I believe Joe really thought about what was best for the school and expressed it in his speech," one student explained. DeCarlo promised more school activities such as sports, clubs, and games. He also appealed to other students to tell him their ideas for school projects and to help him understand their needs. This speech helped to make him the winner.

Of course, some students did not vote for DeCarlo. Many of them still have mixed feelings about on the new president of the school. One disappointed voter complained that the same key points were also stated in the speech of another candidate. Other voters felt that DeCarlo did not really know what the school needed.

However, most students believe he can do the job, as the vote clearly demonstrated. Even the other candidates had good things to say about Joseph DeCarlo. Although they each wanted to be elected, they are standing by the new president. "I wanted to win, but I believe he shows great leadership," commented a former candidate.

Now, it's up to DeCarlo, who takes office next month, to deliver on his promises. Winning is just the beginning! All students are looking forward to seeing what he can accomplish. Electing him was a big step. Most students are hopeful, and their message to Decarlo is a positive one. Congratulations and good luck!

5 PUBLISH Prepare your final draft. Share your essay with your teacher and classmates.

Workbook Page 94

Learn about **Art** *with the*

Smithsonian American Art Museum

SELF-PORTRAITS

*I*n a self-portrait, an artist portrays himself or herself. Artists who make self-portraits are trying to explore who they are and what they have experienced. Before they start, they must ask themselves a lot of questions. These might include questions such as: What have I learned over the years? What is important to me? What information and feelings do I want to share with other people?

There are two self-portraits on these pages. They could not be more different. One shows a stone sculpture of a woman. The other is a print of a man in glasses. Both show artists striving for success while also celebrating their own self-awareness.

Malvina Hoffman, *Self-Portrait* (1929)

Malvina Hoffman has a gentle, thoughtful expression in her *Self-Portrait* carved in limestone. She looks to the side, as though eyeing something of interest, and slings her modeling tool over her shoulder. The smoothness of her face contrasts with the harsh cutting marks on the side of the base, which remind the viewer of the strong strokes required to craft such an effortless pose! Hoffman spent most of her life looking for things of interest around the globe to serve as models for her work. Despite her small build, she embraced the heavy labor required to be an accomplished sculptor, including bending iron, sawing wood, and building supports. Her *Self-Portrait* celebrates both the tools of her trade and her own curious nature.

▲ Malvina Hoffman, *Self-Portrait*, 1929, limestone, 25¾ x 17⅛ x 13 in., Smithsonian American Art Museum

192

▲ Chuck Close, *Self Portrait*, 2000, serigraph, 58½ x 48¼ in., Smithsonian American Art Museum

Chuck Close, *Self Portrait* (2000)

In *Self Portrait*, Chuck Close used a photograph of his own face. Then he divided it up into lots of small squares and rectangles. He then hand-painted each square onto paper. Each square is a tiny piece of art that makes up the larger piece of art. In 1988, he had a terrible health problem that caused him to become partially paralyzed. He could have allowed this disaster to keep him from his art, but he continued to strive for success in his work from his wheelchair.

Both artists created their self-portraits to show what they have been through in their lives, and what they have learned about their art.

Apply What You Learned

1 How does Malvina Hoffman show what she has experienced in her self-portrait?

2 In what way do both artworks illustrate the idea of striving for success?

 Big Question
How would you show success in your self-portrait?

 Workbook
Pages 95–96

193

Can we see change as it happens?

This unit is about personal, social, and global changes. You will read science and social studies articles and literature about changes that affect our daily lives. Reading, writing, and talking about these ideas will give you practice using academic language and help you become a better student.

READING 1: Science Article

■ "Changing Earth"

READING 2: Letters

■ "The Intersection" by Dina Anastasio

READING 3: Social Studies Article

■ From *Through My Eyes* by Ruby Bridges

READING 4: Essay, Art, and Poetry

■ "Harlem: Then and Now" by James Baldwin

■ *Tar Beach* by Faith Ringgold

■ "Harlem" and "Dreams" by Langston Hughes

Listening and Speaking

At the end of this unit, you will choose a topic and present a **speech**. You will persuade people about the need to make changes for a healthy Earth.

Writing

In this unit you will practice **persuasive writing**. In persuasive writing, the writer tries to make readers change their opinions. At the end of the unit, you will write a persuasive essay.

QuickWrite

Make a list of two or three things you would like to change at your school or in your neighborhood.

What You Will Learn

Reading
- Vocabulary building: *Context, dictionary skills, word study*
- Reading strategy: *Scan*
- Text type: *Informational text (science)*

Grammar, Usage, and Mechanics
Present perfect

Writing
Write an advertisement

THE BIG QUESTION

Can we see change as it happens? Think about how people's lives have changed over the years. What things have changed for the better? What things have changed for the worse? Copy the chart into your notebook and complete it.

Things That Have Changed	Good Things about the Change	Bad Things about the Change
world population		
cars	safer and faster	cause pollution, traffic
food we eat		
buildings		
energy (oil and gas)		
computers		

BUILD BACKGROUND

Earth's population is now 6.5 billion people. According to the U.S. Census Bureau, this number has almost doubled since 1960. The population on Earth is nearly four times greater than it was in 1900.

The science article "**Changing Earth**" describes the problems and challenges that population growth is causing on Earth. It also suggests some changes people can make to protect our planet.

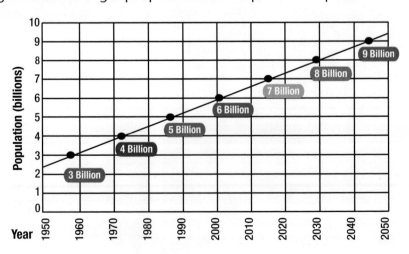

World Population: 1950–2050

Learn Key Words

Read these sentences. Use the context to figure out the meaning of the red words. Use a dictionary to check your answers. Then write each word and its meaning in your notebook.

Key Words

fertilizer
fossil fuels
hybrid
microscopic
resources
solar power

1. Farmers use **fertilizer** to make the soil richer so that plants can grow better.

2. Oil, natural gas, and coal are **fossil fuels**. They are natural materials that form under the ground.

3. **Hybrid** cars run on a combination of gasoline and battery power instead of gasoline alone.

4. Scientists need special instruments to see **microscopic** genes because they are very small.

5. Earth's natural **resources** include things such as food, trees, water, oil, and coal.

6. When people use **solar power**, they are using the sun to produce energy for their houses.

Practice  **Workbook Page 97**

Write the sentences in your notebook. Choose a red word from the box above to complete each sentence. Then take turns reading the sentences aloud with a partner.

1. Population growth has increased the world's need for natural _____ such as food, water, and oil.

2. _____ genes found in the cells of all living things are so tiny we cannot see them.

3. Because _____ such as coal and oil are underground, they can be difficult to locate.

4. New _____ cars use two sources of energy: gasoline and batteries.

5. The sun is a good source of energy. Some people use _____ to heat their houses.

6. Plants often grow better when _____ is added to the soil.

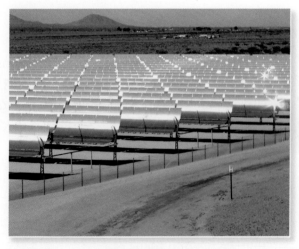

▲ These solar power panels can supply energy to over 50,000 homes.

Learn Academic Words

Study the red words and their meanings. You will find these words useful when talking and writing about informational texts. Write each word and its meaning in your notebook. After you read "Changing Earth," try to use these words to respond to the text.

alternative = something you can use or do instead of something else	➡	Scientists are looking for an **alternative** to fossil fuels because they are difficult to find.
communication = ways of relating, such as speaking or writing	➡	Cell phones and computers make **communication** much easier and faster.
enable = make something possible	➡	Electricity and solar power **enable** us to heat our homes, offices, and schools.
focus on = concentrate on or give special attention to	➡	Students who **focus on** their studies do well in school.
regulation = official rule or order	➡	The government passed a **regulation** that helps keep air and water clean.

Practice  Workbook Page 98

Work with a partner to answer these questions. Try to include the red word in your answer. Write the sentences in your notebook.

1. Walking to school is an alternative to riding in a car. What is another alternative?

2. How has e-mail made communication between people easier?

3. What do cell phones enable us to do in an emergency?

4. What are some important global issues that we need to focus on?

5. What regulation in your school helps keep you safe? Can you name more than one?

▲ Electrical power lines

Word Study: Related Words

In English some nouns and adjectives are related to the base form of a verb. Knowing the meaning of the base form of verbs can help you figure out the meanings of related nouns and adjectives. Look at the chart below.

Verb	Noun	Adjective
pollute = make air, water, or soil dangerously dirty The smoke from the paper mills **pollutes** the air in our city	**pollution** = the process of polluting Engineers think of different ways to reduce **pollution**.	**polluted** = dangerously dirty We could not swim in the **polluted** water.
transport = move or carry goods of people from one place to another Thousands of trucks **transport** goods all over the country.	**transportation** = the process of transporting We take public **transportation** to school instead of driving our car.	**transported** = taken or carried from one place to another The **transported** goods arrived safely from Asia.

Practice  Workbook Page 99

Work with a partner. Copy the headings of the chart above into your notebook. Add the verbs *combine, insert,* and *produce* to the chart. Write the related noun and adjective forms. Use a dictionary to help you check your work.

READING STRATEGY | SCAN

Scanning helps you find the key information you need quickly. When you scan, you look for particular things that you want to know. For example, dates, numbers, ideas, names, and other types of information. To scan, follow these steps:

- Look at the title, visuals, captions, and labels to see if they contain the information you need.
- Start reading the beginning of the text. Move your eyes quickly over the lines.
- Don't stop if you see a word you don't know.
- Look for key words related to the information you want to find.
- Stop scanning and begin reading as soon as you find any of the key words you're looking for.

As you read "Changing Earth," use the scanning strategy to find three or four pieces of information you want to know.

 Workbook Page 100

INFORMATIONAL TEXT

SCIENCE

Set a purpose for reading What kind of changes do people have to make to accommodate Earth's growing population?

Changing Earth

▲ Earth's population is expected to increase to more than 9 billion by 2050.

Growth of Human Population

Earth has changed very quickly over the past 200 years. The human population has grown. Means of transportation have changed. Communication has exploded. People are experimenting with new sources of energy. Even food has changed. What are these changes, and what are their effects?

Until the early 1800s, there were fewer than 1 billion people living on Earth. But since then, improvements in medicine, agriculture, living conditions, and other areas have produced a longer life expectancy and a lower death rate. By 1900, Earth's population had doubled to 2 billion people. The population had grown to 6 billion people by the year 2000. Today, 4.2 people are born and 1.8 people die every second, the United States Census Bureau reports. This means that every minute,144 more people are alive and living on Earth.

living conditions, food, shelter, and cleanliness of environment
life expectancy, length of time a person or an animal is likely to live

This population growth is increasing the demand for Earth's limited natural resources. These resources include food, water, and fossil fuels. More fossil fuels are needed to power our means of transportation. More food is needed to feed hungry people. And more trees are needed for lumber and paper products.

Society has had difficulty keeping up with the increased demand for resources. When fossil fuels were first used as an energy source, people did not know that burning them could affect the environment. This lack of knowledge, as well as limited technologies, led to air and water pollution. Now, thanks to government regulations and industry efforts, scientists have developed ways to reduce air and water pollution.

Our natural resources are extremely valuable. But they are being used up too quickly. We must be careful not to run out of these resources. The choices we make as individuals, as a nation, and as citizens of Earth all affect the environment.

Food

To feed the world's growing population, scientists have been focusing on ways to increase the food supply. One way is through genetic engineering. In the United States, the government and scientists are working to safely regulate the genetic engineering of various plant and animal foods.

Genes are microscopic structures found in cells of every living thing. These genes determine the characteristics of an animal or a plant. In genetic engineering, scientists put genes from one organism, or living thing, into cells of another kind of organism. One way in which scientists are using genetic engineering is to try to make a plant or animal stronger, healthier, or larger. For example, scientists might insert genes from a certain organism into the cells of tomato plants. This is to enable the plants to survive in very cold temperatures or poor soil. If scientists can produce a tomato that can grow in places where a typical tomato cannot survive, then both farmers and consumers will benefit.

◀ Scientists use genetic engineering to increase the food supply.

---

society, people in general
determine, control; decide

BEFORE YOU GO ON

1 How is Earth's population changing?

2 How is Earth's changing population affecting its natural resources?

💡 **On Your Own**
What do you think food will be like in 200 years?

201

Genetic engineering seems like a good idea to some people. But others say that scientists can make mistakes when changing the characteristics of a plant or an animal. Because this is such a new technology, scientists are not sure yet how genetically engineered plants and animals will affect other living things.

Another way to increase the food supply is by using chemicals to produce bigger, stronger crops. The most common types of chemicals that farmers use are fertilizers, herbicides, and pesticides. Fertilizers add nutrients to the soil to help plants grow. Herbicides kill weeds. Pesticides kill insects and other organisms that harm plants.

Chemicals can help foods grow and get rid of harmful insects and weeds. But some chemicals can hurt the environment if used carelessly or incorrectly. Certain pesticides, for example, may also kill insects that do not harm crops. They may also hurt the animals that eat the poisoned insects. Scientists test chemicals used in farming to ensure that they meet safety standards. And farmers are trying other ways of controlling insects, such as by adding an insect's natural enemies to fields where crops are growing.

Sometimes the exact source of chemical pollution is difficult to find. When rain or water from sprinklers falls on crops, the water washes away some of the chemicals on the plants. The chemically polluted water then enters the soil and runs off into streams, rivers, and lakes. Runoff also occurs in cities, where chemicals are carried as runoff to rivers and lakes, polluting them.

---

weeds, unwanted wild plants

▲ A crop-duster plane sprays chemicals on a field.

▲ An experimental solar car

Fuel Supply

We all use some form of energy in our everyday lives, whether by turning on bedroom lights, using a computer, or riding in a car. Whatever energy we use, the source of that energy is fuel. Oil, natural gas, and coal are Earth's most valuable fossil fuels. The cars we drive depend on these resources. The stoves we use for cooking and many power plants that provide our electricity also need these resources.

Fossil fuels are nonrenewable sources of energy. This means that once they are gone, they are gone forever. Fortunately, there are ways to preserve our natural resources. Everyday choices affect the environment. Something as simple as riding a bicycle to school rather than riding in a car saves energy. Reusing valuable resources by recycling saves energy. Throwing an aluminum can into a recycling bin may not seem very important, but if everyone does it, and does it consistently, it will help Earth.

Transportation Changes

Scientists are looking for new ways to power cars and other vehicles, such as by using batteries, solar power, and fuel cells.

---

preserve, keep and protect
batteries, objects that store electricity to power other objects

In an all-electric car, a large, heavy battery stores the electric energy that powers the car. When the battery runs low, the driver must recharge it by plugging it into a special electrical outlet. Recharging the battery takes much longer than refilling a gasoline tank. Even so, electricity is a relatively clean source of energy for cars, so this extra effort benefits the environment.

Some car manufacturers have developed hybrid cars. These cars run on a combination of electricity and gasoline. Their batteries are small and can be recharged by the car's small gasoline engine while the car is being driven.

Scientists are also experimenting with solar-powered cars and hydrogen-powered cars. Solar-powered cars use solar cells to change energy from the sun into electricity. Hydrogen-powered cars use fuel cells that combine two gases—hydrogen and oxygen—to produce electricity. Solar cells and fuel cells are clean energy sources.

---

recharge, put more energy into a battery
engine, machine that makes power from fuel

BEFORE YOU GO ON

1 How do chemicals affect the food supply?

2 What are some new ways to power cars and other vehicles?

On Your Own
What do you think cars might be like in 200 years?

203

Alternative Energy Sources

As the number of people on Earth grows, so does the need for energy to make things work. So scientists are searching for alternative sources of energy. One alternative is nuclear power. Nuclear power does not cause air pollution. However, nuclear power must be handled carefully to prevent accidents that could have long-lasting negative effects on living things. That is why strict safety regulations at nuclear power stations are in place. In addition, much of the unwanted leftover material from nuclear plants is radioactive. It can be dangerous for a very long time if disposed of improperly.

---

radioactive, containing or producing radiation

▲ A solar collector

▲ Wind-powered generators (windmills)

Hot, stale air is vented through louvers. _____

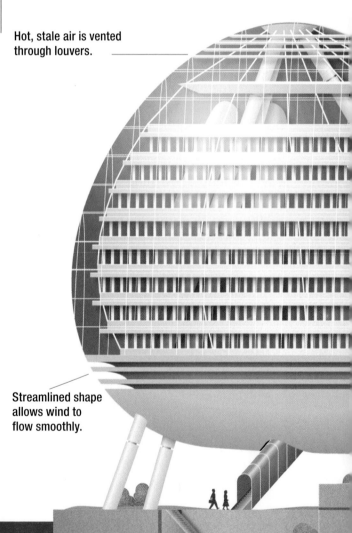

Streamlined shape allows wind to flow smoothly.

Another alternative energy source is solar power. Some solar power stations have hundreds of large mirrors. These mirrors collect and focus sunlight on a large container of water to make the water boil. The boiling water produces steam, which powers machines to produce electricity.

Wind is also an alternative source of power. People once used windmills to grind grains and pump water. Now wind farms use wind to generate electricity. A wind farm is a large area of land, usually a treeless hill or other windy spot, on which groups of modern windmills operate.

Both solar and wind power are clean sources of energy. They depend on natural forces—sunlight and wind—to work effectively. However, sunlight varies with the weather and the time of day, and wind also comes and goes. Therefore, solar and wind power are not always available to generate electricity.

generate, produce; create

Environmentally Friendly Buildings

Many buildings waste energy. They use oil, gas, or electricity for heat in the winter and for air-conditioning in the summer. To save energy, many architects and engineers are changing the way they design buildings. The model office building shown here is environmentally friendly. It uses sunlight and ventilation to heat and cool the building efficiently. In winter, warm air at the top heats cold air coming in at the bottom.

environmentally friendly, not harmful to the environment
ventilation, ways of bringing fresh air into and out of a building
efficiently, without wasting energy or effort

Solar radiation heats air between glass layers.

Mirrors reflect natural light into offices.

A natural ventilation system replaces air-conditioning.

Huge columns support building.

◀ An office building of the future

BEFORE YOU GO ON

1 What is a good reason for using solar and wind power?

2 What do solar and wind power depend on to be effective?

On Your Own
What changes can be made to protect Earth?

205

COMPREHENSION
Workbook Page 101

Right There

1. What has happened to Earth's population in the last 200 years?
2. How has population growth changed our environment?

Think and Search

3. How are scientists changing the food supply? What do some people think about these changes?
4. What's the difference between solar-powered cars and hydrogen-powered cars?

Author and You

5. What other title could the author have used for this article?
6. What other topics could the author have included in this article?

On Your Own

7. Why is it important to find and develop new sources of energy?
8. How does your community help conserve natural resources? What more can it do to conserve?

IN YOUR OWN WORDS

Use the topics and vocabulary below to tell a partner about changes on Earth.

Topics		Vocabulary
Human Population	➡	communication, benefit, growth
Food	➡	nutrients, genetic engineering, fertilizer
Fuel Supply	➡	fossil fuels, hybrid cars, transportation
Alternative Energy Sources	➡	solar power, wind power, regulations

DISCUSSION

Discuss in pairs or small groups.

1. Do you think genetically engineered food is a good way to increase the food supply?

2. How do you think transportation will change in the future? Give examples.

Q **Can we see change as it happens?** Many people believe we need to make changes in our lifestyle, such as saving energy and finding alternative sources for fuel, in order to help protect our environment. But some people don't see the need for change. They continue to waste energy and harm the environment. Why do you think some people ignore the need for change? Does it matter?

Listening TIP

Listen for important details that the speaker includes.

READ FOR FLUENCY

It is often easier to read a text if you understand the difficult words and phrases. Work with a partner. Choose a paragraph from the reading. Identify the words and phrases you do not know or have trouble pronouncing. Look up the difficult words in a dictionary.

Take turns pronouncing the words and phrases with your partner. If necessary, ask your teacher to model the correct pronunciation. Then take turns reading the paragraph aloud. Give each other feedback on your reading.

▲ A traffic jam

EXTENSION

Workbook
Page 101

Fertilizers, herbicides, and pesticides enable farmers to grow more food. But can they be harmful to our environment and to us? Go to the library or do research on the Internet to find out more about fertilizers, herbicides, and pesticides. Use a cause-and-effect chart to help you organize the information you find. For example:

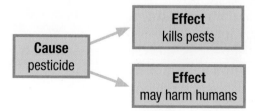

Cause
pesticide

Effect
kills pests

Effect
may harm humans

Grammar and Writing

Present Perfect

Use the present perfect to talk about things that happened (or did not happen) at an unspecified time in the past. To form the present perfect, use *have/has* + the past participle.

> Some car manufacturers **have developed** hybrid cars.
> She **hasn't driven** a hybrid car.

Use the present perfect with adverbs to talk about repeated actions at some unspecified time in the past.

> Nuclear power plants **have** often **failed** safety regulations.
> They **have** always **purchased** cars with good gas efficiency.

Use the present perfect for a situation that began (or didn't begin) in the past and that affects the present.

> Society **has had** difficulty keeping up with the increased demand for resources.
> Solar and wind power **haven't become** popular yet.

Practice

Workbook
Page 102

Work with a partner. Copy the sentences below into your notebook. Complete the sentences using a word from the box in the correct form of the present perfect.

develop	experience	ride	show	use

1. The world _____ a great increase in population.
2. Genetic engineers _____ seedless fruits and vegetables.
3. I _____ in a hybrid car three or four times.
4. Research _____ that hybrid cars are good for the environment.
5. We _____ solar power in our home for many years.

WRITING A PERSUASIVE PARAGRAPH

Write an Advertisement

At the end of this unit, you will write a persuasive essay. In persuasive writing, writers offer an opinion and try to get readers to accept their viewpoint. Persuasive writing should include reasons and examples that support the opinion. One example of persuasive writing is an advertisement. An ad gives you reasons and examples, which persuade you to buy a particular product.

Here is a model of an advertisement. Notice that the writer has stated her opinion and supported it with a reason and examples. She used a graphic organizer to organize her ideas.

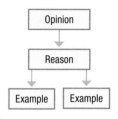

Opinion → Reason → Example / Example

Valeria Morales

Why Choose Hybrid Cars?

Are you shopping for a new car? Have you heard about hybrid cars? They are the best cars. You should consider buying one. Why? First of all, they are better for the environment. They produce 90 percent fewer pollutants than regular cars. In other words, they reduce smog by 90 percent. Hybrids use less fuel, too. They get about 44 miles per gallon, while regular cars get about 29 miles per gallon. Some hybrid cars can even get as much as 50 miles per gallon! Hybrid cars cost a bit more than regular cars, but you'll spend less on gas. So in the long run, if you buy a hybrid car, you can help the environment _and_ save money! These are excellent reasons to buy a hybrid car, so drop by our showroom today.

Practice

Workbook Page 103

Write a persuasive paragraph in the form of an advertisement. Persuade people to buy something that is good for the environment, such as energy-saving light bulbs or recycled notebook paper. Include your opinion, reason, and a few examples. Use a graphic organizer like the one above to organize your ideas. Be sure to use the present perfect correctly.

Writing Checklist

IDEAS:
☑ I stated my opinion clearly.

ORGANIZATION:
☑ I included a reason and examples.

What You Will Learn

Reading

■ Vocabulary building: *Literary terms, dictionary skills, word study*

■ Reading strategy: *Identify author's purpose*

■ Text type: *Literature (letters)*

Grammar, Usage, and Mechanics

Future with *will* or *won't* for prediction

Writing

Write a letter to the editor

THE BIG QUESTION

Can we see change as it happens? A community is a place and the people in it. What type of community do you live in? Do you live in the country, the suburbs, a small town, or a city? Have you noticed changes that have taken place in your community? Were they positive or negative changes? Were you aware of them while they were happening, or later? Discuss with a partner.

BUILD BACKGROUND

In many newspapers, there is a section for letters from people who want to express their opinions, or how they feel about something. Very often the letters are about problems in the community, as is the case for the three fictional letters in "**The Intersection.**" In a story that spans 100 years, the author describes family members from three generations who share a common problem. As the saying goes, "Some things never change."

Below are photographs of an intersection in New York City (Fifth Avenue and Broadway), taken more than 100 years apart. What looks the same in these photographs? What looks different?

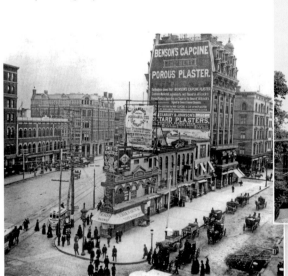

◀ An intersection in the late 1800s

▲ The same intersection today

Learn Literary Words

A **conflict** is a struggle between opposing forces. Authors use conflict to show the main problem in a story. In many cases, it is the conflict that sets the story's plot in motion. Conflict can occur between people or groups of people. Read this excerpt from the text.

Literary Words

conflict
foreshadowing

> Through three generations, the Winthrop family has been in conflict with careless drivers that drove down their tiny street.

Who is having the conflict? How long has it been going on?

Foreshadowing is a hint or clue in a story about what will happen later on. The name of a place or a character may provide foreshadowing. Certain events may also foreshadow other events or conflicts that will happen later. Read this excerpt from the text.

> Every day, from his window, Jason Winthrop saw carriages going too fast around the corner. Sometimes, the drivers were not even looking where they were going.

What do you think might happen next?

▲ A horse-drawn carriage

Practice
Workbook Page 104

With a partner, read the sentences below. Discuss what each sentence might foreshadow.

1. The city grew larger every day. Thousands of people were moving there, and almost all of them drove cars.

2. When the first accident occurred, the horse got stuck in the mud and the carriage tipped over, but no one got hurt.

3. Miguel was very angry. He crumpled a piece of paper and threw it down. It landed near the fireplace. He ran out of the room without looking back.

Learn Academic Words

Study the red words and their meanings. You will find these words useful when talking and writing about literature. Write each word and its meaning in your notebook. After you read "The Intersection," try to use these words to respond to the text.

achieve = succeed in doing or gaining something	➡	We hope we can **achieve** our goal, which is to win the state competition.
consequence = something that happens as a result of a particular action	➡	The **consequence** of his bad driving was a minor car accident.
impact = effect that an event or situation has on someone or something	➡	The new stop sign has had a positive **impact**. Now there are fewer accidents.
incident = something that happens, especially something that is unusual	➡	When the **incident** occurred, the police came quickly to keep the traffic moving.
injured = harmed or wounded in an accident	➡	"I don't want the children to get **injured**," said the crossing guard.
outcome = final result	➡	The **outcome** of the election hasn't been decided yet. We don't know who won.

Practice

Work with a partner to answer these questions. Try to include the red word in your answer. Write the sentences in your notebook.

1. What kinds of things would you like to **achieve** in your lifetime?

2. What is the **consequence** of not studying for a test?

3. What would be the **impact** on traffic if traffic lights stopped working?

4. What is one memorable **incident** that happened in your school or community this year?

5. How can you be safe and not get **injured** at school?

6. When has the **outcome** of a story surprised you?

▲ Heavy traffic has a negative impact on our daily lives.

Word Study: Synonyms

Synonyms are words that have similar meanings. Writers often use synonyms to make their writing more varied, exciting, or precise. Since each synonym has a particular meaning, check a dictionary to make sure you are using the precise word you want. For example, *sluggish* and *unhurried* are synonyms for *slow*. Compare the synonyms below:

> My mother was not in a hurry, so she drove the car at a **slow** pace.
> I was **sluggish** today and got to school late.
> We had a nice, **unhurried** dinner with friends.

Practice

Copy the chart below into your notebook. Use a thesaurus to find synonyms for the words in the chart. Make sure you use the correct part of speech. Then write a sentence using a new synonym that you found. Read your sentences to the class.

Word	Synonyms	Sentence
accident		
home		
hurt		
watch		

READING STRATEGY   IDENTIFY AUTHOR'S PURPOSE

Identifying an author's purpose (or reason for writing) can help you analyze information better. Three of the most common reasons authors write are to inform, to entertain, and to persuade. To identify an author's purpose, follow these steps:

- As you read, ask yourself, Is this entertaining? Am I enjoying it?
- Am I learning new information from what I'm reading?
- Is the author trying to persuade me about something or change my opinion?
- Is there more than one reason the author wrote this? If so, what are the reasons?

An author can have many reasons for writing. As you read "The Intersection," try to identify what the main purpose is, and also how many different reasons the author has for writing.

Set a purpose for reading What major changes do the letter writers describe? How do they affect the intersection and the people who live near it? Could people see the changes while they were happening, or only after time had passed?

THE INTERSECTION

Dina Anastasio

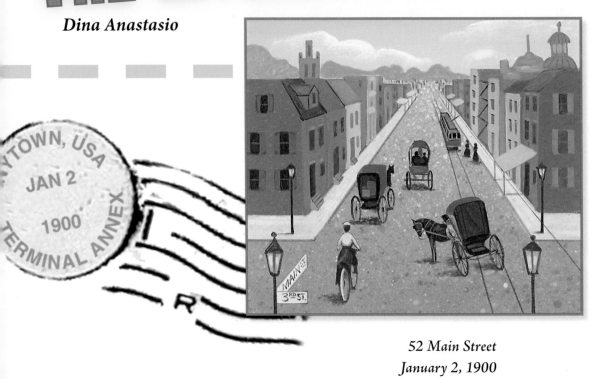

52 Main Street
January 2, 1900

To the Editor:

I am writing this letter to ask your readers for help. I live on the corner of Main and Third Streets. When it rains, this dirt road turns to mud. When it snows, it turns to slush.

From my sitting room window I see carriages race through the intersection. They are going too fast for such a slippery corner. The drivers do not look where they are going. Often another carriage is coming the other way. The horses rear up. The carriages turn over. Too many people are hurt.

---

intersection, place where two roads or streets cross
slush, partly melted snow
carriages, vehicles that horses pull
rear up, rise on back legs

214

Last night, I helped to pull a horse out of the mud again. The carriage had turned over. A woman broke her leg.

We have now moved into the twentieth century. The horseless carriage is about to change our lives. I hear that Mr. Henry Ford is trying to develop one right now. These motor cars will move people faster than we can imagine. Everyone says that they will solve all our traffic problems. But I'm not sure how. They will race past my house from morning to night. If we aren't careful, they will bang into each other on this corner. They will disturb my sleep. . . .

So please try and drive a little slower when you come to the corner of Main and Third.

Yours sincerely,
Jason Winthrop

✔ **LITERARY CHECK**

How does the invention of a motor car foreshadow events to come?

52 Main Street
January 2, 1950

To the Editor:

Fifty years ago, my father wrote to your newspaper. He asked for his neighbors' help. At that time he was concerned about speeding. He was worried about the mud and slush on the road. He wanted people to slow down their horses and carriages.

Since that time, our city has changed. There are now 100,000 people instead of 10,000. Electric lights have replaced gas lights. Houses have been pulled down. Apartment and office buildings have replaced them.

I have watched these changes from my living room window ever since I was a child. I watched workers cover the road in front of my house with cobblestones. And after that I watched them pave it. I remember the day the first stop sign was put up on our corner.

---

concerned, worried

BEFORE YOU GO ON

1. What problems does Jason Winthrop (the writer of the first letter) describe?

2. What changes to the city does Jason Winthrop suggest?

💡 **On Your Own**
What impact do apartment buildings have on a community?

I also remember the day, in 1929, when the first electric traffic light went up. Those lights were needed. Motor cars came speeding by, and they needed to be controlled.

This city is still getting larger. More and more people are moving here. That will mean more and more cars. Although there are trolleys and buses today, traffic is still a problem.

I cannot stop all the accidents. But I would like to stop the accidents that happen on my corner. And that is one reason that I am writing this letter.

Please slow down! I am tired of dragging injured people out of their cars.

I am writing for another reason, too. Cars are polluting our city. There may be nothing that we can do about our polluted air. But there is something that we can do about the noise.

So please stop blowing your horns! I need my sleep!

Best wishes,
Jason Winthrop Jr.

---

52 Main Street

January 2, 2000

To the Editor:

One hundred years ago today, my grandfather wrote a letter to this newspaper. He asked your readers to slow down when they came to the corner of Main Street and Third. Fifty years later, my father wrote a letter, too. He asked your readers to slow down and stop blowing their horns.

Today, I too am asking for help. Our family still lives in the same house, and I have watched our city change over the past fifty years. This is now a big city. All around me are office buildings and parking lots. My home is the only house

---

trolleys, vehicles that use tracks and are powered by electric current from overhead wires

dragging, pulling

left in the whole downtown. Many people have begged me to sell it. But I will not sell.

This is not a fancy house. It is a small wooden house. It is not worth the money that people have offered me. But I do not care about the money. My family has lived here for over one hundred years. I hope we will live here for another hundred.

I would like to tell you what I see from my window. In some ways, the view is the same as my grandfather's view. I still see some of the things that my father saw, too. We have all seen traffic problems. Today, our street has been paved many times. The trolleys are gone. Traffic lights are now run by computers. Best of all, our street is now one-way.

Everyone said that a one-way street would cut the number of accidents in half. But it didn't.

People drive faster because it is one-way. Sometimes they even drag-race here. Beating the light is too often a game. So there are still accidents. People still get very badly hurt, because they go faster. . . .

So my family asks you again, for the third time, to slow down.

Sincerely,
Jason Winthrop III

✔ LITERARY CHECK
What is the ongoing **conflict** *described in these three letters?*

---

begged, asked in an anxious way
fancy, elaborate and often expensive
drag-race, race from a standstill to a fast speed
beating the light, driving quickly through an intersection just as the traffic light turns red

ABOUT THE **AUTHOR**

Dina Anastasio has written many books for children and young adults. Her books include *The Case of the Glacier Park Swallow, Pirates, A Question of Time, The Wolf, The Living Desert,* and *Apollo 13.* She was the editor of *Sesame Street Magazine.*

BEFORE YOU GO ON

1 According to Jason Winthrop III, what has changed in the past fifty years in his neighborhood?

2 Why doesn't he want to sell his house?

On Your Own
Do you have any of these problems in your neighborhood? Explain.

217

DRAMATIC READING

Work in groups of three to reread, discuss, and perform "The Intersection." Identify from whose point of view each letter is written. Tell which words or phrases you feel should be stressed. Discuss how you think the voice in each letter is different from or the same as the one before it. Work together to interpret any difficult words or phrasing. Use a dictionary or ask your teacher for help if you need it.

After your group has reread and examined the letters carefully, choose who will play the part of Jason Winthrop, Jason Winthrop Jr., and Jason Winthrop III. Put the main points of each letter into your own words. Then perform each letter for the class.

Speaking TIPS

Be sure there is emotion in your voice since you are giving your opinion.

COMPREHENSION

Workbook Page 108

Right There

1. When was the first letter written? How do you know this?
2. When were the first electric lights put in?

Think and Search

3. Which writer talks about pollution? What does he say about it?
4. What are the problems facing the writer in the year 2000?

Author and You

5. Do you think the writers of these letters were effective? Did the letters help make changes? Why or why not?
6. Do you think the author would agree with the statement, "The more things change the more they stay the same"? Do you agree? Why or why not?

On Your Own

7. Why are intersections dangerous? How can people make them safer?
8. Do you think writing letters to the editor of a newspaper is an effective way to achieve certain goals?

DISCUSSION

Discuss in pairs or small groups.

1. What impact does too much traffic have on a community? What are some solutions to this problem?

2. Have you ever thought about writing a letter suggesting a change? Give details.

Q Can we see change as it happens? Usually we're aware of events as they happen, but we don't always see the changes they will bring. The writers of these letters, however, were able to see daily events (fast drivers, building construction) *and* predict the consequences of these events (more accidents, more traffic). Why is it helpful to be aware of changes and their consequences?

»))) *Listening* TIP

Give the speaker your attention; don't talk to your classmates.

RESPONSE TO LITERATURE

Workbook
Page 108

The three letters in "The Intersection" all tell about the same problem even though they were written fifty years apart. Imagine that you are Jason Winthrop IV. You live in the same family house in the year 2050. What is the view from your window? Are people still driving automobiles? Are they driving hybrid cars or flying space-age automobiles? Are there still accidents?

Write a letter to the editor of a newspaper about the traffic problem on the corner of Main Street and Third. Give details about the problem and suggest a solution. Include foreshadowing about the future. Share your letter with the class.

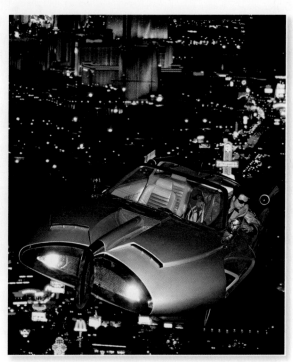

A car of the future? ▶

219

Grammar and Writing

Future with *will* or *won't* for Prediction

Use *will* or *won't* (*will not*) + the base form of a verb to talk about the future. You can also use *will* or *won't* to make predictions or guesses about the future. When you aren't completely sure about your prediction, you can use the adverb *probably*. When you are even less sure, you can use the adverb *maybe*.

> They **will** race past my house from morning to night.
> That **will probably** mean more cars.
> **Maybe** they **will** solve all our problems. **Maybe** they **won't**.

Practice

Workbook
Page 109

Work with a partner. Use the words and phrases below to exchange opinions about the future. Make predictions using *will* or *won't*. Use *probably* or *maybe* when you aren't sure about your prediction. Then write the sentences in your notebook.

1. traffic / become more of a problem
2. cars / become more fuel efficient
3. higher gas prices / solve traffic problems
4. people / take more public transportation
5. there / be more pollution
6. the community / work for safer streets
7. we / drive our cars on the moon
8. the city / become more crowded
9. the neighborhood / change over time
10. the weather / have an impact on the traffic

▲ In the future, traffic lights and cars will be able to communicate with each other.

220

WRITING A PERSUASIVE PARAGRAPH

Write a Letter to the Editor

A letter to the editor of a newspaper or magazine is a form of persuasive writing. The purpose of many letters to the editor is to discuss a problem and offer a solution. For example, in the letters you have just read, the problems that concern the writers are that people are driving too fast and they are polluting the neighborhood. Often writers include in their letters a suggested solution to the problem. In "The Intersection" the writers of the letters offer several solutions. They suggest that people drive slower and stop honking their horns.

Here is a model of a letter to the editor of a publication. Notice that the writer states the problem and solution clearly. He used a T-chart to help organize his ideas.

Problem	Solution

November 18, 2009

To the Editor,

Downtown Jacksonville has had a lot of traffic lately. This is mainly because of the closing of some of the lanes on Matthews Bridge. This is making many of the citizens of Jacksonville late to their jobs and for appointments. Recently my parents had an appointment at the local hospital on the other side of the bridge. The traffic was so bad that they gave up and had to go back home. To solve this problem, I think that construction on the bridge should be done at night. This will prevent a lot of traffic problems. Maybe it won't solve all of the congestion, but it will make it better. I hope the administration of Jacksonville will consider this request.

Sincerely,
Emanuel Bonilla

Practice

Workbook Page 110

Write a letter to the editor of a publication that discusses a problem that concerns you. Express the problem clearly and include a possible solution. Use a graphic organizer like the one above to organize your ideas. Be sure to use the future with *will* and *won't* correctly and put your letter in the correct format.

Writing Checklist

VOICE:
☑ I used language appropriate to a formal letter.

IDEAS:
☑ I included a problem and a possible solution.

221

Prepare to Read

What You Will Learn

Reading
- Vocabulary building: *Context, dictionary skills, word study*
- Reading strategy: *Draw conclusions*
- Text type: *Informational text (social studies)*

Grammar, Usage, and Mechanics
Conjunctions: *and, but, or*

Writing
Write a persuasive paragraph

THE BIG QUESTION

Can we see change as it happens? Think of a time when you were treated unfairly. How did it make you feel? Did you try to change the situation? If anything changed, did the change begin immediately, or did some time pass before you were treated fairly again?

BUILD BACKGROUND

You will read an excerpt from Ruby Bridges's memoir ***Through My Eyes***. Ruby Bridges was involved with the civil rights movement, an important period in American history. Years ago, African Americans did not have the same rights as white Americans. This began to change in the 1950s and 1960s when African Americans began fighting for—and winning—equal rights.

The images and timeline below show how African-American students had to be protected as they entered or exited their previously "all-white" schools.

September 1957

Little Rock Central High
Little Rock, Arkansas

November 1960

McDonogh Elementary School
New Orleans, Louisiana

September 1962

University of Mississippi
Oxford, Mississippi

VOCABULARY

Learn Key Words

Read these sentences. Use the context to figure out the meaning of the red words. Use a dictionary to check your answers. Then write each word and its meaning in your notebook.

1. People who believe in **civil rights** fight for equal social, legal, and economic rights for everyone under the law.

2. The **federal court** does not make laws; it interprets and applies laws in order to find solutions to problems.

3. There are nine **justices** on the Supreme Court, which is the highest court in the United States.

4. **Racism** is wrong. People should not be mistreated because of their race.

5. During the period of **segregation**, many people believed that students of different races should be separated.

6. The President asked the federal **troops**, members of the regular army, to protect the civil rights marchers.

Practice  **Workbook Page 111**

Write the sentences in your notebook. Choose a red word from the box above to complete each sentence. Then take turns reading the sentences aloud with a partner.

1. _____ of the Supreme Court hear cases and make decisions that affect many people.

2. In the 1950s and 1960s, many people fought for _____, or equal treatment of all Americans.

3. Many states in the South practiced _____. They wanted to keep students apart.

▲ The Supreme Court outlawed school segregation in *Brown v. Board of Education of Topeka, Kansas*.

4. The _____ stood in front of the school to protect the entering students.

5. The Supreme Court is part of the United States _____ system.

6. Sadly, there is still _____ in the world, causing unfair treatment.

Learn Academic Words

Study the red words and their meanings. You will find these words useful when talking and writing about informational texts. Write each word and its meaning in your notebook. After you read the excerpt from *Through My Eyes*, try to use these words to respond to the text.

Academic Words

apparent
convince
enormous
integrate
symbol
undertake

apparent = easy to understand; obvious	➡	The need for equal and fair treatment was **apparent** to all of the students.
convince = make someone believe	➡	Civil rights leaders tried to **convince** the people to fight for equal rights.
enormous = very large in size or amount	➡	The **enormous** crowd at the march in Washington, D.C. was an amazing sight.
integrate = unite; end the practice of separating people of different races	➡	The government passed laws that would **integrate** schools and end segregation.
symbol = a picture, a letter, or a sign that means or stands for something else	➡	The flag is a **symbol** of our country.
undertake = start to do something	➡	The students are too busy to **undertake** such a big project.

Practice

Workbook Page 112

Write the sentences in your notebook. Choose a red word from the box above to complete each sentence. Then take turns reading the sentences aloud with a partner.

1. Segregation caused _____ hardship and suffering for African Americans.

2. I'm not sure you're right. You have to _____ me that your opinion is correct.

3. It was important to _____ the schools, because separating students by race was unfair.

4. I'll _____ a new task, but first I have to finish this one.

5. Some of the problems in society are hidden, and some are _____.

6. People often draw a heart as a _____ for love.

▲ An enormous crowd attends the "March on Washington," Washington, D.C., 1963.

Word Study: Capitalizing Proper Nouns

A **proper noun** is a noun that names a specific person, place, or thing and must be capitalized. Study the proper nouns below.

Proper Nouns	Example
Names of individuals	Mrs. Lucille Bridges
Names of ethnic groups, national groups, and languages	African Americans
Organizations, institutions, and political parties	Supreme Court
Monuments, bridges, and buildings	The White House
Documents, awards, and laws	Nobel Peace Prize
Geographical terms	Mississippi River, Arkansas
Historical events, eras, calendar items	Korean War

Practice

Copy the sentences below into your notebook. Capitalize the proper nouns.

1. When I was younger, we lived on north shore drive.
2. dr. Fernandez is the new principal at kennedy middle school.
3. My uncle jim fought in the vietnam war.
4. They went to washington, d.c., to meet president johnson.
5. From the window we could see the rocky mountains.

READING STRATEGY | DRAW CONCLUSIONS

Drawing conclusions helps you figure out the meanings of clues and events in a text. Good readers put together the clues until they can draw a conclusion. To draw a conclusion, follow these steps:

- Look for clues in the text. Does the information make sense?
- Think about what you already know from similar situations that you have read about or experienced.
- Put together the clues and what you know. Use a graphic organizer to list the information.
- Draw your conclusion by looking at the list.

As you read *Through My Eyes*, ask yourself what conclusions you can draw about life for African Americans during the 1950s and 1960s.

Set a purpose for reading Even though Ruby Bridges couldn't see it at the time, her first day of first grade was a historical event. Why? What change did society begin to experience, thanks to this brave young girl and her family?

from # Through My Eyes

Ruby Bridges

Preface to My Story

When I was six years old, the civil rights movement came knocking at the door. It was 1960, and history pushed in and swept me up in a whirlwind. At the time, I knew little about the racial fears and hatred in Louisiana, where I was growing up. Young children never know about racism at the start. It's we adults who teach it.

In spite of the aftereffects of the whirlwind, I feel privileged now to have been a part of the civil rights struggle. The 1950s and 1960s were important decades: Negroes, as African Americans were known then, dared at last to demand equal treatment as American citizens. School integration was only part of the struggle, but an absolutely essential part.

In 1954—coincidentally, the year I was born—the U.S. Supreme Court ordered the end of "separate but equal" education for African-American children. Because of her race, Linda Brown was not allowed to attend her local elementary school. All nine justices of the Supreme Court agreed that Linda had a legal right to go to that school. But for a few years afterward, the Court looked the other way when states in the South ignored its order. Black children in states like Louisiana and Mississippi continued to attend all-black public schools. White children went to separate and usually better schools.

By 1957, less than two percent of southern schools had been integrated. That year, nine black high school students enrolled in a white school in Little Rock, Arkansas. The white segregationists in Arkansas were furious. President Dwight D. Eisenhower ordered federal troops—soldiers with rifles and machine guns mounted on military jeeps—to protect the "Little Rock Nine" in their school.

---

whirlwind, confused rush
aftereffects, results
privileged, proud; honored
essential, important and necessary
coincidentally, two things happening by chance
enrolled, officially joined

◄ *The Problem We All Live With*, 1964, Norman Rockwell

BEFORE YOU GO ON

1 What year did the U.S. Supreme Court order the end of school segregation?

2 Which states in the 1950s continued to have all-white schools?

💡 On Your Own
Describe the painting. How does it make you feel?

227

Even after the events in Little Rock, Louisiana continued to ignore its African-American children. However, the civil rights movement was growing stronger. A federal court gave the city a deadline for school integration: September 1960.

I don't remember everything about that school year, but there are events and feelings I will never forget. In writing this book, I recall how integration looked to me then, when I was six and limited to my own small world. However, as an adult, I wanted to fill in some of the blanks about what was a serious racial crisis in the American South. I have tried to give you the bigger picture—through my eyes.

One Year in an All-Black School

When it was time for me to start kindergarten, I went to Johnson Lockett Elementary School. My segregated school was fairly far from my house, but I had lots of company for the long walk. All the kids on my block went to Johnson Lockett. I loved school that year, and my teacher, Mrs. King, was warm and encouraging. She was black, as all the teachers in black schools were back then. Mrs. King was quite old, and she reminded me of my grandmother.

What I didn't know in kindergarten was that a federal court in New Orleans was about to force two white public schools to admit black students. The plan was to integrate only the first grade for that year. Then, every year after that, the incoming first grade would also be integrated.

In the late spring of my year at Johnson Lockett, the city school board began testing black kindergartners. They wanted to find out which children should be sent to the white schools. I took the test. I was only five, and I'm sure I didn't have any idea why I was taking it. Still, I remember that day. I remember getting dressed up and riding uptown on the bus with my mother, and sitting in an enormous room in the school board building along with about a hundred other black kids, all waiting to be tested.

Apparently the test was difficult, and I've been told that it was set up so that kids would have a hard time passing. If all black children had failed, the white school board might have had a way to keep the schools segregated for a while longer.

▲ Ruby Bridges, age 6

---

deadline, time to end
crisis, turning point; difficult period
admit, allow to enter

That summer, my parents were contacted by the National Association for the Advancement of Colored People (NAACP). The NAACP is an old and well-respected civil rights organization. Its members work to get equal rights for black people.

Several people from the NAACP came to the house in the summer. They told my parents that I was one of just a few black children to pass the school board test, and that I had been chosen to attend one of the white schools, William Frantz Public School. They said it was a better school and closer to my home than the one I had been attending. They said I had the right to go to the closest school in my district. They pressured my parents and made a lot of promises. They said my going to William Frantz would help me, my brothers, my sister, and other black children in the future. We would receive a better education, which would give us better opportunities as adults.

My parents argued about what to do. My father, Abon, didn't want any part of school integration. He was a gentle man and feared that angry segregationists might hurt his family. Having fought in the Korean War, he experienced segregation on the battlefield, where he risked his life for his country. He didn't think that things would ever change. He didn't think I would ever be treated as an equal.

Lucille, my mother, was convinced that no harm would come to us. She thought that the opportunity for me to get the best education possible was worth the risk, and she finally convinced my father.

> *Ruby was special. I wanted her to have a good education so she could get a good job when she grew up. But Ruby's father thought his child shouldn't go where she wasn't wanted.*
>
> *There were things I didn't understand. I didn't know Ruby would be the only black child in the school. I didn't know how bad things would get.*
>
> *I remember being afraid on the first day Ruby went to the Frantz school, when I came home and turned on the TV set and I realized that, at that moment, the whole world was watching my baby and talking about her.*
>
> *At that moment, I was most afraid.*
>
> —*Lucille Bridges (Ruby's mother)*

---

district, particular area of the city
pressured, tried hard to convince
opportunities, chances

BEFORE YOU GO ON

1 Where did Ruby Bridges go to kindergarten?

2 Who persuaded Ruby's parents to allow her to go to an all-white school?

On Your Own
Do you remember how you felt the first day you went to kindergarten?

November 14, 1960

My mother took special care getting me ready for school. When somebody knocked on my door that morning, my mother expected to see people from the NAACP. Instead, she saw four serious-looking white men, dressed in suits and wearing armbands. They were U.S. federal marshals. They had come to drive us to school and stay with us all day. I learned later they were carrying guns.

I remember climbing into the back seat of the marshals' car with my mother, but I don't remember feeling frightened. William Frantz Public School was only five blocks away, so one of the marshals in the front seat told my mother right away what we should do when we got there.

"Let us get out of the car first," the marshal said. "Then you'll get out, and the four of us will surround you and your daughter. We'll walk up to the door together. Just walk straight ahead, and don't look back."

---

armbands, bands of material worn around the arm
federal marshals, government officers

◀ Ruby Bridges had to be escorted by federal marshals to and from school each day.

When we were near the school, my mother said, "Ruby, I want you to behave yourself today and do what the marshals say."

We drove down North Galvez Street to the point where it crosses Alvar. I remember looking out of the car as we pulled up to the Frantz school. There were barricades and people shouting and policemen everywhere. I thought maybe it was Mardi Gras, the carnival that takes place in New Orleans every year. Mardi Gras was always noisy.

As we walked through the crowd, I didn't see any faces. I guess that's because I wasn't very tall and I was surrounded by the marshals. People yelled and threw things. I could see the school building, and it looked bigger and nicer than my old school. When we climbed the high steps to the front door, there were policemen in uniforms at the top. The policemen at the door and the crowd behind us made me think this was an important place.

It must be college, I thought to myself.

---

barricades, objects blocking a road to prevent people from entering
awed, inspired

There was a certain shyness about Ruby. She would appear at the door of our room in the morning and walk in slowly, taking little steps. I would always greet her with a compliment about how nicely she was dressed to help make her feel special as she was, and make her feel more welcome and comfortable. We would hug, and then we would sit down side by side. We had our corner of the room, and it was cozy. I never sat in the front of the classroom apart. If I went to the blackboard, she was always right there with me.

I grew to love Ruby and to be awed by her. It was an ugly world outside, but I tried to make our world together as normal as possible. Neither one of us ever missed a day. It was important to keep going.

—Barbara Henry (Ruby's first grade teacher)

ABOUT THE **AUTHOR**

Ruby Bridges received two honorary college degrees and has become a public speaker. In 1999, she formed The Ruby Bridges Foundation. The goal of the foundation is to inspire and educate children to be tolerant and respectful of differences. Ruby Bridges lives with her husband and sons in New Orleans, Louisiana.

BEFORE YOU GO ON

1 What did Ruby first think when she arrived at her new school? Why?

2 Why did Ruby's mother want her to go to an all-white school?

On Your Own
Can you think of a grade school teacher that had a positive impact on you?

231

Review and Practice

COMPREHENSION

 **Workbook Page 115**

Right There

1. Who were the "Little Rock Nine"? What did they do?
2. Why did Ruby Bridges think her new school was an important place?

Think and Search

3. What did Ruby think of her kindergarten teacher, Mrs. King?
4. How did Ruby Bridges's father feel about Ruby going to an all-white school? Why?

Author and You

5. What does the author mean when she says, "Young children never know about racism at the start"?
6. Why did the author compare her first day at the all-white school to a festival, Mardi Gras?

On Your Own

7. How would you feel if you were Ruby's first grade teacher?
8. When is it easy to stand up for things you believe in? When is it difficult?

IN YOUR OWN WORDS

Use the phrases and vocabulary below to tell a partner about integration.

Civil Rights Movement	➡	equal treatment, integrate
Supreme Court	➡	justices, legal rights
Segregation	➡	convinced, separate, racism
Integration	➡	opportunities, equal

 *Speaking* TIP

If someone doesn't understand you, try using other words to make your point.

DISCUSSION

Discuss in pairs or small groups.

1. Why did U.S. marshals accompany Ruby to and from school?

2. Ruby Bridges was one of the first African Americans to go to an all-white school. How did Ruby make it easier for other African Americans to go to white schools and get a better education?

Q **Can we see change as it happens?** At first, not everyone accepted school integration (when African Americans and whites were allowed to attend the same school). It took time and many sacrifices from people like Ruby Bridges. Can you think of any other problems in society that changed slowly?

READ FOR FLUENCY

Reading with feeling helps make what you read more interesting. Work with a partner. Choose a paragraph from the reading. Read the paragraph. Ask each other how you felt after reading the paragraph. Did you feel happy or sad?

Take turns reading the paragraph aloud to each other with a tone of voice that represents how you felt when you read it the first time. Take turns reading the paragraph aloud and give each other feedback.

EXTENSION 📖 **Workbook** Page 115

The civil rights movement had an enormous impact on the United States. Research one of the events below at the library or on the Internet. Explain why the event was so important.

▲ Rosa Parks

- *Brown vs. the Board of Education*
- Rosa Parks refuses to give up her seat on a bus
- Sit-in at Woolworths, Greensboro, North Carolina
- Martin Luther King Jr. is arrested
- March to Montgomery from Selma, Alabama

Grammar and Writing

Conjunctions: *and, but, or*

A conjunction is a connecting word that joins other words or groups of words. *And* shows connection; *but* shows contrast; *or* shows choice. When connecting two independent clauses (complete sentences), use a comma to separate the clauses.

> I don't remember everything, **but** there are events I will never forget.

When connecting three or more items, use a comma after each item before the conjunction.

> It would help me, my brothers, my sister, **and** other black children in the future.

When connecting two items in a sentence, don't use a comma.

> I knew little about the racial fears **and** hatred in Louisiana.
> The U.S. Supreme Court ordered the end of "separate **but** equal" education.
> Ruby could attend a segregated school **or** an integrated school.

Practice

Workbook Page 116

Work with a partner. Copy the following sentences into your notebook. Complete each sentence with *and, but,* or *or.*

1. The Constitution guarantees our right to life, liberty, _____ the pursuit of happiness.

2. Which person do you agree with? Ruby's mother _____ Ruby's father?

3. The federal court required schools to integrate by 1960, _____ most schools in the South ignored this order.

4. The civil rights movement fought for equal rights _____ social justice.

5. It was apparent to many people that segregation wasn't fair, _____ some people thought it was okay.

WRITING a PERSUASIVE PARAGRAPH

Write a Persuasive Paragraph

At the end of this unit, you will write a persuasive essay. To do this, you'll need to learn some of the skills writers use in persuasive writing. One way of organizing a persuasive piece is to ask and answer a question in a persuasive way. For example, in the selection you just read by Ruby Bridges, a question might be, "Why can't Ruby attend the local school?" In her own words, she answers the question and describes her experience using vivid details.

Here is a model of a persuasive paragraph that uses a question-and-answer format. The writer organized his ideas using a graphic organizer.

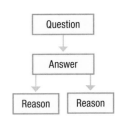

Andrew Tilley

Banning Recess

In order to make time for more classes, our school is considering eliminating recess. Should our school ban recess? I don't think so. Recess is a vital part of the school day. Recess gives students and teachers a chance to relax after working hard all morning. I have read that recess is very important to students because it gives them an opportunity to interact socially without worrying about grades. More importantly, some experts say that recess helps students concentrate better in class. If they don't have a break, students might get bored or have trouble focusing. When that happens, students don't learn as much as they should. Recess is fun for kids, but it also helps them learn. Recess is just as important as any other part of the school day and should not be eliminated.

Practice

Workbook Page 117

Write a persuasive paragraph organized by question and answer. You could write about a situation, rule, or law you believe is unfair. For example, you could write about the need for more performing arts or physical education classes in school. You could also write about the need for more respect and tolerance among your peers. Remember to ask a question, answer it, and include reasons to support your opinion. Use a graphic organizer like the one above.

Writing Checklist

WORD CHOICE:
- ☑ I used language that will appeal to readers' emotions.

VOICE:
- ☑ My voice was clear and my tone was persuasive.

235

What You Will Learn

Reading

- Vocabulary building: *Literary terms, word study*

- Reading strategy: *Recognize sequence*

- Text type: *Literature (essay, art, and poetry)*

Grammar, Usage, and Mechanics
Noun, pronoun, and possessive adjectives

Writing
Write a review

THE BIG QUESTION

Can we see change as it happens? Changes to our neighborhoods, towns, and cities have a big impact on our personal lives. Sometimes the changes happen rapidly, like when there's a natural disaster. But sometimes the changes happen slowly, and we don't even notice they are happening. In these instances, it helps to know the history of where you live. Then you can contrast the past and the present and identify changes. How much do you know about the history of your neighborhood, town, or city? What changes, large or small, fast or slow, do you know about? Discuss with a partner.

BUILD BACKGROUND

You will read an essay by James Baldwin called "**Harlem: Then and Now**." The essay is about the changes that occurred in this famous New York City neighborhood. In the 1920s, African-American art, literature, dance, and music flourished in Harlem. This cultural movement became known as the Harlem Renaissance. You will also read about Harlem-born artist Faith Ringgold and her painted story quilt, *Tar Beach*, plus two poems by the famous writer Langston Hughes, entitled "**Harlem**" and "**Dreams**."

Row houses in Harlem, New York City ▶

Learn Literary Words

Rhyme is the repetition of sounds. End rhyme occurs when the rhyming words come at the ends of lines, as in the stanza below. Poets use rhyme to give a songlike quality to their poem. Rhyme can also emphasize certain words and ideas.

Literary Words

rhyme
theme

> Go home and write
> a page tonight.
> And let that page come out of you—
> Then, it will be true.
> —*Langston Hughes*

The **theme** is the central idea, or message, of a work of literature. A theme can usually be expressed as a generalization, or general statement, about human beings or about life. The theme is not just a summary of the plot. It is the author's point.

Many common themes can be found in literature, such as love and friendship, revenge, journeys, and courage. Although a theme can be directly stated, it is most often presented indirectly. The reader must figure out the theme by looking carefully at what the author is really trying to say in the work of literature.

Practice  Workbook Page 118

Work with a partner. Take turns reading the following stanzas. Identify the words that rhyme.

> All that we see or seem
> Is but a dream within a dream.
>
> I stand amid the roar
> Of a surf-tormented shore,
> And I hold within my hand,
> Grains of the golden sand
> —*Edgar Allan Poe*

Create four rhyming lines. Write your lines in your notebook.

Learn Academic Words

Study the red words and their meanings. You will find these words useful when talking and writing about literature. Write each word and its meaning in your notebook. After you read "Harlem: Then and Now," *Tar Beach*, "Harlem," and "Dreams," try to use these words to respond to the text.

brief = lasting a short time	➡	We only lived in the city for a **brief** period, and then we moved to a small town.
community = all the people who live in the same area or town	➡	The **community** was full of artists who had moved there from all over the country.
published = printed and sold a book, newspaper, or magazine	➡	Katya **published** her poems when she was only fifteen. The book sold many copies.
residential = referring to a place that is made up of homes, not offices or businesses	➡	Micah lives in a **residential** area. He has to drive many miles to get to work.
section = one part of something	➡	The historic district was the only **section** of the city that was old.

Practice  **Workbook** Page 119

Work with a partner to answer these questions. Try to include the red word in your answer. Write the sentences in your notebook.

1. Have you ever lived in a place for a brief period?
2. What kinds of people live in your community?
3. Have you ever published your writing?
4. Do you live in a residential part of town?
5. Is there a section of your town or city that is old?

▲ A residential community

Word Study: Spelling Long *e*

The text you are going to read contains words with the long *e* sound. The letter *e* stands for different sounds. Short *e* is usually spelled *e*. Long *e* has several different spellings: *ee*, *ea*, *e*, and *y*. Read the examples of each long *e* sound-spelling in the chart below.

ee	ea	e	y
three	beach	me	fifty
sweet	reader	we	city
see	neat	be	happy

Practice

Work with a partner. Copy the chart above into your notebook with blank rows. Take turns reading the words in the box. Write the long *e* words in the correct column.

baby	green	need	mean	she	street	tree
daddy	he	many	real	story	team	week

Workbook Page 120

READING STRATEGY | **RECOGNIZE SEQUENCE**

Recognizing sequence will help you understand what you read. Knowing the sequence or order of events in a text is important because it helps you to understand the order in which things happen. To recognize sequence, follow these steps:

- As you read, look for words the author uses to show sequence. For example, *first, then, next, finally, last, while, during,* and *after.*
- Look for dates and times. For example, *morning, afternoon, yesterday, in 2010.*
- Draw a timeline of the events the author describes.

As you read "Harlem: Then and Now," make a note of the sequence in which the events happen. What happened first? What happened next? What happened last?

Workbook Page 121

Set a purpose for reading Think about the way
Harlem has changed over the years. In what ways does
Harlem's past help us understand Harlem's present?

Harlem: *Then and Now*

James Baldwin

James Baldwin wrote this essay in 1937 at age thirteen.

I wonder how many of us have ever stopped to think what Harlem was
two or three centuries ago? Or how it came to be as it is today? Not many of
us. Most of us know in a vague way that the Dutch lived in Harlem "a long
time ago," and let it go at that. We don't think about how the Indians were
driven out, how the Dutch and English fought, or how finally Harlem grew
into what it is today. Now I am going to tell you a little about this.

Listen:

---

vague, not clear

Seventeenth Century

In 1636, inspired by glowing accounts of Harlem, a Dr. Johannes de la Montagne, his family and a handful of settlers landed at 125th Street and the Harlem River. They landed when Harlem was a wilderness. Nature reigned supreme.

Courageously these people set about making a home out of this wilderness. They chopped down trees, they built their homes, and tried to make something out of the land. It was tough going at first. The houses were hard to heat, the crops refused to grow. They were often cold, hungry, and frightened, a feeling not lessened by the sight of Indians running around in the forest. But they stayed because they couldn't and wouldn't go back.

And one day, in the beginning of Spring, a Dutch housewife discovered a little green shoot growing. 'Look!' she cried. 'Corn is growing!' And it grew. All over, it grew. Farms that before had been thought barren yielded up corn by the bushel. People enlarged their farms, planted more seed. A Danish capitalist, Jochem Pieter, had a farm that extended from 125th to 150th Streets, along the Harlem River. All over people were jubilant. They had nothing to fear. This was "good earth."

But the Indians did not like it. The squeak of cart wheels and swish of scythes warned them that their "happy hunting grounds" would soon be taken away from them.

Eighteenth Century

The eighteenth century found Harlem in English hands. She had been conquered in 1664.

Harlem had improved a great deal. The farms were more pretentious. Many people had slaves. All in all, Harlem was a very proper little village. At that time, of course, Seventh Avenue was a mere dirt road, St. Nicholas Park was old "Breakneck Hill" (a very appropriate title), Mt. Morris Park was "Old Snake Hill" and the place where the family went for picnics. There was no Madison Avenue, no Lenox Avenue, and no tenements. There were no sidewalks, no asphalt streets, no large churches and schools, etc. In fact, the schools were just little one-room buildings.

That was Harlem in the eighteenth century.

---

reigned supreme, ruled everything
barren, not able to grow plants
jubilant, very happy
scythes, farming tools with long curved blades
pretentious, seeming to be important or wealthy
tenements, large buildings divided into apartments

BEFORE YOU GO ON

1 How old was James Baldwin when he wrote this essay?

2 What was life like for the settlers in the 1600s?

On Your Own
Would you be brave enough to make a home in the wilderness?

241

▲ *The Terminal* by Alfred Stieglitz

▲ Street cars on 125th Street by Herbert Gehr

Nineteenth Century

Harlem had changed greatly. Now there were streets, or at least public roads. Seventh Avenue was still dirt, though, and people drove up and down in carriages, and in the winter time in sleighs. Men and women on horseback were a common sight. One hundred and twenty-ninth and one hundred and thirtieth streets were residential sections of stately beauty. There were many very fine mansions throughout the section. Where 131st Street playground is now, there once stood an elegant mansion, only recently torn down. Ere a decade had passed, tenements had sprung up. Smooth, dependable asphalt streets replaced rough, muddy roads, and farms and all that goes with them gradually disappeared.

Twentieth Century

Today, as we all know, Harlem is a large, thickly populated urban community—a city within a city, with fine streets and avenues, parks, playgrounds, churches, schools, apartment houses, theatres, etc.

---

sleighs, vehicles pulled by animals, used for traveling in the snow
ere, before
gradually, slowly

▲ Storefronts on Lenox Avenue by Berenice Abbott

However, there is still great room for improvement. The tenements people were once so proud of are now rather dangerous firetraps and should be rebuilt. There has been some effort on the part of the Housing Authorities to improve them, but as yet they have only operated in a very small field.

Now we, who are interested in Harlem, hope that the future will bring a steady growth and improvement.

✔ **LITERARY CHECK**
What is the author's theme, or message, here?

---

firetraps, buildings that would be hard to escape from if they were on fire
steady, even; stable

ABOUT THE **AUTHOR**

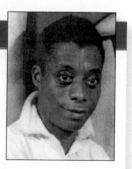

James Baldwin (1924–1987) was a famous novelist and essayist. He was born in the Harlem neighborhood of New York City. Baldwin became one of the most influential American writers of the twentieth century. He is best known for his novel *Go Tell It on the Mountain*. In addition to being a writer, Baldwin was also a civil rights activist and humanitarian.

BEFORE YOU GO ON

1. What replaced the muddy roads in the nineteenth century?

2. Why does the author suggest that the tenements be rebuilt?

💡 **On Your Own**
What city's history would you like to know more about?

Tar Beach

Faith Ringgold is best known for her painted story quilts—art that combines painting, quilted fabric, and storytelling. Her great-great-great-grandmother was a Southern slave who made quilts for plantation owners. So, for Ringgold, quilt-making represents a strong connection between art and her family history. A story quilt is a traditional American craft that also has roots in African culture. *Tar Beach* shows the heroine and narrator Cassie Louise Lightfoot on a summer night in Harlem. "Sleeping on Tar Beach was magical . . .," explains Cassie in the text on the quilt. "Only eight years old and in the third grade and I can fly. That means I am free to go wherever I want to for the rest of my life." For Ringgold, this fantastic flight through the urban night sky symbolizes the potential for freedom and self-possession. "My women," Ringgold has said, "are actually flying. They are just free, totally . . ."

---

quilts, blankets with designs
magical, enjoyable and exciting in a strange way
potential, possibility
self-possession, confidence about one's self

▲ *Tar Beach* (Part I from the *Woman on a Bridge* series), 1988. Acrylic on canvas bordered with printed, painted, quilted, and pieced cloth

ABOUT THE ARTIST

Faith Ringgold was born in Harlem. She began her career in the 1960s as a painter. She has exhibited in major museums throughout the world. She wrote and illustrated many children's books and received numerous awards and honors in addition to many honorary doctorates. Faith Ringgold is a professor of art at the University of California in San Diego.

HaRLeM

What happens to a dream deferred?

Does it dry up
like a raisin in the sun?
Or fester like a sore—
And then run?
Does it stink like rotten meat?
Or crust and sugar over—
like a syrupy sweet?

Maybe it just sags
like a heavy load.

Or does it explode?
                    —Langston Hughes

---

deferred, delayed until a later time
fester, become infected

✔ **LITERARY CHECK**
*Which words **rhyme**
in this poem?*

Dreams

Hold fast to dreams
For if dreams die
Life is a broken-winged bird
That cannot fly.

Hold fast to dreams
For when dreams go
Life is a barren field
Frozen with snow.
                    —Langston Hughes

---

fast, close; near

ABOUT THE **POET**

Langston Hughes (1902–1967) was best
known as a Harlem Renaissance poet,
but he was also a novelist, columnist,
playwright, and essayist. Through his work,
he promoted equality, spoke against racism,
and celebrated African-American culture.

BEFORE YOU GO ON

1 What does flying
mean to Faith
Ringgold's heroine?

2 Why does
Langston Hughes
tell us to "hold fast
to dreams"?

On Your Own
Why do you think
it is important to
have dreams?

245

DRAMATIC READING

One of the best ways to understand the emotional impact of a poem is to learn it by heart, or memorize it. Work with a partner to reread, discuss, and interpret "Harlem" and "Dreams." Describe what you visualize as you read the poems line by line. Identify any rhyme pattern you find. Discuss the theme of the poems and the images the words create in your mind. Work together to interpret any difficult words or phrasing, and which words to stress.

After you and your partner have reread and examined the poems carefully, choose one to memorize. Then recite the poems to each other. Comment on each other's oral reading and make helpful suggestions for improvements. Then recite the poem for the class.

> ∫》 *Speaking* TIP
>
> Have some passion in your voice. If you care about what you're saying, people will be more interested in listening to you.

COMPREHENSION

Workbook
Page 122

Right There

1. What was Harlem like when Dr. Johannes de la Montagne and his family landed?

2. Where was Jochem Pieter's farm?

Think and Search

3. Why are story quilts important to Faith Ringgold?

4. What similes does Langston Hughes use to describe a "dream deferred"?

Author and You

5. Why does James Baldwin call Harlem in the twentieth century a "city within a city"?

6. Why do you think Faith Ringgold called her quilt *Tar Beach*?

On Your Own

7. In your opinion, what makes a particular neighborhood a good place to live?

8. If you created a picture of your community, what would you include?

DISCUSSION

Discuss in pairs or small groups.

1. Why did settlers come to Harlem?

2. How would you describe the changes to Harlem over the three centuries?

3. If you could live in Harlem during any century, which century would you like to live in? Explain.

Q **Can we see change as it happens?** We may not notice changes in our community when we look at it from day to day. But when we compare our community year to year, or century to century, the changes are easier to see. Why is it valuable to know how a place has changed over the years? Will it help prepare us for changes to come?

Listening TIP

Listen for supporting details and reasons. Ask yourself, "Did the speaker explain why these ideas are important?"

RESPONSE TO LITERATURE

Workbook
Page 122

What dreams do you have? Have any of your dreams come true? Have you ever dreamed that you could fly? Write a poem or make a picture about a dream you had. Try to include rhyming words in the poem.

▲ Detail from *Tar Beach*

Grammar and Writing

Nouns, Pronouns, and Possessive Adjectives

Possessive adjectives are used with nouns or pronouns to show possession or ownership. A possessive adjective must agree with the noun or pronoun it refers to. Read the examples below.

Pronoun	Possessive Adjective	Example Sentence
I	my	**I** am going to tell you something about **my** neighborhood, Harlem.
you	your	How much do **you** know about **your** city?
he	his	Dr. Johannes de la Montagne traveled to Harlem. **He** and **his** family landed at 125th Street.
she	her	A Dutch housewife discovered a little green shoot growing in **her** field. **She** cried, "Corn is growing!"
it	its	A Danish capitalist had a farm. **It** stretched from 125th to 150th. **Its** soil was "good earth."
we	our	The residents said, "**We** hope that the future will bring improvements to **our** city."
you	your	**You** should all learn more about **your** hometowns.
they	their	These people set about making a home. **They** chopped down trees and built **their** homes.

Practice

Copy the sentences below into your notebook. Complete each sentence using the correct pronoun or possessive adjective from the chart above.

1. James Baldwin wrote the essay for _____ school newspaper.
2. The Indians were driven out of _____ land.
3. How did Harlem grow into what _____ is today?
4. The people were often cold and hungry, but _____ wouldn't go back.
5. Corn grew where _____ had never grown before.
6. To learn more about Harlem, you can ask _____ teacher.

WRITING A PERSUASIVE PARAGRAPH

Write a Review

A common form of persuasive writing is a review. In a review, the writer states his or her opinion of a book, play, or film. The writer's purpose is to make a recommendation to the reader, either to seek out the work or to avoid it. The writer's recommendation should be clearly stated and backed up with reasons. Also, in order to persuade the reader, the writer must include supporting details.

Here is a model of a book review. The supporting details that the writer includes show us that he has given the book serious thought. He used a graphic organizer to help organize his ideas.

Recommendation

Reason	Reason

Lukas Arbogast

Animal Poems by Langston Hughes

Do you like animals? If so, you won't want to miss this book. In <u>The Sweet and Sour Animal Book</u>, Langston Hughes has written animal poems to match each letter of the alphabet — from ape to zebra. This is sold as a children's book. However, the poems in the book are different from what you would expect. The rhymes are short and simple, but they make you think. They are both fun and serious at the same time (I guess that may be why he calls them "sweet and sour"). Another wonderful feature of this book is the fantastic artwork. The sculptures that illustrate the text were made by the children at the Harlem School of the Arts. Since Langston Hughes loved Harlem, that would have made him happy.

The Sweet and Sour Animal Book

Langston Hughes

Practice

Workbook
Page 124

Write a review of a book you have read. It can be a book you liked or disliked. State your recommendation clearly. Back up your recommendation with reasons. Include details from the text to show that you have given the book serious thought. Be sure that your nouns, pronouns, and possessive adjectives agree in person, gender, and number, and use a graphic organizer to help organize your ideas.

Writing Checklist

IDEAS:
- ☑ I included ideas and details that demonstrate my knowledge of the topic.

CONVENTIONS:
- ☑ I checked my work for errors in spelling and punctuation.

Link the Readings

Critical Thinking

Look back at the readings in this unit. Think about what they have in common. They all tell about change. Yet they do not all have the same purpose. The purpose of one reading might be to inform, while the purpose of another might be to entertain or persuade. In addition, the content of each reading relates to change differently. Now copy the chart below into your notebook and complete it.

Title of Reading	Purpose	Big Question Link
"Changing Earth"	*to inform*	
"The Intersection"		*It describes how a neighborhood changed over 100 years.*
From *Through My Eyes*		
"Harlem: Then and Now" *Tar Beach* "Harlem" and "Dreams"		

Discussion

Discuss in pairs or small groups.

- Compare and contrast "The Intersection" and "Harlem." How are the themes of these selections similar? What makes them different?

- **Q Can we see change as it happens?** Think about the readings. Why is it important to be aware of the changes going on around us? What can we do to prepare ourselves for change, or the consequences of change?

Fluency Check

Work with a partner. Choose a paragraph from one of the readings. Take turns reading it for one minute. Count the total number of words you read. Practice saying the words you had trouble reading. Take turns reading the paragraph three more times. Did you read more words each time? Copy the chart below into your notebook and record your speeds.

	1st Speed	2nd Speed	3rd Speed	4th Speed
Words Per Minute				

Projects

Work in pairs or small groups. Choose one of these projects.

1 Write a poem about a place that is special to you. Use rhyme, if possible. Then read your poem to the class.

2 List the things that you think are changing, have changed, or need to change in your community. Make a poster to show what you predict your community will be like in the future. Then share your poster with the class.

3 What do you think Ruby Bridges and her parents discussed at home after her first day at William Frantz Public School? Write a dialogue and practice it. Then perform it for the class.

4 Look in your local newspaper and choose a letter to the editor. Do you agree with the writer's argument? Write a response to the writer in which you explain why you agree or disagree. Then read your response to the class.

Further Reading

To find out more about the theme of this unit, choose from these reading suggestions.

The Amazon Rainforest, Bernard Smith
There are more kinds of animals and plants in the rainforest than anywhere else on Earth. This Penguin Reader® describes the changing rainforest and how those changes can affect the world we live in.

"The Battle of the Giants" from Tales of the Greek Heroes, Roger Green
Earth made the giants and hid them away in caves in Greece. Now they are strong enough to attack the immortals. Zeus calls upon Heracles, his son, and the great battle begins. Who will win in the epic struggle for power? And what will the world be like after the battle?

Walking on the Boundaries of Courage, Sara Holbrook
These poems are about the problems young people struggle with as they change and their worlds change. The poems focus on difficult choices, new experiences, and the search for what is true.

Put It All Together

LISTENING & SPEAKING WORKSHOP

Speech

You will give a persuasive speech about a change that people need to make.

1 THINK ABOUT IT Talk about "Changing Earth" with a small group. Review the topics covered in that reading.

As a group, discuss what you think the future will be like. Work together to develop a list of topics about things we must change if we want our communities and the world to be healthy in the future. For example:

- We must develop alternative energy sources.
- We must use solar power more.
- We must make sure people don't impact the environment in a bad way.

2 GATHER AND ORGANIZE INFORMATION Choose a topic from your group's list. Think about why this change is important and how you can persuade people to make it. Write down your ideas.

Research Find out all you can about your topic. Go to the library or search the Internet to find information on your topic. Take notes on what you discover.

Order Your Notes Use note cards to record the points you want to make. Put your note cards in the sequence in which you want to present them. Make sure your point of view and reasons for it are clearly stated and well supported with facts and examples.

Use Visuals If possible, find photographs to support your argument. Or create a diagram to illustrate one of your points. Your photographs or diagram should be big enough for everyone to see them easily.

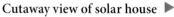

Cutaway view of solar house ▶

3 **PRACTICE AND PRESENT** Use your note cards as the written outline for your speech. You may want to practice standing in front of a podium with your note cards laid out in front of you. Glance at them as you need them, but try to look up, so that you will be able to make eye contact with the audience.

Deliver Your Speech Speak clearly. Take your time, and give special emphasis to your main points. Show your visuals at appropriate times, being careful not to hide behind or face them while speaking. Support your opinion with facts, examples, and details.

4 **EVALUATE THE PRESENTATION** You will improve your skills as a speaker and a listener by evaluating each speech you give and hear. Use this checklist to help you judge your speech and the speeches of your classmates.

- ☑ Were the speaker's topic and point of view clearly stated?
- ☑ Did the speaker use emotion to help persuade the audience?
- ☑ Did the speaker go too fast or too slow, talk too loud or too low?
- ☑ Did the speaker support his or her opinions with facts and details?
- ☑ What suggestions do you have for improving the speech?

 Speaking TIPS

Use both facts and emotion to persuade your audience. Ask your listeners for feedback. Did they understand that the topic was important to you?

Number your note cards, and highlight key points you want to remember.

 Listening TIP

Listen to the speaker's reasons for his or her opinion. Then think about the opposite point of view. What reasons could support that opinion? Which opinion is best supported by the evidence? Make your own decision.

WRITING WORKSHOP

Persuasive Essay

In this workshop you will write a persuasive essay. In a persuasive essay, the writer tries to convince readers to agree with a certain opinion or belief. Sometimes, the writer asks readers to take action on the basis of that opinion or belief. A good persuasive essay begins with an introductory paragraph that states the writer's opinion. The essay includes facts, details, and examples that support the writer's opinion in each paragraph. Opposing arguments are identified and answered. A concluding paragraph restates the writer's opinion in a new and appealing way. Throughout the essay, the writer uses strong, persuasive words to stir readers' feelings.

Your assignment for this workshop is to write a five-paragraph essay that tries to persuade readers to agree with your opinion about a topic.

1 **PREWRITE** Choose an issue that you care about in your school or community. Then make a word web with your topic in the center. Around your topic, write words that tell why you care about this issue. Include words that you think might stir the feelings of your audience.

List and Organize Ideas and Details Use a T-chart to organize your ideas and to anticipate possible opposing arguments. On the left side of your chart, write *For*. On the right side of your chart, write *Against*. A student named Justine decided to write a persuasive essay about the importance of volunteering. Here is the T-chart she created:

For	*Against*
Important to give to others *Helps the community* *Have fun and learn a lot*	*Hard to find right place to volunteer* *Nervous about responsibility*

2 **DRAFT** Use the model on page 257 and your T-chart to help you write a first draft. Remember to state your opinion clearly in the first paragraph and to identify and answer possible arguments against your position in your essay.

254

3 REVISE Read over your draft. As you do so, ask yourself the questions in the writing checklist. Use the questions to help you revise your essay.

SIX TRAITS OF WRITING CHECKLIST

☑ **IDEAS:** Is my opinion stated clearly?

☑ **ORGANIZATION:** Are my facts, details, and examples presented in an order that makes sense?

☑ **VOICE:** Does my writing express my feelings about the issue?

☑ **WORD CHOICE:** Do I include words that will stir my readers' feelings?

☑ **SENTENCE FLUENCY:** Do my sentences flow smoothly?

☑ **CONVENTIONS:** Does my writing follow the rules of grammar, usage, and mechanics?

Here are the changes Justine plans to make when she revises her first draft:

An Important Gift

Volunteering is an important activity, and I am glad *thankful* that so many

people do it. I also want to urge everyone to volunteer who can

possibly find the time. Your school and community need you. You

~~are~~ *will* not only *be* helping others, you ~~are~~ *will* also *be* having fun and learning

something in the process.

Why is volunteering so important? Some *individuals and* organizations need extra

help, but can't afford to hire someone. other organizations, such as

school clubs, are run entirely by volunteers. Without volunteers to

help out, many jobs would not get done.

Don't worry about finding a place to volunteer! There are lots of ^great places that could use your ~~help~~ ^assistance. Here's one example: Guiding eyes for the blind has a program where you take home two or three puppies for a few days to socialize them. Home socializing involves playing with the puppies and encouraging them to be friendly with people and other dogs. Who wouldn't want a job that not only involves playing with puppies, but benefits people with disabilities? Through these activities, you help prepare the puppies for possibly becoming seeing-eye dogs.

Of course, you might feel nervous about the responsibility of volunteering. However, once you find a place where you want to volunteer, people ~~are~~ ^will be there to show you how to do your job. ^And believe me: Whatever time and effort you can give will be very much appreciated.

In conclusion, volunteers make a ^huge contribution to any community. Wouldn't you like the satisfaction of knowing that you ^have made a difference? By volunteering, we can help others, learn a lot about ourselves and feel ~~good~~ ^happy about doing a good job.

4 **EDIT AND PROOFREAD**  Workbook Page 125

Copy your revised draft onto a clean sheet of paper. Read it again. Correct any errors in grammar, word usage, mechanics, and spelling. Here are the additional changes Justine plans to make when she prepares her final draft.

Justine Kefauver

An Important Gift

Volunteering is an important activity, and I am thankful that so many people do it. I also want to urge everyone to volunteer who can possibly find the time. Your school and community need you. You will not only be helping others, you will also be having fun and learning something in the process.

Why is volunteering so important? Some individuals and organizations need extra help, but can't afford to hire someone. other organizations, such as school clubs, are run entirely by volunteers. Without volunteers to help out, many jobs would not get done.

Don't worry about finding a place to volunteer! There are lots of great places that could use your assistance. Here's one example: Guiding Eyes for the Blind has a program where you take home two or three puppies for a few days to socialize them. Home socializing involves playing with the puppies and encouraging them to be friendly with people and other dogs. Through these activities, you help prepare the puppies for possibly becoming seeing-eye dogs. Who wouldn't want a job that not only involves playing with puppies, but also benefits people with disabilities?

Of course, you might feel nervous about the responsibility of volunteering. However, once you find a place where you want to volunteer, people will be there to show you how to do your job. And believe me: whatever time and effort you can give will be very much appreciated.

In conclusion, volunteers make a huge contribution to any community. Wouldn't you like the satisfaction of knowing that you have made a difference? By volunteering, we can help others, learn a lot about ourselves and feel happy about doing a good job.

5 PUBLISH Prepare your final draft. Share your essay with your teacher and classmates.

Workbook
Page 126

Learn about Art with the

Smithsonian American Art Museum

Moving Through Time

*O*ur world changes all the time. The sun moves across the sky and sets. *Another day ends. The seasons change. Soon another year has gone by. Artists have always been interested in our changing world. They work to capture the change in light at sunset, or the way a street or a family looks over a number of years. If we look at a photograph of a family from 1900, for example, we would probably notice their clothes. They are very different from the clothes we wear today. By capturing these details, the artist makes a record.*

Eadweard Muybridge, *Animal Locomotion (Woman Lifting a Basket, Waving a Handkerchief)* (1887)

Today it may seem strange that Eadweard Muybridge wanted to take photographs of everyday events. But in 1887 there were no movies or television. To make *Animal Locomotion*, Muybridge used more than one camera. Each time the woman moved, one of these cameras would take a picture. Muybridge then cut and pasted the pictures onto a moving circular reel. When a person moved the reel in a circle, the pictures would blend together in what looked like a moving picture. This was the first "movie."

With his cameras, Muybridge did more than just make a record of a woman lifting a basket and waving a handkerchief. He changed the way people saw their world. Other artists began to rethink the way they painted people in motion. In time, Muybridge's work would lead to the beginnings of the movie industry as we know it today.

▲ Eadweard Muybridge, *Animal Locomotion (Woman Lifting a Basket, Waving a Handkerchief)*, 1887, collotype, 12⅞ × 9⅞ in., Smithsonian American Art Museum

258

Helen Lundeberg, *Double Portrait of the Artist in Time* (1935)

Many adults save baby portraits of themselves. In *Double Portrait of the Artist in Time*, Helen Lundeberg used a photograph of herself as a child to make the image of the child in the center of this painting. Normally, an adult would have a photograph of herself as a child in an album or in a frame on the wall. But Lundeberg decided to include an image of the *adult* the child would become in a frame on the wall instead.

The child sits with a budding flower. The flower is a symbol of her youth. The woman in the painting has had more life experience. She holds a bold red flower and stares into an empty box. The shadow that stretches between the child and the woman shows the ties between the past and future in a person.

▲ Helen Lundeberg, *Double Portrait of the Artist in Time*, 1935, oil, 47¾ x 40 in., Smithsonian American Art Museum

Both of these artworks try to capture changing time. Muybridge captures "moments" that happen over minutes. Lundeberg's work looks at the passage of years.

Apply What You Learned

1 How is the idea of time important in these artworks?

2 What kind of artwork would you create to show movement through time?

Big Question
How would you show in an artwork that you have changed as you've grown up?

Workbook
Pages 127–128

UNIT 5

THE BIG QUESTION

Why do we explore new frontiers?

This unit is about the North American frontier. A frontier is an area of land where people are just beginning to explore. You will read about the history of the United States and how and why people explore new lands. Reading, writing, and talking about these ideas will give you practice using academic language and help you become a better student.

READING 1: **Novel Excerpt, Song, and Poetry**
- From *River to Tomorrow* by Ellen Levine
- "River Song" by Bill Staines
- "Morning Prayer Song" by Ronald Snake Edmo

READING 2: **Social Studies Article**
- "Maps and Compasses"

READING 3: **Social Studies Article**
- "The Cowboy Era"

READING 4: **Tall Tale Excerpt**
- From *Pecos Bill: The Greatest Cowboy of All Time* by James Cloyd Bowman

Listening and Speaking

At the end of this unit, you will make a **group presentation**. You will describe life on the American frontier.

Writing

In this unit you will write an **expository essay**. After each reading, you will learn a skill to help you write an expository essay. At the end of this unit, you will use these skills to write an instructional essay.

QuickWrite
Write instructions telling how you get to school every day. Make a map.

Visit *LongmanKeystone.com*

What You Will Learn

Reading

- Vocabulary building: *Literary terms, word study*

- Reading strategy: *Make generalizations*

- Text type: *Literature (novel excerpt, song, poetry)*

Grammar, Usage, and Mechanics

The past perfect and the simple past

Writing

Write a cause-and-effect paragraph

THE BIG QUESTION

Why do we explore new frontiers? Rivers are all around us. They move water from the mountains to the ocean. Some rivers are very small and others are very large. What role do rivers play in our exploration of new frontiers?

BUILD BACKGROUND

In the nineteenth century, people explored and settled the southern and western parts of North America. The excerpt you will read from ***River to Tomorrow*** tells about Sacagawea, a young Native American woman who helped the early explorers Meriwether Lewis and William Clark. In 1803, the United States purchased the Louisiana Territory from France. President Thomas Jefferson asked Lewis and Clark to explore this unknown land and find a water route to the Pacific Ocean. Although they did not find a water route, they learned a lot about the continent and Native American cultures. They also drew detailed maps of the area.

"River Song" and **"Morning Prayer Song"** share the theme of exploring nature.

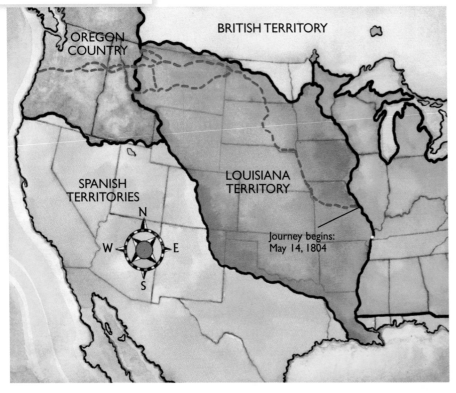

BRITISH TERRITORY

OREGON COUNTRY

SPANISH TERRITORIES

LOUISIANA TERRITORY

N
W — E
S

Journey begins: May 14, 1804

◀ Lewis and Clark's route

VOCABULARY

Learn Literary Words

Dialogue is a conversation between characters. It reveals character traits and it advances the action or plot in a story. Dialogue shows the speaker's exact words and is usually enclosed in quotation marks (" ").

Literary Words

dialogue
flashback

Plot is the sequence of events that happen in a story. These events can be presented in chronological, or time, order. Sometimes, they may be told through flashbacks. A **flashback** is a scene from the past that interrupts the sequence of events. Flashbacks show a character's memories, dreams, or accounts of past events. Read the flashback below. What does it tell you about the woman?

The woman stopped at the river's edge, hesitant to wade across. She saw herself as a young girl and remembered that she was nearly swept away by this river. She felt powerless against it. However, as she watched her friends safely cross, she put her dreadful memory aside and proceeded across the river.

Practice

Workbook Page 129

Work with a partner. Take turns reading the dialogue below from *River to Tomorrow* between the chief of the Shoshone, a Native American tribe, and Meriwether Lewis. What does the conversation tell you about the characters? How does the dialogue advance the action of the story?

"The Shoshone people have herds of horses," the chief answered. "They might be willing to trade." He paused. "And the Frenchman's wife is Shoshone," he said, pointing to Sacagawea.

With excitement in his voice, Lewis turned to Clark. "She will be important to us. When they see her, maybe the Shoshone will be more willing to trade with us!"

Learn Academic Words

Study the **red** words and their meanings. You will find these words useful when talking and writing about literature. Write each word and its meaning in your notebook. After you read the excerpt from *River to Tomorrow*, try to use these words to respond to the text.

accompany = go somewhere with someone	➡	He wanted to **accompany** the hikers on a walk through the woods.
assist = help	➡	The guide had to **assist** the travelers when they lost their way.
goal = something you want to do in the future	➡	The **goal** of the explorer's mission was to find a route to the ocean.
interpreter = someone who translates the spoken words in one language into another language	➡	The **interpreter** translated the conversation from French to English.
locate = find the exact position	➡	It was difficult to **locate** the lake because it was hidden behind some trees.

Practice
Workbook Page 130

Work with a partner to answer these questions. Try to include the **red** word in your answer. Write the sentences in your notebook.

1. Who should **accompany** students on field trips?
2. How can students **assist** one another at school?
3. What is the **goal** of a runner in a race?
4. Why is the work of an **interpreter** important?
5. What tool can help you **locate** north, south, east, and west on a map?

Sacagawea ▶

Word Study: Synonyms

Synonyms are words with the same meaning or almost the same meaning as another word. Many words in English have synonyms. A thesaurus is a reference tool that provides synonyms.

Word	Synonym
explore	search
assist	help

Writers often choose one synonym over another to express a certain feeling. For example, *travel* means to take a trip, but the synonym *trek* has a slightly different and more specific meaning. *Trek* means to make a long and difficult trip on foot. The word *trek* gives you more information about what is happening.

Practice  Workbook Page 131

Work with a partner. Copy the chart below into your notebook. Use a thesaurus to find a synonym for each word. Then write a sentence using the synonym.

	Synonym	Sentence
people		
enemy		
interpret		

READING STRATEGY   MAKE GENERALIZATIONS

Making generalizations helps you form opinions and understand the information that is in a text. A generalization is a statement that can apply to many examples. Here is a generalization: *Many people are honest.* To make generalizations, follow these steps:

- Look for big statements that the author makes.
- Look for examples that support the statement.
- Use what you already know from your own experience.

As you read *River to Tomorrow*, think about what you already know about Native American culture. Then look for sentences that support the statements the author makes. Make generalizations about the topic.

 Workbook Page 132

Set a purpose for reading What reasons can you find for why Sacagawea wanted to travel with Lewis and Clark?

from

River to Tomorrow

Ellen Levine

On their journey west, Meriwether Lewis and William Clark and their "Corps of Discovery" met Sacagawea. Sacagawea was a young Native American woman from the Shoshone tribe who joined Lewis and Clark and acted as their interpreter. This excerpt starts with a conversation between Captain Clark and Sacagawea.

"Quick!" said Captain Clark to his aide. "Bring the Indian woman." George Drewyer ran through the brush to the clearing at the river's edge.

"Sacagawea . . . over here!" he motioned. Sacagawea followed Drewyer through the brush.

"Could your people have camped here?" Captain Clark asked.

"I am not certain," she said slowly, walking the distance between the ash piles. "Perhaps." Five winters had passed since she had been kidnapped from her people. "Perhaps," she repeated.

John Shields, another of Clark's men, asked, "What do you make of this, sir? I found it by a log at the edge of the clearing." He handed a well-worn moccasin to Clark. The captain looked at it and passed it to Sacagawea.

---

corps, group of people who do a particular job
Indian, Native American
brush, small bushes and trees
clearing, area of forest without trees
ash piles, powder left from burned-out
   campfires
make of this, think this is

This time there was no question. "No," she said firmly. Her people did not stitch this way. This was definitely not a Shoshone moccasin.

She turned back to the river. Sadness filled her. Perhaps these white men would never find her people. And if they did, would there be anyone left who knew her? Her mother and many others had been killed in the Minnetaree enemy raid five winters ago. The Minnetaree had taken her to live in a village far away in the east.

For so many winters, so many summers, Sacagawea had thought about tomorrow. *Tomorrow* everything would be better, she told herself. At first she had thought about escaping. Then the Minnetaree warrior who had captured her lost her in a gambling game to a French-Canadian trader named Charbonneau. He took her as one of his wives. That's when Sacagawea stopped thinking about tomorrow. That's when she gave up hope of ever seeing her people again.

Then one day some white men had come to the Minnetaree village in long boats. They came, they said, with orders from the white Chief of the United States. They planned to travel up the great river until they reached the Shining Mountains where the snow never melted. They would cross the mountains and travel down another river to the Great Stinking Lake the whites called the Pacific Ocean.

---

stitch, sew
captured, took as prisoner

✔ **LITERARY CHECK**
*What did Sacagawea recall in this **flashback**?*

BEFORE YOU GO ON

1 How does Sacagawea know that the moccasin is not Shoshone?

2 When was Sacagawea kidnapped?

On Your Own
What were Sacagawea's duties on the journey?

267

The captains had hired Charbonneau as an interpreter. When Charbonneau told Sacagawea about the trip, she had turned away. Her heart had pounded so loudly, she was certain he would see and hear it. The Shining Mountains, he had said. They were her mountains! And her people were there.

Several nights later, she had stood with Charbonneau in the Minnetaree chief's lodge, listening to the white men talk about their trip.

"The Missouri River will take us to the Rocky Mountains," Captain Clark had said, as the chief drew a map in the dust.

"This is where the waters flow to the setting sun." The chief pointed as he drew the line of another river to the ocean.

"We must have horses for the portage across the mountains from the Missouri to the Columbia River," Captain Lewis said. "We cannot get across on foot with all our supplies."

"The Shoshone people have herds of horses," the chief answered. "They might be willing to trade." He paused. "And the Frenchman's wife is Shoshone," he said, pointing to Sacagawea.

With excitement in his voice, Lewis turned to Clark. "She will be important to us. When they see her, maybe the Shoshone will be more willing to trade with us!"

And so Sacagawea, her two-month-old baby, Pomp, and Charbonneau joined thirty others in the Lewis and Clark expedition to the Pacific. That had been in the spring.

---

lodge, Native American home
portage, act of carrying boats and canoes
    overland from one river to another

It was midsummer now, and the canoes and flat-bottomed boats had traveled upriver for many miles. Some days the men rowed, or even put up a sail if the wind was right. Often they walked along the shoreline, pulling long ropes attached to the bow.

The men had blistered and cut their feet on the sharp stones on the river bottom. They ached from the piercing prickly pear thorns that tore their clothes and flesh. They had lost supplies and canoes crossing treacherous rapids. They had faced rattlesnakes and grizzly bears, and still they traveled on.

The canoes traveled upriver. Then the men stopped to hunt for food. As the group walked to a clearing on shore, Sacagawea gasped and pointed to a grove of pine trees. The bark had been stripped from many of them.

"My people," she said. "They have been here."

"How do you know?" asked Captain Clark, as the men gathered around.

"When food is scarce, we eat the soft wood under the bark. It is filling," she said as she touched the torn edge.

They traveled on through the hot day. Sacagawea felt a nervous excitement. She scanned the riverbank.

Suddenly, she motioned to the bank. "I have been here! We used that white earth for paint. The place where the water parts in three is not far!"

---

bow, front of the boat
blistered, wounded, or hurt, by continual rubbing
treacherous rapids, dangerous part of a river where water moves quickly
grove, small group of trees that are close together
scanned, quickly looked at

✔ LITERARY CHECK

What surprising thing did Sacagawea see that led to this dialogue?

BEFORE YOU GO ON

1 Who did Lewis and Clark hire as an interpreter?

2 What do the explorers need in order to cross the mountains?

💡 **On Your Own**
What do you think might happen next?

269

That night she told Captain Clark that her people often camped at the three forks. It was there that she had been kidnapped by the Minnetarees.

Captain Lewis immediately planned a search party. "We *must* find the Shoshone and get horses before the snows close the mountain passes. Everything depends on it," he said.

Sacagawea explained to Captain Lewis the Shoshone signs of peace. "Hold a blanket this way," she said, gripping two corners. Then she flung it over her head and down to the ground. "Three times you must do this. Then my people will know that you come in friendship."

A few days later, Captain Lewis set off on foot with Drewyer and three other men in search of Sacagawea's people. Captain Clark remained with the others, and they continued their struggle up the river in the boats.

To lighten the boat load, one day Sacagawea walked on the shore carrying Pomp. Suddenly, a small cloud of dust rose ahead.

A group of riders swept down to the river's edge. Sacagawea quickly scanned their faces. Their clothes and riding ways had told her they were Shoshone, but she recognized no one except Drewyer, who had ridden back with the warriors.

"The Indians feared Captain Lewis was setting a trap for them," Drewyer told Captain Clark.

---

search party, group of people who look for someone
depends on, is affected by
struggle, difficult effort
setting a trap, trying to catch a person or an animal

"But we were coming with supplies," said Clark.

"Yes, but not everyone believed that," answered Drewyer.

When they reached the camp, the Shoshone were gathered at the edge of the lodges. An old woman pointed at Sacagawea.

The chief of the Shoshone, standing next to Captain Lewis, stepped forward to greet Captain Clark. Then he led the two men and a group of Shoshone into a tent where they sat around a grass circle. The chief lit a long-stemmed pipe. He pointed the stem to the four corners of the earth, then to the sky and the earth below. He took three puffs and repeated the ceremony three times. Then he passed the pipe around to the group.

Drewyer explained in sign language that the Shoshone woman with them would act as interpreter. Captain Lewis then sent Drewyer to get Sacagawea. She came into the tent and sat near the captains. She scarcely looked at anyone.

The chief began to speak. Sacagawea slowly looked up. She paid no attention to the words. All she could hear was the tone, the voice, the way the man spoke. She leaned forward. The chief gestured as he spoke. She knew that gesture. She knew that voice. She swayed forward and caught herself before she fell. Then she leapt up and ran to him. She took the blanket from off her shoulders and threw it around him.

"Cameahwait! Cameahwait!" Tears ran down her cheeks as she hugged her brother. He, too, wept. Then, straightening up, he placed his hands on her shoulders.

"We must hear what the white men have to say, little sister," he said in a low voice. "Later we will talk."

Sacagawea returned to her seat. She was filled with a peace. She sang a silent song to the river, for the river had brought her home. The river had brought her tomorrow.

---

sign language, communication using signs, such as hand movements
gestured, used hands, head, or arms to communicate without words

ABOUT THE **AUTHOR**

Ellen Levine enjoys writing fiction, but she is best known for her nonfiction books for young readers. She also enjoys telling students about different ways to get interesting information. She wants students to understand that research can be exciting. Ellen Levine lives in New York City and Salem, New York.

BEFORE YOU GO ON

1 What place does Sacagawea recognize?

2 How does Sacagawea feel at the end of the story? Why?

On Your Own
What do you think it takes to explore new frontiers? Explain.

271

River Song

I was born in the path of the winter wind
And raised where the mountains are old.
Their springtime waters came dancing
   down:
I remember the tales they told.

The whistling ways of my younger days
Too quickly have faded on by,
But all of their memories linger on
Like the light in a fading sky.

Chorus:
River, take me along,
In your sunshine sing me your song.
Ever moving and winding and free,
You rolling old river,
You changing old river,
Let's you and me, river,
Run down to the sea.

I've been to the city and back again;
I've been moved by some things that I've
   learned,

Met a lot of good people, and I've called
   them friends,
Felt the change when the seasons turned.
I've heard all the songs that the children sing
And listened to love's melodies;
I've felt my own music within me rise
Like the wind in the autumn trees.

[Repeat Chorus]

Someday when the flowers are
   blooming still,
Someday when the grass is still green,
My rolling waters will round the bend
And flow into the open sea.

So here's to the rainbow that's followed
   me here,
And here's to the friends that I know,
And here's to the song that's within me now:
I will sing it where'er I go.

[Repeat Chorus]

—*Bill Staines*

---

winding, turning and twisting

melodies, songs or tunes
blooming, opening

ABOUT THE **ARTIST**

Bill Staines is a songwriter and folk singer from New England who has traveled across North America singing his songs. He has made twenty-two albums, and many famous artists have recorded his songs. Staines has appeared on radio and television and won a national yodeling contest.

Morning Prayer Song

I face the rising sun,
Good morning, Grandfather Spirit.
All is well.

I face South,
Grandfather Spirit, look kindly on our Elders.
Protect our children.

I face West,
Grandfather Spirit, warm our Mother Earth.

I face North,
Grandfather Spirit, walk with our people today.

I touch the earth,
Mother Earth, bring life to us.
All is well.
—*Ronald Snake Edmo*

ABOUT THE **POET**

Ronald Snake Edmo is a poet and the author of *Spirit Rider: A Collection of Contemporary Poetry in the Shoshoni Language.* He is a Tribal Elder of the Shoshone-Bannock Tribes. Edmo is a war veteran and received a degree in anthropology in 2001. He currently lives on the Fort Hall Indian Reservation in Idaho.

BEFORE YOU GO ON

1 What does "River Song" compare memories to?

2 Where will the river in "River Song" eventually end?

On Your Own
In which direction does the sun rise? In which direction does the sun set?

Review and Practice

DRAMATIC READING

One of the best ways to understand characters in a story is to think about their dialogue. Work in groups to reread, discuss, and interpret the dialogue in the excerpt from *River to Tomorrow*. Discuss what the dialogue tells you about the characters. Work together to interpret any difficult words or phrasing. Use a dictionary or ask your teacher to help if needed.

After your group has reread and examined the story carefully, assign the roles of Sacagawea, Captain Clark, the Minnetaree chief, Cameahwait, Captain Lewis, Drewyer, and John Shields. Have one student act as a narrator and read all the lines that are not in quotations. Choose several pages from the story to read aloud, giving emotion to the dialogue as if it were a play. Practice reading aloud several times, then perform your "play" for the class.

🔊 *Speaking* TIP

Use expressions and movements that go with the dialogue.

COMPREHENSION

Workbook
Page 133

Right There

1. Who accompanied Lewis and Clark on their expedition to the Pacific?
2. What are the Shoshone signs of peace?

Think and Search

3. Why was Sacagawea important to the explorers?
4. How difficult was the trip upriver? Describe.

Author and You

5. What do you think the author means by the statement "The river had brought her tomorrow"?
6. What can you infer about the Shoshone people from their behavior toward the explorers?

On Your Own

7. Do you think Lewis and Clark could have made their journey without the help of Native Americans? Explain.

8. What do you think were the most difficult things for the explorers in Lewis and Clark's group? What do you think were the most interesting and exciting things?

DISCUSSION

 **Listening TIP**

Think about what you are hearing. Try to relate what you hear to what you already know.

Discuss in pairs or small groups.

1. What kind of person was Sacagawea? How would you describe her abilities and strengths? Give examples from the excerpt.

2. What does the river symbolize in the story and the song?

Q Why do we explore new frontiers? Are rivers as important for travel and exploration today as they were in the past? Explain.

RESPONSE TO LITERATURE

Workbook
Page 133

In the excerpt from *River to Tomorrow,* Sacagawea's brother Cameahwait promises her "later we will talk." Work with a partner and discuss what the brother and sister might have said to each other in this conversation. Write a short dialogue in your notebook. Then read it aloud to the class.

Native Americans from
the Shoshone tribe ▶

Grammar and Writing

GRAMMAR, USAGE, AND MECHANICS

The Past Perfect and the Simple Past

Use the past perfect to describe something that happened before a certain time in the past. The past perfect is formed with *had* + the past participle. Sentences in the past perfect are often used with phrases such as *by (summer)* and *at first*.

> **By midsummer** the canoes **had traveled** upriver for many miles.
> **At first** she **had thought** about escaping.

Use the past perfect with the simple past to show which of the two past events happened first. The clause in the past perfect shows the first action. The clause in the simple past shows the second action. The clause in the simple past is often used with conjunctions such as *when* and *before*.

> **When** Lewis and Clark **reached** the camp, the Shoshone **had gathered** together.
> [First the Shoshone gathered together. Then Lewis and Clark reached the camp.]
> **Before** Sacagawea **learned** of the trip, she **had given up** hope of ever seeing her people again.
> [First she gave up hope. Then she learned of the trip.]

Practice
Workbook
Page 134

Work with a partner. Discuss the events in Sacagawea's life that occurred *before* her journey with Lewis and Clark. Copy the paragraph below into your notebook. Complete the paragraph using the past perfect.

> The Minnetaree _____ (kill) Sacagawea's family and _____ (take) her far from her people. She _____ (want) to escape. However, she couldn't because the warrior who _____ (capture) her lost her in a game. Then Sacagawea learned that some white men _____ (come) with orders to travel to the Pacific Ocean. Sacagawea helped the white men because she thought she might see her people again.

276

WRITING AN EXPOSITORY PARAGRAPH

Write a Cause-and-Effect Paragraph

At the end of this unit, you will write an expository essay. In an expository essay, a writer presents facts and explains ideas. Often the writer will need to explain causes and effects.

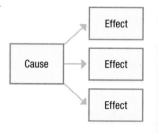

A cause is the reason something happens; an effect is the result. The relationship between cause and effect must be made clear. To help accomplish this, writers use words and phrases such as *because*, *as a result of*, and *therefore*.

Here is a model of a cause-and-effect paragraph. Before writing, the writer used a graphic organizer to help organize his ideas.

Lukas Arbogast

Consequences

There is a problem in our school that has been happening all year: bad behavior. Kids are not listening to the teachers. Sometimes they are talking with friends when they are not supposed to be, for example, at an assembly or during class. This affects the other students because they can't hear what is going on. Other times, kids just don't follow the rules. One time during a special show in our theater, a kid interrupted the performance by clapping when he had been told not to clap until the end. Then, as a result of the first kid's clapping, other kids joined in. These kids created a distraction for everyone. The assembly ended early, and we all had to return to our classrooms. One kid's actions led to consequences for the whole school.

Practice
Workbook Page 135

Think about a problem in your neighborhood, school, or community. For example, if there is a lot of litter on the streets, what are the causes of the problem? What are the effects?

Write a cause-and-effect paragraph in which you clearly describe how an event or situation leads to certain results or effects. Use a graphic organizer like the one above to help organize your ideas. Include words such as *because* to make the relationships clear. Be sure to use the past perfect correctly.

Writing Checklist

IDEAS:
☑ I showed cause-and-effect relationships clearly.

WORD CHOICE:
☑ I used words and phrases that signal cause and effect.

277

What You Will Learn

Reading

- Vocabulary building: *Context, dictionary skills, word study*

- Reading strategy: *Take notes*

- Text type: *Informational text (social studies)*

Grammar, Usage, and Mechanics
Imperatives

Writing
Write instructions

THE BIG QUESTION

Why do we explore new frontiers? Have you ever hiked, camped, or explored? Did you follow a trail? Did you use a map or a compass? What are some other things people use to find their way?

BUILD BACKGROUND

"Maps and Compasses" is a social studies article. It explains how to read a relief map and gives a brief introduction about the compass. A relief map is a type of map that shows the elevation of land with contour lines or with three-dimensional figures. A compass is a magnetic tool that shows direction. At the end of the article, you'll learn how to make your own compass.

▼ Hikers using a map and compass

VOCABULARY

Learn Key Words

Read these sentences. Use the context to figure out the meaning of the red words. Use a dictionary to check your answers. Then write each word and its meaning in your notebook.

Key Words

elevation
geographical
kilometer
relief
scale
sea level

1. The **elevation** of Mount McKinley is 6,194 meters (20,320 ft.). It is the tallest mountain in North America.

2. Mountains, valleys, rivers, and lakes are all **geographical** features that are seen on a map.

3. A **kilometer** is a measurement in the metric system. It equals 1,000 meters, or .6 miles.

4. To find out the height of a mountain range, you can look at a **relief** map.

5. We used the **scale** on a map to measure the distance between our starting point and the base of the mountain.

6. The city of New Orleans is below **sea level**; levees were built to keep the water from pouring into the city.

Practice  **Workbook** Page 136

Work with a partner to answer these questions. Try to include the red word in your answer. Write the sentences in your notebook.

1. Have you ever been at a high **elevation**?

2. What are three examples of **geographical** features?

3. Do you live more than a **kilometer** from school?

4. When might you need to use a **relief** map?

5. Why do maps include a **scale**?

6. Is your town located above or below **sea level**?

◀ Mt. McKinley, Denali National Park, Alaska

279

Learn Academic Words

Study the red words and their meanings. You will find these words useful when talking and writing about informational texts. Write each word and its meaning in your notebook. After you read "Maps and Compasses," try to use these words to respond to the text.

Academic Words

adjacent
chart
erode
found
labels
physical

adjacent = very close or next to	➡	You can see on the map that the lake is **adjacent** to the meadow.
chart = information that is shown in the form of pictures, graphs, etc.	➡	The weather **chart** shows that it is raining on the west coast.
erode = destroy gradually by wind, rain, or acid	➡	Strong rain and wind began to **erode** the mountainside over the years.
found = discovered by searching or by chance	➡	We **found** our way up the mountain by following a trail and using a compass.
labels = written words or phrases that name or describe something	➡	The largest **labels** on the map were the names of countries.
physical = relating to the body, not the mind	➡	Hiking is very good **physical** exercise.

Practice  Workbook Page 137

Write the sentences in your notebook. Choose a red word from the box above to complete each sentence. Then take turns reading the sentences aloud with a partner.

1. The _____ on the chart describe the elevation of each place.
2. Years of harsh weather began to _____ the old building.
3. The _____ showed all the different kinds of animals and plants in the state.
4. You must be in good _____ shape to climb a mountain.
5. The lakes are close together; they are _____ to one another.
6. Early explorers _____ a new route from Europe to North America.

Word Study: Spelling *ie / ei*

Learning letter-sound correspondence will help you read more fluently. The vowel combination *ie* can stand for the long *e* sound. The vowel combination *ei* can stand for the long *a* sound.

Long *e / ie*	Long *a / ei*
rel**ie**f	fr**ei**ght
bel**ie**f	w**ei**ght

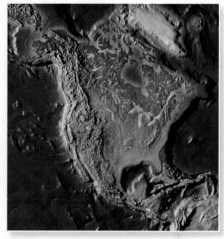

▲ A relief map of North America

Practice

Copy the chart above into your notebook. Add three blank rows. Practice pronouncing the words in the box below. Then add the words to the correct column of the chart.

achieve	chief	eight	neighbor	shriek	sleigh

READING STRATEGY TAKE NOTES

Taking notes keeps you focused on what you're reading. It also helps you understand and remember new information. To take notes, follow these steps:

- Think about your purpose for reading the text.
- Read one paragraph at a time and make a note about it.
- Don't write in complete sentences. Use short notes, for example: *sea level is 0.*
- Write notes about the most important facts you need, not the details.

As you read "Maps and Compasses," think about the information you want to remember. Take notes while you read. Review your notes and check that they're correct.

Workbook
Page 139

Set a purpose for reading Think about why you might use a relief map or a compass. When would a relief map or compass be useful?

Maps and Compasses

Reading a Relief Map

A relief map shows the geographical features of a region. It shows the differences in a region's elevation, or height. For example, by looking at a relief map, you can see whether the land in a region has plains, hills, or mountains.

Relief maps have a key—a box with different colors that show elevation, or how high the land is above sea level. Sea level is the level of the surface of the sea where it meets the land. We measure sea level in meters and in feet.

Maps have scales. The scale on a map looks like a ruler. It shows how many kilometers or miles equal a certain distance on the map. You can use the scale to figure out the distance between places on the map.

---

features, parts
region, particular area
measure, find the size, weight, or
   amount of something

ELEVATION

Meters	Feet
Over 4,000	Over 13,000
2,000–4,000	6,600–13,000
1,000–2,000	3,300–6,600
500–1,000	1,650–3,300
200–500	650–1,650
0–200	0–650
Below sea level	

0   150   300 miles

0   150   300 kilometers

▲ Western United States, Canada, and Mexico

BEFORE YOU GO ON

1 What do the colors in the key tell you?

2 What is the elevation of Ciudad Juárez?

On Your Own
Does your region have plains, hills, or mountains?

283

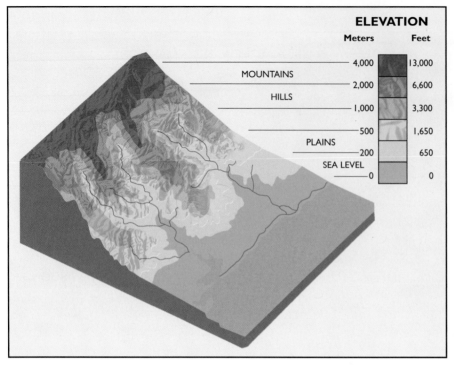

Land regions above sea level

Sea level is always 0 on a relief map. Most land in the United States is above—higher than—sea level. For example, the city of Denver, Colorado, is about 1,609 meters (5,280 ft.) above sea level. Dallas, Texas, is about 141 meters (463 ft.) above sea level. Cities that are on a seacoast, such as San Francisco, California, and Boston, Massachusetts, have some land that is at sea level and some land that is higher. San Francisco, for example, is about 20 meters (65 ft.) above sea level in some places. Some land is below—lower than—sea level. For example, Death Valley in California is 86 meters (282 ft.) below sea level.

The Compass

A map is a useful tool for a traveler, but it does not tell the direction that you are facing. You can find this out by using a compass. A compass is a simple instrument that consists of a small magnet. Anywhere on Earth you can hold a compass in your hand and it will point toward the North Pole. It reacts to Earth's magnetic field.

Over 2,000 years ago, the Chinese discovered a special black stone called a lodestone. The discovery of the lodestone brought about the invention of the first compass.

Meriwether Lewis used this compass during his expedition. ▼

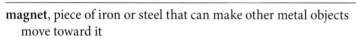

magnet, piece of iron or steel that can make other metal objects move toward it
reacts, behaves in a particular way because of what has been done

Early explorers used the lodestone to make their own compasses. They rubbed the tip of a needle against a lodestone to magnetize it. The needle moved toward north. By the sixteenth century, round cards were fixed to the needle. This allowed explorers to take accurate readings from the compass points.

▲ **A modern compass**

How to Make a Compass

You can make your own simple compass.
You will need:

- A sewing needle

- A magnet

- A small cork, or one cut in half

- A plastic container filled with water

1. Magnetize the needle by moving the magnet over the tip of the needle twenty-five to fifty times in the same direction.
2. Carefully push the needle through the side of the cork.
3. Place the container of water on a table or desk. Gently place the cork on the surface of the water.
4. Watch as the needle points north. Now you can determine south, east, and west.

BEFORE YOU GO ON

1 Where does the compass point?

2 What did early explorers use to make compasses?

On Your Own
In what direction is your home from your school?

285

COMPREHENSION  Workbook Page 140

Right There

1. What is a key on a map?
2. What discovery led to the invention of the first compass?

Think and Search

3. What can you learn by studying a relief map?
4. How is a relief map different from a road map? How is it similar?

Author and You

5. In what types of places or situations would it be useful to know how to read a relief map?
6. Does the author of this article think that the invention of the compass was important? Explain.

On Your Own

7. What would you take on a hiking trip?
8. Have you ever been lost? How did you find your way back?

▲ Reading a map and using a compass

IN YOUR OWN WORDS

Use the phrases and vocabulary in the chart below to tell a partner how to read a relief map and use a compass.

Geographical features	➡	elevation, sea level
Scale	➡	kilometers, miles
Labels	➡	places, compass points

DISCUSSION

Discuss in pairs or small groups.

1. What knowledge is useful for hiking or camping? What abilities and skills does an explorer need to have?

2. How do people find their way when they don't have a map?

3. What does it mean to "have a sense of direction"? Do you have a sense of direction? How do you keep from getting lost?

Q **Why do we explore new frontiers?** How do you think frontiers were explored before the relief map and compass were invented? How did these things make exploration easier?

»)) *Listening* TIP

As you listen, take note of new and interesting information.

READ FOR FLUENCY

It is often easier to read a text if you understand the difficult words and phrases. Work with a partner. Choose a paragraph from the reading. Identify the words and phrases you do not know or have trouble pronouncing. Look up the difficult words in a dictionary.

Take turns pronouncing the words and phrases with your partner. If necessary, ask your teacher to model the correct pronunciation. Then take turns reading the paragraph aloud. Give each other feedback.

EXTENSION  Workbook Page 140

We use many types of maps every day—road maps, public transit maps, relief maps—to help us understand the geographical features of a region, locate places, and learn about the natural resources in an area. Find one or two different types of maps. Then copy the chart below into your notebook and complete it.

Type of Map	Details Shown on Map

Grammar and Writing

Imperatives

In the text "How to Make a Compass," the author uses imperatives. An imperative can be used to give instructions. The subject of the sentence is *you*, but it is not stated. Use the simple present in imperatives.

> **Magnetize** the needle.
> Carefully **push** the needle through the side of the cork.
> **Place** the container of water on a table or desk.
> **Watch** as the needle points north.

An imperative can also be used to give directions.

> **Go** to the next corner. Then **turn** right.

You can also use an imperative to make a request using the word *please*.

> **Please** give me the map. Give me the map, **please**.

Practice

Workbook Page 141

Work with a partner. Think about a well-known place in your community. Give your partner directions on how to get there. Use the imperatives in the box below. Write the directions in your notebook.

cross	follow	go	turn	walk

Turn left on Main Street. ▶

WRITING AN EXPOSITORY PARAGRAPH

Write Instructions

You've learned that expository writing involves explaining something. When you write step-by-step instructions, you are explaining how to do something by following particular steps. Instructions should be easy to understand, and the steps should follow a logical sequence. Use words such as *first*, *then*, *next*, and *finally* to explain the sequence.

Here is a model of a paragraph of instructions on how to make a compass. Notice that the writer uses logical sequence and makes the instructions easy to understand. Before writing, the writer used a graphic organizer to help organize her ideas.

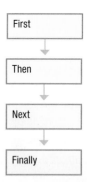

First → Then → Next → Finally

Justine Kefauver

How to Make a Floating Compass

So you want to make a compass! Well, here are some easy steps to start you on your way. You will need one magnet, a needle, one cup or bowl filled about halfway with water, and a cork. First, take the magnet and rub the needle with it about thirty times. This will magnetize the needle. Make sure that the needle is magnetized by letting it stick to a refrigerator or by picking up a pin with it. Next, take the cork and push the needle all the way through it. Finally, put the cork and needle in the middle of the bowl of water. When the needle has come to a rest, it will point north. Congratulations! You have just made your first compass!

Practice

 **Workbook** Page 142

Write a paragraph giving instructions on how to do something, such as how to prepare a meal or make an arts-and-crafts project. Use a graphic organizer like the one above to help organize your ideas. Be sure to use imperatives correctly in your instructions.

Writing Checklist

SENTENCE FLUENCY:

☑ I made sure my sentences flowed so that the steps were easy to follow and understand.

VOICE:

☑ I used an enthusiastic tone that would encourage readers to use my instructions.

What You Will Learn

Reading

■ Vocabulary building:
Context, dictionary skills, word study

■ Reading strategy:
Summarize

■ Text type:
Informational text (social studies)

Grammar, Usage, and Mechanics
Modals: *could* for past ability; *could* and *might* for possibility

Writing
Write a summary

THE BIG QUESTION

Why do we explore new frontiers? A ranch is land used for growing food or raising animals such as cows and sheep. The people who work on ranches are called cowboys. In the past, cowboys settled new frontiers. What do you think life is like on a ranch? Do you think the life of a cowboy was exciting? Can you identify some of the cowboy equipment below? What was the equipment used for?

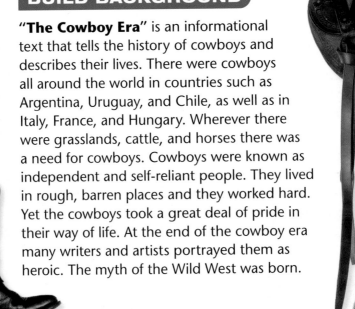

▼ A saddle

BUILD BACKGROUND

"The Cowboy Era" is an informational text that tells the history of cowboys and describes their lives. There were cowboys all around the world in countries such as Argentina, Uruguay, and Chile, as well as in Italy, France, and Hungary. Wherever there were grasslands, cattle, and horses there was a need for cowboys. Cowboys were known as independent and self-reliant people. They lived in rough, barren places and they worked hard. Yet the cowboys took a great deal of pride in their way of life. At the end of the cowboy era many writers and artists portrayed them as heroic. The myth of the Wild West was born.

Boots and spurs ▼

▼ A wide-brimmed hat

▲ A canteen

◀ A lariat

▲ A bandanna

VOCABULARY

Learn Key Words

Read these sentences. Use the context to figure out the meaning of the red words. Use a dictionary to check your answers. Then write each word and its meaning in your notebook.

Key Words

harvested
independence
missionaries
ranching
settlers
sharecroppers

1. When the corn was ready, the farmer harvested the crop.
2. The Republic of Texas was established after declaring independence from Mexico in 1836.
3. The Church sent Spanish missionaries to California to spread Christianity.
4. Raising animals and herding cows are part of cattle ranching.
5. The settlers moved from one place to another and made homes in a new territory.
6. The landowner paid the sharecroppers for the crops they grew.

Practice  Workbook Page 143

Write the sentences in your notebook. Choose a red word from the box above to complete each sentence. Then take turns reading the sentences aloud with a partner.

1. The Spanish brought horses and cows to Mexico, and established cattle _____.
2. It was difficult for the _____ to buy the land they farmed from the landowner.
3. _____ traveled west in wagon trains looking for a better life.
4. The farmers grew and _____ their crops every year.
5. The _____ came from far away to spread their religion.
6. The United States celebrates its _____ on the fourth of July.

▲ African-American sharecroppers picking cotton after the Civil War

Learn Academic Words

Study the **red** words and their meanings. You will find these words useful when talking and writing about informational texts. Write each word and its meaning in your notebook. After you read "The Cowboy Era," try to use these words to respond to the text.

Academic Words

maintain
survey
tradition
ultimate
widespread

maintain = continue in the same way as before	➡	It is expensive to **maintain** a large cattle ranch.
survey = a set of questions designed to get information	➡	The school **survey** showed that the students came from ten different countries.
tradition = belief or custom that has existed for a long time	➡	Telling stories by the campfire at night was a cowboy **tradition**.
ultimate = better, bigger, worse, etc., than others of the same kind	➡	The **ultimate** dream for sharecroppers was to own their own land.
widespread = happening in many places among many people or in many situations	➡	Cattle ranching became **widespread** throughout Texas and in parts of California.

Practice  Workbook Page 144

Work with a partner to answer these questions. Try to include the **red** word in your answer. Write the sentences in your notebook.

1. How do you **maintain** a healthy diet?
2. Have you ever done a **survey**? What were the results?
3. What is a **tradition** in your family?
4. What is your **ultimate** goal in life?
5. What music styles have become **widespread** in recent years?

▲ A painting of a cowboy by Frederic Remington

Word Study: Compound Words

Compound words are made up of two or more words. You can form a compound word by adding a noun to another noun or to an adjective, a verb, or a preposition.

Compound Words		
noun + noun	➡	grass + lands = grasslands
adjective + noun	➡	black + bird = blackbird
noun + verb	➡	hair + cut = haircut
preposition + noun	➡	under + foot = underfoot

Practice
Work with a partner. Make compound words from the words in the box below. Use a dictionary if you need help.

bare	foot	horn	rail	rise	sun
fire	hide	long	raw	road	wood

READING STRATEGY | SUMMARIZE

Summarizing helps you to see how much you understand in a text. It also helps you remember the most important points. When you summarize, you find the main ideas in the text and put them in a few short sentences. To summarize, follow these steps:

- Read the text. Then reread each paragraph or section. What is the author writing about?
- Decide what the main idea is in each paragraph or section. Make notes.
- Leave out details. Just focus on the most important points.
- Write a few sentences that summarize the main ideas. Use your own words.

As you read "The Cowboy Era," stop from time to time and make a note of the main ideas. Summarize the text in two or three sentences.

293

Set a purpose for reading How did the cowboy era begin and why did it end?

The Cowboy Era

The Vaqueros

Cattle ranching began in North America in the early 1500s. The Spanish settlers brought the first domesticated horses and cattle to Mexico from Spain. The animals flourished and ran free. Huge Spanish ranches were scattered across northern Mexico. The ranchers taught local Native Americans to ride horses and take care of cattle. Often they rode barefoot. These ranchers were called *vaqueros*, from the Spanish word *vaca* for "cow." Ranching spread from Mexico to Texas and California.

Ranches in California

Spanish missionaries introduced cattle ranching to California in the 1700s. Father Junípero Serra established twenty-one missions. Raising cattle became California's main industry. When Mexico declared independence from Spain in 1821, Mexicans of Spanish descent received land grants on which to raise cattle. Some of the ranches were very large—40,000 acres or more.

▲ Mission Basilica San Diego de Alcala, California

Cotton and Cattle

Both cotton and cattle were important to the Texas economy when Texas became a state in 1845. Growing cotton was a lot of work. Most farmers planted and harvested their own cotton. Others were slaveholders, and enslaved Africans did much of the work. After the Civil War (1861–1865), the slaves were freed. Many former slaves became

---

cattle, cows raised on a ranch
domesticated, animals that live or work
   with people
flourished, grew well
descent, family origin

---

economy, a state's or nation's business and
   money system

sharecroppers. Others joined the growing number of Texans who became cowboys. They herded cattle on the large, open grasslands, called ranges.

Why were cattle important to the Texas economy? Beef was a popular food among Americans. In 1865, people in the northern and eastern United States didn't raise many cattle. Cattle there cost up to forty dollars a head. However, there were more than 4 million longhorn cattle in southern Texas. Cattle in Texas were worth only about four dollars a head. Ranchers quickly realized that they could make a lot of money by selling their cattle elsewhere. First, they could drive the cattle to Kansas or Missouri. There they could ship them to the northern or eastern United States by train. This idea led to the first cattle drives.

---

herded, moved animals together as a group
a head, an animal
drives, acts of herding large groups of animals to another place

▼ Cowboys herding cattle in the 1880s

The Great Cattle Drives

In 1866, the great cattle drives began. In that year, cowboys drove more than a quarter of a million Texas cattle through what is now Oklahoma to Kansas and Missouri. This was a journey of about 1,609 to 2,414 kilometers (1,000 to 1,500 mi.), and it took from three to six months to complete. The cowboys and cattle usually traveled on trails that already existed. About 2 million cattle were driven up the Chisholm Trail to Kansas between 1867 and 1871.

Three trails on which cowboys drove cattle north from Texas ▼

BEFORE YOU GO ON

1 Who brought the first horses to Mexico?

2 Why was cattle ranching important to the Texas economy in 1865?

On Your Own
How are cattle transported from place to place today?

295

Cowboy Life

Cowboys did not have an easy job. Cattle drives were difficult and sometimes dangerous. Cowboys got little pay, worked long days, and got little sleep. River crossings and stampedes were particularly dangerous. Cowboys and cattle might drown crossing a river or get trampled to death in a stampede. Cowboys sometimes had to fight rustlers who tried to steal their cattle.

---

stampedes, sudden movements of large groups of running animals

crown

brim

bandanna

lariat

cuff

belt

chaps

cowboy boots

spurs

▲ A cowboy's clothing and gear

Some days were scorching hot, and some nights were freezing cold. Cowboys wore practical clothes to help them withstand these temperatures.

Cowboy hats had to be strong and long lasting. On hot days, the high top part of the hat kept the head cool, while the broad brim shaded the eyes and neck. On rainy or snowy days, the hats worked as umbrellas. The hats also protected cowboys from thorns and low-hanging branches. Cowboys even used them to carry water, to fan or put out fires, and as pillows.

The cowboys' other clothing was also practical. Their shirts and pants were made of strong material. They lasted a long time and protected the cowboys' skin. When it was dusty, cowboys covered their noses and mouths with the bandannas they wore around their necks.

When riding horses, cowboys used their boot heels to prevent their feet from slipping out of the stirrups. When roping cattle, the cowboys could dig their boot heels into the ground.

Many cowboys were native Texans. Others came from the South, East, and Midwest. Some were African American, Native American, and Mexican. One in four cowboys in the late nineteenth century was African American. They all had excellent riding skills, enabling them to herd cattle on long drives.

---

practical, useful and sensible
protected, kept safe from damage or harm
stirrups, metal rings where you put your feet when you ride a horse
roping, catching an animal with a circle of rope (lariat)

◄ Cowboys using lariats

The most important tools for a cowboy were his horse and his rope, or lariat (from the Spanish word *la reata*, meaning "rope"). The lariat is used for catching, or "roping," a cow or steer. It was originally made from braided rawhide, 18 meters (60 ft.) long and about as thick as a pencil. One end was slipped through the honda, or eyelet (made of metal or cow horn), to make a large loop. The honda allowed the rope to slide so the loop could become bigger or smaller. The cowboy held the main line and the loop in his throwing hand, while the rest of the rope was coiled in his other hand, ready to be let out. He also had to hold the reins and steer the horse with that hand. It took a lot of practice to perfect this roping skill.

---

braided, three or more pieces twisted together
coiled, twisted into a round shape
reins, bands of leather around the horse's neck used to control it

End of the Cowboy Era

The golden era of the cowboy lasted only about twenty years. During that time, thousands of cowboys worked on cattle drives. What caused the end of the cowboy era? Until the 1870s, the ranges were open; there were no fences to stop the movement of cattle. However, in 1874 barbed wire was invented. Farmers and ranchers began fencing their land with barbed wire, so the ranges became closed. In addition, many railroads were built in Texas in the 1880s. Then ranchers could send their cattle to market directly by train, so cattle drives became unnecessary.

---

barbed wire, wire with short, sharp points
fencing, building wood or wire structures to stop people or animals from entering or leaving an area
unnecessary, not needed

BEFORE YOU GO ON

1 How did a cowboy's clothing help him?

2 How long did the golden era of the cowboy last?

On Your Own
Would you like to be a cowboy? Why or why not?

297

Review and Practice

Right There

1. Who brought cattle ranching to California in the 1700s?

2. What caused the end of the cowboy era?

Think and Search

3. What were cattle drives? Why did they become widespread during the late 1860s?

4. How was cowboy life dangerous?

Author and You

5. Would you agree with the author that cowboys had a difficult job? Explain.

6. Do you think the author would agree that cowboys played an important role on the American frontier? Explain.

On Your Own

7. Do you think that you'd enjoy going on a cattle drive? Why or why not?

8. Why do you think filmmakers, artists, and writers often portray cowboys as heroes?

IN YOUR OWN WORDS

Work with a partner. Use the phrases and vocabulary in the chart below to discuss the cowboy era.

Missionaries	➡	cattle ranching
Settlers	➡	domesticated
Former slaves	➡	sharecroppers, cowboys, harvested
Clothes	➡	practical, stirrups
The great cattle drives	➡	ranchers, stampedes, sell, roping

DISCUSSION

Discuss in pairs or small groups.

1. Have any parts of cowboy culture survived today? Explain.

2. The life of a cowboy was full of danger and discomfort. Why do you think men still wanted to become cowboys?

3. Would you like to have lived in Texas during the golden era of the cowboys? Why or why not?

Q **Why do we explore new frontiers?** What do you think the "frontier spirit" means? In what ways did cowboys have a frontier spirit? How did the cowboy era affect American culture?

»)⌇ _Listening_ TIP

In your mind, summarize what the speaker says.

READ FOR FLUENCY

When we read aloud to communicate meaning, we group words into phrases, pause or slow down to make important points, and emphasize important words. Pause for a short time when you reach a comma and for a longer time when you reach a period. Pay attention to rising and falling intonation at the end of sentences.

Work with a partner. Choose a paragraph from the reading. Discuss which words seem important for communicating meaning. Practice pronouncing difficult words. Take turns reading the paragraph aloud and give each other feedback.

EXTENSION

Workbook
Page 147

The cowboy way of life has had a great impact on American culture. Research cowboys of the past and today. Think about what parts of cowboy life are still with us. Copy the chart below into your notebook. Work with a partner to complete the chart.

	Cowboys of the Past	Cowboys Today
Traditions		
Food		
Clothing		
Landscape		
Equipment		

Grammar and Writing

Modals: *could* for Past Ability; *could* and *might* for Possibility

Modals are auxiliary, or "helping," verbs. A modal is always used with the base form of the verb. Modals have only one form. Do not use *-s* in the third-person singular.

Use the modal *could* to express past ability. The negative form of *could* is *could not* or *couldn't*.

> When roping cattle, they **could** dig their boot heels into the ground.
>
> The honda allowed the rope to slide so the loop **could** become bigger or smaller.

Use *could* or *might* to express possibility. The negative form of *might* is *might not*.

> Ranchers quickly realized that they **could** make a lot of money by selling their cattle elsewhere.
>
> Cowboys and cattle **might** drown crossing a river.

Practice  **Workbook Page 148**

Talk about the cowboy way of life using the modals *could* and *might* with a partner. Complete the sentence starters on the left of the chart with a phrase on the right. Write the sentences in your notebook.

	carry water in their hats
Cowboys might . . .	come from the South
	drown crossing a river
Cowboys could . . .	get hurt during a stampede
	ride long distances

▲ A cowboy's boot in a stirrup

300

WRITING AN EXPOSITORY PARAGRAPH

Write a Summary

You've learned that expository writing involves presenting facts and explaining ideas. Often, expository writing involves summarizing. When a writer summarizes a piece of writing, he or she includes the main ideas and a few of the most important details. To tell whether a detail is important, try leaving it out of your summary. If you find that your summary is hard to understand without the detail, then it is important enough to include.

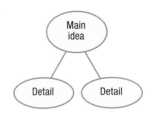

Here is a paragraph summarizing "The Cowboy Era." Notice how the writer includes the main ideas and only the most important details. Before writing, he organized his ideas using a main-idea-and-details web.

Ben Berman

History of the Cowboy Era

Cattle ranching in North America was started by the Spanish in the early 1500s. The Spanish brought horses to Mexico and taught Native Americans how to ride and look after cattle. Ranching soon spread from Mexico to Texas and then to California. Raising cattle was important because beef was a very popular food in America. It was the job of cowboys to herd cattle to places such as Kansas or Missouri, where the cattle could then be brought by train to other markets. When a large group of cattle was moved by cowboys, it was known as a cattle drive. Soon, however, the cowboy era came to a close. This might be because railroads were expanding, so cattle drives weren't needed. There was also the invention of barbed wire, which could fence in cattle at ranches.

Practice  **Workbook** Page 149

Write a paragraph in which you summarize an article or story. You could summarize the excerpt from *River to Tomorrow*, "Maps and Compasses," or another selection from this book. Include the main ideas and only the most important details. Use a main-idea-and-details web to organize your ideas. Be sure to use the modals *could* and *might* correctly.

Writing Checklist

IDEAS:

☑ I included facts and only the most important details.

ORGANIZATION:

☑ My summary uses the same organization as the reading it summarizes.

301

Prepare to Read

What You Will Learn

Reading
- Vocabulary building: *Literary terms, word study*
- Reading strategy: *Skim*
- Text type: *Literature (tall tale)*

Grammar, Usage, and Mechanics
Comparison structures

Writing
Write a classifying paragraph

THE BIG QUESTION

Why do we explore new frontiers? You are going to read a tall tale about a boy who grows up on the Texas frontier. A tall tale is funny story that has characters with exaggerated and unusual abilities. Why do you think people made up tall tales about the American frontier?

BUILD BACKGROUND

Pecos Bill: The Greatest Cowboy of All Time is a tall tale about a young boy who becomes separated from his family and is raised by coyotes. Storytelling has been used throughout history to entertain, teach, make sense of the world, communicate experiences, and remember and record events. Storytelling has a rich and diverse history in the United States. The early settlers on the American frontier invented the tall tale. Many tall tales were based on real figures in history or on actual events and places.

▲ *The Legend of Pecos Bill* by Harold von Schmidt

VOCABULARY

Learn Literary Words

Onomatopoeia is the use of words that imitate the sounds they represent. Examples include words such as *splash*, *zip*, and *slurp*. Find the words in these sentences that imitate sounds.

Literary Words

onomatopoeia
hyperbole

> The flies buzzed around the cattle.
> The fire was crackling and popping all night long.

Hyperbole is a way of describing something by exaggerating on purpose—saying that it is much bigger, smaller, faster, slower, or in some other way more than it really is. Tall tales use hyperbole to exaggerate the qualities of the setting and the characters. How is hyperbole used in this paragraph?

> Ben was the strongest and fastest carpenter in the village. He was so strong that if you wanted a new house, he would rip your old house down and throw it over his shoulder. Then he could build you a new one in less than an hour!

Practice

Workbook
Page 150

Read these paragraphs about the giant Paul Bunyan, an American folk hero. Work with a partner and find at least three examples of hyperbole in the excerpt below.

> When Paul Bunyan was just one week old, he was wearing his father's clothes. His crib was a lumber wagon pulled by a team of horses.
> Paul Bunyan was a lumberjack. It was said that he could take down sixteen trees in one swing. Some claim he and Babe created Minnesota's 10,000 lakes with their footprints and the Grand Canyon by dragging an axe.

▲ Paul Bunyan with Babe, his blue ox

303

Learn Academic Words

Study the red words and their meanings. You will find these words useful when talking and writing about literature. Write each word and its meaning in your notebook. After you read the excerpt from *Pecos Bill: The Greatest Cowboy of All Time,* try to use these words to respond to the text.

Academic Words

instruct
invisible
partnership
rigid
substitute
unique

instruct = teach	➡	The forest ranger tried to **instruct** the students in how to survive in the wild.
invisible = not able to be seen	➡	The coyote was the same color as the dusty earth. It was almost **invisible** to see from afar.
partnership = relationship in which two or more people work together	➡	The two new students formed a **partnership** to complete the project.
rigid = stiff and still	➡	The coyote stopped and became **rigid** as the hunters approached.
substitute = use something new or different instead of something else	➡	You can **substitute** an axe for a saw when cutting up trees.
unique = unusually good and special	➡	She had a **unique** ability to find her way in the wilderness.

Practice  Workbook Page 151

Write the sentences below in your notebook. Choose a red word from the box above to complete each sentence. Then take turns reading the sentences aloud with a partner.

1. The teacher had to _____ the students to follow the new rules in the classroom.

2. Although he was shaking inside, the boy remained _____ and unmoving on the outside.

3. The animal blended in with the surroundings so well it seemed _____.

4. Coyotes have a _____ ability to adapt to different environments.

5. The two hikers worked together to form a _____ so that they could get to the top of the mountain.

6. People who are successful agree: There is no _____ for hard work.

▲ A coyote

304

Word Study: Frequently Misspelled Words

The English language contains many confusing words, such as *there*, *their*, and *they're*. These words are sometimes pronounced the same or are pronounced very similarly. But each different spelling of the word changes the meaning.

Word	Definition	Sentence
their	belonging to a group	They lost one of **their** children.
they're	contraction with *they* and *are*	**They're** trying to help Pecos Bill.
there	used to refer to a place	He liked it **there**.
to	tell the direction or position	They were migrating **to** the West.
too	also	Pecos liked Grandy, **too**.
who's	contraction with *who* and *is*	**Who's** going to look for him?
whose	the person something belongs to	**Whose** saddle is that?

Practice

Work with a partner. Take turns reading the words in the box below. Copy the words into your notebook. Look up the definition of each word in the dictionary. Then write a sentence using each word.

bought / brought   it's / its   then / than   your / you're

READING STRATEGY   SKIM

Skimming a text helps you get a general understanding of what the text is about before you read it more carefully. It also helps you set a purpose for reading the text a second time. To skim a text, follow these steps:

- Look at the title and any visuals to get an idea of what the text is about.
- Read the first paragraph quickly. Then read the first sentence of the paragraphs that follow.
- Read the last paragraph quickly.
- Don't stop at any words you don't know—skip over them.

As you read the selection from *Pecos Bill: The Greatest Cowboy of All Time*, skim the text quickly to see what it's about. Then stop reading and think about the subject of what you read. What is the text about? How do you know this?

305

Set a purpose for reading Look for ways in which Pecos Bill's frontier family is different from families today. Look for ways in which they are similar.

from

PECOS BILL:
The Greatest Cowboy of All Time

James Cloyd Bowman

▲ Pecos Bill falls out of the wagon.

▲ Pecos Bill meets Grandy.

Pecos Bill had the strangest and most exciting experience any boy ever had. He became a member of a pack of wild Coyotes, and until he was a grown man, believed that his name was Cropear, and that he was a full-blooded Coyote. Later he discovered that he was a human being and very shortly thereafter became the greatest cowboy of all time. This is how it all came about.

Pecos Bill's family was migrating westward through Texas in the early days, in an old covered wagon with wheels made from cross sections of a sycamore log. His father and mother were riding in the front seat, and his father was driving a wall-eyed, spavined roan horse and a red and white spotted milch cow hitched side by side. The eighteen children in the back of the wagon were making such a medley of noises that their mother said it wasn't possible even to hear the thunder.

Just as the wagon was rattling down to the ford across the Pecos River, the rear left wheel bounced over a great piece of rock, and Bill, his red hair bristling like porcupine quills, rolled out of the rear of the wagon, and landed, up to his neck, in a pile of loose sand. He was only four years old at the time, and he lay dazed until the wagon had crossed the river and disappeared into the sagebrush. It wasn't until his mother rounded up the family for the noonday meal that Bill was missed. The last anyone remembered seeing him was just before they had forded the river.

Cropear, the name given to Pecos Bill because he had short, or cropped, ears
wall-eyed, having eyes that turn outward
spavined, old and weak
roan, reddish brown mixed with white
milch cow, cow that gives milk
ford, shallow place where you cross a river
porcupine quills, sharp needles on the back of a porcupine

✔ **LITERARY CHECK**
*Where does the author use **hyperbole** here?*

BEFORE YOU GO ON

1 Why did Pecos Bill have such a strange childhood?

2 How did Pecos Bill become separated from his family?

💡 **On Your Own**
What frontier were Bill and his family going to? Why?

307

The mother and eight or ten of the older children hurried back to the river and hunted everywhere, but they could find no trace of the lost boy. When evening came, they were forced to go back to the covered wagon, and later, to continue their journey without him. Ever after, when they thought of Bill, they remembered the river, and so they naturally came to speak of him as Pecos Bill.

What had happened to Bill was this. He had strayed off into the mesquite, and a few hours later was found by a wise old Coyote, who was the undisputed leader of the Loyal and Approved Packs of the Pecos and Rio Grande Valleys. He was, in fact, the Granddaddy of the entire race of Coyotes, and so his followers, out of affection to him, called him Grandy.

When he accidentally met Bill, Grandy was curious, but shy. He sniffed and he yelped, and he ran this way and that, the better to get the scent, and to make sure there was no danger. After a while he came quite near, sat up on his haunches, and waited to see what the boy would do. Bill trotted up to Grandy and began running his hands through the long shaggy hair.

"What a nice doggy you are," he repeated again and again.

"Yes, and what a nice Cropear you are," yelped Grandy joyously.

And so, ever after, the Coyotes called the child Cropear.

Grandy was much pleased with his find and so, by running ahead and stopping and barking softly, he led the boy to the jagged side of Cabezon, or the Big Head, as it was called. This was a towering mass of mountain that rose abruptly, as if by magic, from the prairie. Around the base of this mountain the various families of the Loyal and Approved Packs had burrowed out their dens.

Here, far away from the nearest human dwelling, Grandy made a home for Cropear, and taught him all the knowledge of the wild out-of-doors. He led Cropear to the berries that were good to eat, and dug up roots that were sweet and spicy. He showed the boy how to break open the small nuts from the piñon. . . .

Grandy became his teacher and schooled him in the knowledge that had been handed down through thousands of generations of the Pack's life.

---

mesquite, common trees or bushes in the southwestern United States
undisputed leader, someone everybody agrees is the leader
yelped, made a sharp, high bark
scent, smell that animals or human beings leave behind
haunches, back legs
towering, very tall
abruptly, suddenly; steeply
burrowed, dug

▲ Pecos Bill learns from Grandy.

He taught Cropear the many signal calls, and the code of right and wrong, and the gentle art of loyalty to the leader. He also trained him to leap long distances and to dance; and to flip-flop and to twirl his body so fast that the eye could not follow his movements. And most important of all, he instructed him in the silent, rigid pose of invisibility, so that he could see all that was going on around him without being seen.

As Cropear grew tall and strong, he became the pet of the Pack. The Coyotes were always bringing him what they thought he would like to eat, and were ever showing him the many secrets of the fine art of hunting. They taught him where the Field-mouse nested, where the Song Thrush hid her eggs, where the Squirrel stored his nuts; and where the Mountain Sheep concealed their young among the towering rocks. . . .

---

signal, movement or sound telling someone something
loyalty, support; faithfulness
rigid pose of invisibility, keeping one's body still so that others do not see it

✔ **LITERARY CHECK**
What are some examples of **hyperbole** *in this paragraph?*

BEFORE YOU GO ON

1 Who found Pecos Bill?

2 What does Pecos Bill learn to eat?

💡**On Your Own**
Why do you think Grandy calls Bill "Cropear"?

▲ Grandy introduces Pecos Bill to the Mountain Lion, the Grizzly
Bear, the Skunk, the Porcupine, and the Bull Rattlesnake.

Grandy took pains to introduce Cropear to each of the animals and
made every one of them promise he would not harm the growing man-
child. "Au-g-gh!" growled the Mountain Lion. "I will be as careful as I can.
But be sure to tell your child to be careful, too!"

"Gr-r-r!" growled the fierce Grizzly Bear. "I have crunched many a
marrow bone, but I will not harm your boy. Gr-r-r!"

"Yes, we'll keep our perfumery and our quills in our vest pockets,"
mumbled the silly Skunk and Porcupine, as if suffering from adenoids.

✔ LITERARY CHECK
*Where does
the author use
onomatopoeia here?*

But when Grandy talked things over with the Bull Rattlesnake, he
was met with the defiance of hissing rattles. "Nobody will ever make me
promise to protect anybody or anything! S-s-s-s-ss! I'll do just as I please!"

"Be careful of your wicked tongue," warned Grandy, "or you'll be
very sorry."

But when Grandy met the Wouser, things were even worse. The Wouser
was a cross between the Mountain Lion and the Grizzly Bear, and was ten
times larger than either. Besides that, he was the nastiest creature in the
world. "I can only give you fair warning," yowled the Wouser, "and if you
prize your man-child, as you say you do, you will have to keep him out of
harm's way!"

---

took pains, was very careful
marrow, the soft substance in the hollow center of a bone
adenoids, growths in the throat that sometimes make breathing difficult
defiance, disobedient or disrespectful behavior

And as the Wouser continued, he stalked back and forth, lashing his tail and gnashing his jaws, and acting as if he were ready to snap somebody's head off. "What's more, you know that nobody treats me as a friend. Everybody runs around behind my back spreading lies about me. Everybody says I carry hydrophobia—the deadly poison—about on my person, and because of all these lies, I am shunned like a leper. Now you come sneaking around asking me to help you. Get out of my sight before I do something I will be sorry for!"

"I'm not sneaking," barked Grandy in defiance, "and besides, you're the one who will be sorry in the end."

So it happened that all the animals, save only the Bull Rattlesnake and the Wouser, promised to help Cropear bear a charmed life so that no harm should come near him. And by good fortune, the boy was never sick. The vigorous exercise and the fresh air and the constant sunlight helped him to become the healthiest, strongest, most active boy in the world.

---

hydrophobia, rabies (a deadly disease that people can get from animals)
shunned, avoided
leper, someone who has leprosy (an infectious skin disease)
vigorous, active and energetic

▲ Grandy introduces Pecos Bill to the Wouser.

ABOUT THE **AUTHOR**

James Cloyd Bowman (1880–1961) was born and grew up in Ohio. He was a college professor. He wrote several books for children, including tall tales about Pecos Bill, John Henry, and Paul Bunyan. Bowman received a Newbery Honor award in 1938 for *Pecos Bill: The Greatest Cowboy of All Time.*

BEFORE YOU GO ON

1 Why does the Bull Rattlesnake refuse to protect Pecos Bill?

2 What is the Wouser's reaction to Grandy's request?

On Your Own
Do you believe that this story is true? Why or why not?

311

READER'S THEATER

Speaking TIP

Use a strong tone of voice. Change your tone to emphasize certain points.

With a partner, act out the following imagined scene between Pecos Bill's Ma and Pa when they found him missing.

Ma: Children, it's time for the noonday meal! Come eat. Let's see now . . . [*counting the children*] that's sixteen, seventeen . . . Only seventeen children! Can that be? Pa, count them again!

Pa: [*counting*] Fifteen, sixteen, seventeen . . . There are only seventeen children here. We're missing one. Who are we missing? Let's see now, it's mighty quiet. Why, Bill's not here!

Ma: How could that be? He was on the wagon this morning when we left our campsite.

Pa: It was mighty rough going over that river. Do you reckon he could have fallen out?

Ma: Fallen out! My poor little Bill!

Pa: Now that I think of it, it was pretty quiet once we crossed the river. That must be what happened.

Ma: How terrible. Hurry everyone! We've lost your brother! We must go back to the river to search for him.

COMPREHENSION

Workbook Page 154

Right There

1. Why did Bill's family always think of him as Pecos Bill?
2. How did Grandy get his name?

Think and Search

3. What helped Pecos Bill become the "healthiest, strongest, and most active boy in the world"?
4. How did Grandy help young Pecos Bill?

Author and You

5. What does the author suggest about life among the wild Coyotes?
6. How do you think the Coyotes felt about Pecos Bill? Support your answer with evidence from the text.

On Your Own

7. What do you think everyday life was like for families migrating westward? What problems did they have to solve?

8. Have you ever gotten lost? What happened?

DISCUSSION

Listening TIP

Pay attention to the speaker's tone of voice, gestures, and expressions.

Discuss in pairs or small groups.

1. Which event in this story do you think is the most exaggerated? Why?

2. What elements of this story could be realistic or true to life?

3. What are the benefits of hyperbole in a story? How can it make a story more interesting?

Q Why do we explore new frontiers? Read the title of the tale again. Do you think Pecos Bill's time with the Coyotes had anything to do with his wanting to be a cowboy? Explain.

RESPONSE TO LITERATURE

Workbook Page 154

Write a tall tale about this illustration. Make up a character and a place. Explain what he is doing and why he is doing it. Then include the final results— what has occurred from his action. Make sure to include hyperbole and onomatopoeia.

Grammar and Writing

Comparison Structures
(-er / -est, more / the most + adjective)

Comparison structures show how things are different. Use comparative adjectives to compare one noun to another noun.

> The Wouser is **nastier than** the Bull Rattlesnake.
> Bill is **more famous than** his brothers and sisters.

Use superlative adjectives to compare one noun in a group to the rest of those in that group.

> These things helped him to become **the healthiest**, **strongest**, **most active** boy [out of all the other boys] in the world.

Notice the spelling changes for comparative and superlative adjectives. Some comparative and superlative adjectives are irregular.

		Comparative	Superlative
One-syllable adjectives: + -er / -est	sad	sadd**er** (than)	(the) sadd**est**
	strange	strang**er** (than)	(the) strang**est**
Two-syllable adjectives ending in *y*: change *y* to *i* + -er / -est	pretty	prett**ier** (than)	(the) prett**iest**
	busy	bus**ier** (than)	(the) bus**iest**
Most adjectives with two or more syllables: *more / most*	famous	**more** famous (than)	(the) **most** famous
	generous	**more** generous (than)	(the) **most** generous
Irregular adjectives	good	**better** (than)	(the) **best**
	bad	**worse** (than)	(the) **worst**

Practice

Workbook Page 155

Work with a partner. Write sentences in your notebook comparing the characters from *Pecos Bill: The Greatest Cowboy of All Time.* Use the adjectives below in the comparative and superlative form.

clever	dangerous	funny	helpful	kind	loyal	nasty	tough	tricky

314

WRITING AN EXPOSITORY PARAGRAPH

Write a Classifying Paragraph

You've learned that expository writing involves presenting facts and explaining ideas. Expository writing can also classify specific subject matter. When you classify something, you tell which group or category it belongs to. To do this, you must first list the categories that apply to your subject and then describe the characteristics of each category.

Here is a model of a paragraph that classifies different kinds of animals. Notice how the writer clearly presents and describes the categories. The writer used a three-column chart to organize his ideas.

Characteristics		
Wild animal	Farm animal	Pet

Emanuel Bonilla

Different Kinds of Animals

Animals are very different from one another. Let me explain. There are wild animals, farm animals, and pets. Some animals in the wild animal category are lions, tigers, sharks, alligators, anacondas, wild cats, bears, and wolves. These animals live in the jungle, the forest, or the ocean. The animals that belong in the wild animal category are very dangerous. Farm animals include pigs, chickens, cows, horses, donkeys, and ducks. These animals are tamer and are not very dangerous, but you don't usually have them as pets. And pet animals are the tamest. You can keep them in your house. You can also train them and even have fun with them. Examples of some pets are cats, dogs, hamsters, guinea pigs, fish, and birds. So remember, wild animals are the most dangerous animals in the world.

Practice

Workbook Page 156

Write a paragraph explaining how something is classified. For example, you might classify different types of sports or hobbies. Show the categories clearly and use a chart like the one above to organize your ideas. Be sure to use comparison structures correctly.

Writing Checklist

ORGANIZATION:
☑ I organized my writing so that the categories are clearly defined.

CONVENTIONS:
☑ I used comparison structures correctly.

Link the Readings

Critical Thinking

Look back at the readings in this unit. Think about what they have in common. They all tell about the frontier. Yet they do not all have the same purpose. The purpose of one reading might be to inform, while the purpose of another might be to entertain or persuade. In addition, the content of each reading relates to the frontier differently. Now copy the chart below in your notebook and complete it.

Title of Reading	Purpose	Big Question Link
From *River to Tomorrow* "River Song" "Morning Prayer Song"		
"Maps and Compasses"	*to inform*	
"The Cowboy Era"		
From *Pecos Bill: The Greatest Cowboy of All Time*		*tells a story about a boy whose family was traveling across the frontier*

Discussion

Discuss in pairs or small groups.

- Compare and contrast "Maps and Compasses" and "The Cowboy Era." Which text gave you more information?

- **Q Why do we explore new frontiers?** Think about the readings. Why do people explore new frontiers? How has exploring changed? How can exploring new frontiers be dangerous? How can it be exciting?

Fluency Check

Work with a partner. Choose a paragraph from one of the readings. Take turns reading it for one minute. Count the total number of words you read. Practice saying the words you had trouble reading. Take turns reading the paragraph three more times. Did you read more words each time? Copy the chart below into your notebook and record your speeds.

	1st Speed	2nd Speed	3rd Speed	4th Speed
Words Per Minute				

Projects

Work in pairs or small groups. Choose one of these projects.

1 Use the library or Internet to learn more about the journey of Lewis and Clark and Sacagawea. Make a map of their route. Include interesting facts and details. Then present your map to the class.

2 Write a poem about a river. Use the literary elements you have learned in this unit—flashback, dialogue, hyperbole, onomotopoeia—as well as symbolism and figurative language in your poem. Read your poem to the class.

3 Make a collage about the cowboy era. Print out photographs and maps from the Internet or copy them from reference books. Share your collage and explain why you chose each image.

4 Use the library or Internet to find several tall tales about American heroes such as Johnny Appleseed, Annie Oakley, Ezekiel Williams, and Paul Bunyan. Retell the tall tales to the class using your own words. Then compare and contrast the heroes.

Further Reading

To find out more about the theme of this unit, choose from these reading suggestions.

The Road Ahead, Bill Gates
This Penguin Reader® original describes Bill Gates's vision of the future. He describes how he thinks the information revolution will change the way we buy, work, learn, and communicate.

Sarah, Plain and Tall, Patricia Maclachlan
In the late nineteenth century, a widowed Midwestern farmer with two children advertises for a wife. Sarah applies and gets the job. Soon after she moves from her home in Maine, she becomes homesick. Will Sarah stay to make a home on the new frontier?

The Jungle Book, Rudyard Kipling
A family of wolves takes a young child into its jungle home and names him Mowgli. The child plays with the wolf cubs and makes friends with Bagheera, the panther, and Baloo, the bear. But can Mowgli live in the jungle and learn how to speak and hunt the way the animals do?

Put It All Together

LISTENING & SPEAKING WORKSHOP

Group Presentation

You will give a group presentation describing an aspect of life on the American frontier.

1 **THINK ABOUT IT** Review the readings from this unit. Then, in small groups, discuss the cultures, traditions, and values of the characters in the readings. Talk about the lifestyle of a cowboy, a Native American, and a pioneer.

Work together to develop a list of possible topics for a group presentation about frontier life. For example:
- A day in the life of a cowboy
- How Native Americans lived in harmony with the land
- Traveling the Oregon trail

2 **GATHER AND ORGANIZE INFORMATION** As a group, choose a topic from your list. Then brainstorm everything you know about the topic. Use a word web or other graphic organizer to record and organize your ideas. Divide your topic into sections (such as the duties of a cowboy, cowboy meals, and what cowboys did for fun) and assign one section to each group member.

Research Use the library and the Internet to find more information about your topic. Take notes on what you find.

Order Your Notes Share your notes with the group, and discuss which details to include in your presentation. Decide how to begin and end the presentation, and choose a logical order for presenting the different sections. Write your plans in outline form. Arrange your notes for your own part of the presentation in an appropriate order. For example, you could use chronological order to describe a cowboy's daily tasks.

Use Visuals Make or find visual aids such as photos and maps to enhance your presentation. Make sure they're big enough for the audience to see easily.

3 **PRACTICE AND PRESENT** Follow your outline and practice your presentation as a group. Listen to each other and offer suggestions for improvement. Keep practicing until all group members know their parts well. Work on making smooth transitions between speakers. Invite a friend or family member to listen to your group and offer feedback. Ask if the listener can hear and understand each speaker.

Deliver Your Presentation Speak loudly enough so that everyone in the class can hear you. Say each word carefully and clearly. Look at the audience as you speak, and don't hide behind your notes! Hold up your visuals so everyone can see them.

4 **EVALUATE THE PRESENTATION**

You will improve your skills as a speaker and a listener by evaluating each presentation you give and hear. Use this checklist to help you judge your group's presentation and the presentations of other groups.

- ☑ Was the group's topic clear?
- ☑ Could you hear the speakers easily?
- ☑ Could you understand the speakers' words?
- ☑ Were the transitions between speakers smooth and logical?
- ☑ What suggestions do you have for improving the presentation?

 Speaking TIPS

Think of a way to grab the audience's attention and introduce your topic. You might use a quote, make a surprising statement, or ask a question.

Pronounce names and numbers carefully. Write these important details on your visuals so the audience can both see them and hear them.

Listening TIPS

Show interest in what your fellow group members are saying. This will encourage the audience to pay attention, too.

Think about what you are hearing. Try to relate new information to what you already know.

WRITING WORKSHOP

Instructional Essay

In this workshop you will write an instructional essay. An instructional essay provides directions explaining how to do something. For example, an instructional essay might explain how to play a sport, how to bake a cake, or how to build a model airplane. A good instructional essay begins with a paragraph that tells what is going to be taught. The essay includes step-by-step directions presented in a sequence that is easy for readers to follow. Sequence words such as *first*, *next*, and *finally* show the order in which steps happen. Details help readers understand exactly what to do. A concluding paragraph sums up the process taught in the essay.

Your writing assignment for this workshop is to expand the instructional paragraph you wrote for this unit into an instructional essay.

1 PREWRITE Writers need to understand something completely to explain it clearly. Write a list of questions readers might have about the activity explained in your instructional paragraph. Answer these questions clearly and completely when you expand your paragraph into an essay.

List and Organize Your Ideas and Details To organize ideas for your essay, list the steps involved in doing the activity. Make sure the steps are presented in a logical sequence. A student named Caleb wrote about fixing a bike tire. Here is his list.

1. Remove wheel from bike
2. Remove rubber tube from wheel
3. Submerge tube in water
4. Find source of leak
5. Remove tube from water
6. Allow tube to dry
7. Put rubber patch on leak
8. Replace tube on wheel
9. Replace wheel on bike
10. Pump air in tire

2 DRAFT Use the model on page 323 and your numbered list of steps to help you write a first draft. Remember to include enough details to help readers understand exactly how to do the activity.

3 **REVISE** Read over your draft. As you do so, ask yourself the questions in the writing checklist. Use the questions to help you revise your essay.

SIX TRAITS OF WRITING CHECKLIST

☑ **IDEAS:** Does my first paragraph introduce what I am going to teach?

☑ **ORGANIZATION:** Are the directions presented in a logical sequence?

☑ **VOICE:** Does my writing show my interest in the activity?

☑ **WORD CHOICE:** Do I include sequence words to clarify the steps?

☑ **SENTENCE FLUENCY:** Do my sentences vary in length and type?

☑ **CONVENTIONS:** Does my writing follow the rules of grammar, usage, and mechanics?

Here are the changes Caleb plans to make when he revises his first draft:

How to Fix a Bike Tire

Have you ever sprung a leak in your bike tire? Did you have enough
money to buy a new tire? You ~~were~~ not able to afford one. Well, your
[might] [have been]

in luck because this essay will teach you how to patch

a hole in the punctured tube (the rubber part of the tire) with

minimal labor.
[First,]
~~You~~ unscrew the valve stem cap, [which is located on the interior rim of the tire,] releasing all the air from the tube
[Second,]
of the leaking tire. ~~You~~ unscrew the bolt and remove the wheel from
[from]
the bike. Then use a tire lever to separate the rubber tube ~~and~~ the

rest of the wheel. Afterwards, fill a sink with enough water to

---

submerge the tube. ^Next, Watch the tube. You are looking for small air

bubbles escaping the tube. Find the source of the bubbles and put a

small peice of visible tape next to the source

After that, take the tube out of the water and allow it to dry for a

couple of hour. If you want to speed up the drying process you can

use a hair dryer ~~to dry it quicker~~ for a faster result. Once the tube has ^completely dried, remove the

tape. Place a rubber patch over the leak on the tube. ^

Then put the dry and patched tube back on the wheel. Put the

wheel back on the bike and screw in the bolt. Finally, attach a tire

pump to the wheel and pump in the air. ^until the tire feels hard Now you can go outside and

have fun on your repaired bike.

Remember that is how you fix a leak. Remove the tube, place a

patch on the hole, place the tube back in the wheel, put the wheel back

on the bike, and fill it with air. From now on, if you puncture a tire on

your bike, you know how to fix the punctured tube.

4 EDIT AND PROOFREAD  Workbook Page 157

Copy your revised essay onto a clean sheet of paper. Read it again. Correct
any errors in grammar, word usage, mechanics, and spelling. Here are the
additional changes Caleb plans to make when he prepares his final draft.

Caleb Robinson

How to Fix a Bike Tire

Have you ever sprung a leak in your bike tire? Did you have enough
money to buy a new tire? You might not have been able to afford one.
Well, you're in luck because this essay will teach you how to patch a
hole in the punctured tube (the rubber part of the tire) with minimal
labor.

First, unscrew the valve stem cap, which is located on the interior
rim of the tire, releasing all the air from the tube of the leaking tire.
Second, unscrew the bolt and remove the wheel from the bike. Then
use a tire lever to separate the rubber tube from the rest of the wheel.
Afterwards, fill a sink with enough water to submerge the tube. Next,
watch the tube. You are looking for small air bubbles escaping the
tube. Find the source of the bubbles and put a small piece of visible
tape next to the source.

After that, take the tube out of the water and allow it to dry for a
couple of hours. If you want to speed up the drying process, you can use
a hair dryer for a faster result. Once the tube has completely dried,
place a rubber patch over the leak on the tube. Remove the tape.

Then put the dry and patched tube back on the wheel. Put the
wheel back on the bike and screw in the bolt. Finally, attach a tire
pump to the wheel and pump in the air until the tire feels hard. Now
you can go outside and have fun on your repaired bike.

Remember that is how you fix a leak. Remove the tube, place a
patch on the hole, place the tube back in the wheel, put the wheel back
on the bike, and fill it with air. From now on, if you puncture a tire on
your bike, you know how to fix the punctured tube.

5 **PUBLISH** Prepare your final draft. Share your essay with your
teacher and classmates.

Workbook
Page 158

323

The Roots of Frontier Culture

*T*oday we no longer call the land west of the Mississippi River "the frontier." This is because many people live there now. But artists continue to look at what the frontier has meant in American culture.

Norman S. Chamberlain, *Corn Dance, Taos Pueblo* (1934)

Norman Chamberlain saw many Native American ceremonies while visiting Taos, New Mexico, in the 1920s and 1930s. In *Corn Dance, Taos Pueblo*, he paints a harvest dance. The Native Americans in this area often grew corn, and they needed rain. Without rain there would be no crops, and without crops there would be no food. Corn was grown by Native Americans long before settlers arrived on the frontier.

In the painting, Native Americans gather around a single ear of corn. Women on the left hold ears of corn. The men on the right, painted liked spotted cattle, shake maracas, or dried gourds. They make a beat for everyone to dance to. The large figure at the bottom of the painting plays a drum. He is trying to wake up the clouds so they will bring rain.

Chamberlain painted a pink and blue spiral in the center to add even more motion to the painting. The light and dark colors symbolize hope, celebration, and the seriousness of the event.

Norman S. Chamberlain, *Corn Dance, Taos Pueblo*, 1934, oil, 50¼ x 40¼ in., Smithsonian American Art Museum

Luis Jiménez, *Vaquero*,
modeled 1980/cast 1990, urethane
and fiberglass, 199 × 114 × 67 in.,
Smithsonian American Art Museum ▶

Luis Jiménez, *Vaquero* (modeled 1980/cast 1990)

Luis Jiménez's *Vaquero* is a huge fiberglass sculpture. It shows a Mexican-American cowboy. They are called *vaqueros*. The blue-colored horse and active rider is more than 5 meters (16 ft.) high!

Jiménez was born in Texas and first learned to work with his hands as a boy. He helped his father in his neon-sign-making shop. In *Vaquero*, Jiménez captures the energy of the original cowboys from Mexico who worked on the frontier. Most statues of men on horseback show the horse standing still. Jiménez decided to portray a bucking horse. This makes the sculpture dramatic and playful at the same time. The artist chose this subject because he thought it was a "really American image." The cowboys that we often see in the movies actually modeled their clothes and saddles on the ones Mexican cowboys already used.

In both of these artworks, the artists show that new settlers on the frontier borrowed a lot from the people who already lived there.

Apply What You Learned

1 What did the people Chamberlain and Jiménez portray share with others on the frontier?

2 Do you agree with Luis Jiménez that this man on a horse is a "really American image"? Why or why not?

Big Question
Which of these two artworks do you feel is more successful at capturing the spirit of the frontier? Why?

Workbook
Pages 159–160

How do we know what is true?

THE BIG
QUESTION

This unit asks the question: *How do we know what is true?* You will read literature, science, and social studies texts about early astronomers, the seasons, and Earth's movements. Learning about this topic will help you become a better student. It will also help you practice the language you will need to use in school.

READING 1: Myths
- "How Glooskap Found the Summer"
- "Persephone and the Pomegranate Seeds"

READING 2: Social Studies Article
- "Early Astronomers"

READING 3: Play Excerpt
- From *The War of the Worlds* by H. G. Wells, adapted by Howard Koch

READING 4: Science Article
- "Earth's Orbit"

Listening and Speaking

At the end of this unit, you will write and perform a **dramatic scene** in a play.

Writing

In this unit you will practice writing a **research report**. A research report is a type of expository writing. After each reading you will learn a skill that will help you write a research report. At the end of the unit, you will choose one of your paragraphs and develop it into a research report.

QuickWrite

Use a T-chart to compare what you see in the sky during the day with what you see at night.

Visit *LongmanKeystone.com*

327

Prepare to Read

What You Will Learn

Reading

■ Vocabulary building:
*Literary terms,
dictionary skills,
word study*

■ Reading strategy:
*Compare and
contrast*

■ Text type:
Literature (myth)

**Grammar, Usage,
and Mechanics**
Modals to express
ability, necessity, and
permission

Writing
Write an introductory
paragraph

THE BIG QUESTION

How do we know what is true? For thousands of years, people have created stories and myths to try to make sense of the world. Do you think there could be some truth in these made-up stories? Do you ever wonder what causes things like earthquakes and thunderstorms? Or how lakes and mountains were created? Discuss these questions with a partner.

BUILD BACKGROUND

You will read two myths about seasons. These myths come from different times and different cultures. People who lived on opposite sides of the world told the myths you are about to read. Both myths try to explain why Earth has different seasons.

"**How Glooskap Found the Summer**" is a Native American myth that explains why we have summer. "**Persephone and the Pomegranate Seeds**" is an ancient Greek myth that explains why the seasons change.

VOCABULARY

Learn Literary Words

A **myth** is a fictional story. It explains natural events such as wind and rain. Long ago, many people believed that gods controlled these events. People told stories about the gods and their actions as a way of making sense of nature. Parents told these stories to their children, who told them to their children. In this way myths were passed down from generation to generation as part of the spoken, or oral, tradition.

Read the myth below. What event does it try to explain?

> Once there was a boy named Nikolai who was very sensitive. Whenever he saw anyone be mean or cruel, he would cry long and loud. One day, the god of the sky told Nikolai that he was bringing him to live in the heavens. Now Nikolai sits above and watches everyone below. And when he has seen too much cruelty, he cries and cries, and water falls down on Earth.

A **hero** or **heroine** is a character in a story whose actions are inspiring or noble. The word *hero* describes male characters, and *heroine* describes female characters. Heroes and heroines often have to struggle in order to overcome problems.

Read the description below of the most famous Greek hero, Hercules.

> Hercules possessed tremendous bravery, but like all great heroes, he had to endure terrible hardships. He faced and conquered many problems that tested his physical and mental strength. He once came face to face with a lion.

▲ Hercules and the Nemean lion

Practice

Workbook Page 161

Work in small groups. Copy this chart into your notebook. Make a list of heroes or heroines that you have read about or seen in movies.

Hero / Heroine	Details / Characteristics	Book or Movie

Learn Academic Words

Study the **red** words and their meanings. You will find these words useful when talking and writing about literature. Write each word and its meaning in your notebook. After you read "How Glooskap Found the Summer" and "Persephone and the Pomegranate Seeds," try to use these words to respond to the text.

Academic Words

despite
enforce
manipulate
occupy
restore
role

despite = even though (something is known)	Astronauts plan to go to Mars someday **despite** the many challenges and dangers.
enforce = make someone obey	The principal's job is to **enforce** the rules of the school and make sure the students obey them.
manipulate = make someone do exactly what you want by deceiving or influencing him or her	In Greek mythology, the god Zeus wanted to control people and **manipulate** their lives.
occupy = live, work, etc., in a place	The astronauts and scientists who **occupy** the space station often spend many months in space.
restore = make something as good as it was before	They had to **restore** the broken camera lens on the Hubble telescope.
role = function or part	The Greek gods played a major **role** in people's lives.

Practice  Workbook Page 162

Work with a partner to answer these questions. Try to include the **red** word in your answer. Write the sentences in your notebook.

1. Have you ever been nice to someone **despite** their mean behavior?
2. Is the threat of punishment a good way to **enforce** the law?
3. Do you think it is fair to **manipulate** someone to get what you want?
4. What different kinds of people **occupy** a school building?
5. What can people do to help **restore** a town after a flood?
6. What is the **role** of the teacher in your class?

▲ The god Zeus

Word Study: Antonyms

An antonym is a word that means the opposite of another word. The antonym for the word *same* is *different*. Knowing antonyms builds your vocabulary and helps you become a better reader and writer.

Word	Antonym
cold	hot
south	north
winter	summer
sadly	happily

Practice

Copy the chart below into your notebook and complete it by yourself. Then share it with a partner. Did you find the same antonyms? Check a thesaurus to see if there are other antonyms for each word.

Word	Antonym
sit	
found	
wild	
stay	
strong	

READING STRATEGY | COMPARE AND CONTRAST

Comparing and contrasting helps you to understand what you read more clearly. When you compare, you see how things are similar. When you contrast, you see how things are different. To compare and contrast, follow these steps:

- How are the two stories and the characters in the stories similar?
- Can you find any similar events in the stories? Are the outcomes of the events similar?
- What makes the two stories different from each other?
- How are the characters and settings different?

Compare and contrast the characters, the settings, and the events in the two myths "How Glooskap Found the Summer" and "Persephone and the Pomegranate Seeds."

Set a purpose for reading What are the similarities between these two myths? What do these similarities say about how Native Americans and the Greeks explained the seasons? Why do you think they believed their explanations were true?

How Glooskap Found the Summer

Long ago, the Wawaniki people lived in the northeastern part of North America. Their leader's name was Glooskap.

One time, it grew very cold. Snow and ice were everywhere, and plants could not grow. The Wawaniki began to die from the cold and famine. Glooskap traveled far north, where the land was all ice. He came to a wigwam, where he found Winter. Winter was a giant with icy breath. Winter's breath was so cold, it had frozen all the land. Glooskap entered Winter's wigwam and sat down. Winter told him stories of the old times, when he, Winter, ruled Earth, when all the land was white and beautiful. As Winter talked, Glooskap fell asleep. Winter put a charm on Glooskap, and he slept for six months.

Finally, Glooskap woke up. A wild bird named Tatler the Loon came and told him about a country in the south that was always warm. The bird said that a queen lived there who could make Winter go away. "I must save my people," Glooskap thought. So he decided to go south and find the queen.

Glooskap traveled south until he came to a warm forest with many flowers and trees. There he found Summer, the fairy queen. Glooskap knew that Summer could make Winter go away, so he said to her, "Come with me to the land in the far north." Summer agreed to go with Glooskap.

---

famine, time when there is not enough food
wigwam, home that Native Americans often made by covering a frame with bark or animal skins
giant, very large, strong person
put a charm on, used his power on

When they reached Winter's wigwam, Winter welcomed them. "I'll make them fall asleep," Winter thought. But this time, Glooskap's power was stronger because Summer was with him. First, Glooskap and Summer made sweat run down Winter's face. Winter started to cry because he was losing his power. Next, Winter's icy wigwam melted. Then Summer used her power, and everything woke up: The grass and flowers grew, leaves appeared on trees, and the snow ran down the rivers. "My power is gone!" Winter cried.

Then Summer said, "I have proved that I am stronger than you. So now I will give you all the country to the far north. Six months of every year you may come back to Glooskap's country. During the other six months, I will come back to his land."

"I accept your offer," Winter whispered sadly. So every autumn, Winter returns to Glooskap's country and brings cold and snow. When he comes, Summer runs home to her land in the south. But at the end of six months, Summer always returns to drive Winter away and bring back the grass, leaves, and flowers.

---

sweat, liquid that comes out of your skin when you are hot
melted, changed ice to water by heat
drive Winter away, make Winter go away

✔ **LITERARY CHECK**
What does this myth explain?

BEFORE YOU GO ON

1 What problem do the Wawaniki people have?

2 How does Summer help Glooskap?

💡**On Your Own**
Have you ever read a story in which there was a "charm" put on a character? If so, describe it.

333

Persephone and the Pomegranate Seeds

Long ago, Demeter, the goddess of agriculture, had a beautiful daughter named Persephone. Demeter helped trees and plants grow on Earth. Pluto, the god of the underworld, lived under Earth, where it was always dark and cold. Pluto wanted a wife, but no one wanted to leave the sunshine to live in Pluto's dark world underground.

One day Pluto saw Persephone while she was picking flowers. He wanted to marry her, but he knew that Demeter would say no. So he rode a chariot and took Persephone to the underworld. As they were crossing a river, Persephone dropped her flowers into the water.

---

agriculture, farming, especially growing crops
underworld, place where the spirits of the dead lived (in ancient
    Greek mythology)
chariot, ancient vehicle that horses pulled

334

The river took the flowers to Demeter. Demeter asked Zeus, the king of the gods, to help her get Persephone back. Zeus answered, "I'll send my messenger, Hermes, to the underworld. But if Persephone eats anything there, she cannot return to Earth."

Pluto knew that if Persephone ate anything, she must stay with him. So he gave her twelve pomegranate seeds. She was very hungry and started to eat. While she was eating, Hermes arrived.

"Persephone, did you eat the twelve seeds?" he inquired.

"I ate only six," she replied. Hermes didn't know what to do, so he returned to Zeus.

Zeus said, "Persephone ate six seeds, so she must stay in the underworld six months a year. She can spend the other six months on Earth with Demeter."

And that is why there are six cold months of autumn and winter each year, and six warm months of spring and summer.

messenger, someone who takes information from one person to another

✔ LITERARY CHECK

Who is the hero or heroine of this story?

BEFORE YOU GO ON

1 What does Pluto give Persephone? Why?

2 What does Zeus decide?

On Your Own
What does this myth explain?

335

READER'S THEATER

Act out this retelling of "How Glooskap Found the Summer."

Glooskap: Summer, I'm so glad to have found you. I need your help.

Summer: What is it, Glooskap? What's the problem?

Glooskap: Winter is ruining the lives of my people. We can't grow any plants. Many people are dying.

Summer: Oh, that Winter! He thinks he is so powerful. We'll show him that he's not. I'll help you, Glooskap. Take me to him.

Glooskap: Thank you, Summer. He lives in the far north.

[Summer and Glooskap travel to Winter's wigwam.]

Winter: Summer and Glooskap, it's so nice to see you.

Glooskap: You can't manipulate me with your power this time, Winter.

Winter: Aaaah! What's happening to me? I am dripping and sweating. And why aren't you falling asleep?

Glooskap: Summer is with me and your powers are no match for hers.

Winter: What's happening? My wigwam is disappearing! Everything's melting. Where's my power?

Summer: As you can see, I am stronger than you, Winter. So now you must do as I say. You can come back to Glooskap's country for six months and then you must leave.

Winter: Fine. I'll agree to your demand. I have no other choice.

COMPREHENSION

Workbook
Page 165

Right There

1. How did Glooskap find out about the warm land in the south?
2. What was Demeter's role on Earth?

Think and Search

3. In the first myth, how are the powers of Winter and Summer similar? How are they different?
4. In the second myth, what did the twelve pomegranate seeds stand for? What happens during winter and summer?

Author and You

5. What can you infer about the culture and beliefs of the Native Americans who created the myth about Glooskap?

6. What does the myth of "Persephone and the Pomegranate Seeds" suggest about the gods and their relationship to Earth?

On Your Own

7. What are winter and summer like where you live?

8. Do you prefer winter or summer? Explain.

DISCUSSION

Discuss in pairs or small groups.

1. Do you agree with Zeus's decision to allow Persephone to stay in the underworld for six months? How would you resolve the conflict?

2. Compare and contrast the two myths. How are they similar? What do the similarities suggest? In what ways are the myths different?

3. Why do you think both the Native American and Greek cultures created myths about the seasons?

Q **How do we know what is true?** Ancient cultures depended on oral traditions such as myths to understand the world. What are our sources today for understanding natural events and why things happen? How do we know if the information is true?

 *Speaking* TIP

Share personal experiences that illustrate your ideas. This will help make your response more interesting and persuasive.

RESPONSE TO LITERATURE

 **Workbook** Page 165

Both myths explain why Earth has different seasons. Work with a partner to find myths from other cultures that explain the seasons. Share the myths with the class.

▲ Spring   ▲ Summer   ▲ Fall   ▲ Winter

Grammar and Writing

GRAMMAR, USAGE, AND MECHANICS

Modals to Express Ability, Necessity, and Permission

Modals are helping verbs. They have only one form and do not take an -*s* in the third-person singular. Always use a modal + the base form of the verb.

Can / *Could* to Express Ability
Summer **can** travel with Glooskap to the north. A queen lived there who **could** make Winter go away.

Must / *Have to* / *Had to* to Express Necessity
I **must** save my people. They **have to** obey the gods. Demeter **had to** find her daughter.

Can / *Could* / *May* to Ask and Give Permission
She **can** spend the other six months on Earth with Demeter. **Could** you please help Persephone? Six months of every year you **may** come back to Glooskap's country.

Practice  Workbook Page 166

Work with a partner. Copy the sentences into your notebook. Choose the correct modal for each sentence.

1. You **can** / **may** learn a lot from myths.

2. You **must** / **could** eat to survive.

3. You **may** / **have to** write about any myth you choose.

4. **Can** / **May** Demeter help her daughter?

5. Myths **could** / **had to** help ancient cultures to explain nature.

338

WRITING A RESEARCH REPORT

Write an Introductory Paragraph

At the end of this unit, you will write a research report. On this page you'll learn to choose and narrow a topic. Then you'll do some research and write an introductory paragraph.

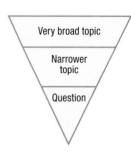

Very broad topic

Narrower topic

Question

Suppose your topic was Native American masks. You might narrow it by choosing a Native American group, such as the Kwakiutl. To narrow it further, write a question to direct your research: *What features do authentic Kwakiutl masks share?* Once you write a question, choose resources and begin your research.

After you have researched your topic and have organized your ideas, you can begin writing. The introductory paragraph should present your topic clearly and grab the reader's attention.

Here is a model of an introductory paragraph. Before writing, the writer narrowed his topic using a graphic organizer. He also did some research to find out the answer to his question.

Caleb Robinson

Masks of the Kwakiutl

The Kwakiutl Native Americans created some of the greatest masks ever. They wore these masks to ceremonies and special occasions. To be authentic Kwakiutl masks, the masks must be made of red and yellow cedar. Cedar is a soft wood, so the Kwakiutl could easily carve it. The masks have curves and rigid lines to show nostrils. Some of these masks are called transformation masks. The Kwakiutl believed that animals and humans shared a bond and could take the form of one another. The transformation masks show this by having movable parts. When the mask is closed, it can look like a bird or another animal. But when it is open, it shows a human form.

Practice

Workbook Page 167

Select a topic related to the arts or crafts of a culture other than your own. Use a graphic organizer like the one above to narrow your topic, and write a question to direct your research. Then do some research to answer your question. Write an introductory paragraph for a research paper on the topic. Be sure to use modals correctly.

Writing Checklist

IDEAS:
☑ I clearly stated the topic of my report.

CONVENTIONS:
☑ I used modals correctly.

What You Will Learn

Reading

■ Vocabulary building: *Context, dictionary skills, word study*

■ Reading strategy: *Evaluate new information*

■ Text type: *Informational text (social studies)*

Grammar, Usage, and Mechanics
Participial adjectives

Writing
Suppport the main idea with facts and details

THE BIG QUESTION

How do we know what is true? Throughout history, people have believed many things that we now know are not true. For example, people once believed that the sun revolved around Earth. The development of science and technology has answered many questions. Are there still things about the universe that we don't know about? Do you think one day we will know everything? Discuss these questions with a partner.

BUILD BACKGROUND

Astronomers are scientists who study the sky to learn about planets, stars, and other objects. The social studies article **"Early Astronomers"** tells about some of the first people who studied the stars and planets. By studying the stars, astronomers made discoveries such as how to count days, predict seasons, and tell direction.

◀ A fifteenth-century Aztec calendar

Learn Key Words

Read these sentences. Use the context to figure out the meaning of the red words. Use a dictionary to check your answers. Then write each word and its meaning in your notebook.

1. When you look at the night sky, you sometimes see groups of stars that form **constellations**, such as the Big Dipper and Orion.

2. Scientists today study the sky and hope to make new **discoveries** about stars and planets.

3. A **galaxy** consists of billions of stars and planets, as well as gases and dust. Our galaxy is called the Milky Way.

4. Falling stars are an unusual **phenomenon** that few people see.

5. The sun is the center of our **solar system**. Our solar system is made up of Earth and seven other planets.

6. A **telescope** helps us to see objects in the sky much larger and clearer than we can see with the naked eye.

▲ The solar system

Practice

Workbook Page 168

Write the sentences in your notebook. Choose a red word from the box above to complete each sentence. Then take turns reading the sentences aloud with a partner.

1. The _____ is a very helpful tool for studying the sky.

2. Early astronomers looked at the night sky and made _____ about the stars.

3. When you look at the night sky, try to find groups of stars that might be _____.

4. Three of the planets in our _____ are Mercury, Venus, and Jupiter.

5. There are many billions of stars in a _____.

6. Astronomers can now explain the _____ of why planets go around the sun.

Learn Academic Words

Study the red words and their meanings. You will find these words useful when talking and writing about informational texts. Write each word and its meaning in your notebook. After you read "Early Astronomers," try to use these words to respond to the text.

Academic Words

identified
location
philosopher
predictable
theory

identified = knew; recognized	➡	Some early astronomers **identified** the objects in the sky as planets, not stars.
location = place or position	➡	A sundial is a very old clock that measures time by the **location** of the sun.
philosopher = a person who studies life and what it means, how we should live, and what knowledge is	➡	The famous Greek **philosopher** Socrates was interested in seeking knowledge by asking questions.
predictable = usual, expected, or obvious	➡	He studied hard, so it was **predictable** that he would do well on the test.
theory = idea that tries to explain something, but it may or may not be true	➡	The **theory** that the sun revolved around Earth was proved false.

Practice  Workbook Page 169

Work with a partner to complete these sentences using the sentence starters. Include the red word in your sentence. Then write the sentence in your notebook.

1. The scientist identified . . .
2. The location of the constellation . . .
3. A philosopher asks . . .
4. The weather is predictable in . . .
5. The astronomer's theory was . . .

A sundial ▶

Word Study: Spelling Long *i*

The letter *i* stands for different sounds. Short *i* is usually spelled *i*.
Long *i* has several different spellings: *i_e*, *igh*, *ie*, and *y*. Read the
examples of each long *i* sound-spelling in the chart below.

i_e	igh	ie	-y
kite	night	pie	sky
ride	high	cried	why
hike	light	ties	fly

Practice  **Workbook** Page 170

Work with a partner. Copy the chart above into your notebook with
additional rows. Take turns reading the words in the box below. Write
each word in the correct column.

bike	dry	price	shy	slight	try
dried	five	right	sigh	spied	wife

READING STRATEGY | EVALUATE NEW INFORMATION

Evaluating new information helps you connect new information to
information you already know. It also helps you understand the content
of a text more easily. To evaluate new information, follow these steps:

- Before you read, ask yourself, "What do I know about this subject?"
- As you read, make a note of the new information you find.
- Compare the new information to what you already know. Is it similar
  or different from what you know?
- Does the new information help you understand the subject better?

Before you read "Early Astronomers," think about what you know
about astronomy. As you read, make a note of new and interesting
information. Use a T-chart to list what you knew already and what
you learn.

 **Workbook** Page 171

343

Set a purpose for reading How did early astronomers discover the truth about the movements of the sun and Earth?

Early Astronomers

Imagine a time thousands of years ago. You are looking at the night sky. You don't have a watch on your wrist, a map in your hands, or a calendar on your wall. You've never seen a globe or a picture of the solar system. Above you are dazzling points of light scattered across the darkness. You are amazed, but you don't understand what you see.

The night sky fascinated the first philosophers and astronomers. They were intrigued by its beauty and mystery. They studied the sky and made drawings of what they saw. Over time, they began to notice that the points of light moved in regular, predictable patterns. They wanted to identify and understand these points of light and their patterns.

People's ability to tell time, count days, predict seasons, and tell direction came as a result of studying the stars. By noting the positions of stars in the sky over periods of time, people developed ways to tell direction. This was very important for nomadic people especially. Noting the changes in the sun's position in the sky enabled people to predict the change of seasons. This was important for people like the ancient Maya. They created their own calendar, as accurate as the one we use today. Having a calendar helped them know when to plant and when to harvest.

▲ An ancient Maya calendar

---

globe, ball with a map of the world on it
dazzling, very bright
intrigued, very interested
nomadic, wandering or roaming

Aristotle (384–322 B.C.E.)

The ancient Greeks were extraordinary astronomers. They were responsible for many discoveries that form the basis of what we know today. For example, they discovered that some of the bright objects in the sky were not stars but planets. In fact, the word *planet* comes from the Greek word *planetes*. The Greeks also identified and recorded the locations of constellations in the sky. Constellations are groups of stars that form a pattern. Sometimes these patterns look like pictures. The Greeks named constellations after their gods, such as Orion the hunter. They were the first astronomers to name and catalogue everything they could see in the sky.

One of the most famous men of his time was the Greek philosopher Aristotle. His writings covered a wide variety of subjects, such as logic and astronomy. Aristotle believed that Earth was the center of the solar system and did not move. This view of the world lasted for over 1,000 years.

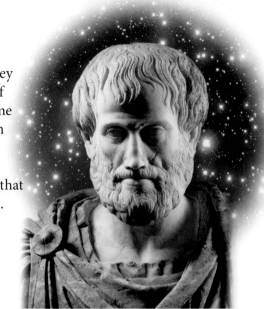

▲ Aristotle

Al-Sufi (908–986 C.E.)

People throughout the Middle East also studied the sky. In Persia (modern-day Iran) during the tenth century, the astronomer Al-Sufi translated many of the Greek works on astronomy. Through his own studies, he located and identified more than 1,000 different stars.

In 964 C.E., Al-Sufi published a book called *The Book of Fixed Stars*. It illustrates the color, brightness, and position of stars in the sky. This book describes a galaxy of stars and planets beyond our own galaxy. Al-Sufi and his work were unknown in Europe. Europeans learned about the stars 600 years later when the telescope was developed.

---

pattern, regular arrangement
catalogue, list

Al-Sufi ▶

BEFORE YOU GO ON

1 Why was having a calendar important to the ancient Maya?

2 What did Al-Sufi's book illustrate?

On Your Own
Why do you think people throughout history have been fascinated with astronomy?

345

▲ Nicolas Copernicus

Nicolas Copernicus (1473–1543)

At the end of the Middle Ages, a Polish astronomer named Nicolas Copernicus sparked a revolution in scientific thinking. He believed that the sun—not Earth—was the center of the solar system, and that Earth moved around the sun in a perfect circle. The idea of the sun as the center of the solar system contradicted the beliefs of the time, including the beliefs of the Roman Catholic Church. The Church condemned Copernicus during his lifetime, but today he is considered the founder of modern astronomy.

Johannes Kepler (1571–1630)

Like Copernicus, German mathematician and astronomer Johannes Kepler believed that the sun was the center of the solar system. Kepler found the mathematical calculations to support this belief. However, he also discovered that the orbits of the planets around the sun could not be perfect circles, as Copernicus had believed. They had to be elliptical, or oval shaped. Kepler knew from the calculations that this was true, but he didn't know why. The answer came later from the work of the astronomers who followed after him.

---

sparked, activated or set off
contradicted, was the opposite of
condemned, disapproved of

▲ Johannes Kepler

▲ Galileo Galilei

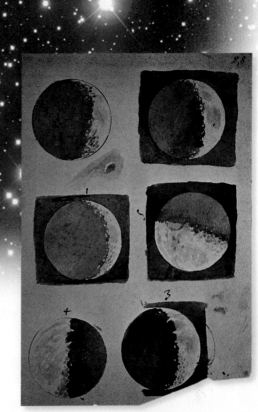

▲ Sketches of the moon by Galileo, from his book *The Starry Messenger,* 1616

Galileo Galilei (1564–1642)

Galileo, the Italian physicist, mathematician, astronomer, and philosopher is often called the father of modern science. He asked questions, made observations, and tested his theories. This would later be known as "the scientific method" of investigation.

In 1609, Galileo learned about the invention of the telescope. He improved the design of the telescope so that it gave a much better view of the stars and planets. His telescope magnified objects to thirty times their real size. He discovered that the Milky Way is made up of millions of stars. He also discovered Saturn's rings and Jupiter's moons. Amazingly, no additional moons of Jupiter were discovered until 400 years later, in 2002.

Galileo believed that Earth traveled around the sun. He published his theories and findings in the book *Dialogue on the Two Great World Systems.* Galileo was warned by the Roman Catholic Church to stop teaching his theories, but Galileo refused. He was brought before the Inquisition, a religious court. The court found him guilty of speaking against the Church's beliefs. In 1633, Galileo was sentenced to stay inside his house for the rest of his life.

---

method, planned way of doing something
warned, told something bad might happen

BEFORE YOU GO ON

1 What did Johannes Kepler discover about the shape of the planets' orbits?

2 Who is called "the father of modern science"?

On Your Own
Why do you think the Church was angry about Galileo's theories?

COMPREHENSION  **Workbook** Page 172

Right There

1. What was Aristotle's theory about the solar system? How long did people consider this view of the world to be true?

2. What discoveries did Galileo make using his telescope?

Think and Search

3. How did knowing the location of the stars and the sun in the sky help early astronomers?

4. What was Copernicus's belief about the solar system and why was it so important?

Author and You

5. Why do you think people believed that Earth was the center of the solar system? Why was it difficult for people to accept the belief that Earth moved around the sun?

6. Do you think the author of this article would agree or disagree with the following statement: "There were no important advances in the science of astronomy before the development of the telescope."

On Your Own

7. Do you know about any recent discoveries that astronomers have made using telescopes?

8. What do you think astronomers might discover in the future?

IN YOUR OWN WORDS

Think about the information you have just read. Did you learn something new? Copy the chart below into your notebook. Then write the most important facts you learned from the text. Include details that support the facts. Compare your chart with a partner.

Facts	Details

DISCUSSION

Discuss in pairs or small groups.

1. What characteristics did the astronomers you read about share? Why are these characteristics important for an astronomer to have?

2. The astronomers in the reading lived during different time periods. Imagine if Copernicus, Kepler, and Galileo had met to discuss their theories. What do you think they might have said to each other?

Q **How do we know what is true?** What truth about the solar system did the early astronomers discover? How do you think their work has helped today's astronomers?

READ FOR FLUENCY

When we read aloud to communicate meaning, we group words into phrases, pause or slow down to make important points, and emphasize important words. Pause for a short time when you reach a comma and for a longer time when you reach a period. Pay attention to rising and falling intonation at the end of sentences.

Work with a partner. Choose a paragraph from the reading. Discuss which words seem important for communicating meaning. Practice pronouncing difficult words. Take turns reading the paragraph aloud and give each other feedback.

EXTENSION  **Workbook** Page 172

Choose the astronomer that you find the most interesting. Research the person on the Internet or go to the library to learn more about his life and work. Write some notes about the astronomer and share them with the class.

Isaac Newton (1642–1727), English physicist, mathematician, and astronomer ▶

Grammar and Writing

Participial Adjectives

Participial adjectives—adjectives ending in *-ing* and *-ed*—describe nouns or pronouns.

Adjectives ending in *-ing* describe the cause of a feeling.
The points of light are **dazzling**. [describes *the points of light*] The solar system is **amazing**. [describes *the solar system*] The night sky's beauty was **intriguing**. [describes *the night sky's beauty*]

Adjectives ending in *-ed* describe how a person feels.
We are **dazzled** by the points of light. [describes how *we* feel] You are **amazed**, but you don't understand it. [describes how *you* feel] They were **intrigued** by the night sky's beauty. [describes how *they* felt]

Practice  **Workbook Page 173**

Copy the chart below into your notebook. Then write a sentence for each adjective. Work with a partner and compare your sentences.

-ing	Sentence	-ed	Sentence
exciting		excited	
fascinating		fascinated	
interesting		interested	
thrilling		thrilled	

The night sky ▶

350

WRITING A RESEARCH REPORT

Support the Main Idea with Facts and Details

You've learned that in a research report, a writer chooses a topic and then narrows it down. After the introduction, each paragraph contains a main idea supported by facts and details. The main idea is the most important point in a paragraph. The details and facts that follow should support the main idea. As you research, take notes that list facts and details about your main idea. You can arrange the facts and details you've found in a word web and consult it as you write your paragraph.

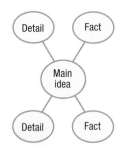

Here is a model paragraph by a student whose favorite hobby is astronomy. Notice how he supports the main idea with facts and details. He used a word web to help organize his ideas.

> *Sebastian Z. Mitchell*
>
> ### Astronomy for the Amateur
>
> Amateur astronomy is a hobby that is interesting and exciting for all ages. I like amateur astronomy because you get to use telescopes to view celestial objects like planets and comets. Not only is it fun, but it also helps you learn about our universe. You can practice amateur astronomy on your own, or with a group of people or club. Sometimes astronomy clubs have star parties, where astronomers gather, look at stars and planets, talk, and participate in activities. Some amateurs even practice astrophotography, where they take pictures of the night sky with high-quality cameras. You don't have to be a scientist to join a local astronomy group. You don't even need a telescope. So give amateur astronomy a try. You'll be amazed.

Practice

Workbook Page 174

Write a paragraph for a research report in which you present a main idea and include facts and details that support it. For your topic, you may want to develop the main idea from your introductory paragraph, or come up with a new one. List your details and facts before writing. Use a word web like the one above to help organize your ideas. Be sure to include participial adjectives.

Writing Checklist

VOICE:
☑ I chose a tone appropriate to fact-based writing.

WORD CHOICE:
☑ I chose words that make my facts and details clear.

351

Prepare to Read

What You Will Learn

Reading

■ Vocabulary building: *Literary terms, word study*

■ Reading strategy: *Analyze text structure*

■ Text type: *Literature (radio play)*

Grammar, Usage, and Mechanics
Punctuation of quoted speech

Writing
Include quotations and citations

THE BIG QUESTION

How do we know what is true? We get our news and information from many different sources, such as newspapers, television, radio, and the Internet. How can we be sure that what we read and hear is true? Do you think the people who provide news and information have a responsibility to tell the truth? Discuss these questions with a partner.

BUILD BACKGROUND

You will read an excerpt from a radio play based on the novel **The War of the Worlds** by H. G. Wells. The novel is a work of fiction, written in 1898, about a spacecraft from Mars that crashes into Earth. Aliens—creatures from outer space—invade our planet. Forty years later, the Hollywood writer, actor, and director Orson Welles and actors from the Mercury Theatre performed the play on the radio.

In the 1930s, before television was invented, radio was a very important source of news and information for ordinary people. When this play was first performed, many listeners thought it was a real news report. They were frightened because they believed aliens were really invading Earth. As you read this selection, you will see why people mistook this play for a real news report.

Orson Welles (1915–1987) ▶

VOCABULARY

Learn Literary Words

The radio play based on *The War of the Worlds* is science fiction.
Science fiction is a type of literature with imaginary events that
involve science and technology. Science fiction stories often
occur in the future and have aliens or other fantastic creatures as
characters. Science fiction is sometimes called fantasy because
the setting, plot, and characters are not true to life.

Which words in this passage tell you that it is science fiction?

> **Professor Pierson:**   I don't know what to think. The metal casing is definitely
> extraterrestrial . . . not found on this earth. Friction with the earth's
> atmosphere usually tears holes in a meteorite. This thing is smooth and, as
> you can see, of cylindrical shape.

Like most plays, the radio play based on *The War of the Worlds* has
stage directions. **Stage directions** are notes included in a play to
describe how the work is supposed to be performed. These instructions
are printed in *italics* and are set off by parentheses ( ) or brackets [ ].
Stage directions are used to describe sets, lighting, sound effects, and
the movements of characters. Because a radio play is meant to be
listened to instead of watched, many of the stage directions tell what
kinds of sound effects are to be made.

> **Announcer Two:**   We take you now to Grovers Mill, New Jersey.
>   [*crowd noises . . . police sirens*]

Practice

Workbook
Page 175

Work with a partner. Look at the excerpt from *The War of the
Worlds* on page 356. Answer the following questions:

1. How can you tell that this is a play?
2. Who are some of the characters?
3. Which lines are not spoken?
4. Where and when does the action of the play take place?
5. What details might tell you that this is science fiction?

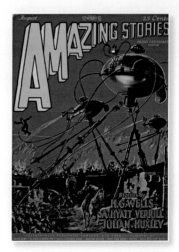

A science fiction magazine cover, 1927 ▶

Learn Academic Words

Study the **red** words and their meanings. You will find these words useful when talking and writing about literature. Write each word and its meaning in your notebook. After you read the excerpt from *The War of the Worlds*, try to use these words to respond to the text.

Academic Words

conferring
evidently
occurrence
version
visible

conferring = discussing with other people	→	The students were **conferring** loudly about the news report they heard on the radio.
evidently = easily noticed or understood	→	The movie was **evidently** science fiction because the spaceship came from Mars.
occurrence = something that happens	→	The Northern Lights are a common **occurrence** in the skies over Alaska.
version = copy of something that has been slightly changed	→	The movie **version** of the book was very exciting.
visible = able to be seen	→	On a clear night, the moon and the stars are **visible** in the sky.

Practice  **Workbook Page 176**

Work with a partner to complete these sentences using the sentence starters. Include the **red** word in your sentence. Then write the sentence in your notebook.

1. When Liz saw her friends **conferring** quietly without her, she . . .
2. Class is cancelled tomorrow because **evidently** . . .
3. Jim had never seen such an **occurrence** . . .
4. That's what I remember. Your **version** . . .
5. Some planets are only **visible** . . .

▲ The Northern Lights

Word Study: Words Ending in *-ible / -able*

Many words end in *-ible* and *-able*. It is sometimes difficult to know which ending to use. Most of the time, if the root is not a complete word, add *-ible*. If the root is a complete word, add *-able*.

-ible	-able
vis**ible**, horr**ible**, poss**ible**	comfort**able**, suit**able**, laugh**able**

If the root is a complete word that ends with an *e*, drop the *e* and add *-able*.

describe + *able* = *describable*

Practice  Workbook Page 177

Work with a partner. Copy the sentences below into your notebook. Fill in the correct ending. Take turns reading the sentences aloud.

1. The announcer said, "This is an incred_____ sight!"
2. They asked for help from anyone who was avail_____.
3. It was a terr_____ looking creature.
4. The scientist's information was accurate and depend_____.
5. We ran away. It was the sens_____ thing to do.

READING STRATEGY   ANALYZE TEXT STRUCTURE

Analyzing text structure can help you understand what kind of text you're reading. It can also help you set a purpose for reading. There are many different types of text structure, including poems, plays, and stories. To analyze text structure, read these descriptions:

- Stories are written in paragraphs. Dialogue is enclosed within quotation marks.
- Poems are usually written in lines and groups of lines. The punctuation may be different from other types of text.
- Plays are mainly written in dialogue. The dialogue has the speakers' names, followed by colons, and then the words the speaker says. Stage directions are usually in parentheses or brackets.

Review the text structure of the excerpt from the radio play *The War of the Worlds*. Discuss it with a partner.

 Workbook Page 178

Set a purpose for reading Why do you think people believed that the events in this play were true?

from

THE *War* OF THE *Worlds*

H. G. Wells,
adapted for radio by Howard Koch

On October 30, 1938, a "news bulletin" interrupted a music program on the radio. It was announced that a spaceship from the planet Mars had landed in New Jersey.

CARL PHILLIPS: Ladies and gentlemen, I shall read you a wire addressed to Professor Pierson from Dr. Gray of the National History Museum, New York. "9:15 P.M. Eastern Standard Time. Seismograph registered shock of almost earthquake intensity occurring within a radius of twenty miles of Princeton. Please investigate. Signed, Lloyd Gray, Chief of Astronomical Division," . . . Professor Pierson, could this occurrence possibly have something to do with the disturbances observed on the planet Mars?

PROF. PIERSON: Hardly, Mr. Phillips. This is probably a meteorite of unusual size and its arrival at this particular time is merely a coincidence. However, we shall conduct a search, as soon as daylight permits.

CARL PHILLIPS: Thank you, Professor. Ladies and gentlemen, for the past ten minutes we've been speaking to you from the observatory at Princeton, bringing you a special interview with Professor Pierson, noted astronomer. This is Carl Phillips speaking. We are returning you now to our New York studio.

---

seismograph, instrument that measures movement of
   the ground during an earthquake
intensity, strength
radius, distance from the center to the edge of a circle
meteorite, piece of rock or metal that comes
   from space

[fade in piano playing]

ANNOUNCER TWO: Ladies and gentlemen, here is the latest bulletin from the Intercontinental Radio News. Toronto, Canada: Professor Morse of McGill University reports observing a total of three explosions on the planet Mars, between the hours of 7:45 P.M. and 9:20 P.M., Eastern Standard Time. This confirms earlier reports received from American observatories. Now, nearer home, comes a special bulletin from Trenton, New Jersey. It is reported that at 8:50 P.M. a huge, flaming object, believed to be a meteorite, fell on a farm in the neighborhood of Grovers Mill, New Jersey, twenty-two miles from Trenton.

The flash in the sky was visible within a radius of several hundred miles and the noise of the impact was heard as far north as Elizabeth.

We have dispatched a special mobile unit to the scene, and will have our commentator, Carl Phillips, give you a word description as soon as he can reach there from Princeton.

In the meantime, we take you to the Hotel Martinet in Brooklyn, where Bobby Millette and his orchestra are offering a program of dance music.

[swing band for twenty seconds . . . then cut]

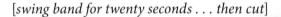

bulletin, official statement
confirms, proves
dispatched, sent out
mobile, able to move

BEFORE YOU GO ON

1 Where does Dr. Gray work? What is his title?

2 Where is Carl Phillips speaking from?

On Your Own
Have you ever heard an important news bulletin? How did it make you feel?

357

ANNOUNCER TWO: We take you now to Grovers Mill, New Jersey. [*crowd noises . . . police sirens*]

CARL PHILLIPS: Ladies and gentlemen, this is Carl Phillips again, out at the Wilmuth farm, Grovers Mill, New Jersey. Professor Pierson and myself made the eleven miles from Princeton in ten minutes. Well, I . . . I hardly know where to begin, to paint for you a word picture of the strange scene before my eyes, like something out of a modern "Arabian Nights." Well, I just got here. I haven't had a chance to look around yet. I guess that's it. Yes, I guess that's the . . . thing, directly in front of me, half buried in a vast pit. Must have struck with terrific force. The ground is covered with splinters of a tree it must have struck on its way down. What I can see of the . . . object itself doesn't look very much like a meteor, at least not the meteors I've seen. It looks more like a huge cylinder. It has a diameter of . . . what would you say, Professor Pierson?

PROF. PIERSON: [*off-mike*] What's that?

CARL PHILLIPS: What would you say . . . what is the diameter?

PROF. PIERSON: About thirty yards.

---

splinters, sharp pieces
meteor, piece of rock or metal in space
cylinder, long round shape like a tube
diameter, length of the straight line through the center of a circle

358

CARL PHILLIPS: About thirty yards . . . The metal on the sheath is . . . well, I've never seen anything like it. The color is sort of yellowish-white. Curious spectators now are pressing close to the object in spite of the efforts of the police to keep them back. They're getting in front of my line of vision. Would you mind standing to one side, please?

POLICEMAN: One side, there, one side.

CARL PHILLIPS: While the policemen are pushing the crowd back, here's Mr. Wilmuth, owner of the farm here. He may have some interesting facts to add . . . Mr. Wilmuth, would you please tell the radio audience as much as you remember of this rather unusual visitor that dropped in your backyard? Step closer, please. Ladies and gentlemen, this is Mr. Wilmuth.

MR. WILMUTH: Well, I was listenin' to the radio.

CARL PHILLIPS: Closer and louder please.

MR. WILMUTH: Pardon me?

CARL PHILLIPS: Louder, please, and closer.

MR. WILMUTH: Yes, sir—I was listening to the radio and kinda drowsin', that Professor fellow was talkin' about Mars, so I was half dozin' and half . . .

CARL PHILLIPS: Yes, yes, Mr. Wilmuth. Then what happened?

MR. WILMUTH: As I was sayin', I was listenin' to the radio kinda halfways . . .

CARL PHILLIPS: Yes, Mr. Wilmuth, and then you saw something?

MR. WILMUTH: Not first off. I heard something.

---

sheath, cover
spectators, people watching an event
drowsin', falling asleep
dozin', sleeping

BEFORE YOU GO ON

1 Where is Carl Phillips now?

2 Who is the owner of the farm?

On Your Own
Have you ever been in a crowd watching an event? Describe it.

359

CARL PHILLIPS: And what did you hear?

MR. WILMUTH: A hissing sound. Like this: Sssssssss . . . kinda like a fourt' of July rocket.

CARL PHILLIPS: Yes?

MR. WILMUTH: Turned my head out the window and would have swore I was to sleep and dreamin'.

CARL PHILLIPS: Then what?

MR. WILMUTH: I seen a kinda greenish streak and then zingo! Somethin' smacked the ground. Knocked me clear out of my chair!

CARL PHILLIPS: Well, were you frightened, Mr. Wilmuth?

MR. WILMUTH: Well, I—I ain't quite sure. I reckon I—I was kinda riled.

CARL PHILLIPS: Thank you, Mr. Wilmuth. Thank you very much.

MR. WILMUTH: Want me to tell you some more?

CARL PHILLIPS: No . . . That's quite all right, that's plenty.

Ladies and gentlemen, you've just heard Mr. Wilmuth, owner of the farm where this thing has fallen. I wish I could convey the atmosphere . . . the background of this . . . fantastic scene. Hundreds of cars are parked in a field in back of us. Police are trying to rope off the roadway leading into the farm. But it's no use. They're breaking right through. Cars' headlights throw an enormous spot on the pit where the object's half buried. Some of the more daring souls are now venturing near the edge. Their silhouettes stand out against the metal sheen.

[*faint humming sound*]

One man wants to touch the thing . . . he's having an argument with a policeman. The policeman wins . . . Now, ladies and gentlemen, there's something I haven't mentioned in all this excitement, but now it's becoming more distinct. Perhaps you've caught it already on your radio. Listen, please: [*long pause*] . . .

Do you hear it? It's a curious humming sound that seems to come from inside the object. I'll move the microphone nearer. [*pause*] Now we're not more than twenty-five feet away. Can you hear it now? Oh, Professor Pierson!

Prof. Pierson: Yes, Mr. Phillips?

✔ **LITERARY CHECK**

How do the the stage directions add to the suspense of the radio play?

---

fourt', fourth
zingo, all of a sudden
reckon, think
riled, upset
venturing, going somewhere when it could be dangerous
sheen, smooth, shiny appearance

CARL PHILLIPS: Can you tell us the meaning of that scraping noise inside the thing?

PROF. PIERSON: Possibly the unequal cooling of its surface.

CARL PHILLIPS: I see, do you still think it's a meteor, Professor?

PROF. PIERSON: I don't know what to think. The metal casing is definitely extraterrestrial . . . not found on this earth. Friction with the earth's atmosphere usually tears holes in a meteorite. This thing is smooth and, as you can see, of cylindrical shape.

CARL PHILLIPS: Just a minute! Something's happening! Ladies and gentlemen, this is terrific! This end of the thing is beginning to flake off! The top is beginning to rotate like a screw! The thing must be hollow!

VOICES: She's movin'! Look, the darn thing's unscrewing! Keep back, there! Keep back, I tell you! Maybe there's men in it trying to escape! It's red hot, they'll burn to a cinder! Keep back there. Keep those idiots back!

[suddenly the clanking sound of a huge piece of falling metal]

VOICES: She's off! The top's loose! Look out there! Stand back!

CARL PHILLIPS: Ladies and gentlemen, this is the most terrifying thing I have ever witnessed . . . Wait a minute! Someone's crawling out of the hollow top. Someone or . . . something. I can see peering out of that black hole two luminous disks . . . are they eyes? It might be a face. It might be . . .

[shout of awe from the crowd]

CARL PHILLIPS: Good heavens, something's wriggling out of the shadow like a gray snake. Now it's another one, and another. They look like tentacles to me. There, I can see the thing's body. It's large, large as a bear and it glistens like wet leather. But that face, it . . . Ladies and gentlemen, it's indescribable. I can hardly force myself to keep looking at it. The eyes are black and gleam like a serpent. The mouth is V-shaped with saliva dripping from its rimless lips that seem to quiver and pulsate. The monster or whatever it is can hardly move. It seems weighed down by . . . possibly gravity or something. The thing's rising up. The crowd falls back now.

---

casing, outer layer
extraterrestrial, from another planet
cylindrical, cylinder-like
cinder, small piece of burnt material
luminous, brightly shining
tentacles, long thin parts of a creature, such as an octopus
indescribable, too strange or frightening to be described
quiver, tremble slightly
pulsate, beat

BEFORE YOU GO ON

1 What kinds of sounds came from the object?

2 What came crawling out of the top?

On Your Own
Did you ever interview someone? If so, who?

361

They've seen plenty. This is the most extraordinary experience. I can't find words . . . I'll pull this microphone with me as I talk. I'll have to stop the description until I can take a new position. Hold on, will you please, I'll be right back in a minute.

[*fade into piano*]

ANNOUNCER: We are bringing you an eyewitness account of what's happening on the Wilmuth farm, Grovers Mill, New Jersey.

[*more piano*]

ANNOUNCER: We now return you to Carl Phillips at Grovers Mill.

CARL PHILLIPS: Ladies and gentlemen (Am I on?). Ladies and gentlemen, here I am, back of a stone wall that adjoins Mr. Wilmuth's garden. From here I get a sweep of the whole scene. I'll give you every detail as long as I can talk. As long as I can see. More state police have arrived. They're drawing up a cordon in front of the pit, about thirty of them. No need to push the crowd back now. They're willing to keep their distance.

The captain is conferring with someone. We can't quite see who. Oh yes, I believe it's Professor Pierson. Yes, it is. Now they've parted. The Professor moves around one side, studying the object, while the captain and two policemen advance with something in their hands. I can see it now.

✔ **LITERARY CHECK**
*How do you know that this radio play is **science fiction**?*

It's a white handkerchief tied to a pole . . . a flag of truce. If those creatures know what that means . . . what anything means! . . . Wait! Something's happening!

[*hissing sound followed by a humming that increases in intensity*]

CARL PHILLIPS: A humped shape is rising out of the pit. I can make out a small beam of light against a mirror. What's that? There's a jet of flame springing from the mirror, and it leaps right at the advancing men. It strikes them head on! Good Lord, they're turning into flame!

[*screams and unearthly shrieks*]

CARL PHILLIPS: Now the whole field's caught fire.

[*explosion*]

CARL PHILLIPS: The woods . . . the barns . . . the gas tanks of automobiles . . . it's spreading everywhere. It's coming this way. About twenty yards to my right . . .

[*dead silence*]

ANNOUNCER: Ladies and gentlemen, due to circumstances beyond our control, we are unable to continue the broadcast from Grovers Mill. Evidently there's some difficulty with our field transmission. However, we will return to that point at the earliest opportunity. . . .

---

truce, an agreement to stop fighting
humped, rounded
circumstances, events

ABOUT THE **AUTHORS**

Howard Koch (1902–1995) was an American writer most famous for writing screenplays. He received an Academy Award in 1942 for co-writing the screenplay of the movie *Casablanca.* Koch taught writing and wrote several books about his days in Hollywood.

H. G. Wells (1866–1946) was a British writer, teacher, and historian. He is known as one of the fathers of modern science fiction. Some of his most famous novels are *The Time Machine, The War of the Worlds,* and *The Invisible Man.*

BEFORE YOU GO ON

1 Why was the crowd no longer pushing to get closer?

2 What came rising out of the pit?

On Your Own
Do you think there is life on other planets? Explain why or why not.

DRAMATIC READING

One of the best ways to understand and appreciate a play is to perform it. Because a radio play is meant to be read aloud, performers need to think about how they speak their lines. For example, a news broadcast sounds different from a casual conversation.

In small groups, read the excerpt from *The War of the Worlds* aloud. Pay close attention to the stage directions and make sure to assign someone the task of creating sound effects. Take turns performing a scene from the radio play for the class.

COMPREHENSION

Workbook
Page 179

Right There

1. According to the radio announcer, what happened at 8:50 P.M. in Grovers Mill, New Jersey?

2. How does Carl Phillips describe the scene?

Think and Search

3. How does the crowd react after the object crashes?

4. What makes Professor Pierson think the object is not from Earth?

Author and You

5. Do you think the play is realistic? Do you think you would have believed it was a real news report if you were listening in 1938?

6. What do you think would have happened if the play had been performed on television instead of on the radio?

▲ Orson Welles directing a rehearsal

On Your Own

7. How do you think people would react to this play if it were put on the radio today? Why?

8. Do you think we will be able to travel to other planets? If so, when?

DISCUSSION

»))⌣ *Listening* TIP

Be patient. Give the speaker enough time to express his or her ideas clearly.

Discuss in pairs or small groups.

1. Why do you think creatures from outer space or other planets are a popular theme in science fiction stories?

2. What could the radio station have done to make sure people knew that the events in the play were not real? Was the radio station responsible for the misunderstanding?

3. What is your favorite way to learn about what is happening in the world? Why?

Q How do we know what is true? Do you think it is acceptable to portray fictional events as if they were true? Why or why not?

RESPONSE TO LITERATURE

Workbook
Page 179

Work with a partner. Imagine that you are writing a science fiction story about aliens. Copy the chart below into your notebook and complete it. Then draw a picture of your aliens and present your ideas and drawing to the class.

What do the aliens look like?	
How do the aliens travel?	
Where do the aliens come from?	
What do the aliens sound like?	
What did the aliens do after they got here?	
How do people react to the aliens?	

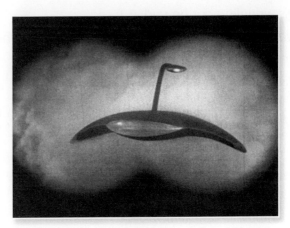

A Martian war machine from the movie *The War of the Worlds,* 1953 ▶

365

Grammar and Writing

Punctuation of Quoted Speech

Quoted speech is a speaker's exact words enclosed in quotation marks (" ").

Look at the example below. Note that a comma comes after *Professor Pierson said.* The final quotation mark comes after the period at the end of the sentence.

> Professor Pierson said, "I don't know what to think."

A sentence that includes quoted speech may begin either with the speaker or the quoted speech. The punctuation changes depending on which comes first.

Note that a comma, not a period, is used at the end of the quoted sentence because it comes before *stated the announcer.*

> The announcer stated, "This confirms earlier reports."
> "This confirms earlier reports," stated the announcer.

Practice
Workbook
Page 180

Work with a partner. Copy the sentences below into your notebook. Add quotation marks, correct punctuation, and capitalization to show the speaker's exact words.

1. Mr. Wilmuth said let me tell you some more
2. Something's wriggling out he said.
3. It must have struck with tremendous force stated Carl Phillips
4. The announcer said the flash in the sky was visible
5. Professor Pierson stated the object was huge

Include Quotations and Citations

When you write a research report, you support your ideas with facts and details. An effective research report includes quotations and citations from individuals involved in the topic or from people, such as historians or authors, who have previously written about the topic. Quotations can make the facts and ideas you present more accurate and compelling. Quotations can also add to the persuasiveness of the argument you are making. The source of each quotation should be cited, or named. There are many ways to cite sources. See pages 449–450 for some common methods.

Here is an example of a paragraph with a quotation and a citation. Notice how the writer clearly named the person being quoted and the source for the quotation. The writer used a main idea web to organize her ideas.

Justine Kefauver

How Will the World End?

There are many good science fiction stories about how the world will end. An interesting idea comes from a book called _The Bar Code Tattoo_. This book takes place in the year 2025. When people reach the age of 17 the popular thing to do is to get a bar code tattoo, which is like a credit card on their skin. But there is something strange and sinister about it. When the main character, Kayla, meets a bar code resister, the woman says, "The dark times that were foretold are being fully expressed." (Weyn) And bad things are about to happen.

Works Consulted List

Weyn, Suzanne. _The Bar Code Tattoo_. Scholastic Paperbacks, 2004.

Practice

Workbook
Page 181

Write a paragraph that includes quotations and citations. As a topic, you may continue the research you started for one of the paragraphs you have written earlier. Use a graphic organizer like the one above to organize your quotations and citations. Be sure to punctuate quotations properly.

Writing Checklist

SENTENCE FLUENCY:
- ☑ I made sure my sentences flow smoothly.

CONVENTIONS:
- ☑ I checked to make sure my quotations are punctuated correctly.

367

What You Will Learn

Reading
- Vocabulary building: *Context, dictionary skills, word study*
- Reading strategy: *Classify*
- Text type: *Informational text (science)*

Grammar, Usage, and Mechanics
Cause and effect structures

Writing
Support the main idea with examples and explanations

THE BIG QUESTION

How do we know what is true? Why do you think for thousands of years people have wanted to learn about the solar system and Earth's place in the universe? Why do we want to learn about the unknown? Discuss these questions with a partner.

BUILD BACKGROUND

"Earth's Orbit" is a science article. It explains why the amount of daylight we receive is controlled by Earth's orbit around the sun. Many people live in places where there are dramatic differences in daytime and nighttime hours. For example, the Inuit people, who live in the Arctic region, receive only a few hours of daylight during the middle of winter. During the summer, they receive about twenty hours of daylight, and the sky is never totally dark.

You will also learn why the seasons are controlled by the tilt of Earth's axis. Why does Earth tilt? Some astronomers believe that Earth was hit by a Mars-sized planet about five billion years ago. If Earth did not tilt, places near the North and South poles would be cold and dark all year round. If Earth tilted too much, the seasons would be very extreme. On the planet Uranus, for example, winters are forty-two years of total darkness.

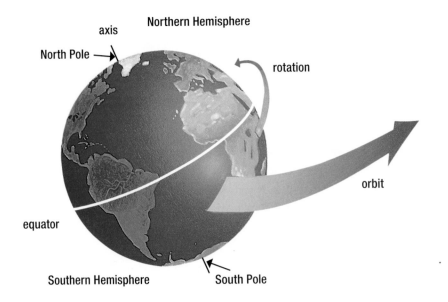

368

VOCABULARY

Learn Key Words

Read these sentences. Use the context to figure out the meaning of the red words. Use a dictionary to check your answers. Then write each word and its meaning in your notebook.

Key Words

axis
equator
equinox
hemisphere
rotation
solstice

1. Earth spins on its **axis**, the imaginary line that goes through Earth's center from the North Pole to the South Pole.

2. The **equator** is another imaginary line. It divides Earth into the northern half and the southern half.

3. On the **equinox**, the length of day and night everywhere on Earth is the same—twelve hours each. This happens twice a year, in March and September.

4. The Northern **Hemisphere** is the northern half of Earth.

5. Earth makes one **rotation**, or complete spin, on its axis every twenty-four hours.

6. In the Northern Hemisphere, June 21 is the summer **solstice** and the longest day of the year because the sun is at its highest path through the sky. December 21 is the winter solstice and the shortest day of the year because the sun is at its lowest path through the sky.

▲ A view of Earth from space

Practice  Workbook Page 182

Write the sentences in your notebook. Choose a red word from the box above to complete each sentence. Then take turns reading the sentences aloud with a partner.

1. The Southern _____ is the half of Earth south of the equator.

2. Some people celebrate in March and September on the _____, when the length of day and night are the same everywhere.

3. In the Southern Hemisphere, June 21 is the winter _____.

4. Every twenty-four hours, Earth completes one _____.

5. Earth rotates by spinning on its _____.

6. It is usually hot near the _____, the imaginary line that divides Earth into two halves, northern and southern.

Learn Academic Words

Study the **red** words and their meanings. You will find these words useful when talking and writing about informational texts. Write each word and its meaning in your notebook. After you read "Earth's Orbit," try to use these words to respond to the text.

parallel = two lines side by side and always the same distance apart	➡	The two bright yellow lines on a street are **parallel** to each other.
parameters = limits that control the way something should be done	➡	The **parameters** for the project were very strict. Only certain materials could be used.
phase = a stage in a process	➡	During one **phase** of the moon's cycle, the moon looks like a crescent.
revolves = moves around a central point	➡	The sun does not move around Earth; Earth **revolves** around the sun.
sphere = solid round shape like a ball	➡	When you see a picture of Earth from space, it looks like a **sphere**.
transmits = sends out signals	➡	A satellite in space **transmits** information back to Earth. We use these signals for television and radio.

Practice  Workbook Page 183

Work with a partner to answer these questions. Try to include the **red** word in your answer. Write the sentences in your notebook.

1. Look around your classroom. What objects do you see with **parallel** lines?
2. Have you ever worked on a science project that had strict **parameters**?
3. How can you tell which **phase** the moon is in?
4. How does daylight change as Earth **revolves** around the sun?
5. What object besides Earth is a **sphere**?
6. What **transmits** information into your home?

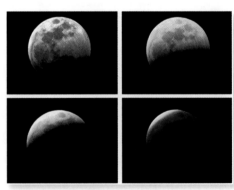

▲ The four phases of the moon

Word Study: Word Roots *astro-*, *cycl-*, *equ-*

Understanding the meaning of a word's root can help you understand the word's meaning. Knowing the root also helps you spell the word. Many English words, especially science words, have Greek or Latin roots.

Root	Meaning	Word	Definition
astro-	stars, outer space	astronomy	the study of stars and outer space
cycl-	circle, ring	cycle	a sequence that is repeated
equ-	equal, equally	equinox	time when the length of day and night are equal everywhere on Earth

Practice

Work with a partner. Copy the chart below into your notebook. Write the definition of each word. Check a dictionary if you need to.

Root	Meaning	Word	Definition
rota-	wheel	rotation	
geo-	earth	geography	
kilo-	thousand	kilometer	
rev-	turn	revolution	

READING STRATEGY | CLASSIFY

Classifying information helps you organize new ideas and facts. It also makes it easier for you to understand the text. To classify, follow these steps:

- As you read, make a list of new information that you learn.
- Think about how the ideas or facts are similar and different.
- Decide which ideas belong together. Think about how they are related.
- Think about how you could group the facts and ideas together.

As you read "Earth's Orbit," list all the new information that you learn. When you finish reading, group similar information together. Use a graphic organizer to help you.

Set a purpose for reading What are some things people believed in the past that astronomers proved were not true?

Earth's Orbit

Earth's Rotation: Measuring Day and Night

The study of the planets, stars, and other objects in space is called astronomy. The word *astronomy* comes from two Greek words: *ástron*, which means "star," and *nomos*, which means "a system of knowledge about a subject." An astronomer is someone who studies the stars.

Ancient astronomers also studied the movements of the sun and moon. They thought that the sun and moon were moving around Earth. In fact, the sun and moon seem to move across the sky each day because Earth is rotating, or turning, on its axis. Earth's axis is the imaginary line that goes through Earth's center and the North Pole and South Pole. The turning of Earth on its axis is called its rotation.

Earth's rotation on its axis causes day and night. As Earth rotates to the east, the sun appears to move to the west across

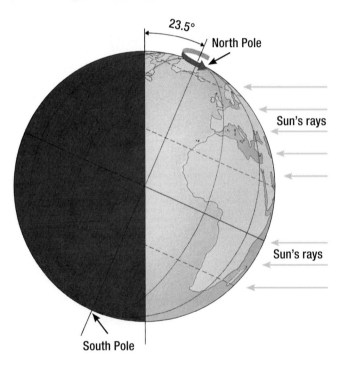

▲ Earth rotates on its axis every twenty-four hours. Earth's rotational axis tilts at a 23.5-degree angle in relation to the sun.

---

imaginary, not real

the sky. It is day on the side of Earth that faces the sun. As Earth continues to rotate to the east, the sun appears to set in the west. Sunlight can't reach the side of Earth that faces away from the sun, so it is dark (night) there. It takes Earth 24 hours to rotate one complete turn on its axis. This 24-hour cycle is called a day.

Earth's Revolution: Measuring a Year

As well as rotating on its axis, Earth is traveling around the sun. The movement of one object around another object is called a revolution. Earth's path as it revolves around the sun is called its orbit. Earth's orbit is not really a circle. It is actually an oval, or egg, shape.

Earth's orbit around the sun takes about 365 days. In measuring four years of Earth's orbit, three years have 365 days and the fourth year has 366 days. This fourth year with an extra day is known as a leap year. During a leap year, February has 29 days instead of the usual 28 days.

Long ago, people tried to divide the year into smaller parts. They used moon cycles—the time between full moons —as a kind of calendar. There are about 29.5 days between full moons. However, a year of 12 moon cycles, or months, adds up to only 354 days. The ancient Egyptians created a calendar that had 12 months of 30 days each, with 5 days left over. The ancient Romans borrowed this calendar and made changes to it. With more changes, the Roman calendar finally became the calendar we use today. It consists of 11 months of 30 or 31 days each, plus 1 month of 28 or 29 days.

---

faces, points or looks toward
cycle, series of events that happen again and again in a repeating pattern
as well as, in addition to

---

full moons, times when the moon looks completely round

▲ Earth revolves around the sun in an oval orbit.

BEFORE YOU GO ON

1 How long does Earth take to rotate on its axis?

2 How long does Earth take to revolve around the sun?

On Your Own
When is the next full moon? Find it on a calendar.

373

How Sunlight Hits Earth

The equator is an imaginary line around Earth, halfway between the North and South poles. The equator divides Earth into two parts—the Northern Hemisphere and the Southern Hemisphere. It is always cold around the North and South poles and hot around the equator. The warm area around the equator is sometimes called the tropics. Most places outside the tropics have four seasons: winter, spring, summer, and autumn (also called fall).

Why are there different temperatures in different places on Earth? In the tropics, sunlight travels to Earth's surface most directly. As a result, the sun's energy—in the form of heat—is very strong. Closer

---

directly, in a straight line or path

to the North and South poles, sunlight hits Earth's surface more indirectly—at an angle. Near the poles, sunlight is spread out over a greater area. Therefore, its energy and heat are less strong, and the temperatures are much colder.

Why Earth Has Seasons

Why do temperatures around the world change with the seasons? Earth's axis is tilted as it revolves around the sun. The axis always points in the same direction. For part of the year, Earth's axis is tilted away from the sun. For another part of the year, the axis is tilted toward the sun.

---

indirectly, not directly
at an angle, not upright or straight
tilted, with one side higher than the other; leaning

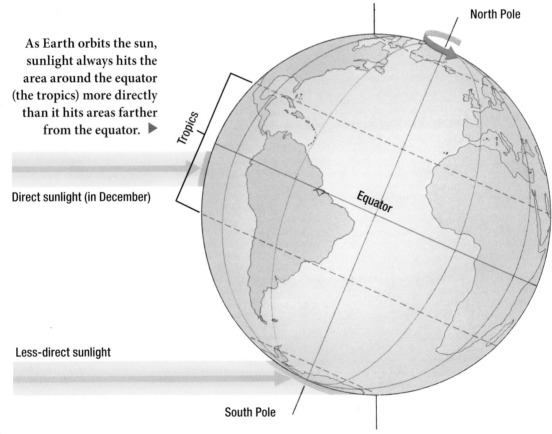

As Earth orbits the sun, sunlight always hits the area around the equator (the tropics) more directly than it hits areas farther from the equator. ▶

Tropics

Direct sunlight (in December)

Less-direct sunlight

North Pole

Equator

South Pole

374

June

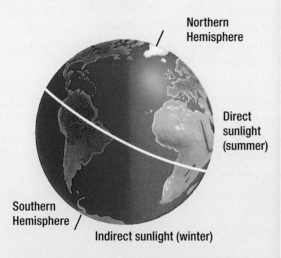

Northern
Hemisphere

Direct
sunlight
(summer)

Southern
Hemisphere

Indirect sunlight (winter)

▲ In June, the Northern Hemisphere is tilted toward the sun. The sun's energy hits the Northern Hemisphere more directly, so it is summer there. The sun's energy hits the Southern Hemisphere less directly, so it is winter there.

December

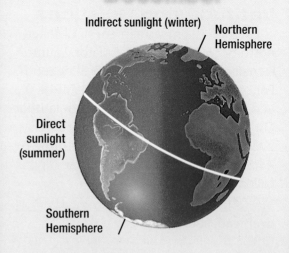

Indirect sunlight (winter)

Northern
Hemisphere

Direct
sunlight
(summer)

Southern
Hemisphere

▲ In December, the Southern Hemisphere is tilted toward the sun. The sun's energy hits the Southern Hemisphere more directly, so it is summer there. The sun's energy hits the Northern Hemisphere less directly, so it is winter there.

When the north part of Earth's axis is tilted toward the sun, it is summer in the Northern Hemisphere and winter in the Southern Hemisphere. When the south part of Earth's axis is tilted toward the sun, it is summer in the Southern Hemisphere and winter in the Northern Hemisphere.

Summer and Winter in the Northern and Southern Hemispheres

In June, the north part of Earth's axis is tilted toward the sun. The hemisphere that is tilted toward the sun has more hours of daylight than the hemisphere tilted away from the sun. The combination of direct sunlight and more hours of daylight creates summer in the Northern Hemisphere. At the same time, the Southern Hemisphere has fewer hours of daylight and indirect sunlight. The combination of indirect sunlight and fewer hours of daylight creates winter in the Southern Hemisphere.

In December, the Southern Hemisphere has more direct sunlight, so it is summer there. At the same time, the Northern Hemisphere has indirect sunlight and fewer hours of daylight. It is winter there.

BEFORE YOU GO ON

1 Why is the area near the equator hot?

2 When is it summer in the Northern Hemisphere? In the Southern Hemisphere?

On Your Own
Describe how the seasons are affected by Earth's tilt.

375

Latitude and Solstices

Latitude is a measurement of distance north or south from the equator. Latitude is measured in degrees (°) north or south. For example, the equator is at latitude 0°, and the North Pole is at 90° north latitude. On two days each year, the noon sun is overhead at either 23.5° south latitude or 23.5° north latitude. Each of these days is called a solstice.

---

overhead, above your head

Each year on or about December 21, the noon sun is overhead at 23.5° south latitude. This is the winter solstice in the Northern Hemisphere and the summer solstice in the Southern Hemisphere. It is the shortest day of the year in the Northern Hemisphere and the longest day of the year in the Southern Hemisphere. Similarly, on about June 21, the noon sun is overhead at 23.5° north latitude. This is the summer solstice in the Northern Hemisphere and the winter solstice in the Southern Hemisphere.

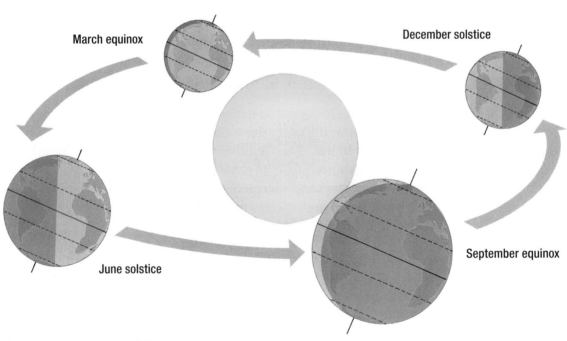

March equinox

December solstice

June solstice

September equinox

▲ Earth's seasons: Earth has seasons because its axis is tilted as it revolves around the sun.

▲ In about 1500 B.C.E., ancient peoples in what is now England completed Stonehenge, a giant stone monument. It is thought that they arranged the stones to record the sun's movements, such as the summer and winter solstices and the spring autumnal equinoxes.

Equinoxes

On two days each year, the noon sun is directly overhead at the equator. Neither hemisphere is closer to or farther from the sun. Each of these days is called an equinox, which means "equal night." During an equinox, night and day are about the same length of time. The vernal equinox (spring equinox) occurs on or about March 21 and marks the beginning of spring in the Northern Hemisphere. The autumnal equinox occurs on or about September 23. It marks the beginning of autumn (fall) in the Northern Hemisphere.

---

neither, not one and not the other

autumnal, related to autumn, or fall

BEFORE YOU GO ON

1 What is a solstice?

2 What is an equinox?

💡**On Your Own**
What is the latitude of your city or town? Find it on a map.

377

COMPREHENSION

Workbook
Page 186

Right There

1. How long does it take Earth to orbit the sun?
2. What is latitude? How is it measured?

Think and Search

3. How does Earth's rotation on its axis cause day and night?
4. What happens during an equinox?

Author and You

5. What does the text suggest about the similarities and differences between climate at the North and South poles?
6. What does the text suggest about the relationship between the sun's energy and Earth's tilt?

On Your Own

7. How does the sun affect your life every day?
8. Would you rather live far from the equator or close to it? Why?

IN YOUR OWN WORDS

Pretend you are explaining to a younger person why we have day and night and why seasons change. Use the Key Words and the diagrams and illustrations in the article to help you.

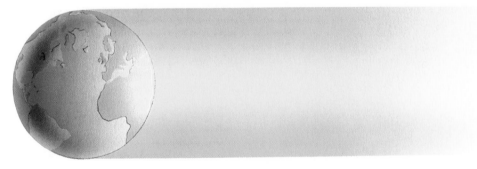

▲ The rays shown in bright yellow heat the equator, the place on Earth closest to the sun. The rays in orange reach the poles, which are farther away and receive less heat.

DISCUSSION

Discuss in pairs or small groups.

● Some places in the world are either always hot or always cold. Would you like to live in this kind of place or would you prefer living in a place with four different seasons?

Q **How do we know what is true?** Early astronomers discovered that Earth was really revolving around the sun. How did their discoveries surprise people? Why?

»⟩ Listening TIP

As you listen to your classmates, evaluate the facts they present. You may want to question their source of information.

READ FOR FLUENCY

It is often easier to read a text if you understand the difficult words and phrases. Work with a partner. Choose a paragraph from the reading. Identify the words and phrases you do not know or have trouble pronouncing. Look up the difficult words in a dictionary.

Take turns pronouncing the words and phrases with your partner. If necessary, ask your teacher to model the correct pronunciation. Then take turns reading the paragraph aloud. Give each other feedback on your reading.

EXTENSION

Workbook
Page 186

Work with a partner. Imagine that you are an astronomer who is transported back into the past to explain to the people of the 1400s what we now know about the way Earth moves. Write a short speech explaining:

- Earth's rotation
- Earth's revolution
- The two equinoxes
- The two solstices

When you have finished, present your speech to the class.

▲ Planets in orbit around the sun

379

Grammar and Writing

GRAMMAR, USAGE, AND MECHANICS

Cause and Effect Structures

Writers often connect ideas by using cause and effect structures. The cause is an action that makes something happen. The effect is what happens because of the cause.

Therefore and *as a result* are phrases used to tell the effect. They often begin a sentence and are followed by a comma.

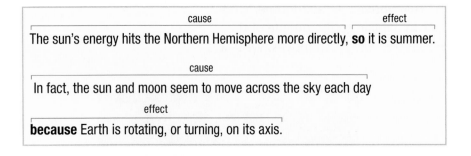

cause	effect

Near the poles, sunlight is spread out. **Therefore,** its energy and heat are less strong, and the temperatures are much colder.

cause

In the tropics, sunlight travels to Earth's surface most directly.

effect

As a result, the sun's energy is very strong.

So and *because* connect two independent clauses (complete sentences). Use a comma before *so,* but don't use a comma with *because.*

cause · effect

The sun's energy hits the Northern Hemisphere more directly, **so** it is summer.

cause

In fact, the sun and moon seem to move across the sky each day

effect

because Earth is rotating, or turning, on its axis.

Practice  Workbook Page 187

Work with a partner. Use each word or phrase from the box to create your own cause-and-effect sentences. Write the sentences in your notebook. Be sure to use correct punctuation and capitalization. Label the cause and the effect in each sentence.

as a result	because	so	therefore

380

WRITING A RESEARCH REPORT

Support the Main Idea with Examples and Explanations

In a research report some main ideas are better supported by examples and explanations than with facts and details. An example can give the reader a clear image of the main idea. The example should be clearly explained so that it relates to the main idea. For example, to show the results of not taking care of a bicycle, you could provide the following information: *As a result of failing to check the air in the bicycle tires, he discovered that the tires were flat.*

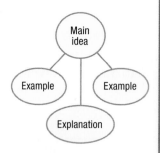

Here is a model paragraph in which the writer presents a main idea, and then supports it with examples and explanations. She used a word web to help her organize her ideas.

Muniphe Green

A Comet's Orbit

An orbit is the path of an object that travels around another object, usually in space. Comets are objects in space and, like Earth, their orbit is around the sun. Because comets come in different shapes and sizes, they have different types of orbits: short-period orbits and long-period orbits. Short-period orbits generally take less than 200 years. Some long-period orbits can take as long as a thousand years. How long a comet's orbit takes also depends on its eccentricity. If the orbit has a high eccentricity, then the comet will move faster. When a comet gets closer to the sun, the sun melts the icy outer layer of the comet and causes a jet-like reaction. As a result, the comet speeds up. However, a lower eccentricity makes the comet move more slowly.

Practice

Workbook Page 188

Write a paragraph for a research report in which you present a main idea and include examples and explanations that support it. You may wish to continue the research you started for one of the paragraphs you have written earlier. List your examples and explanations before writing. Use a word web like the one above to help organize your ideas. Be sure to use words and phrases such as *so*, *because*, and *as a result* to show cause and effect.

Writing Checklist

ORGANIZATION:
☑ I organized my writing by stating a main idea, then following it with examples.

CONVENTIONS:
☑ I used connecting ideas correctly.

Link the Readings

Critical Thinking

Look back at the readings in this unit. Think about what they have in common. They all ask the question: *What is true?* Yet they do not all have the same purpose. The purpose of one reading might be to inform, while the purpose of another might be to entertain. In addition, the content of each reading relates to the subject differently. Now copy the chart below into your notebook and complete it.

Title of Reading	Purpose	Big Question Link
"How Glooskap Found the Summer" "Persephone and the Pomegranate Seeds"		*explains why seasons change*
"Early Astronomers"	*to inform*	
From *The War of the Worlds*		
"Earth's Orbit"		

Discussion

Discuss in pairs or small groups.

- How does the purpose of "Early Astronomers" differ from the purpose of *The War of the Worlds*? What does the radio play convey that the article does not?

- **Q How do we know what is true?** Think about the readings. Why did some cultures try to explain natural occurrences through myths? How does science help us learn the truth? How do we know what is accurate or real?

Fluency Check

Work with a partner. Choose a paragraph from one of the readings. Take turns reading it for one minute. Count the total number of words you read. Practice saying the words you had trouble reading. Take turns reading the paragraph three more times. Did you read more words each time? Copy the chart below into your notebook and record your speeds.

	1st Speed	2nd Speed	3rd Speed	4th Speed
Words Per Minute				

Projects

Work in pairs or small groups. Choose one of these projects:

1 Write a myth explaining a natural phenomenon such as the phases of the moon or the cycle of day and night. Use heroes and heroines, if possible. Then read your myth to the class.

2 Create a poster showing constellations. Use illustrations from textbooks, magazines, or websites, or draw your own. Then share your poster with the class.

3 What do you predict will happen next in the radio play based on *The War of the Worlds*? In small groups, write an ending for the radio play and assign roles. Perform your play for the class.

4 Make a model or mobile of one of the planets. Include moons, if it has any. Explain your planet's orbit. Does it rotate? Write a brief report to tell the interesting facts you discovered.

Further Reading

To find out more about the theme of this unit, choose from these reading suggestions.

Stargate, from the screenplay and novelization by Dean Devlin and Roland Emmerich, adapted by Sheila Black
In this Penguin Reader® adaptation, archaeologists find a mysterious stone in 1928. Sixty years later, a scientist decodes the stone and finds Stargate, a 10,000-year-old machine that can transport humans across space. What's on the other side of the gate?

When Jaguars Ate the Moon: and Other Stories about Animals and Plants of the Americas, Maria Cristina Brusca and Tona Wilson
Traditional Native American stories that explain how animals and plants of North and South America came to be the way they are.

A Wrinkle in Time, Madeleine L'Engle
Meg Murry's father has disappeared while experimenting with time travel. Meg, her brother, and their friend go on a dangerous and fantastic journey where they must battle the forces of evil to try to find him.

Put It All Together

LISTENING & SPEAKING WORKSHOP

Play

With a group, you will write and perform a short dramatic play.

1 **THINK ABOUT IT** In a small group, discuss the radio play based on *The War of the Worlds*. What makes it so exciting and dramatic?

Work together to develop a list of stories or events that could be presented as a dramatic play. For example:

- An exciting event at your school
- A myth
- A surprising discovery

2 **GATHER AND ORGANIZE INFORMATION** As a group, choose a story or event from your list and think about how you can present it as a dramatic play. Write down the main characters, setting, and time period for your play.

▲ Orson Welles performs the radio drama *The War of the Worlds* in 1938.

Plan In paragraph form, write a brief plot summary of what will happen in your play. If you need to, review the lesson about plot on page 71. Decide what role each group member will play. Choose one person to be the director.

Prepare a Script Write a script for your play based on your plot summary. Show the dialogue by putting a character's name at the left side of the paper, followed by a colon and then the exact words he or she will say. Do not use quotation marks. Include stage directions to tell where the characters are, what actions they should do, and possible sound effects.

Use Visuals Find or make the props and costumes you need for your play. Simple objects such as a hat or a treasure map can give the audience important information about the characters, setting, and plot.

3 **PRACTICE AND PRESENT** Read your script aloud several times. When all group members are comfortable with their parts, practice acting out the scene using props and stage movements. Keep practicing until your parts are memorized and the director is satisfied with your actions and speech. You may want to invite friends or family members to watch your play and give you feedback: *Can they hear all your words? Can they understand the plot?* Make changes as needed so that your play is successful and exciting.

Perform Your Play Pay attention to the other actors, and be ready when it's your turn to speak or move. Try to express your character's thoughts and feelings as you say your lines. Speak loudly enough so that everyone in the class can hear you.

4 **EVALUATE THE PRESENTATION**
You will improve your skills as a speaker and a listener by evaluating each presentation you give and hear. Use this checklist to help you judge your play and the plays given by your classmates.

☑ Could you understand the story?

☑ Did the actors know their parts well?

☑ Were the costumes and props helpful and appropriate?

☑ Could you hear and understand the actors' words?

☑ What suggestions do you have for improving the play?

Speaking TIPS

Always face the audience when you speak, even when you are talking to another character. If you turn away from the audience, people may not be able to hear or understand you.

Speak naturally and with feeling. Use your voice, face, and hands to communicate information about your character.

Listening TIPS

Listen carefully to the other actors so that you know when to say your lines. Learn your cues.

When you watch a play, look for actions and gestures to help you understand what people are saying.

WRITING WORKSHOP

Research Report

Researching a topic means studying it thoroughly. In a research report, writers explain a topic they have investigated. They include information gathered from different sources. A good research report begins with a paragraph that clearly presents the writer's controlling idea or focus. Each body paragraph presents a main point that develops the controlling idea. Facts, details, and examples support the writer's main points. A concluding paragraph sums up what the writer has explained. The report includes an accurate, complete list of all the sources the writer used.

Your assignment for this workshop is to write a five-paragraph research report about a person, place, or thing that interests you. You may choose to write about a topic related to astronomy or space. Use the following steps and models to help you.

1 PREWRITE Select a topic. Then, narrow it down to make sure it isn't too general. Use a graphic organizer like the one page 339 to find your focus.

Write a question to direct your research. Possible sources include books about your topic, newspapers, magazines, encyclopedias, and online websites. Take notes on note cards and list your sources.

List and Organize Ideas and Details Use a question-and-answer outline to organize your ideas. A student named Andrew decided to write about the Milky Way. Here is

> I. What is the Milky Way?
>   A. a galaxy of mystery
>   B. scientists have many unanswered questions
> II. Why is the Milky Way special to us?
>   A. looks like a splash of milk
>   B. the home of our solar system
> III. What is the shape of the Milky Way?
>   A. a spiral galaxy
>   B. a wheel with spokes
> IV. How large is the Milky Way?
>   A. about 80,000 to 100,000 light years long
>   B. actual size not measured
> V. What happens when we learn more about the Milky Way?
>   A. the more we learn, the more questions we have
>   B. some of its mysteries may never be solved

2 **DRAFT** Use the model on pages 390–391 and your outline to help you write a draft of your report. Remember to begin with a paragraph that states your controlling idea. Be sure to use your own words when you write your report. If you use exact words from a source, punctuate the quotation correctly. List all your sources at the end of your report.

Citing Sources Look at the style, punctuation, and order of information in the following sources. Use these examples as models.

Book
Stanchak, John. Civil War. New York: Dorling Kindersley, 2000.

Magazine article
Kirn, Walter. "Lewis and Clark: The Journey That Changed America Forever." Time 8 July 2002: 36–41.

Internet website
Smith, Gene. "The Structure of the Milky Way." Gene Smith's Astronomy Tutorial. 28 April 1999. Center for Astrophysics & Space Sciences, University of California, San Diego. 20 July 2009 <http://casswww.ucsd.edu/public/tutorial/MW.html>.

Encyclopedia article
Siple, Paul A. "Antarctica." World Book Encyclopedia. 1991 ed.

---

3 **REVISE** Read over your draft. As you do so, ask yourself the questions in the writing checklist. Use the questions to help you revise your report.

SIX TRAITS OF WRITING CHECKLIST

☑ **IDEAS:** Does my first paragraph clearly state my controlling idea?

☑ **ORGANIZATION:** Does each main point develop my controlling idea?

☑ **VOICE:** Does my writing have energy?

☑ **WORD CHOICE:** Do I use linking words to connect ideas?

☑ **SENTENCE FLUENCY:** Do my sentences begin in different ways?

☑ **CONVENTIONS:** Does my writing follow the rules of grammar, usage, and mechanics?

Here are the changes Andrew plans to make when he revises his first draft:

The Milky Way

The Milky Way is a galaxy of ~~dazzled~~ *dazzling* wonder and mystery. ^*It is mysterious because* There are many questions that we can't answer about it. Scientists have learned many facts about the Milky Way‚ but many other facts still need to be discovered.

A galaxy is a group of billion of stars. Although there are many different galaxies, the Milky Way is special to people on planet Earth. As we look up at it from Earth, the Milky Way looks like a splash of milk. ^*Therefore,* We gave this galaxy its special name. Sometimes, the Milky Way is also called the Galaxy, with a capital G. We refer to it this way because it is where our solar system lives (Hermans-Killam). Our solar system includes Earth and all the other planets and matter that revolve around the sun. The Milky Way is one of many galaxies in the universe, but it is our solar system's only galaxy.

A spiral galaxy has a nucleus with arms coming out of the center, which makes it look like a wheel with spokes. The Milky Way is a spiral galaxy (Hatchett 40). The gravitational pull of the Milky Way holds our solar system on one of its arms. Scientists are having trouble finding how long the MilkyWay has been in existence, but it is believed that this marvelos galaxy has kept our solar system on its arm since the beginning of time.

The size of the Milky Way also hasn't been measured. Experts have made estimates that it is 80,000 to 100,000 light years long, but that isn't the exact length (Hermans-Killam). Estimating the size is, to quote Neil Armstrong, "one small step for man, one giant leap for mankind. However, finding the actual size would be a bigger step and a bigger leap. In the future we might be able to determine the actual size.

The more we learn about the Milky Way, the more questions scientists may come across. Some of these question may never be answered. This magnificent group of stars has many secrets, and even if we discover some of them, this vast galaxy is sure to have more.

Works Consulted List

Berger, Melvin. <u>Planets, Stars, and Galaxies</u>. New York: G.P. Putnum's Sons, 1978.

Branley, Franklyn M. <u>A Book of the Milky Way Galaxy for You</u>. New York: Thomas Y. Crowell Company, 1965.

Hatchet, Clint. <u>Stars and Galaxies</u>. Grolier Educational, 1998.

Hermans-Killam, Linda. "What is the Milky Way?" <u>Ask an Astronomer for Kids</u>. Cool Cosmos at the Infrared Processing and Analysis Center. 20 July 2009 <http://coolcosmos.ipac.caltech.edu/cosmic_kids/AskKids/milkyway.shtml>.

4 EDIT AND PROOFREAD

Workbook
Page 189

Copy your revised draft onto a clean sheet of paper. Read it again. Correct any errors in grammar, word usage, mechanics, and spelling. Here are the additional changes Andrew plans to make when he prepares his final draft.

Andrew Tilley

The Milky Way

The Milky Way is a galaxy of dazzling wonder and mystery. It is mysterious because there are many questions that we can't answer about it. Scientists have learned many facts about the Milky Way, but many other facts still need to be discovered.

A galaxy is a group of billion**s** of stars. Although there are many different galaxies, the Milky Way is special to people on planet Earth. As we look up at it from Earth, the Milky Way looks like a splash of milk. Therefore, we gave this galaxy its special name. Sometimes, the Milky Way is also called the Galaxy, with a capital G. We refer to it this way because it is where our solar system lives (Hermans-Killam). Our solar system includes Earth and all the other planets and matter that revolve around the sun. The Milky Way is one of many galaxies in the universe, but it is our solar system's only galaxy.

The Milky Way is a spiral galaxy (Hatchett 40). A spiral galaxy has a nucleus with arms coming out of the center, which makes it look like a wheel with spokes. The gravitational pull of the Milky Way holds our solar system on one of its arms. Scientists are having trouble finding how long the Milky **#** Way has been in existence, but it is believed that this marvel**u**os galaxy has kept our solar system on its arm since the beginning of time.

The size of the Milky Way also hasn't been measured. Experts have made estimates that it is 80,000 to 100,000 light years long, but that isn't the exact length (Hermans-Killam). Estimating the size is, to quote

Neil Armstrong, "one small step for man, one giant leap for mankind." However, finding the actual size would be a bigger step and a bigger leap. In the future, we might be able to determine the actual size.

The more we learn about the Milky Way, the more questions scientists come across. Some of these questions may never be answered. This magnificent group of stars has many secrets, and even if we discover some of them, this vast galaxy is sure to have more.

Works Consulted List

Berger, Melvin. <u>Planets, Stars, and Galaxies</u>. New York: G.P. Putnum's Sons, 1978.

Branley, Franklyn M. <u>A Book of the Milky Way Galaxy for You</u>. New York: Thomas Y. Crowell Company, 1965.

Hatchet, Clint. <u>Stars and Galaxies</u>. Grolier Educational, 1998.

Hermans-Killam, Linda. "What is the Milky Way?" <u>Ask an Astronomer for Kids</u>. Cool Cosmos at the Infrared Processing and Analysis Center. 20 July 2009 <http://coolcosmos.ipac.caltech.edu/cosmic_kids/AskKids/milkyway.shtml>.

5 **PUBLISH** Prepare your final draft. Share your research report with your teacher and classmates.

Workbook
Page 190

Otherworldly Art

*T*o understand the mysteries of Earth and the sky, many cultures have created myths. These are stories that try to explain things that people once could not explain, such as thunder and lightning. Today, we rely on science to help us explain many of the world's mysteries. But even with all of the knowledge collected by people over thousands of years, there is much we still do not know. For example, no one knows what angels look like, but artists often give them wings and a special glow. This is because these are the characteristics people expect to see. It's all part of the human need to make sense of the world and our place in it.

Abbott Handerson Thayer, *Angel* (1887)

Abbott Handerson Thayer's young daughter Mary was the model for his painting of an angel. She is in the center of the painting and wears a flowing gown. Wings rise like clouds behind her. Her figure fills the frame so we can't really see where she is. Even her arms seem to fade off in the distance. Thayer painted Mary's face very carefully, but everything else about her is much lighter in color. We don't know where she's standing (or flying).

Abbott Handerson Thayer,
Angel, 1887, oil, 36¼ x 28⅛ in.,
Smithsonian American Art Museum ▶

Bruce Conner, *Arachne* (1959)

Torn pieces of nylon stretch and strain like a fractured spider's web in Bruce Conner's *Arachne*. The title, *Arachne*, refers to a Greek myth about a woman of that name who was a great weaver. She believed she could out-perform the gods. The goddess Athena did not appreciate such arrogance and destroyed Arachne's loom and tapestries. According to one version of the tale, Athena then turned Arachne into a spider.

Conner used discarded nylon stockings against a cardboard support to create this layered piece. The dripping paint in the background just adds to the mysterious mood! He was first inspired to work with cloth in his art after seeing rag pickers selling old pieces of clothing and fabric near his apartment. He was frustrated with using just paint, which he felt was a "pretty limited medium for spontaneity."

▲ Bruce Conner, *Arachne*, 1959, mixed media, 48 x 65½ in., Smithsonian American Art Museum

Like Thayer's *Angel,* Conner's *Arachne* has an otherworldly quality to it, but of course, there's nothing as realistic as a girl in Conner's artwork, just threads, darkness, and light.

Apply What You Learned

1 How are these two artworks similar? How are they different?

2 Why did Bruce Conner title his piece *Arachne*?

Big Question
Why do you think people make art to try to explain certain mysteries?

Workbook
Page 191–192

393

Contents
Handbooks and Resources

Study Skills and Language Learning
How to Learn Language 396
How to Build Vocabulary 398
How to Use Reference Books 400
How to Take Tests 402
Study Skills and Learning Strategies 404

Grammar Handbook 406

Reading Handbook
What Is Reading Comprehension? 424
What Are Reading Strategies? 425
How to Improve Reading Fluency 426

Viewing and Representing
What Are Viewing and Representing? 428
How to Read Maps and Diagrams 428
How to Read Graphs 430
How to Use Graphic Organizers 432

Writing Handbook
Modes of Writing 433
The Writing Process 436
Rubrics for Writing 440
Writing Letters 443
Filling In Forms 445
Conducting Research 447
Proofreading 448
Citing Sources 449

Technology Handbook
What Is Technology? 451
How to Use the Internet for Research 452
How to Evaluate the Quality of Information 453
How to Use Technology in Writing 455

Glossary 456
Index 462
Acknowledgments 468
Credits 470
Smithsonian American Art Museum
    List of Artworks 473

Study Skills and Language Learning

HOW TO LEARN LANGUAGE

Learning a language takes time, but, just like learning to swim, it can be fun. Whether you're learning English for the first time or adding to your knowledge of English by learning academic or content-area words, you're giving yourself a better chance of success in your studies and in your everyday life.

Learning any language is a skill that requires you to be active. You listen, speak, read, and write when you learn a language. Here are some tips that will help you learn English more actively and efficiently.

Listening

1. Set a purpose for listening. Think about what you hope to learn from today's class. Listen for these things as your teacher and classmates speak.

2. Listen actively. You can think faster than others can speak. This is useful because it allows you to anticipate what will be said next. Take notes as you listen. Write down only what is most important, and keep your notes short.

3. If you find something difficult to understand, listen more carefully. Do not give up and stop listening. Write down questions to ask afterward.

4. The more you listen, the faster you will learn. Use the radio, television, and Internet to practice your listening skills.

Speaking

1. Pay attention to sentence structure as you speak. Are you saying the words in the correct order?

2. Think about what you are saying. Don't worry about speaking fast. It's more important to communicate what you mean.

3. Practice speaking as much as you can, both in class and in your free time. Consider reading aloud to improve your pronunciation. If possible, record yourself speaking.

4. Do not be afraid of making mistakes. Everyone makes mistakes!

Reading

1. Read every day. Read as many different things as possible: Books, magazines, newspapers, and websites will all help you improve your comprehension and increase your vocabulary.

2. Try to understand what you are reading as a whole, rather than focusing on individual words. If you find a word you do not know, see if you can figure out its meaning from the context of the sentence before you look it up in a dictionary. Make a list of new vocabulary words and review it regularly.

3. Read texts more than once. Often your comprehension of a passage will improve if you read it twice or three times.

4. Try reading literature, poems, and plays aloud. This will help you understand them. It will also give you practice pronouncing new words.

Writing

1. Write something every day to improve your writing fluency. You can write about anything that interests you. Consider keeping a diary or a journal so that you can monitor your progress as time passes.

2. Plan your writing before you begin. Use graphic organizers to help you organize your ideas.

3. Be aware of sentence structure and grammar. Always write a first draft. Then go back and check for errors before you write your final version.

HOW TO BUILD VOCABULARY

1. Improving Your Vocabulary
Listening and Speaking

The most common ways to increase your vocabulary are listening, reading, and taking part in conversations. One of the most important skills in language learning is listening. Listen for new words when talking with others, joining in discussions, listening to the radio or audio books, or watching television.

You can find out the meanings of the words by asking, listening for clues, and looking up the words in a dictionary. Don't be embarrassed about asking what a word means. It shows that you are listening and that you want to learn. Whenever you can, use the new words you learn in conversation.

Reading Aloud

Listening to texts read aloud is another good way to build your vocabulary. There are many audio books available, and most libraries have a collection of them. When you listen to an audio book, you hear how new words are pronounced and how they are used. If you have a printed copy of the book, read along as you listen so that you can both see and hear new words.

Reading Often

Usually, people use a larger variety of words when they write than when they speak. The more you read, the more new words you'll find. When you see new words over and over again, they will become familiar to you and you'll begin to use them. Read from different sources—books, newspapers, magazines, Internet websites—in order to find a wide variety of words.

2. Figuring Out What a Word Means
Using Context Clues

When you come across a new word, you may not always need to use a dictionary. You might be able to figure out its meaning using the context, or the words in the sentence or paragraph in which you found it. Sometimes the surrounding words contain clues to tell you what the new word means.

Here are some tips for using context clues:

- Read the sentence, leaving out the word you don't know.
- Find clues in the sentence to figure out the new word's meaning.
- Read the sentence again, but replace the word you don't know with another possible meaning.
- Check your possible meaning by looking up the word in the dictionary. Write the word and its definition in your vocabulary notebook.

3. Practicing Your New Words

To make a word part of your vocabulary, study its definition, use it in your writing and speaking, and review it to make sure that you really understand its meaning.

Use one or more of these ways to remember the meanings of new words.

Keep a Vocabulary Notebook

Keep a notebook for vocabulary words. Divide your pages into three columns: the new words; hint words that help you remember their meanings; and their definitions. Test yourself by covering either the second or third column.

Word	Hint	Definition
zoology	zoo	study of animals
fortunate	fortune	lucky
quizzical	quiz	questioning

Make Flashcards

On the front of an index card, write a word you want to remember. On the back, write the meaning. You can also write a sentence that uses the word in context. Test yourself by flipping through the cards. Enter any hard words in your vocabulary notebook. As you learn the meanings, remove these cards and add new ones.

Say the Word Aloud

A useful strategy for building vocabulary is to say the new word aloud. Do not worry that there is no one to say the word to. Just say the word loud and clear several times. This will make you feel more confident and help you to use the word in conversation.

Record Yourself

Record your vocabulary words. Leave a ten-second space after each word, and then say the meaning and a sentence using the word. Play the recording. Fill in the blank space with the meaning and a sentence. Replay the recording until you memorize the word.

HOW TO USE REFERENCE BOOKS

The Dictionary

When you look up a word in the dictionary, you find the word and information about it. The word and the information about it are called a dictionary entry. Each entry tells you the word's spelling, pronunciation, part of speech, and meaning. Many English words have more than one meaning. Some words, such as *handle*, can be both a noun and a verb. For such words, the meanings, or definitions, are numbered. Sometimes example sentences are given in italics to help you understand how the word is used.

Here is part of a dictionary page with its important features labeled.

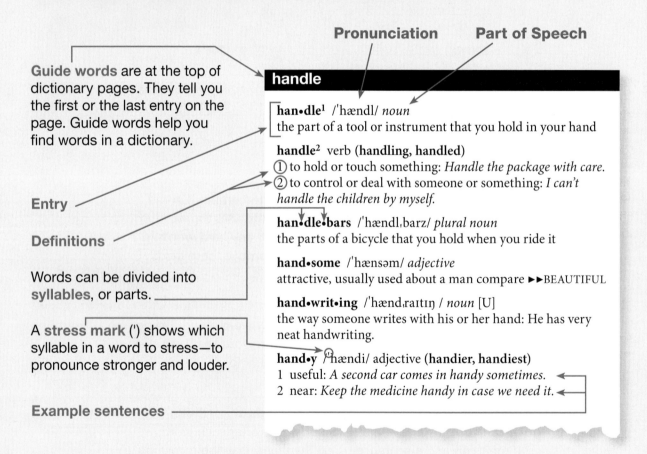

Pronunciation

Part of Speech

Guide words are at the top of dictionary pages. They tell you the first or the last entry on the page. Guide words help you find words in a dictionary.

Entry

Definitions

Words can be divided into **syllables**, or parts.

A **stress mark** (') shows which syllable in a word to stress—to pronounce stronger and louder.

Example sentences

handle

han•dle¹ /ˈhændl/ *noun*
the part of a tool or instrument that you hold in your hand

handle² *verb* (**handling, handled**)
① to hold or touch something: *Handle the package with care.*
② to control or deal with someone or something: *I can't handle the children by myself.*

han•dle•bars /ˈhændl̩ˌbarz/ *plural noun*
the parts of a bicycle that you hold when you ride it

hand•some /ˈhænsəm/ *adjective*
attractive, usually used about a man compare ▶▶BEAUTIFUL

hand•writ•ing /ˈhændˌraɪtɪŋ / *noun* [U]
the way someone writes with his or her hand: *He has very neat handwriting.*

hand•y /ˈhændi/ *adjective* (**handier, handiest**)
1 useful: *A second car comes in handy sometimes.*
2 near: *Keep the medicine handy in case we need it.*

400

The Thesaurus

A thesaurus is a kind of dictionary. It is a specialized dictionary that lists synonyms, or words with similar meanings, for words. You can use a print thesaurus (a book) or an online thesaurus on the Internet.

A thesaurus is a useful writing tool because it can help you avoid repeating the same word. It can also help you choose more precise words. Using a thesaurus regularly can help build your vocabulary by increasing the number of words you know that are related by an idea or concept.

In a thesaurus, words may either be arranged alphabetically or be grouped by theme. When the arrangement is by theme, you first have to look up the word in the index to find out in which grouping its synonyms will appear. When the thesaurus is arranged alphabetically, you simply look up the word as you would in a dictionary.

The entry below is from a thesaurus that is arranged alphabetically.

> sad *adjective* Tending to cause sadness or low spirits : blue, cheerless, depressed, depressing, dismal, dispiriting, downcast, gloomy, heartbreaking, joyless, melancholy, miserable, poignant, sorrowful, unhappy. See **happy** (antonym) in index.
> —See also **depressed, sorrowful**.

Choose synonyms carefully. You can see from the thesaurus entry above that there are many synonyms for the word *sad*. However, not all of these words may be the ones you want to use. For example, *depressed* can mean that you have an illness called depression, but it can also mean that you feel sad. If you are not sure what a word means, look it up in a dictionary to check that it is, in fact, the word you want to use.

HOW TO TAKE TESTS

In this section, you will learn some ways to improve your test-taking skills.

1. Taking Tests

Objective tests are tests in which each question has only one correct answer. To prepare for these tests, you should study the material that the test covers.

Preview the Test

1. Write your name on each sheet of paper you will hand in.
2. Look over the test to get an idea of the kinds of questions being asked.
3. Find out whether you lose points for incorrect answers. If you do, do not guess at answers.
4. Decide how much time you need to spend on each section of the test.
5. Use the time well. Give the most time to questions that are hardest or worth the most points.

Answer the Questions

1. Answer the easy questions first. Put a check next to harder questions and come back to them later.
2. If permitted, use scratch paper to write down your ideas.
3. Read each question at least twice before answering.
4. Answer all questions on the test (unless guessing can cost you points).
5. Do not change your first answer without a good reason.

Proofread Your Answers

1. Check that you followed the directions completely.
2. Reread questions and answers. Make sure you answered all the questions.

2. Answering Different Kinds of Questions

This section tells you about different kinds of test questions and gives you specific strategies for answering them.

True-or-False Questions

True-or-false questions ask you to decide whether or not a statement is true.

1. If a statement seems true, make sure that it is *all* true.
2. Pay special attention to the word *not*. It often changes the meaning of a statement entirely.
3. Pay attention to words that have a general meaning, such as *all, always, never, no, none,* and *only.* They often make a statement false.
4. Pay attention to words that qualify, such as *generally, much, many, most, often, sometimes,* and *usually.* They often make a statement true.

Multiple-Choice Questions

This kind of question asks you to choose from four or five possible answers.

1. Try to answer the question before reading the choices. If your answer is one of the choices, choose that answer.
2. Eliminate answers you know are wrong. Cross them out if you are allowed to write on the test paper.

Matching Questions

Matching questions ask you to match items in one group with items in another group.

1. Count each group to see whether any items will be left over.
2. Read all the items before you start matching.
3. Match the items you know first, and then match the others. If you can write on the paper, cross out items as you use them.

Fill-In Questions

A fill-in question asks you to give an answer in your own words.

1. Read the question or exercise carefully.
2. If you are completing a sentence, look for clues in the sentence that might help you figure out the answer. If the word *an* is right before the missing word, this means that the missing word begins with a vowel sound.

Short-Answer Questions

Short-answer questions ask you to write one or more sentences in which you give certain information.

1. Scan the question for key words, such as *explain, compare,* and *identify*.
2. When you answer the question, give only the information asked for.
3. Answer the question as clearly as possible.

Essay Questions

On many tests, you will have to write one or more essays. Sometimes you are given a choice of questions that you can answer.

1. Look for key words in the question or questions to find out exactly what information you should give.
2. Take a few minutes to think about facts, examples, and other types of information you can put in your essay.
3. Spend most of your time writing your essay so that it is well planned.
4. Leave time at the end of the test to proofread and correct your work.

1. Understanding the Parts of a Book

The Title Page

Every book has a **title page** that states the title, author, and publisher.

The Table of Contents and Headings

Many books have a **table of contents**. The table of contents can be found in the front of the book. It lists the chapters or units in the book. Beside each chapter or unit is the number of the page on which it begins. A **heading** at the top of the first page of each section tells you what that section is about.

The Glossary

While you read, you can look up unfamiliar words in the **glossary** at the back of the book. It lists words alphabetically and gives definitions.

The Index

To find out whether a book includes particular information, use the **index** at the back of the book. It is an alphabetical listing of names, places, and subjects in the book. Page numbers are listed beside each item.

The Bibliography

The **bibliography** is at the end of a nonfiction book or article. It tells you the other books or sources where an author got information to write the book. The sources are listed alphabetically by author. The bibliography is also a good way to find more articles or information about the same subject.

2. Using the Library

The Card Catalog

To find a book in a library, use the **card catalog**—an alphabetical list of authors, subjects, and titles. Each book has a **call number**, which tells you where to find a book on the shelf. Author cards, title cards, and subject cards all give information about a book. Use the **author card** when you want to find a book by an author but do not know the title. The **title card** is useful if you know the title of a book but not the author. When you want to find a book about a particular subject, use the **subject card**.

The Online Library Catalog

The **online library catalog** is a fast way to find a book using a computer. Books can be looked up by author, subject, or title. The online catalog will give you information on the book, as well as its call number.

3. Learning Strategies

Strategy	Description and Examples
Organizational Planning	Setting a learning goal; planning how to carry out a project, write a story, or solve a problem
Predicting	Using parts of a text (such as illustrations or titles) or a real-life situation and your own knowledge to anticipate what will occur next
Self-Management	Seeking or arranging the conditions that help you learn
Using Your Knowledge and Experience	Using knowledge and experience to learn something new, brainstorm, make associations, or write or tell what you know
Monitoring Comprehension	Being aware of how well a task is going, how well you understand what you are hearing or reading, or how well you are conveying ideas
Using/Making Rules	Applying a rule (phonics, decoding, grammar, linguistic, mathematical, scientific, and so on) to understand a text or complete a task; figuring out rules or patterns from examples
Taking Notes	Writing down key information in verbal, graphic, or numerical form, often as concept maps, word webs, timelines, or other graphic organizers
Visualizing	Creating mental pictures and using them to understand and appreciate descriptive writing
Cooperation	Working with classmates to complete a task or project, demonstrate a process or product, share knowledge, solve problems, give and receive feedback, and develop social skills
Making Inferences	Using the context of a text and your own knowledge to guess meanings of unfamiliar words or ideas
Substitution	Using a synonym or paraphrasing when you want to express an idea and do not know the word(s)
Using Resources	Using reference materials (books, dictionaries, encyclopedias, videos, computer programs, the Internet) to find information or complete a task
Classification	Grouping words, ideas, objects, or numbers according to their attributes; constructing graphic organizers to show classifications
Asking Questions	Negotiating meaning by asking for clarification, confirmation, rephrasing, or examples
Summarizing	Making a summary of something you listened to or read; retelling a text in your own words
Self-evaluation	After completing a task, judging how well you did, whether you reached your goal, and how effective your problem-solving procedures were

Grammar Handbook

THE PARTS OF SPEECH

In English there are eight **parts of speech**: nouns, pronouns, adjectives, verbs, adverbs, prepositions, conjunctions, and interjections.

Nouns

Nouns name people, places, or things. There are two kinds of nouns: **common nouns** and **proper nouns**.

A **common noun** is a general person, place, or thing.

person	thing	place

The **student** brings a **notebook** to **class**.

A **proper noun** is a specific person, place, or thing. Proper nouns start with a capital letter.

person	place	thing

Joseph went to **Paris** and saw the **Eiffel Tower.**

A noun that is made up of two words is called a **compound noun**. A compound noun can be one word or two words. Some compound nouns have hyphens.

One word: **newspaper, bathroom**
Two words: **vice president, pet shop**
Hyphens: **sister-in-law, grown-up**

Articles identify nouns. *A, an,* and *the* are articles.

A and *an* are called **indefinite articles**. Use the article *a* or *an* to talk about one general person, place, or thing.

Use *an* before a word that begins with a vowel sound.

I have **an** idea.

Use *a* before a word that begins with a consonant sound.

May I borrow **a** pen?

The is called a **definite article**. Use *the* to talk about one or more specific people, places, or things.

Please bring me **the** box from your room. **The** books are in my backpack.

Pronouns

Pronouns are words that take the place of nouns or proper nouns. In this example, the pronoun *she* replaces, or refers to, the proper noun *Angela*.

Pronouns can be subjects or objects. They can be singular or plural.

	Subject Pronouns	**Object Pronouns**
Singular	I, you, he, she, it	me, you, him, her, it
Plural	we, you, they	us, you, them

A **subject pronoun** replaces a noun or proper noun that is the subject of a sentence. A **subject** is who or what a sentence is about. In these sentences, *He* replaces *Daniel*.

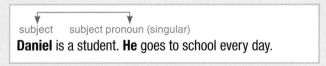

In these sentences, *We* replaces *Heather* and *I*.

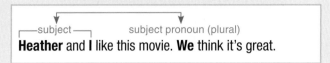

407

An **object pronoun** replaces a noun or proper noun that is the object of a verb. A verb tells the action in a sentence. An **object** receives the action of a verb.

In these sentences the verb is *gave*. *Him* replaces *Ed*, which is the object of the verb.

object   object pronoun (singular)

Lauren gave **Ed** the notes. Lauren gave **him** the notes.

An object pronoun can also replace a noun or proper noun that is the **object of a preposition**. Prepositions are words like *for, to,* or *with*. In these sentences, the preposition is *with*. *Them* replaces *José* and *Yolanda*, which is the object of the preposition.

object of a preposition   object pronoun (plural)

I went to the mall with **José and Yolanda**. I went to the mall with **them**.

Pronouns can also be possessive. A **possessive pronoun** replaces a noun or proper noun. It shows who owns something.

	Possessive Pronouns
Singular	mine, yours, hers, his
Plural	ours, yours, theirs

In these sentences, *hers* replaces the words *Kyoko's coat*. It shows that Kyoko owns the coat.

It is **Kyoko's coat**. It is **hers**.

Adjectives

Adjectives describe nouns. An adjective usually comes before the noun it describes.

tall grass **big** truck **two** kittens

An adjective can also come *after* the noun it describes.

The bag is **heavy**. The books are **new**.

Do not add -*s* to adjectives that describe plural nouns.

the **red** houses the **funny** jokes the **smart** teachers

Verbs

Verbs express an action or a state of being.

subject verb subject verb Jackie **walks** to school. The school **is** near her house.

An **action verb** tells what someone or something does or did. You cannot always see the action of an action verb.

Verbs That Tell Actions You Can See		Verbs That Tell Actions You Cannot See	
dance	swim	know	sense
play	talk	remember	name
sit	write	think	understand

A **linking verb** shows no action. It links the subject with another word that describes the subject.

Linking Verbs		
look	is	appear
smell	are	seem
sound	am	become
taste	were	
feel		

In this sentence, the adjective *tired* tells something about the subject, *dog*. *Seems* is the linking verb.

Our dog **seems** tired.

In this sentence, the noun *friend* tells something about the subject, *brother*. *Is* is the linking verb.

Your brother **is** my friend.

A **helping verb** comes before the main verb. It adds to the main verb's meaning. Helping verbs can be forms of the verbs *be*, *do*, or *have*.

	Helping Verbs
Forms of *be*	am, was, is, were, are
Forms of *do*	do, did, does
Forms of *have*	have, had, has
Other helping verbs	can, must, could, have (to), should, may, will, would

In this sentence, *am* is the helping verb; *walking* is the action verb.

helping action
verb   verb
I **am walking** to my science class.

In this sentence, *has* is the helping verb; *completed* is the action verb.

helping   action
verb   verb
He **has completed** his essay.

In questions, the subject comes between a helping verb and a main verb.

person
Did Liang **give** you the CD?

Adverbs

Adverbs describe the action of verbs. They tell *how* an action happens. Adverbs answer the question *Where? When? How? How much?* or *How often?*

Many adverbs end in *-ly.*

easily	slowly	carefully

Some adverbs do not end in *-ly.*

seldom	fast	very

In this sentence, the adverb *everywhere* modifies the verb *looked.* It answers the question *Where?*

verb   adverb
Nicole looked **everywhere** for her cell phone.

In this sentence, the adverb *quickly* modifies the verb *walked.* It answers the question *How?*

verb   adverb
They walked home **quickly**.

Adverbs also modify adjectives. They answer the question *How much?* or *How little?*

In this sentence, the adjective *dangerous* modifies the noun *road.* The adverb *very* modifies the adjective *dangerous.*

adverb adjective noun
This is a **very** dangerous road.

Adverbs can also modify other adverbs. In this sentence, the adverb *fast* modifies the verb *runs.* The adverb *quite* modifies the adverb *fast.*

verb adverb adverb
John runs **quite** fast.

Prepositions

Prepositions can show time, place, and direction.

Time	Place	Direction
after	above	across
before	below	down
during	in	into
since	near	to
until	under	up

In this sentence, the preposition *above* shows where the bird flew. It shows place.

> preposition
> A bird flew **above** my head.

In this sentence, the preposition *across* shows direction.

> preposition
> The children walked **across** the street.

A **prepositional phrase** starts with a preposition and ends with a noun or pronoun.

In this sentence, the preposition is *near* and the noun is *school.*

> prepositional phrase
> The library is **near the new school**.

Conjunctions

A **conjunction** joins words, groups of words, and whole sentences.

Conjunctions			
and	for	or	yet
but	nor	so	

In this sentence, the conjunction *and* joins two proper nouns: *Jonah* and *Teresa*.

> noun   noun
> Jonah **and** Teresa are in school.

In this sentence, the conjunction *or* joins two prepositional phrases: *to the movies* and *to the mall*.

> prepositional   prepositional
> ┌─ phrase ─┐   ┌─ phrase ─┐
> They want to go to the movies **or** to the mall.

In this sentence, the conjunction *and* joins two independent clauses: *Amanda baked the cookies*, and *Eric made the lemonade*.

> ┌── independent clause ──┐   ┌── independent clause ──┐
> Amanda baked the cookies, **and** Eric made the lemonade.

Interjections

Interjections are words or phrases that express emotion.

Interjections that express strong emotion are followed by an exclamation point.

> **Wow!** Did you see that catch?
> **Hey!** Watch out for that ball.

Interjections that express mild emotion are followed by a comma.

> **Gee,** I'm sorry that your team lost.
> **Oh,** it's okay. We'll do better next time.

CLAUSES

Clauses are groups of words with a subject and a verb. Some clauses form complete sentences; they tell a complete thought. Others do not.

This clause is a complete sentence. Clauses that form complete sentences are called **independent clauses**.

> subject verb
> The dog's **tail wagged**.

This clause is not a complete sentence. Clauses that don't form complete sentences are called **dependent clauses**.

> subject verb
> when the **boy patted** him.

Independent clauses can be combined with dependent clauses to form a sentence.

In this sentence, *The dog's tail wagged* is an independent clause. *When the boy patted him* is a dependent clause.

> ┌──independent clause──┐┌──dependent clause──┐
> The dog's tail wagged when the boy patted him.

SENTENCES

Sentences have a subject and a verb, and tell a complete thought. A sentence always begins with a capital letter. It always ends with a period, question mark, or exclamation point.

> subject action verb
> The **cheetah runs** very fast.
>
> helping
> verb   subject   action verb
> **Do you play** soccer?
>
> subject linking verb
> **I am** so late!

Simple Sentences and Compound Sentences

Some sentences are called simple sentences. Others are called compound sentences. A **simple sentence** has one independent clause. Here is an example.

> ┌──── independent clause ────┐
> The dog barked at the mail carrier.

Compound sentences are made up of two or more simple sentences, or independent clauses. They are joined together by a **conjunction** such as *and* or *but*.

> ┌──── independent clause ────┐   ┌──── independent clause ────┐
> The band has a lead singer, **but** they need a drummer.

Sentence Types

Sentences have different purposes. There are four types of sentences: declarative, interrogative, imperative, and exclamatory.

Declarative sentences are statements. They end with a period.

> We are going to the beach on Saturday.

Interrogative sentences are questions. They end with a question mark.

> Will you come with us?

Imperative sentences are commands. They usually end with a period. If the command is strong, the sentence may end with an exclamation point.

> Put on your life jacket. Now jump into the water!

Exclamatory sentences express strong feeling. They end with an exclamation point.

> I swam all the way from the boat to the shore!

MECHANICS

End Marks

End marks come at the end of sentences. There are three kinds of end marks: periods, question marks, and exclamation points.

Use a **period** to end a statement (declarative sentence).

The spacecraft *Magellan* took pictures of Jupiter.

Use a **period** to end a command or request (imperative sentence) that isn't strong enough to need an exclamation point.

Please change the channel.

Use a **question mark** to end a sentence that asks a question. (interrogative sentence).

Where does Mrs. Suarez live?

Use an **exclamation point** to end a sentence that expresses strong feeling (exclamatory sentence).

That was a great party! Look at that huge house!

Use an **exclamation point** to end an imperative sentence that gives an urgent command.

Get away from the edge of the pool!

Periods are also used after initials and many abbreviations.

Use a **period** after a person's initial or abbreviated title.

Ms. Susan Vargas	Mrs. Fiske	J. D. Salinger
Gov. Lise Crawford	Mr. Vargas	Dr. Sapirstein

Use a **period** after the abbreviation of streets, roads, and so on.

Avenue	Ave.	Road	Rd.
Highway	Hwy.	Street	St.

Use a **period** after the abbreviation of many units of measurement. Abbreviations for metric measurements do *not* use periods.

inch	in.	centimeter	cm
foot	ft.	meter	m
pound	lb.	kilogram	kg
gallon	gal.	liter	l

Commas

Commas separate, or set off, parts of a sentence, or phrase.

Use a comma to separate two independent clauses linked by a conjunction. In this sentence, the comma goes before the conjunction *but*.

⌐independent clause⌐ ⌐independent clause⌐
We went to the museum, **but** it is not open on Mondays.

Use commas to separate the parts in a series. A series is a group of three or more words, phrases, or very brief clauses.

	Commas in Series
To separate words	Lucio's bike is red, white, and silver.
To separate phrases	Today, he rode all over the lawn, down the sidewalk, and up the hill.
To separate clauses	Lucio washed the bike, his dad washed the car, and his mom washed the dog.

Use a comma to set off an introductory word, phrase, or clause.

	Commas with Introductory Words
To separate words	Yes, Stacy likes to go swimming.
To set off a phrase	In a month, she may join the swim team again.
To set off a clause	If she joins the swim team, I'll miss her at softball practice.

Use commas to set off an interrupting word, phrase, or clause.

	Commas with Interrupting Words
To set off a word	We left, finally, to get some fresh air.
To set off a phrase	Carol's dog, a brown pug, shakes when he gets scared.
To set off a clause	The assignment, I'm sorry to say, was too hard for me.

Use a comma to set off a speaker's quoted words in a sentence.

Jeanne asked, "Where is that book I just had?"
"I just saw it," said Billy, "on the kitchen counter."

In a direct address, one speaker talks directly to another. Use commas to set off the name of the person being addressed.

Thank you, Dee, for helping to put away the dishes.
Phil, why are you late again?

Use a comma between the day and the year.

My cousin was born on September 9, 2003.

If the date appears in the middle of a sentence, use a comma before and after the year.

Daria's mother was born on June 8, 1969, in New Jersey.

Use a comma between a city and a state and between a city and a nation.

My father grew up in Bakersfield, California.
We are traveling to Acapulco, Mexico.

If the names appear in the middle of a sentence, use a comma before *and* after the state or nation.

My friend Carl went to Mumbai, India, last year.

Use a comma after the greeting in a friendly letter. Use a comma after the closing in both a friendly letter and formal letter. Do this in e-mail letters, too.

Dear Margaret,	Sincerely,	Yours truly,

Semicolons and Colons

Semicolons can connect two independent clauses. Use them when the clauses are closely related in meaning or structure.

The team won again; it was their ninth victory. Ana usually studies right after school; Rita prefers to study in the evening.

Colons introduce a list of items or important information.

Use a colon after an independent clause to introduce a list of items. (The clause often includes the words *the following, these, those,* or *this*.)

The following animals live in Costa Rica: monkeys, lemurs, toucans, and jaguars.

Use a colon to introduce important information. If the information is in an independent clause, use a capital letter to begin the first word after the colon.

There is one main rule: Do not talk to anyone during the test. You must remember this: Stay away from the train tracks!

Use a colon to separate hours and minutes when writing the time.

1:30	7:45	11:08

Quotation Marks

Quotation Marks set off direct quotations, dialogue, and some titles. A **direct quotation** is the exact words that somebody said, wrote, or thought.

Commas and periods *always* go inside quotation marks. If a question mark or exclamation point is part of the quotation, it is also placed *inside* the quotation marks.

> "Can you please get ready?" Mom asked.
> My sister shouted, "Look out for that bee!"

If a question mark or exclamation point is *not* part of the quotation, it goes *outside* the quotation marks. In these cases there is no punctuation before the end quotation marks.

> Did you say, "I can't do this"?

Conversation between two or more people is called **dialogue**. Use quotation marks to set off spoken words in dialogue.

> "What a great ride!" Pam said. "Let's go on it again."
> Julio shook his head and said, "No way. I'm feeling sick."

Use quotation marks around the titles of short works of writing or other art forms. The following kinds of titles take quotation marks:

Chapters	"The Railroad in the West"
Short Stories	"The Perfect Cat"
Articles	"California in the 1920s"
Songs	"This Land Is Your Land"
Single TV episodes	"Charlie's New Idea"
Short poems	"The Bat"

Titles of all other written work and artwork are underlined or set in italic type. These include books, magazines, newspapers, plays, movies, TV series, and paintings.

Apostrophes

Apostrophes can be used with singular and plural nouns to show ownership or possession. To form the possessive, follow these rules:

For singular nouns, add an apostrophe and an *s*.

| Maria's eyes | hamster's cage | the sun's warmth |

For singular nouns that end in *s*, add an apostrophe and an *s*.

| her boss's office | Carlos's piano | the grass's length |

For plural nouns that do not end in *s*, add an apostrophe and an *s*.

| women's clothes | men's shoes | children's books |

For plural nouns that end in *s*, add an apostrophe.

| teachers' lounge | dogs' leashes | kids' playground |

Apostrophes are also used in **contractions**. A contraction is a shortened form of two words that have been combined. The apostrophe shows where a letter or letters have been taken away.

> I will
> **I'll** be home in one hour.
> do not
> We **don't** have any milk.

Capitalization

There are five main reasons to use capital letters:

1. To begin a sentence and in a direct quotation
2. To write the word *I*
3. To write a proper noun (the name of a specific person, place, or thing)
4. To write a person's title
5. To write the title of a work (artwork, written work, magazine, newspaper, musical composition, organization)

Use a capital letter to begin the first word in a sentence.

Cows eat grass. They also eat hay.

Use a capital letter for the first word of a direct quotation. Use the capital letter even if the quotation is in the middle of a sentence.

Carlos said, "We need more lettuce for the sandwiches."

Use a capital letter for the word *I*.

How will I ever learn all these things? I guess I will learn them little by little.

Use a capital letter for a proper noun: the name of a specific person, place, or thing. Capitalize the important words in names.

Robert E. Lee   Morocco   Tuesday   Tropic of Cancer

Capital Letters in Place Names	
Streets	Interstate 95, Center Street, Atwood Avenue
City Sections	Greenwich Village, Shaker Heights, East Side
Cities and Towns	Rome, Chicago, Fresno
States	California, North Dakota, Maryland
Regions	Pacific Northwest, Great Plains, Eastern Europe
Nations	China, Dominican Republic, Italy
Continents	North America, Africa, Asia
Mountains	Mount Shasta, Andes Mountains, Rocky Mountains
Deserts	Mojave Desert, Sahara Desert, Gobi Desert
Islands	Fiji Islands, Capri, Virgin Islands
Rivers	Amazon River, Nile River, Mississippi River
Lakes	Lake Superior, Great Bear Lake, Lake Tahoe
Bays	San Francisco Bay, Hudson Bay, Galveston Bay
Seas	Mediterranean Sea, Sea of Japan
Oceans	Pacific Ocean, Atlantic Ocean, Indian Ocean

Capital Letters for Specific Things	
Historical Periods, Events	Renaissance, Battle of Bull Run
Historical Texts	Constitution, Bill of Rights
Days and Months	Monday, October
Holidays	Thanksgiving, Labor Day
Organizations, Schools	Greenpeace, Central High School
Government Bodies	Congress, State Department
Political Parties	Republican Party, Democratic Party
Ethnic Groups	Chinese, Latinos
Languages, Nationalities	Spanish, Canadian
Buildings	Empire State Building, City Hall
Monuments	Lincoln Memorial, Washington Monument
Religions	Hinduism, Christianity, Judaism, Islam
Special Events	Boston Marathon, Ohio State Fair

Use a capital letter for a person's title if the title comes before the name. In the second sentence below, a capital letter is not needed because the title does not come before a name.

I heard **S**enator Clinton's speech about jobs. The **s**enator may come to our school.

Use a capital letter for the first and last word and all other important words in titles of books, newspapers, magazines, short stories, plays, movies, songs, paintings, and sculptures.

Lucy wants to read <u>**T**he **L**ord of the **R**ings</u>.
The newspaper my father reads is <u>**T**he **N**ew **Y**ork **T**imes</u>.
Did you like the painting called <u>**W**ork in the **F**ields</u>?
This poem is called "**T**he **B**irch **T**ree."

Reading Handbook

People often think of reading as a passive activity—that you don't have to do much, you just have to take in words—but that is not true. Good readers are active readers.

Reading comprehension involves these skills:

1. Understanding what you are reading.
2. Being part of what you are reading, or engaging with the text.
3. Evaluating what you are reading.
4. Making connections between what you are reading and what you already know.
5. Thinking about your response to what you have read.

Understanding What You Are Reading

One of the first steps is to recognize letters and words. Remember that it does not matter if you do not recognize all the words. You can figure out their meanings later. Try to figure out the meaning of unfamiliar words from the context of the sentence or paragraph. If you cannot figure out the meaning of a word, look it up in a dictionary. Next, you activate the meaning of words as you read them. That is what you are doing now. If you find parts of a text difficult, stop and read them a second time.

Engaging with the Text

Good readers use many different skills and strategies to help them understand and enjoy the text they are reading. When you read, think of it as a conversation between you and the writer. The writer wants to tell you something, and you want to understand his or her message.

Practice using these tips every time you read:

• Predict what will happen next in a story. Use clues you find in the text.
• Ask yourself questions about the main idea or message of the text.
• Monitor your understanding. Stop reading from time to time and think about what you have learned so far.

Evaluating What You Are Reading

The next step is to think about what you are reading. First, think about the author's purpose for writing. What type of text are you reading? If it is an informational text, the author wants to give you information about a subject, for example, about science, social science, or math. If you are reading literature, the author's purpose is probably to entertain you.

When you have decided what the author's purpose is for writing the text, think about what you have learned. Use these questions to help you:

- Is the information useful?
- Have you changed your mind about the subject?
- Did you enjoy the story, poem, or play?

Making Connections

Now connect the events or ideas in a text to your own knowledge or experience. Think about how your knowledge of a subject or your experience of the world can help you understand a text better.

- If the text has sections with headings, notice what these are. Do they give you clues about the main ideas in the text?
- Read the first paragraph. What is the main idea?
- Now read the paragraphs that follow. Make a note of the main ideas.
- Review your notes. How are the ideas connected?

Thinking about Your Response to What You Have Read

You read for a reason, so it is a good idea to think about how the text has helped you. Ask yourself these questions after you read:

- What information have I learned? Can I use it in my other classes?
- How can I connect my own experience or knowledge to the text?
- Did I enjoy reading the text? Why or why not?
- Did I learn any new vocabulary? What was it? How can I use it in conversation or in writing?

WHAT ARE READING STRATEGIES?

Reading strategies are specific things readers do to help them understand texts. Reading is like a conversation between an author and a reader. Authors make decisions about how to effectively communicate through a piece of writing. Readers use specific strategies to help them understand what authors are trying to communicate. Ten of the most common reading strategies are Previewing, Predicting, Skimming, Scanning, Comparing and Contrasting, Identifying Problems and Solutions, Recognizing Cause and Effect, Distinguishing Fact from Opinion, Identifying Main Idea and Details, and Identifying an Author's Purpose.

HOW TO IMPROVE READING FLUENCY

1. What Is Reading Fluency?

Reading fluency is the ability to read smoothly and expressively with clear understanding. Fluent readers are better able to understand and enjoy what they read. Use the strategies that follow to build your fluency in these four key areas: accuracy and rate, phrasing, intonation, expression.

2. How to Improve Accuracy and Rate

Accuracy is the correctness of your reading. Rate is the speed of your reading.

- Use correct pronunciation.
- Emphasize correct syllables.
- Recognize most words.

3. How to Read with Proper Rate

- Match your reading speed to what you are reading. For example, if you are reading a mystery story, read slightly faster. If you are reading a science textbook, read slightly slower.
- Recognize and use punctuation.

4. Test Your Accuracy and Rate

- Choose a text you are familiar with, and practice reading it multiple times.
- Keep a dictionary with you while you read, and look up words you do not recognize.
- Use a watch or clock to time yourself while you read a passage.
- Ask a friend or family member to read a passage for you so you know what it should sound like.

5. How to Improve Intonation

Intonation is the rise and fall in the pitch of your voice as you read aloud. Pitch means the highness or lowness of the sound. Follow these steps:

- Change the sound of your voice to match what you are reading.
- Make your voice flow, or sound smooth, while you read.
- Make sure you are pronouncing words correctly.
- Raise the pitch of your voice for words that should be stressed, or emphasized.
- Use proper rhythm and meter.
- Use visual clues.

Visual Clue and Meaning	Example	How to Read It
Italics: draw attention to a word to show special importance	He is *serious*.	Emphasize "serious."
Dash: shows a quick break in a sentence	He is—serious.	Pause before saying "serious."
Exclamation point: can represent energy, excitement, or anger	He is serious!	Make your voice louder at the end of the sentence.
All capital letters: can represent strong emphasis or yelling	HE IS SERIOUS.	Emphasize the whole sentence.
Boldfacing: draws attention to a word to show importance	He is **serious**.	Emphasize "serious."
Question mark: shows curiosity or confusion	Is he serious?	Raise the pitch of your voice slightly at the end of the sentence.

6. How to Improve Phrasing

Phrasing is how you group words together. Follow these steps:

- Use correct rhythm and meter by not reading too fast or too slow.
- Pause for key words within the text.
- Make sure your sentences have proper flow and meter, so they sound smooth instead of choppy.
- Make sure you sound like you are reading a sentence instead of a list.
- Use punctuation to tell you when to stop, pause, or emphasize.

7. How to Improve Expression

Expression in reading is how you express feeling. Follow these steps:

- Match the sound of your voice to what you are reading. For example, read louder and faster to show strong feeling. Read slowly and more quietly to show sadness or seriousness.
- Match the sound of your voice to the genre. For example, read a fun, fictional story using a fun, friendly voice. Read an informative, nonfiction article using an even tone and a more serious voice.
- Avoid speaking in monotone, or using only one tone in your voice.
- Pause for emphasis and exaggerate letter sounds to match the mood or theme of what you are reading.

Viewing and Representing

WHAT ARE VIEWING AND REPRESENTING?

Viewing

Viewing is something you do every day. Much of what you read and watch includes visuals that help you understand information. These visuals can be maps, charts, diagrams, graphs, photographs, illustrations, and so on. They can inform you, explain a topic or an idea, entertain you, or persuade you.

Websites use visuals, too. It is important for you to be able to view visuals critically in order to evaluate what you are seeing or reading.

Representing

Representing is creating a visual to convey an idea. It is important for you to be able to create and use visuals in your own written work and presentations. You can use graphic organizers, diagrams, charts, posters, and artwork to illustrate and explain your ideas. Following are some examples of visuals.

HOW TO READ MAPS AND DIAGRAMS

Maps

Maps help us learn more about our world. They show the location of places such as countries, states, and cities. Some maps show where mountains, rivers, and lakes are located.

Many maps have helpful features. For example, a **compass rose** shows which way is north. A **scale** shows how miles or kilometers are represented on the map. A **key** shows what different colors or symbols represent.

◀ Three trails on which cowboys drove cattle north from Texas

Diagrams

Diagrams are drawings or plans used to explain things or show how things work. They are often used in social studies and science books. Some diagrams show pictures of how objects look on the outside or on the inside. Others show the different steps in a process.

   This diagram shows what a kernel of corn looks like on the inside.

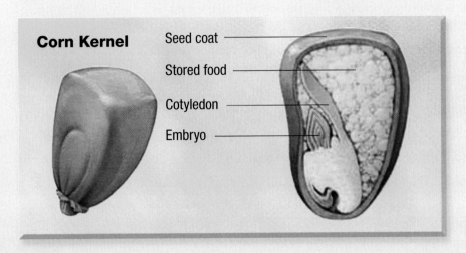

Corn Kernel

Seed coat

Stored food

Cotyledon

Embryo

A **flowchart** is a diagram that uses shapes and arrows to show a step-by-step process. The flowchart below shows the steps involved in baking chicken fingers. Each arrow points to the next step.

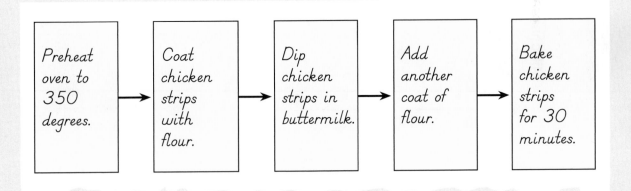

| Preheat oven to 350 degrees. | → | Coat chicken strips with flour. | → | Dip chicken strips in buttermilk. | → | Add another coat of flour. | → | Bake chicken strips for 30 minutes. |

HOW TO READ GRAPHS

Graphs organize and explain information. They show how two or more kinds of information are related, or how they are alike. Graphs are often used in math, science, and social studies books. Three common kinds of graphs are **line graphs**, **bar graphs**, and **circle graphs**.

Line Graphs

A line graph shows how information changes over a period of time. This line graph explains how, over a period of about 100 years, the Native-American population of Central Mexico decreased by more than 20 million people. Can you find the population in the year 1540? What was it in 1580?

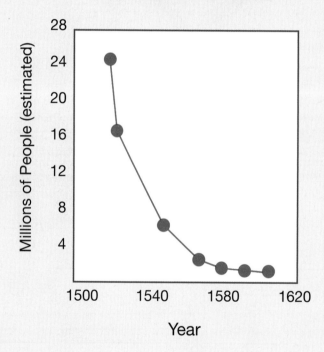

Native-American Population
of Central Mexico

Bar Graphs

We use bar graphs to compare information. For example, this bar graph compares the populations of the thirteen United States in 1790. It shows that, in 1790, Virginia had over ten times as many people as Delaware.

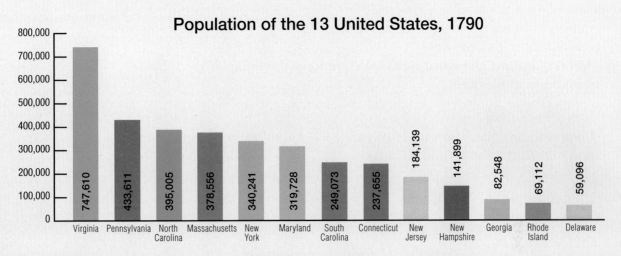

Population of the 13 United States, 1790

State	Population
Virginia	747,610
Pennsylvania	433,611
North Carolina	395,005
Massachusetts	378,556
New York	340,241
Maryland	319,728
South Carolina	249,073
Connecticut	237,655
New Jersey	184,139
New Hampshire	141,899
Georgia	82,548
Rhode Island	69,112
Delaware	59,096

Circle Graphs

A circle graph is sometimes called a pie chart because it looks like a pie cut into slices. Circle graphs are used to show how different parts of a whole thing compare to one another. In a circle graph, all the "slices" add up to 100 percent. This circle graph shows that only 29 percent of the earth's surface is covered by land. It also shows that the continent of Asia takes up 30 percent of the earth's land.

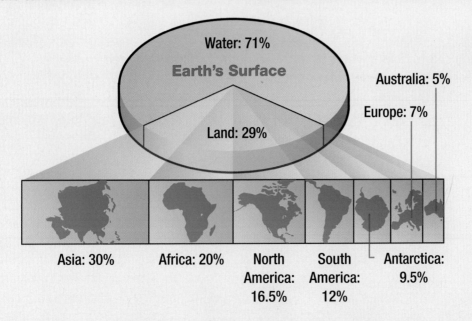

Earth's Surface

Water: 71%
Land: 29%

Australia: 5%
Europe: 7%

Asia: 30%   Africa: 20%   North America: 16.5%   South America: 12%   Antarctica: 9.5%

HOW TO USE GRAPHIC ORGANIZERS

A graphic organizer is a diagram that helps you organize information and show relationships among ideas. Because the information is organized visually, a graphic organizer tells you—in a quick snapshot—how ideas are related. Before you make a graphic organizer, think about the information you want to organize. How are the ideas or details related? Choose a format that will show those relationships clearly.

Venn diagrams and word webs are commonly used graphic organizers. Here is an example of each.

Venn Diagrams

A Venn diagram shows how two thing are alike and different. The diagram below compares oranges and bananas.

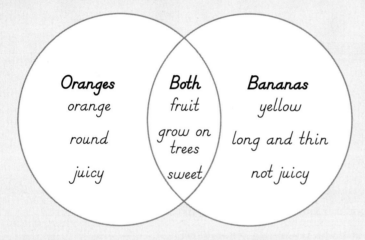

Word Webs

A word web is often used to help a writer describe something. The word web below lists five sensory details that describe popcorn.

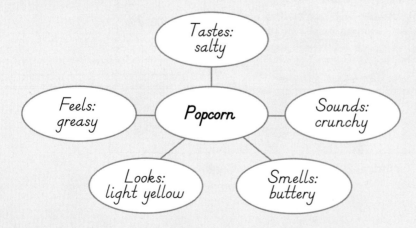

Writing Handbook

Narration

When writers tell a story, they use narration. There are many kinds of narration. Most include characters, a setting, and a sequence of events. Here are some types of narration.

A **short story** is a short, creative narrative. Most short stories have one or more characters, a setting, and a plot. A few types of short stories are realistic stories, fantasy stories, science-fiction stories, and adventure stories.

Autobiographical writing is a factual story of a writer's own life, told by the writer, usually in the first-person point of view. An autobiography may tell about the person's whole life or only a part of it.

Biographical writing is a factual story of a person's life told by another person. Most biographies are written about famous or admirable people.

Description

Description, or descriptive writing, is writing that gives the reader a mental picture of whatever is being described. To do this, writers choose their words carefully. They use figurative language and include vivid sensory details.

Persuasion

Writers use persuasion to try to persuade people to think or act in a certain way. Forms of persuasive writing include advertisements, essays, letters, editorials, speeches, and public-service announcements.

Exposition

Exposition, or expository writing, is writing that gives information or explains something. The information that writers include in expository writing is factual. Here are some types of expository writing.

A **compare-and-contrast essay** analyzes the similarities and differences between or among things.

A **cause-and-effect essay** explains causes or effects of an event. For example, a writer might examine several causes of a single effect or several effects of a single cause.

Writers use a **problem-and-solution essay** to describe a problem and offer one or more solutions to it.

A **how-to essay** explains how to do or make something. The process is broken down into steps, which are explained in order.

A **summary** is a brief statement that gives the main ideas of an event or a piece of writing. One way to write a summary is to read a text and then reread each paragraph or section. Next put the text aside and write the main ideas in your own words in a sentence or two.

Research Writing

Writers often use research to gather information about topics, including people, places, and things. Good research writing does not simply repeat information. It guides the readers through a topic, showing them why each fact matters and creating a complete picture of the topic. Here are some types of research writing.

Research report A research report presents information gathered from reference books, interviews, or other sources.

Biographical report A biographical report includes dates, details, and main events in a person's life. It can also include information about the time in which the person lived.

Multimedia report A multimedia report presents information through a variety of media, including text, slides, photographs, prerecorded music and sound effects, and digital imaging.

Responses to Literature

A **literary essay** is one type of response to literature. In a literary essay, a writer discusses and interprets what is important in a book, short story, essay, article, or poem.

Literary criticism is another type of response to literature. Literary criticism is the result of a careful examination of one or more literary works. The writer makes a judgment by looking carefully and critically at various important elements in the work.

A book **critique** gives readers a summary of a book, encouraging the reader either to read it or to avoid reading it. A movie critique gives readers a summary of a movie, tells if the writer enjoyed the movie, and then explains the reasons why or why not.

A **comparison of works** compares the features of two or more works.

Creative Writing

Creative writing blends imagination, ideas, and emotions, and allows the writer to present a unique view of the world. Poems, plays, short stories, dramas, and even some cartoons are examples of creative writing.

434

Practical and Technical Documents

Practical writing is fact-based writing that people do in the workplace or in their day-to-day lives. A business letter, memo, school form, job application, and a letter of inquiry are a few examples of practical writing.

Technical documents are fact-based documents that identify a sequence of activities needed to design a system, operate machinery, follow a procedure, or explain the rules of an organization. You read technical writing every time you read a manual or a set of instructions.

In the following descriptions, you'll find tips for tackling several types of practical and technical writing.

Business letters are formal letters that follow one of several specific formats.

News releases, also called press releases, announce factual information about upcoming events. A writer might send a news release to a local newspaper, local radio station, TV station, or other media that will publicize the information.

Guidelines give information about how people should act or how to do something.

Process explanations are step-by-step explanations of how to do something. The explanation should be clear and specific and can include diagrams or other illustrations. Below is an example.

KEYSTONE
CD-ROM

Usage Instructions
1. Insert the *Keystone* CD-ROM into your CD drive.
2. Open "My Computer."
3. Double-click on your CD-ROM disk drive.
4. Click on the *Keystone* icon. This will launch the program.

435

THE WRITING PROCESS

The **writing process** is a series of steps that can help you write effectively.

Step 1: Prewrite

During **prewriting**, you collect topic ideas, choose a topic, plan your writing, and gather information.

A good way to get ideas for a topic is to **brainstorm**. Brainstorming means writing a list of all the topic ideas you can think of.

Look at your list of topic ideas. Choose the one that is the most interesting to you. This is your **topic**, the subject you will write about.

Plan your writing by following these steps:

- First, decide on the **type** of writing that works best with your topic. For example, you may want to write a description, a story, or an essay.
- The type of writing is called the **form** of writing.
- Then think about your **audience**. Identifying your audience will help you decide whether to write formally or informally.
- Finally, decide what your reason for writing is. This is your **purpose**. Is your purpose to inform your audience? To entertain them?

How you gather information depends on what you are writing. For example, for a report, you need to do research. For a description, you might list your ideas in a graphic organizer. A student named Becca listed her ideas for a description of her week at art camp in the graphic organizer below.

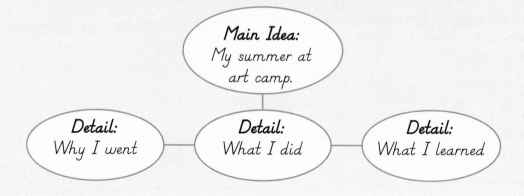

436

Step 2: Draft

In this step, you start writing. Don't worry too much about spelling and punctuation. Just put your ideas into sentences.

Here is the first paragraph that Becca wrote for her first draft.

> I saw an art contest advertised in the newspaper last spring. I entered my best drawing. I have always loved art. The prize was a week at an art camp in June with 9 other kids. I was very happy when I won.

Step 3: Revise

Now it's time to revise, or make changes. Ask yourself these questions:
- Are my ideas presented in the order that makes the most sense?
- Does my draft have a beginning, a middle, and an end?
- Does each paragraph have a main idea and supporting details?

If you answered *no* to any of these questions, you need to revise. Revising can mean changing the order of paragraphs or sentences. It can mean changing general words for specific words. It can mean correcting errors.

Once you decide what to change, you can mark the corrections on your draft using editing marks. Here's how Becca marked up her first paragraph.

> When I saw an art contest advertised in the newspaper last spring, I entered my best drawing. I have always loved art. The prize was a week at an art camp in June with nine other kids. I was very excited happy when I won.

Step 4: Edit and Proofread

In this step, you make a second draft that includes the changes you marked on your first draft. You can also add details you may have thought of since writing your first draft. Now you're ready to **proofread**, or check your work for errors and make final corrections.

Here's Becca's first draft after she finished proofreading.

My Week at Art Camp

I have always loved art. When I saw an art contest advertised in the newspaper last spring, I entered my best drawing. The prize was a week at an art camp in June with nine other students. I was very excited when I won.

The camp was located at the Everson museum of art. On the first day, we looked at paintings by different artists. My favorite was by a painter named Monet. He painted colorful land scapes of boats and gardens. On the second day we began our own paintings. I choose to paint a picture of the duck pond on the campus. I worked hard on my painting because we were going to have an art show of all our work at the end of the week.

I learned alot about painting at camp. I especially liked learning to use watercolors. For example I found out that you can make interesting designs by sprinkling salt on a wet watercolor painting.

I had a great time at art camp. The show at the end of the week was a big success, and I made some new friends. I hope to go again next year.

Step 5: Publish

Prepare a final copy of your writing to **publish**, or share with your audience. Here are some publishing tips.

- Photocopy and hand out your work to your classmates.
- Attach it to an e-mail and send it to friends.
- Send it to a school newspaper or magazine for possible publication.

Here is the final version of Becca's paper.

My Week at Art Camp

I have always loved art. When I saw an art contest advertised in the newspaper last spring, I entered my best drawing. The prize was a week at an art camp in June with nine other students. I was very excited when I won.

The camp was located at the Everson Museum of Art. On the first day, we looked at paintings by different artists. My favorite was by a painter named Monet. He painted colorful landscapes of boats and gardens. On the second day, we began our own paintings. I chose to paint a picture of the duck pond on the campus. I worked hard on my painting because we were going to have an art show of all our work at the end of the week.

I learned a lot about painting at camp. I especially liked learning to use watercolors. For example, I found out that you can make interesting designs by sprinkling salt on a wet watercolor painting.

I had a great time at art camp. The show at the end of the week was a big success, and I made some new friends. I hope to go again next year.

Once you have shared your work with others, you may want to keep it in a **portfolio**, a folder or envelope with your other writing. Each time you write something, add it to your portfolio. Compare recent work with earlier work. See how your writing is improving.

RUBRICS FOR WRITING

What Is a Rubric?

A **rubric** is a tool, often in the form of a chart or a grid, that helps you assess your work. Rubrics are helpful for writing and speaking assignments.

To help you or others assess your work, a rubric offers several specific criteria to be applied to your work. Then the rubric helps you indicate your range of success or failure according to those specific criteria. Rubrics are often used to evaluate writing for standardized tests.

Using a rubric will save you time, focus your learning, and improve your work. When you know the rubric beforehand, you can keep the specific criteria for the writing in your mind as you write. As you evaluate the essay before giving it to your teacher, you can focus on the specific criteria that your teacher wants you to master—or on areas that you know present challenges for you. Instead of searching through your work randomly for any way to improve or correct it, you will have a clear and helpful focus.

How Are Rubrics Structured?

Rubrics can be structured in several different ways:

1. Your teacher may assign a rubric for a specific assignment.
2. Your teacher may direct you to a rubric in your textbook.
3. Your teacher and your class may structure a rubric for a particular assignment together.
4. You and your classmates may structure a rubric together.
5. You can create your own rubric with your own specific criteria.

How Will a Rubric Help Me?

A rubric will help you assess your work on a scale. Scales vary from rubric to rubric but usually range from 6 to 1, 5 to 1, or 4 to 1, with 6, 5, or 4 being the highest score and 1 being the lowest. If someone else is using the rubric to assess your work, the rubric will give your evaluator a clear range within which to place your work. If you are using the rubric yourself, it will help you improve your work.

What Are the Types of Rubrics?

A **holistic rubric** has general criteria that can apply to a variety of assignments. An **analytic rubric** is specific to a particular assignment. The criteria for evaluation address the specific issues important in that assignment. The following pages show examples of both types of rubrics.

440

Holistic Rubrics

Holistic rubrics such as this one are sometimes used to assess writing assignments on standardized tests. Notice that the criteria for evaluation are focus, organization, support, and use of conventions.

Points	Criteria
6 Points	• The writing is focused and shows fresh insight into the writing task. • The writing is marked by a sense of completeness and coherence and is organized with a logical progression of ideas. • A main idea is fully developed, and support is specific and substantial. • A mature command of the language is evident. • Sentence structure is varied, and writing is free of fragments. • Virtually no errors in writing conventions appear.
5 Points	• The writing is focused on the task. • The writing is organized and has a logical progression of ideas, though there may be occasional lapses. • A main idea is well developed and supported with relevant detail. • Sentence structure is varied, and the writing is free of fragments. • Writing conventions are followed correctly.
4 Points	• The writing is focused on the task, but unrelated material may intrude. • Clear organizational pattern is present, though lapses occur. • A main idea is adequately supported, but development may be uneven. • Sentence structure is generally fragment free but shows little variation. • Writing conventions are generally followed correctly.
3 Points	• Writing is focused on the task, but unrelated material intrudes. • Organization is evident, but writing may lack a logical progression of ideas. • Support for the main idea is present but is sometimes illogical. • Sentence structure is free of fragments, but there is almost no variation. • The work demonstrates a knowledge of conventions, with misspellings.
2 Points	• The writing is related to the task but generally lacks focus. • There is little evidence of an organizational pattern. • Support for the main idea is generally inadequate, illogical, or absent. • Sentence structure is unvaried, and serious errors may occur. • Errors in writing conventions and spellings are frequent.
1 Point	• The writing may have little connection to the task. • There has been little attempt at organization or development. • The paper seems fragmented, with no clear main idea. • Sentence structure is unvaried, and serious errors appear. • Poor diction and poor command of the language obscure meaning. • Errors in writing conventions and spelling are frequent.
Unscorable	• The response is unrelated to the task or is simply a rewording of the prompt. • The response has been copied from a published work. • The student did not write a response. • The response is illegible. • The words in the response are arranged with no meaning. • There is an insufficient amount of writing to score.

441

Analytic Rubrics

This analytic rubric is an example of a rubric to assess a persuasive essay. It will help you assess presentation, position, evidence, and arguments.

Presentation	Position	Evidence	Arguments
6 Points Essay clearly and effectively addresses an issue with more than one side.	Essay clearly states a supportable position on the issue.	All evidence is logically organized, well presented, and supports the position.	All reader concerns and counterarguments are effectively addressed.
5 Points Most of essay addresses an issue that has more than one side.	Essay clearly states a position on the issue.	Most evidence is logically organized, well presented, and supports the position.	Most reader concerns and counterarguments are effectively addressed.
4 Points Essay adequately addresses issue that has more than one side.	Essay adequately states a position on the issue.	Many parts of evidence support the position; some evidence is out of order.	Many reader concerns and counterarguments are adequately addressed.
3 Points Essay addresses issue with two sides but does not present second side clearly.	Essay states a position on the issue, but the position is difficult to support.	Some evidence supports the position, but some evidence is out of order.	Some reader concerns and counterarguments are addressed.
2 Points Essay addresses issue with two sides but does not present second side.	Essay states a position on the issue, but the position is not supportable.	Not much evidence supports the position, and what is included is out of order.	A few reader concerns and counterarguments are addressed.
1 Point Essay does not address issue with more than one side.	Essay does not state a position on the issue.	No evidence supports the position.	No reader concerns or counterarguments are addressed.

442

Friendly Letters

A friendly letter is less formal than a business letter. It is a letter to a friend, a family member, or anyone with whom the writer wants to communicate in a personal, friendly way. Most friendly letters are made up of five parts: the **date**, the **greeting** (or salutation), the **body**, the **closing**, and the **signature**. The greeting is followed by a comma, and the paragraphs in the body are indented.

The purpose of a friendly letter is usually to share personal news and feelings, to send or to answer an invitation, or to express thanks.

In this letter, Maité tells her friend Julio about her new home.

Greeting   **Date**

March 2, 2009

Dear Julio,

I was so happy to receive your letter today. I am feeling much better. My mom and I finally finished decorating my room. We painted the walls green and the ceiling pink. At first, my mom was nervous to paint the ceiling something other than white, but I knew it would look good. Now that my bedroom is finished, Manhattan is starting to feel more like home.

Over the weekend I went to the Museum of Natural History. The whale exhibit made me think of back home and how you and I would spend hours at the beach. I am starting to adjust to city life, but I miss the smell of salt in the air and collecting sea glass on the shore.

My parents said I can spend the summer with my grandparents at their beach house. They said I could invite you for a couple of weeks. We'll go swimming every day. I can't wait!

Body

Your friend, ⟵ **Closing**

Maité ⟵ **Signature**

443

Business Letters

Business letters follow one of several formats. In **block format**, each part of the letter begins at the left margin. A double space is used between paragraphs. In **modified block format**, some parts of the letter are indented to the center of the page. No matter which format is used, all letters in business format have a date, an inside address, a greeting (or salutation), a body, a closing, and a signature. These parts are shown on the model business letter below, formatted in block style.

June 11, 2009 ← **Date**

Edward Sykes, Vice President
Animal Rights Group ← **Inside Address**
154 Denver Street
Syosset, NY 11791

Dear Mr. Sykes: ← **Greeting**

Many students at Bellevue High School would like to learn about animal rights for a project we're starting next fall. We've read about your program on your website and would like to know more about your activities.

Would you send us some information about your organization? We're specifically interested in learning what we as students can do to help protect animals. About 75 students have expressed interest so far—I think we'll have the people power to make the project a success and have an impact. ← **Body**

Please help us get started. Thank you for your time and consideration.

Sincerely, ← **Closing**

Pedro Rodriguez ← **Signature**

Pedro Rodriguez

The **inside address** shows where the letter will be sent. The **greeting** is punctuated with a colon. The **body** of the letter states the writer's purpose. The **closing** "Sincerely" is common, but "Yours truly" or "Respectfully yours" are also acceptable. The writer types his or her name and writes a **signature**.

FILLING IN FORMS

Forms are preprinted documents with spaces for the user to enter specific information. Some include directions; others assume that users will follow the labels and common conventions. Two common forms in the workplace are fax cover sheets and applications. When you fill out forms, it is important to do the following:

- Fill them out accurately and completely.
- Write neatly in blue or black ink.
- Include only information that is asked for on the form.

Forms usually have limited space in which to write. Because space is limited, you can use standard symbols and abbreviations, such as *$10/hr.* to mean "10 dollars per hour."

FAX COVER SHEET

To: *Mr. Robert Thompson*   **From:** *Laura Rivas*

Fax: *(001) 921-9833*   **Pages:** *2 (including cover sheet)*

Date: *12/04/09*

Re: *Job Application*

Message:

Dear Mr. Thompson:

Thank you for meeting with me today about the sales associate position at Story Land Bookshop. The following page is my completed application form.

Sincerely,

Laura Rivas

Story Land Bookshop

PRE-EMPLOYMENT QUESTIONNAIRE
EQUAL OPPORTUNITY EMPLOYER
Date: 12/04/2009

PERSONAL INFORMATION

Name (last name first)
Rivas, Laura

Social Security No.
145-53-6211

Present Address	**City**	**State**	**Zip Code**
351 Middleton Road	Osborne	TX	78357

Permanent Address	**City**	**State**	**Zip Code**
Same			

Phone No.
(001) 661-1567

Referred by
Josh Logan

EMPLOYMENT DESIRED

Position	**Start Date**	**Salary Desired**
Sales associate	Immediately	$10/hr.

Are you presently employed? ☐ Yes ☑ No
May we contact your former employer? ☑ Yes ☐ No
Were you ever employed by this company? ☐ Yes ☑ No

EDUCATION

Name and Location of School	**Yrs Attended**	**Did you graduate?**
Osborne High School, Osborne, TX	3	Expect to graduate 2010

FORMER EMPLOYERS

Name and Address of Employer	**Salary**	**Position**
Blue River Summer Camp 127 Horse Lane Millwood, TX 78721	$195 per week	Junior camp counselor

Date Month and Year	**Reason for Leaving**
6/20/09 to 9/20/09	Summer ended

CONDUCTING RESEARCH

Reference Skills
There is a wide range of print and electronic references you can use to find many different kinds of information.

Encyclopedias
Encyclopedias contain facts on a great many subjects. They provide basic information to help you start researching a topic. Use encyclopedias for basic facts, background information, and suggestions for additional research.

Periodicals
Periodicals are magazines and journals. Once you've used a periodical index to identify the articles you want to read, ask a librarian to help you locate the periodicals. Often, past issues of magazines are stored electronically on microfilm, a database, or CD-ROMs. The librarian can help you use these resources. Use the table of contents, the titles, and other magazine features to help you find information.

Biographical References
These books provide brief life histories of famous people in many different fields. Biographical references may offer short entries similar to those in dictionaries or longer articles more like those in encyclopedias. Most contain an index to help you locate entries.

Nonfiction Books
Nonfiction books about your topic can also be useful reference tools. Use titles, tables of contents, prefaces, chapter headings, glossaries, indexes, and appendixes to locate the information you need.

Almanacs
Almanacs are published annually. They contain facts and statistics about many subjects, including government, world history, geography, entertainment, business, and sports. To find a subject in a printed almanac, refer to the index in the front or back. In an electronic almanac, you can usually find information by typing a subject or key word.

Electronic Databases
Available on CD-ROMs or online, electronic databases provide quick access to a wealth of information on a topic. Using a search feature, you can easily access any type of data, piece together related information, or look at the information in a different way.

PROOFREADING

All forms of writing—from a letter to a friend to a research paper—are more effective when they are error-free. Once you are satisfied with the content of your writing, polish the grammar, usage, and mechanics.

Challenge yourself to learn and apply the skills of proofreading to everything you write. Review your writing carefully to find and correct all errors. Here are the broad categories that should direct your proofreading:

☑ **CHECK YOUR SPELLING:** Use a dictionary or an electronic spelling checker to check any spelling of which you are unsure.

☑ **CHECK YOUR GRAMMAR AND USAGE:** Use a writing handbook to correct problems in grammar or usage.

☑ **REVIEW CAPITALIZATION AND PUNCTUATION:** Review your draft to be sure you've begun each sentence with a capital letter and used proper end punctuation.

☑ **CHECK THE FACTS:** When your writing includes facts gathered from outside sources, confirm the accuracy of your work. Consult reference materials. Check names, dates, and statistics.

Editing Marks		
To:	**Use This Mark:**	**Example:**
add something	∧	We ate rice, bean_s and corn.
delete something	℮	We ate rice, beans, and corns.
start a new paragraph	¶	¶We ate rice, beans, and corn.
add a comma	⌄	We ate rice, beans and corn.
add a period	⊙	We ate rice, beans, and corn⊙
switch letters or words	∼	We ate rice, baehs, and corn.
change to a capital letter	a̲	we ate rice, beans, and corn.
change to a lowercase letter	A̸	WE ate rice, beans, and corn.

CITING SOURCES

Proofreading and Preparing Manuscript

Before preparing a final copy, proofread your manuscript.

- Choose a standard, easy-to-read font.
- Type or print on one side of unlined 8 1/2" x 11" paper.
- Set the margins for the side, top, and bottom of your paper at approximately one inch. Most word-processing programs have a default setting that is appropriate.
- Double-space the document.
- Indent the first line of each paragraph.
- Number the pages in the upper right corner.

Follow your teacher's directions for formatting formal research papers. Most papers will have the following features: Title page, Table of Contents or Outline, Works Consulted List.

Crediting Sources

When you credit a source, you acknowledge where you found your information and you give your readers the details necessary for locating the source themselves. Within the body of the paper, you provide a short citation, a footnote number linked to a footnote, or an endnote number linked to an endnote reference. These brief references show the page numbers on which you found the information. Prepare a reference list at the end of the paper to provide full bibliographic information on your sources. These are two common types of reference lists:

A **bibliography** provides a listing of all the resources you consulted during your research. A **works consulted list** lists the works you have referenced in your paper.

The chart on the next page shows the Modern Language Association format for crediting sources. This is the most common format for papers written in the content areas in middle school and high school. Unless instructed otherwise by your teacher, use this format for crediting sources.

MLA Style for Listing Sources

Book with one author	Pyles, Thomas. *The Origins and Development of the English Language.* 2nd ed. New York: Harcourt Brace Jovanovich, Inc., 1971.
Book with two or three authors	McCrum, Robert, William Cran, and Robert MacNeil. *The Story of English.* New York: Penguin Books, 1987.
Book with an editor	Truth, Sojourner. *Narrative of Sojourner Truth.* Ed. Margaret Washington. New York: Vintage Books, 1993.
Book with more than three authors or editors	Donald, Robert B., et al. *Writing Clear Essays.* Upper Saddle River, NJ: Prentice Hall, Inc., 1996.
Single work from an anthology	Hawthorne, Nathaniel. "Young Goodman Brown." *Literature: An Introduction to Reading and Writing.* Ed. Edgar V. Roberts and Henry E. Jacobs. Upper Saddle River, NJ: Prentice-Hall, Inc., 1998. 376–385. [Indicate pages for the entire selection.]
Introduction in a published edition	Washington, Margaret. Introduction. *Narrative of Sojourner Truth.* By Sojourner Truth. New York: Vintage Books, 1993, pp. v–xi.
Signed article in a weekly magazine	Wallace, Charles. "A Vodacious Deal." *Time* 14 Feb. 2000: 63.
Signed article in a monthly magazine	Gustaitis, Joseph. "The Sticky History of Chewing Gum." *American History* Oct. 1998: 30–38.
Unsigned editorial or story	"Selective Silence." Editorial. *Wall Street Journal* 11 Feb. 2000: A14. [If the editorial or story is signed, begin with the author's name.]
Signed pamphlet or brochure	[Treat the pamphlet as though it were a book.]
Pamphlet with no author, publisher, or date	*Are You at Risk of Heart Attack?* n.p. n.d. ["n.p. n.d." indicates that there is no known publisher or date.]
Filmstrips, slide programs, videocassettes, DVDs, and other audiovisual media	*The Diary of Anne Frank.* Dir. George Stevens. Perf. Millie Perkins, Shelly Winters, Joseph Schildkraut, Lou Jacobi, and Richard Beymer. Twentieth Century Fox, 1959.
Radio or television program transcript	"Nobel for Literature." Narr. Rick Karr. *All Things Considered.* National Public Radio. WNYC, New York. 10 Oct. 2002. Transcript.
Internet	*National Association of Chewing Gum Manufacturers.* 19 Dec. 1999 <http://www.nacgm.org/consumer/funfacts.html> [Indicate the date you accessed the information. Content and addresses at websites change frequently.]
Newspaper	Thurow, Roger. "South Africans Who Fought for Sanctions Now Scrap for Investors." *Wall Street Journal* 11 Feb. 2000: A1+ [For a multipage article, write only the first page number on which it appears, followed by a plus sign.]
Personal interview	Smith, Jane. Personal interview. 10 Feb. 2000.
CD (with multiple publishers)	Simms, James, ed. *Romeo and Juliet.* By William Shakespeare. CD-ROM. Oxford: Attica Cybernetics Ltd.; London: BBC Education; London: HarperCollins Publishers, 1995.
Signed article from an encyclopedia	Askeland, Donald R. "Welding." *World Book Encyclopedia.* 1991 ed.

Technology Handbook

Technology is a combination of resources that can help you do research, find information, and write. Good sources for research include the Internet and your local library. The library contains databases where you can find many forms of print and nonprint resources, including audio and video recordings.

The Internet

The Internet is an international network, or connection, of computers that share information with each other. It is a popular source for research and finding information for academic, professional, and personal reasons. The World Wide Web is a part of the Internet that allows you to find, read, and organize information. Using the Web is a fast way to get the most current information about many topics.

Words or phrases can be typed into the "search" section of a search engine, and websites that contain those words will be listed for you to explore. You can then search a website for the information you need.

Information Media

Media is all the organizations, such as television, radio, and newspapers that provide news and information for the public. Knowing the characteristics of various kinds of media will help you to spot them during your research. The following chart describes several forms of information media.

Types of Information Media	
Television News Program	• Covers current news events • Gives information objectively
Documentary	• Focuses on one topic of social interest • Sometimes expresses controversial opinions
Television Newsmagazine	• Covers a variety of topics • Entertains and informs
Commercial	• Presents products, people, or ideas • Persuades people to buy or take action

Other Sources of Information

There are many other reliable print and nonprint sources of information to use in your research. For example: magazines, newspapers, professional or academic journal articles, experts, political speeches, press conferences.

Most of the information from these sources is also available on the Internet. Try to evaluate the information you find from various media sources. Be careful to choose the most reliable sources for this information.

HOW TO USE THE INTERNET FOR RESEARCH

Keyword Search

Before you begin a search, narrow your subject to a keyword or a group of **keywords**. These are your search terms, and they should be as specific as possible. For example, if you are looking for information about your favorite musical group, you might use the band's name as a keyword. You might locate such information as band member biographies, the group's history, fan reviews of concerts, and hundreds of sites with related names containing information that is irrelevant to your search. Depending on your research needs, you might need to narrow your search.

How to Narrow Your Search

If you have a large group of keywords and still don't know which ones to use, write out a list of all the words you are considering. Then, delete the words that are least important to your search, and highlight those that are most important.

Use search connectors to fine-tune your search:

AND: narrows a search by retrieving documents that include both terms.
For example: *trumpets AND jazz*

OR: broadens a search by retrieving documents including any of the terms.
For example: *jazz OR music*

NOT: narrows a search by excluding documents containing certain words.
For example: *trumpets NOT drums*

Good Search Tips

1. Search engines can be case-sensitive. If your first try at searching fails, check your search terms for misspellings and search again.
2. Use the most important keyword first, followed by the less important ones.
3. Do not open the link to every single page in your results list. Search engines show pages in order of how close it is to your keyword. The most useful pages will be located at the top of the list.
4. Some search engines provide helpful tips for narrowing your search.

Respecting Copyrighted Material

The Internet is growing every day. Sometimes you are not allowed to access or reprint material you find on the Internet. For some text, photographs, music, and fine art, you must first get permission from the author or copyright owner. Also, be careful not to plagiarize while writing and researching. Plagiarism is presenting someone else's words, ideas, or work as your own. If the idea or words are not yours, be sure to give credit by citing the source in your work.

HOW TO EVALUATE THE QUALITY OF INFORMATION

Since the media presents large amounts of information, it is important to learn how to analyze this information critically. Analyzing critically means you can evaluate the information for content, quality, and importance.

How to Evaluate Information from Various Media

Sometimes the media tries to make you think a certain way instead of giving all the facts. These techniques will help you figure out if you can rely on information from the media.

- ☑ Ask yourself if you can trust the source, or if the information you find shows any bias. Is the information being given in a one-sided way?

- ☑ Discuss the information you find from different media with your classmates or teachers to figure out its reliability.

- ☑ Sort out facts from opinions. Make sure that any opinions given are backed up with facts. A fact is a statement that can be proved true. An opinion is a viewpoint that cannot be proved true.

- ☑ Be aware of any loaded language or images. Loaded language and images are emotional words and visuals used to persuade you.

- ☑ Check surprising or questionable information in other sources. Are there instances of faulty reasoning? Is the information adequately supported?

- ☑ Be aware of the kind of media you are watching. If it's a program, is it a documentary? A commercial? What is its purpose? Is it correct?

- ☑ Read the entire article or watch the whole program before reaching a conclusion. Then develop your own views on the issues, people, and information presented.

How to Evaluate Information from the Internet

There is so much information available on the Internet that it can be hard to understand. It is important to be sure that the information you use as support or evidence is reliable and can be trusted. Use the following checklist to decide if a Web page you are reading is reliable and a credible source.

☑ The information is from a well-known and trusted website. For example, websites that end in **.edu** are part of an educational institution and usually can be trusted. Other cues for reliable websites are sites that end in **.org** for "organization" or **.gov** for "government." Sites with a **.com** ending are either owned by businesses or individuals.

☑ The people who write or are quoted on the website are experts, not just everyday people telling their ideas or opinions.

☑ The website gives facts, not just opinions.

☑ The website is free of grammatical and spelling errors. This is often a hint that the site was carefully made and will not have factual mistakes.

☑ The website is not trying to sell a product or persuade people. It is simply trying to give correct information.

☑ If you are not sure about using a website as a source, ask your teacher for advice. Once you become more aware of the different sites, you will become better at knowing which sources to trust.

HOW TO USE TECHNOLOGY IN WRITING

Personal Computers

A personal computer can be an excellent writing tool. It enables a writer to create, change, and save documents. The cut, copy, and paste features are especially useful when writing and revising.

Organizing Information

Create a system to organize the research information you find from various forms of media, such as newspapers, books, and the Internet.

Using a computer and printer can help you in the writing process. You can change your drafts, see your changes clearly, and keep copies of all your work. Also, consider keeping an electronic portfolio. This way you can store and organize copies of your writing in several subject areas. You can review the works you have completed and see your improvement as a writer.

It is easy to organize electronic files on a computer. The desktop is the main screen, and holds folders that the user names. For example, a folder labeled "Writing Projects September" might contain all of the writing you do during that month. This will help you find your work quickly.

As you use your portfolio, you might think of better ways to organize it. You might find you have several drafts of a paper you wrote, and want to create a separate folder for these. Every month, take time to clean up your files.

Computer Tips

1. Rename each of your revised drafts using the SAVE AS function. For example, if your first file is "essay," name the first revision "essay2" and the next one "essay3."
2. If you share your computer with others, label a folder with your name and keep your files separate by putting them there.
3. Always back up your portfolio on a server or a CD.

Personal computer ▶

Glossary

abandon leave someone or something that you are responsible for

accompany go somewhere with someone

achieve succeed in doing or gaining something

adapt change something so that it is suitable for a new situation

adjacent very close or next to

adjust make a change in something to make it better

affect influence; produce a change

aid assistance, especially in the form of money, food, equipment

alternative something you can use or do instead of something else

apparent easy to understand; obvious

approaches moves closer

assist help

atmosphere the mixture of gases that surrounds the earth

attain succeed in getting something you want

available able to be used or seen

awareness knowledge or understanding

axis the imaginary line around which something turns

biologists scientists who study living things

brief lasting a short time

capable able to do something

challenge a difficult task or problem

character motivation why a character in a book, play, or movie does something

character a person who takes part in the action of a story

chart information that is shown in the form of pictures, graphs, etc.

civilizations societies that are well organized and developed

civil rights legal rights that every person living in a particular country has

collapse fall down suddenly

commitment a promise and a determination to do something

communication ways of relating, such as speaking or writing

community all the people who live in the same area or town

concluded made a decision based on evidence

condensation small drops of water that appear when steam or hot air touches something that is cool, such as a window

conducted led or guided

conferring discussing with other people

conflict a struggle between opposing forces

consequence something that happens as a result of a particular action

considerable large enough to be noticed or have an effect

consist be made up of

constellations groups of stars that form particular patterns and have names

consume eat or use something

contribution money or help that is offered or given

convince make someone believe

corporation a large business

create make something new

cultural related to a particular society and its way of life (arts, language, etc.)

cycle a set of events that happen again and again

design a plan or sketch

despite even though (something is known)

dialogue a conversation in a book, play, or movie

discoveries things that were hidden or not known before

displayed put things where people could see them easily

distinctive clearly marking a person or thing different from others

dramatic sudden and noticeable

elevation a height above the level of the sea

emphasize show that something is important

enable make something possible

enforce make someone obey

engineer a person who plans the way machines, roads, etc. are built

enormous very large in size or amount

enterprise the ability to work hard and think of new ideas, especially in business

environment the world of land, sea, and air that we live in

equator an imaginary line around the middle of the Earth

equinox one of the two times each year when day and night are the same length everywhere

erode destroy gradually by wind, rain, or acid

established started something new

evaporation vapor that forms when a liquid is heated below the temperature at which it will boil, or the process by which this happens

evidently easily noticed or understood

excelled did something really well, or better than most people

expand become larger

expeditions long difficult trips, especially to dangerous places

exploration a trip to a place to learn about it

extended metaphor a comparison that continues for several lines or an entire poem, book, etc.

famine a time when there is not enough food for people to eat

federal court a court established under a federal government

fertilizer a substance put on soil to help crops grow

figurative language writing or speech that is not meant to be read as fact

finally after a long time

financed gave money for something

flashback part of a movie, play, book, etc. that shows something that happened earlier

focus on concentrate on or give special attention to

foreshadowing a hint or clue in a story about what will happen later on

fossil fuels fuels such as oil or gas that have been formed from plants and animals that lived millions of years ago

found discovered by searching or chance

galaxy one of the large groups of stars that are in the universe

geographical relating to the study of countries, oceans, cities, populations, etc. of the world or a particular area

global affecting or relating to the whole world

goal something you want to do in the future

harvested gathered crops from the fields

hemisphere one of the halves of Earth, especially the northern or southern parts above and below the equator

herd a group of animals of the same kind

hero a male character in a story whose actions are inspiring or noble

heroine a female character in a story whose actions are inspiring or noble

hybrid something that is a mixture of two or more things

hyperbole a way of describing something by saying that it is much bigger, smaller, heavier, etc. than it really is

identified knew; recognized

imagery descriptive language that creates word pictures for readers

immigration the act of going to live in another country

impact effect that an event or situation has on someone or something

incident something that happens, especially something that is unusual

independence political freedom from the control of others

injured harmed or wounded in an accident

innovation using new ideas, methods, or inventions

instruct teach

integrate unite; end the practice of separating people of different races

interact have an effect on each other

interpret explain or translate

interpreter someone who translates the spoken words in one language into another language

investigate search for information by looking or asking questions

invisible not able to be seen

journey a trip, usually a long one

justices judges in a law court, especially the Federal Supreme Court of the U.S.

kilometer a measure of length equal to 1,000 meters

labels written words or phrases that name or describe something

landscape a view of an area of land

locate find the exact position

location place or position

magnetic having the power of a magnet

maintain continue in the same way as before

manipulate make someone do exactly what you want by deceiving or influencing him or her

markets places where people buy and sell goods

metaphor a way of describing something by comparing it to something else that has similar qualities, without using the words *like* or *as*. "A river of tears" is a metaphor.

microscopic extremely small

migrate move from one place to another

missionaries people who go to another country to teach others about his or her religion

myth a fictional story that explains natural events such as wind or rain

navigator someone on a ship or plane who plans the way it should go

nonliving not alive

nutrients chemicals that help plants, animals, or people to live and grow

objective goal; something that you are working hard to achieve

occupy live, work, etc., in a place

occurrence something that happens

onomatopoeia the use of words that imitate the sounds they represent

organism a living thing

outcome final result

parallel two lines side by side and always the same distance apart

parameters limits that control the way something should be done

participate be involved in a particular activity

partnership relationship in which two or more people work together

percent an amount out of every hundred

personification the representation of a thing or a quality as a person

phase a stage in a process

phenomenon something that happens in society, science, or nature that is unusual or difficult to understand

philosopher a person who studies life and what it means, how we should live, and what knowledge is

photosynthesis the way that green plants make their food using the light from the sun

physical relating to the body, not the mind

physicist a scientist who studies physical objects and substances, and natural forces such as light, heat, and movement

plot a sequence of connected events in a story

point of view the perspective from which a story is told

precipitation rain or snow that falls to the ground

precise exact and correct in every detail

predictable usual, expected, or obvious

previous happening before something else

priority the thing that you think is most important

process series of actions

project a plan to do something

published printed and sold a book, newspaper, or magazine

pursue continue doing an activity or trying to achieve something

racism mistreatment of people because of their race

ranching act of raising cattle, horses, or sheep

react behave in a certain way because of what someone has done or said to you

region large area

regulation official rule or order

relief raised areas on a surface

rely trust someone or something

repetition the act of doing or saying something again

reproduce to produce offspring (young plants or animals)

residential referring to a place that is made up of homes, not offices or businesses

resources things such as land, minerals, oil, etc. that exist in a country

restore make something as good as it was before

reverse change something so that it is the opposite of what it was before

revolves spins around a central point

rhyme the repetition of sounds at the ends of words

rigid stiff and still

robotics the study of how robots are made and used

role function or part

rotation a movement around and around like a wheel

route way from one place to another

satellite an object sent into space to receive signals from one part of the world and send them to another

scale a set of marks on an instrument used for measuring something

scholarships money given to students to pay for their education

science fiction books and stories about imaginary things in science such as space travel

sea level the average height of the ocean, used as a standard for measuring other heights and depths

section one part of something

segregation separation of one group of people from another because of race, sex, religion, etc.

self-portrait a picture that you make of yourself

sensory details details of sight, sound, smell, taste, or touch in a story or poem

setting the time and place of a story's action

settlers people who go to live in a new place, usually where there were few before

sharecroppers tenant farmers who are provided with credit for seed, tools, living quarters, and food, who work on the land and receive an agreed share of the value of the crops minus charges

similar almost the same, but not exactly the same

simile an expression in which you compare two things using the words *like* or *as*, for example, "as red as blood"

solar power energy produced by the sun

solar system the earth and all the moons and planets that move around the sun solstice the longest or shortest day of the year

source person, place, or thing that something comes from

species a group of plants or animals of the same type

sphere solid round shape like a ball

stage directions instructions that tell the actors what they should do and how they should do it

stanza a group of lines that forms part of a poem

starvation death or feeling very weak caused by not having enough to eat

strategy set of plans and skills to gain success

substitute use something new or different instead of something else

sufficient as much as one needs; enough

survey a set of questions designed to get information

survive continue to live

suspense a feeling of excitement about what is going to happen next in a piece of literature

symbol a picture, a letter, or a sign that means or stands for something else

telescope an object that you look through to see things that are very small or far away

temporary existing or happening for a short time only

theme the main idea or subject in a book, movie, speech, etc.

theories ideas that try to explain something, but may not be true

theory idea that tries to explain something, but it may or may not be true

trade to buy and sell goods

tradition belief or custom that has existed for a long time

transmits sends out signals

transport move or carry goods from one place to another

troops groups of soldiers

ultimate better, bigger, worse, etc. than others of the same kind

undertake start to do something

unique unusually good and special

vapor a lot of small drops of liquid that float in the air

varied consisting of many different kinds of things

version copy of something that has been slightly changed

visible able to be seen

water cycle continuous series of related events in which the water on the ground becomes heated by the sun and changes into very small drops of liquid. These drops rise into the air then fall back onto the ground or into ocean as rain

widespread happening in many places, among many people, or in many situations

Index of Skills

Further Readings, 59, 121, 185, 251, 317, 383

Grammar, Usage, and Mechanics
Adjectives
  comparative, 314
  order of, 14
  participial, 350
  prenominal and postnominal, 104
Adverbs
  clauses of time, 118
Cause and effect structures, 380
Clauses
  independent and dependent, 142
  of time, 118
Comparison structures, 28, 314
Conjunctions *and, but, or*, 234
Expressions of quantity, 182
Gerunds as subject or object, 154
Imperatives, 288
Infinitives and infinitives of purpose, 170
Modals
  could for past ability; *could* and *might* for possibility, 300
  to express ability, necessity, and permission, 338
Nouns, pronouns, and possessive adjectives, 248
Passive voice
  omitting the *by*-phrase, 92
Punctuation of quoted speech, 366
Sentences
  simple and compound, 44
Subject/verb agreement
  in simple present, 56

Tense
  future with *will* or *won't* for prediction, 220
  past perfect and simple past, 276
  present perfect, 208
  simple present, 56
Verbs
  helping, 300, 338
  regular and irregular in simple past, 80
  will or *won't* for prediction in future, 220

Language Development
Language functions
  comprehension, 12, 26, 42, 54, 78, 90, 102, 116, 140, 152, 168, 180, 206, 218, 232, 246, 274–275, 286, 298, 312-313, 336-337, 348, 364, 378
Language learning strategies
  dramatic reading, 116, 152, 218, 246, 274, 364
  listening and speaking workshop, 60–61, 122–123, 186–187, 252–253, 318–319, 384–385
  reader's theater, 12, 42, 78, 168, 312, 336

Listening and Speaking
Dramatic reading, 116, 152, 218, 246, 274, 364
Gathering and organizing information, 60, 122, 186, 252, 318, 384
Listening and speaking workshop
  group presentation, 318–319
  interview, 186–187
  personal narrative, 122–123
  play, 384–385
  presentation, 60–61
  speech, 252–253
Reader's theater, 12, 42, 78, 168, 312, 336

Literary Analysis
Genre
  essay, 240–243
  historical fiction, 110–115
  interview, 148–150
  letters, 214–217
  myth, 74–77, 332–335
  novel excerpt, 8–11, 266–271
  poetry, 41, 151, 245, 273
  radio play, 356–363
  science text, 20–25, 50–53, 98–101, 176–179, 200–205, 372–377
  short story, 160–167
  social studies text, 86–89, 136–139, 226–231, 282–285, 294–297, 344–347,
  song lyrics, 272
  tall tales, 306–311
Literary response and evaluation
  finding myths, 337
  ideas for science fiction story, 365
  making charts, 13, 153, 169, 180
  writing letters to editor, 219
  writing poem or making picture about dreams, 247
  writing thank-you letters, 43
Literary terms
  character, 71
  character motivation, 157
  conflict, 211
  dialogue, 263
  extended metaphor, 145
  figurative language, 31
  flashback, 263
  foreshadowing, 211
  hero, 329
  heroine, 329
  hyperbole, 303
  imagery, 5
  metaphor, 107
  myth, 329

onomatopoeia, 303
personification, 31
plot, 71
point of view, 71
repetition, 145
rhyme, 237
science fiction, 353
sensory details, 5
setting, 31
simile, 107
stage directions, 353
stanza, 145
suspense, 157
theme, 237

Media and Technology
Internet use, 55, 60, 79, 91, 141, 185, 207, 233, 317, 349
Library use, 55, 60, 79, 91, 141, 185, 207, 233, 317, 349

Reading
Comprehension, 12, 26, 42, 54, 78, 90, 102, 116, 140, 152, 168, 180, 206, 218, 232, 246, 274–275, 286, 298, 312-313, 336-337, 348, 364, 378
Critical thinking, 58, 120, 184, 250, 316, 382
Fluency, 27, 55, 58, 90, 103, 120, 141, 181, 184, 207, 233, 250, 287, 299, 316, 349, 379, 382
Strategies
analyze text structure, 355
ask questions, 175
classify, 371
compare and contrast, 331
connect ideas, 135
draw conclusions, 225
distinguish fact from opinion, 147
evaluate new information, 343
identify author's purpose, 213
identify main idea and details, 49

identify problems and solution, 73
make generalizations, 265
make inferences, 109
predict, 7, 159
preview, 19
recognize cause and effect, 92
recognize sequence, 239
scan, 149
skim, 305
summarize, 293
take notes, 281
use visuals, 85
visualize, 33
Text structure
essay, 240–243
historical fiction, 110–115
interview, 148–150
informational text, 20–25, 50–53, 86–89, 98–101, 136–139, 176–179, 200–205, 226–231, 282–285, 294–297, 344–347, 372–377
letter, 214–217
myth, 74–77, 332–335
novel excerpt, 8–11, 266–271
poetry, 41, 151, 245, 273
radio play, 356–363
short story, 160–167
song lyrics, 272
stage directions, 353
stanza, 145
tall tale, 306–311

Research and Study Skills
Community exploration, 27
Research report, 386–391
Using Internet or library to find information, 55, 60, 79, 91, 141, 185, 207, 233, 317, 349

Vocabulary
Academic words
abandon, 72
accompany, 264
achieve, 212
adapt, 32
adjacent, 280
adjust, 108
affect, 174
aid, 134
alternative, 198
apparent, 224
approaches, 96
assist, 264
attain, 174
available, 48
awareness, 174
brief, 238
capable, 32
challenge, 174
chart, 280
collapse, 72
commitment, 134
communication, 198
community, 238
concluded, 32
conducted, 84
conferring, 354
consequence, 212
considerable, 158
consist, 48
consume, 18
contribution, 134
convince, 224
create, 48
cultural, 146
cycle, 6
design, 174
despite, 330
displayed, 158
distinctive, 146
dramatic, 6
emphasize, 108
enable, 198
enforce, 330
enormous, 224
environment, 18

erode, 280
established, 84
evidently, 354
expand, 108
finally, 72
financed, 84
focus on, 198
found, 280
global, 134
goal, 264
identified, 342
immigration, 108
impact, 212
incident, 212
injured, 212
instruct, 304
integrate, 224
interact, 18
interpret, 146
interpreter, 264
investigate, 72
invisible, 304
labels, 280
locate, 264
location, 342
maintain, 292
manipulate, 330
migrate, 96
objective, 158
occupy, 330
occurrence, 354
outcome, 212
parallel, 370
parameters, 370
participate, 158
partnership, 304
percent, 6
phase, 370
philosopher, 342
physical, 280
precise, 146
predictable, 342
previous, 158
priority, 134
process, 48
project, 6
published, 238

pursue, 146
react, 72
region, 84
regulation, 198
rely, 32
residential, 238
restore, 330
reverse, 48
revolves, 370
rigid, 304
role, 330
route, 32
section, 238
similar, 18
source, 48
sphere, 370
strategy, 72
substitute, 304
sufficient, 96
survey, 292
survive, 18
symbol, 224
temporary, 108
theory, 342
tradition, 292
transmits, 370
transport, 96
ultimate, 292
undertake, 224
unique, 304
varied, 84
version, 354
visible, 354
widespread, 292

Key words
  atmosphere, 47
  axis, 369
  biologists, 95
  civilizations, 83
  civil rights, 223
  condensation, 47
  constellations, 341
  corporation, 173
  discoveries, 341
  elevation, 279
  engineer, 173
  enterprise, 133

equator, 369
equinox, 369
evaporation, 47
excelled, 133
expeditions, 83
exploration, 83
famine, 133
federal court, 223
fertilizer, 197
fossil fuels, 197
galaxy, 341
geographical, 279
harvested, 291
hemisphere, 369
herd, 95
hybrid, 197
independence, 291
innovation, 173
journey, 95
justices, 223
kilometer, 279
landscape, 95
magnetic, 95
markets, 83
microscopic, 197
missionaries, 291
navigator, 83
nonliving, 17
nutrients, 17
organism, 17
phenomenon, 341
photosynthesis, 17
physicist, 173
precipitation, 47
racism, 223
ranching, 291
relief, 279
reproduce, 17
resources, 197
robotics, 173
rotation, 369
satellite, 133
scale, 279
scholarships, 133
sea level, 279
segregation, 223
self-portrait, 133

settlers, 291
sharecroppers, 291
solar power, 197
solar system, 341
solstice, 369
species, 17
starvation, 95
telescope, 341
theories, 173
trade, 83
troops, 223
vapor, 47
water cycle, 47
Literary terms
character, 71
character motivation, 157
conflict, 211
dialogue, 263
extended metaphor, 145
figurative language, 31
flashback, 263
foreshadowing, 211
hero, 329
heroine, 329
hyperbole, 303
imagery, 5
metaphor, 107
myth, 329
onomatopoeia, 303
personification, 31
plot, 71
point of view, 71
repetition, 145
rhyme, 237
science fiction, 353
sensory details, 5
setting, 31
simile, 107
stage directions, 353
stanza, 145
suspense, 157
theme, 237

Word Study
Antonyms, 331
Capitalizing proper nouns, 225
Compound nouns, 33
Compound words, 293
Foreign words, 175
Frequently misspelled words, 305
Homophones, 147
Inflections -*ed* and -*ing*, 159
Prefixes *under-*, *re-*, *multi-*, *inter-*, 135
Prefixes *in-*, *re-*, *over-*, *un-*, 7
Related words, 199
Roots *astro*, *cycl*, *equ*, 371
Roots *vict*, *laps*, *vis*, *mem*, *mand*, 73
Spelling *ie/ei*, 281
Spelling long *a*, 49
Spelling long *e*, 239
Spelling long *i*, 343
Spelling regular plurals, 19
Suffixes -*er/-or*, 85
Synonyms, 213, 265
Words as multiple parts of speech, 97
Words ending in -*ible/-able*, 355
Words ending in *y*, 109

Writing
Applications
    Descriptive writing
        essay, 62–65
        of event or experience, 57
        of object, 15
        of person, 45
        of place, 29
    Expository writing
        cause and effect, 277
        classifying
            paragraph, 315
        compare and
            contrast, 143
        critique, 171
        instructions, 289
        instructional essay, 320–323

news article, 183, 188–191
        problem and solution, 155
        summary, 301
    Narrative writing
        from characters point of view, 81
        fictional, 124–127
        personal letter, 119
        personal narrative, 93
        using story starter, 105
    Persuasive writing
        advertisement, 209
        ask questions, 235
        essay, 254–257
        letter to the editor, 221
        review, 249
    Research report
        main idea with examples and explanations, 381
        main idea with facts and details, 351
        introductory paragraph, 339
Organization
    ask and answer a question, 235
    cause and effect, 277
    chronological order, 57, 119
    classify, 315
    compare and contrast, 143
    gather and organize information, 60, 122, 186, 252, 318, 384
    graphic organizers, 15, 29, 45, 57, 62, 81, 93, 105, 119, 124, 143, 155, 171, 183, 188, 209, 221, 235, 249, 254, 277, 289, 301, 315, 320, 339, 351, 367, 381, 386
    question-and-answer outline, 386
    problem and solution, 155, 221

spatial order, 29

step-by-step instructions,
  289, 320–323

story chart, 124

Skills and strategies

Descriptive

character traits, 45

physical traits, 45

sensory details, 15,
  62–65

sequence words, 57

Expository

5Ws, 183, 188–191

logical sequence, 289,
  320–323

summarizing, 301

supporting reasons and
  examples, 171

Narrative

character traits, 93

fictional, 124–127

point of view, 81

setting, 105

transition words, 119

Persuasive

opinions, 254–257

recommendations, 221

supporting reasons and
  examples, 209

vivid details, 235

Research

narrowing a topic, 339

quotations and citations,
  367, 386–391

supporting main idea
  with examples and
  explanations, 381,
  386–391

supporting main idea
  with facts and details,
  351, 386–391

Traits of writing

checklists, 15, 29, 45, 57,
  63, 81, 93, 105, 119,
  125, 143, 155, 171, 183,
  189, 209, 221, 235,
  249, 255, 277, 289,
  301, 315, 321, 339, 351,
  367, 381, 387

Writing workshop

descriptive essay, 62–65

expository essay,
  188–191

fictional narrative,
  124–127

instructional essay,
  320–323

persuasive essay,
  254–257

research report, 386–391

Index of Authors, Titles, Art, and Artists

Ali, Child of the Desert (London), 34–40

Among the Sierra Nevada, California (Bierstadt), 66–67

Anastasio, Dina, 214–217

Angel (Thayer), 393

Animal Locomotion (Woman Lifting a Basket, Waving a Handkerchief) (Muybridge), 258

"An Interview with Naomi Shihab Nye" (Barenblat), 148–150

Arachne (Conner), 392

Baldwin, James, 240–243

Barenblat, Rachel, 148–150

Bierstadt, Albert, 66–67

Bland, Karina, 176–179

Bowman, James Cloyd, 306–311

Bridges, Ruby, 226–231

Chamberlain, Norman S., 324

"Changing Earth," 200–205

Close, Chuck, 193

Conner, Bruce, 392

Corn Dance, Taos Pueblo (Chamberlain), 324

"The Cowboy Era," 294–297

Desert Women (Mora), 41

Double Portrait of the Artist in Time (Lundeberg), 259

Dreams (Hughes), 245

"Early Astronomers," 344–347

"Early Explorers," 86–89

"Earth's Orbit," 372–377

"Ecosystems: The Systems of Nature," 20–25

Edmo, Ronald Snake, 273

Electronic Superhighway: Continental U.S., Alaska, Hawaii, 128–129

The Frame (Kahlo), 136

"Harlem: Then and Now" (Baldwin), 240–243

Harlem (Hughes), 245

Henry, Barbara, 231

Hoffman, Malvina, 192

How Glooskap Found the Summer, 332–333

Hughes, Langston, 237, 245

"The Intersection" (Anastasio), 214–217

Irving, Washington, 145

Jiménez, Luis, 325

The Journal of Wong Ming-Chung (Yep), 110–115

Kahlo, Frida, 136

Koch, Howard, 356–363

Levine, Ellen, 266–271

London, Jonathan, 34–40

Lundeberg, Helen, 259

"Magnets in Animals" (Stille), 101

Making a Mosaic (Nye), 151

"Maps and Compasses," 282–285

The Marble Champ (Soto), 160–167

"Migrating Caribou," 98–100

Mora, Pat, 41

Morning Prayer Song (Edmo), 273

Moving Through Time, 258–259

Muybridge, Eadweard, 258–259

Nye, Naomi Shibab, 151

Osborne, Mary Pope, 74–77

Otherworldly Art, 392–393

Paik, Nam June, 128–129

Painting the American Landscape, 66–67

Park, Linda Sue, 8–11

Pecos Bill: The Greatest Cowboy of All Time (Bowman), 306–311

Persephone and the Pomegranate Seeds, 334–335

Poe, Edgar Allan, 237

Project Mulberry (Park), 8–11

Ringgold, Faith, 244

River Song (Staines), 272

River to Tomorrow (Levine), 266–271

The Roots of Frontier Culture, 324–325

Rossetti, Christina, 31

Self-Portrait (Close), 193

Self-Portrait (Hoffman), 192-193

Self-Portraits, 192–193

Shakespeare, William, 145

Soto, Gary, 160–167

Staines, Bill, 272

Stille, Darlene R., 101

"Students Win Robotics Competition" (Bland), 176–179

"Success Stories," 136–139

Tales from the Odyssey (Osborne), 74–77

Tar Beach (Ringgold), 244

Thayer, Abbott Handerson, 393

Through My Eyes (Bridges), 226–231

Traveling the Electronic Superhighway, 128–129

Vaquero (Jiménez), 325

The War of the Worlds (Wells/ Koch), 356–363

"Water and Living Things," 50–53

Wells, H. G., 356–363

Wordsworth, William, 5

Yep, Laurence, 110–115

Acknowledgments

UNIT 1

Excerpt from *Project Mulberry* by Linda Sue Park. Copyright © 2005 by Linda Sue Park. Reprinted by permission of Clarion Books, an Imprint of Houghton Mifflin Company. All rights reserved.

"Ecosystems: The Systems of Nature." Copyright © Pearson Longman, 10 Bank Street, White Plains, NY 10606.

"Ali, Child of the Desert" by Jonathan London, Lothrop, Lee and Shepard Books, a Division of William Morrow and Company. Copyright © 1997 by Jonathan London. Reprinted by permission.

"Desert Women" from *My Own True Name* by Pat Mora. Reprinted with permission of Arte Publico Press, University of Houston, 2000.

"Water and Living Things." Copyright © Pearson Longman, 10 Bank Street, White Plains, NY 10606.

UNIT 2

Excerpt from *Tales from the Odyssey Book One: The One Eyed Giant* by Mary Pope Osborne. Copyright © 2002 by Mary Pope Osborne. Reprinted with permission of Hyperion Books for Children.

"Early Explorers." Copyright © Pearson Longman, 10 Bank Street, White Plains, NY 10606.

"Migrating Caribou." Copyright © Pearson Longman, 10 Bank Street, White Plains, NY 10606.

"Magnets in Animals" from *Magnetism* by Darlene R. Stille. Copyright © 2005 by The Child's World®. Reprinted by permission.

Excerpt from *My Name is America: The Journal of Wong Ming-Chung, A Chinese Miner* by Laurence Yep. Copyright © 2000 by Laurence Yep. Reprinted by permission of Scholastic Inc.

UNIT 3

"Success Stories." Copyright © Pearson Longman, 10 Bank Street, White Plains, NY 10606.

"An Interview with Naomi Shihab Nye" by Rachel Barenblat. Reprinted by permission of the author.

"Making a Mosaic" from *Amaze Me* by Naomi Shihab Nye. Copyright © 2005 by Naomi Shihab Nye. Used by permission of HarperCollins Publishers.

"The Marble Champ" from *Baseball in April and Other Stories* by Gary Soto. Copyright © 1990 by GarySoto. Reprinted by permission of Harcourt, Inc.

"Students Win Robotics Competition" by Karina Bland. Published as "Robot Victory Just Part of Story for Hayden Students" from *The Arizona Republic*, March 25, 2006. Reprinted by permission.

UNIT 4

"Changing Earth." Copyright © Pearson Longman, 10 Bank Street, White Plains, NY 10606.

"The Intersection" from *American Expressions: Changes* by Dina Anastasio. Copyright © 1997 by Pearson Education, Inc., publishing as AGS Globe. Used by permission.

Excerpt from *Through My Eyes* by Ruby Bridges. Copyright © 1999 by Ruby Bridges. Reprinted by permission of Scholastic Inc.

Excerpt from "Theme for English B", from *The Collected Poems of Langston Hughes* by Langston Hughes, edited by Arnold Rampersad with David Roessel, associate editor. Copyright © 1994 by The Estate of Langston Hughes, Used by permission of Alfred A. Knopf, a division of Random House, Inc. and Harold Ober Associates Incorporated.

Excerpt from "A Dream Within a Dream" by Edgar Allan Poe. Public domain.

"Harlem: Then and Now" by James Baldwin. Reprinted by arrangement with the James Baldwin Estate.

Credits

471

Faith Ringgold, Tar Beach. 1988. Acrylic on Canvas, tie dyed and pieced fabric. 74" x 69". The Solomon R. Guggenheim Museum, New York. Photo © Faith Ringgold; 244 bottom-right, Grace Matthews/Faith Ringgold, Inc.; 245 bottom, Nicholas Muray/Amistad Research Center; 247 bottom, Faith Ringgold, Inc./Faith Ringgold, "Tar Beach". 1988. Acrylic on Canvas, tie dyed and pieced fabric. 74" x 69". The Solomon R. Guggenheim Museum, New York.; Photo © Faith Ringgold; 249 right, Kenneth Pelka; 252 bottom, Chris Forsey/Dorling Kindersley.

UNIT 5: 260–261 background, John Kelly/Getty Images; 260 top-left, CORBIS; 260 top-center, Dorling Kindersley; 260 bottom-left, David Muir/Masterfile; 260–261 bottom, SuperStock, Inc.; 263 center, Willard Clay/Taxi/Getty Images; 264 Hulton Archive Photos/Getty Images; 271 bottom, Courtesy of A.P. Koedt; 272 background, © Chad Ehlers/Stock Connection; 272 bottom, author/B. Staines; 273 background, © Joe Sohm/Chromosohm/Stock Connection; 273 bottom, author/Ronald Snake Edmo; 275 bottom, CORBIS; 277 right, David de Lossy, Ghislain & Marie/Image Bank/Getty Images; 278 bottom, © Bill Stevenson/Stock Connection; 279 bottom, © John W. Warden/Stock Connection; 281 Dale Sloat/Phototake NYC; 282 top-center, Dorling Kindersley; 284 bottom, National Museum of American History, Smithsonian Institution; 285 top, Dorling Kindersley; 286 right, David Young-Wolff/PhotoEdit; 288 bottom, © Joe Sohm/Chromosohm/Stock Connection; 289 Andy Crawford/Dorling Kindersley; 290 left, Dorling Kindersley; 290 top-right, Geoff Brightling/Dorling Kindersley; 290 bottom, Geoff Brightling/Dorling Kindersley; 290 bottom-right, Geoff Brightling/Dorling Kindersley; 291 bottom, Courtesy of the Library of Congress; 292 bottom, North Wind Picture Archives; 294 Darrell Gulin/Getty Images; 295 bottom, Courtesy of the Library of Congress; 296 Geoff Brightling/Dorling Kindersley; 297 top, Bettmann/CORBIS; 294–297 background, Bonnie Harper Lore/Lady Bird Johnson Wild Flower Center; 298 top, Geoff Brightling/Dorling Kindersley; 300 bottom, Randy Wells/Stone Allstock/Getty Images; 301 right, Jeffrey Greenberg/Photo Researchers, Inc.; 302 bottom, Nicky L. Olson/Museum of Texas Tech University/The Legend of Pecos Bill, 1948, Harold von Schmidt, oil on canvas, 32 1/8 x 38 1/8", Museum of Texas Tech University, Photo by Nicky L. Olson; 303 Bettmann/CORBIS/© Lake County Museum; 304 Michael S. Quinton/National Geographic Image Collection; 311 bottom, Courtesy of Little Brown & Company; 313 bottom, Images.com; 315 right, T.J.

RICH/Nature Picture Library.

UNIT 6: 326–327 background, Chris Butler/Photo Researchers, Inc.; 326 top-left, Dagli Orti/The Art Archive; 326 top-center, Sustermans, Justus (1597–1681)/The Bridgeman Art Library International/Galleria degli Uffizi, Florence, Italy; 326 top-right, Bettmann/CORBIS; 326 bottom-left, The Granger Collection, New York; 326 bottom-right, Altrendo Travel/Getty Images; 327 top, Yann Arthus-Bertrand/CORBIS; 327 center, The Granger Collection, New York; 327 bottom, New York Times Agency/The New York Times; 328 Gay Bumgarner/Stone Allstock/Getty Images; 329 Dagli Orti/The Art Archive; 330 Francesca Yorke/Dorling Kindersley/Courtesy of the Royal Ontario Museum, Toronto; 337 Rich Iwasaki/Stone Allstock/Getty Images; 339, Lynton Gardiner/Dorling Kindersley/Courtesy of The American Museum of Natural History; 340 Gianni Dagli Orti/Bettmann/CORBIS; 341 Jon Weiman; 342 Robert W. Ginn/PhotoEdit; 344 Sachsische Landesbibliothek/Fagan, People of the Earth, 11/ed, 2004; 344–347 background, Jean-Charles Cuillandre/CFHT/Photo Researchers, Inc.; 345 top, Dagli Orti/Museo Nazionale Romano Rome/The Art Archive; 345 bottom, Dorling Kindersley/Courtesy of the National Maritime Museum, London; 346 top-left, The Granger Collection/O. Brausewetter, "Nicolaus Copernicus (1473–1543), Polish Astronomer, Observing the skies at night". The Granger Collection, New York; 346 bottom, Bettmann/CORBIS; 347 Sustermans, Justus (1597–1681)/The Bridgeman Art Library International/Galleria degli Uffizi, Florence, Italy/The Bridgeman Art Library; 347 The Granger Collection, New York; 349 Bettmann/CORBIS; 350 Peter Bull/Dorling Kindersley; 351, Tony Freeman/PhotoEdit; 352 The Granger Collection, New York; 353 The Granger Collection, New York; 354 Paul Nicklen/National Geographic Image Collection; 363 top, George Skadding/Time & Life Pictures/Getty Images; 363 bottom, Hulton Archive Photos/Getty Images; 364 Bettmann/CORBIS; 365 Haywood Magee/Picture Post/Hulton Archive Photos/Getty Images; 367 right, Duane Rieder/Stone Allstock/Getty Images; 369, NASA/Digital image/Bettmann/CORBIS; 370 bottom, Reuters/CORBIS; 372–377, background, Eurelios/Phototake, NYC; 372 Peter Bull/Dorling Kindersley; 373 Sebastian Quigley/Dorling Kindersley; 374 Peter Bull/Dorling Kindersley; 376 Peter Bull/Dorling Kindersley; 377, Yann Arthus-Bertrand/CORBIS; 301 Adam Woolfitt/CORBIS; 378 Richard Ward/Dorling Kindersley; 379 Ambient Images/Mira; 381 Shutterstock; 384 Bettmann/CORBIS.

Smithsonian American Art Museum List of Artworks

UNIT 1 Painting the American Landscape
Page 67
Albert Bierstadt
Among the Sierra Nevada, California
1868
oil on canvas
72 x 120⅛ in.
Smithsonian American Art Museum, Bequest of Helen Huntington Hull,
granddaughter of William Brown Dinsmore, who acquired the painting in 1873
for "The Locusts," the family estate in Dutchess County, New York

UNIT 2 Traveling the Electronic Superhighway
Page 129
Nam June Paik
Electronic Superhighway: Continental U.S., Alaska, Hawaii
1995
49-channel closed-circuit video installation
approx. 15 x 40 x 4 ft.
Smithsonian American Art Museum, Gift of the artist
©1995 Nam June Paik

UNIT 3 Self-Portraits
Page 192
Malvina Hoffman
Self-Portrait
1929
limestone
25¾ x 17⅛ x 13 in.
Smithsonian American Art Museum, Gift of the Charles Lamson Hoffman Family

Page 193
Chuck Close
Self Portrait
2000
color serigraph on paper
58½ x 48¼ in.
Smithsonian American Art Museum, Museum purchase
© 2000 Chuck Close

UNIT 4 Moving Through Time
Page 258
Eadweard Muybridge
Animal Locomotion (Woman Lifting a Basket, Waving a Handkerchief)
ca. 1887
collotype on paper
sheet: 12⅞ x 9⅞ in.
Smithsonian American Art Museum, Gift of Paul and Laurette Laessle

Page 259
Helen Lundeberg
Double Portrait of the Artist in Time
1935
oil on fiberboard
47¾ x 40 in.
Smithsonian American Art Museum, Museum purchase

UNIT 5 The Roots of Frontier Culture
Page 324
Norman S. Chamberlain
Corn Dance, Taos Pueblo
1934
oil on canvas
50¼ x 40¼ in.
Smithsonian American Art Museum, Transfer from the U.S. Department of Labor

Page 325
Luis Jiménez
Vaquero
modeled 1980/cast 1990
acrylic urethane and fiberglass
199 x 114 x 67 in.
Smithsonian American Art Museum, Gift of Judith and Wilbur L. Ross
Jr., Anne and Ronald Abramson, Thelma and Melvin Lenkin
© 1980 Luis Jiménez

UNIT 6 Otherworldly Art
Page 392
Abbott Handerson Thayer
Angel
1887
oil on canvas
36¼ x 28⅛ in.
Smithsonian American Art Museum, Gift of John Gellatly

Page 393
Bruce Conner
Arachne
1959
Mixed media: nylon stockings, collage, cardboard
48 x 65½ in.
Smithsonian American Art Museum, Bequest of Edith S. and Arthur J. Levin